Principles of Diabetes Care
evidence-based management for
health professionals

Principles of Diabetes Care
evidence-based management for health professionals

edited by

Anne Phillips

QUAY BOOKS

A division of MA Healthcare Ltd

Quay Books Division, MA Healthcare Ltd, St Jude's Church, Dulwich Road, London
SE24 0PB

British Library Cataloguing-in-Publication Data
A catalogue record is available for this book

© MA Healthcare Limited 2012

ISBN-10: 1-85642-432-4
ISBN-13: 978-1-85642-432-5

Cover design: Louise Wood, Fonthill Creative

Publishing Manager: Andy Escott

Printed by Mimeo, Huntingdon, Cambridgeshire

This textbook is firstly dedicated to all my colleagues who work with people with diabetes and who strive to make things better accordingly.

Also, for Steve, Beth & Edward whose constant support and love can never be underestimated.

Contents

Foreword   viii

1   **Diagnosis of diabetes**   1
    Clare MacArthur
2   **Intensity of glycaemic management in type 2 diabetes mellitus** 15
    Dr Ram Kela and Professor Melanie Davies
3   **Promoting healthy eating and weight loss**   23
    Paul Pipe-Thomas
4   **Physical activity and health**   33
    Francesca Annan
5   **Assessing and communicating risk with people with diabetes**   41
    Dr Gillian Hawthorne
6   **Supporting individuals after a diagnosis of diabetes**   51
    Mandy Edwards
7   **Person-centred planning**   59
    Phil Holdich
8   **Diabesity: aims of treatment and a multidisciplinary**
    practice team approach   73
    Dr Chinnadori Rajeswaran, Jo Bissell, Dr Ravi Bachuwar
    and Dr Balasubramanian Thiagarajan Srinivasan
9   **Anti-diabetic treatment options**   85
    Dr Paul Jennings and Dr Myint Myint Aye
10 **Optimising insulin therapy to individual need**   101
    Kim Hamson
11 **Blood pressure and lipid management: a primary care approach**   109
    Dr Andrew Inglis
12 **Psychosocial support for people with diabetes**   121
    Anne Phillips and Jerome Wright
13 **Have diabetes, can and will travel**   133
    Rebecca Owen
14 **Hypoglycaemia in type 1 and type 2 diabetes and recognising**
    hypoglycaemic unawareness   139
    Clare MacArthur and Helen Gibson
15 **Managing foot complications in people with diabetes**   161
    Dawn Bowness

16 **Assessment of retinopathy**   173
    Dr Warren Gillibrand and Phil Holdich
17 **Diabetic nephropathy**   183
    Dr Victoria Robins and Dr Paul Laboi
18 **Recognising sexual dysfunction in people with diabetes**   195
    Anne Phillips, Karen Khan and Dr Roger Fisken
19 **Neuropathic presentations of diabetes**   211
    Dr Ewan Masson
20 **Skin complications in diabetes**   221
    Anne Phillips
21 **Preconception care in diabetes**   231
    Dr Gillian Hawthorne
22 **Caring for children and young people with diabetes**   241
    Carole Gelder
23 **Caring for vulnerable adults with diabetes**   253
    Julie Oldroyd
24 **Suspecting diabetes in people living with a learning disability**   267
    Anne Phillips
25 **Supporting people with diabetes-related stress, anxiety and depression**   277
    Phil Holdich and Dr Warren Gillibrand
26 **Diabetes and older people: ensuring individualised practice**   289
    Stephen Phillips
27 **Reassessing people who have been diagnosed with diabetes below age 25**   299
    Julie Cropper and Maggie Shepherd
28 **Managing diabetes in palliative and end of life care**   311
    Theresa Smyth and Dion Smyth
29 **Leadership and successful team working in diabetes care**   323
    Lorna Storr and Anne Phillips

Index   331

Foreword

The increasing prevalence of diabetes in the UK and elsewhere poses enormous challenges to the NHS, particularly in this time of financial stringency. In addition, the reorganisation of primary care commissioning is leading to a complete reevaluation of the provision of care for long-term conditions such as diabetes. It is therefore very timely that this book is produced, outlining the basic principles of diabetes care with a focus on primary care services. The continuing strand of the book is based upon the highly successful MSc course in diabetes that has been running at the University of York for many years. Consequently, the chapters are up-to-date (nothing keeps you more on your toes more than having to deliver regular lectures to enthusiastic colleagues) and cover the broad sweep of topics that all those working in primary care will confront sooner or later when looking after people with diabetes. This book has been put together in bite-size chapters, which focus solidly on a particular aspect of diabetes care. As such, I am sure it will prove to be a very useful resource and reference for commissioners and providers of diabetes care.

Professor R W Bilous
The James Cook University Hospital
Middlesbrough, UK
October 2011

List of contributors

Francesca Annan is a Paediatric Diabetes Dietitian and Diabetes Service Lead, Alder Hey Children's Hospital NHS Foundation Trust, Eaton Road, Liverpool.

Dr Myint Myint Aye is a Clinical Research Fellow, Department of Diabetes, Endocrinology & Metabolism, Hull York Medical School, University of Hull.

Dr Ravi Bachuwar is a Specialist Register in Diabetes and Endocrinology, Kirklees Weight Management Service, Dewsbury & District Hospital, The Mid Yorks NHS Trust.

Jo Bissell is a Diabesity Specialist Nurse, Dewsbury & District Hospital, The Mid Yorks NHS Trust.

Dawn Bowness is the Principal Podiatrist Diabetes at the Brocklehurst Building, Hull Diabetes Centre, Hull Royal Infirmary.

Julie Cropper is a genetic diabetes nurse covering Yorkshire and the Humber, and a Children's Diabetes Nurse Specialist at Leeds Teaching Hospitals Trust.

Professor Melanie Davies is a Professor of Diabetes Medicine, Department of Diabetes, Leicester Royal Infirmary, Leicester.

Marilyn Edwards is an Advanced Nurse Practitioner, Rising Brook Surgery, Stafford.

Dr Roger Fisken is a retired consultant in diabetes and endocrinology, The Friarage Hospital, Northallerton, South Tees Hospitals NHS Foundation Trust.

Carole Gelder is a Lecturer Practitioner in Diabetes at the University of York and a Children's Diabetes Specialist Nurse/Clinical Educator, Leeds Teaching Hospitals NHS Trust.

Helen Gibson is an honorary lecturer at the University of York and is a senior Diabetes Specialist Nurse at York Diabetes and Endocrine Centre, York Teaching Hospital NHS Foundation Trust.

Dr Warren Gillibrand is a Senior Lecturer in Adult Nursing, University of Huddersfield, Queensgate, Huddersfield

Kim Hamson is a Primary Care Diabetes Specialist Nurse, Diabetes Centre, Scunthorpe General Hospital, North Lincolnshire.

Dr Gillian Hawthorne is a Consultant Community Diabetologist & Head of the Clinical Diabetes Service, Newcastle Diabetes Service, Newcastle General Hospital, Westgate Road, Newcastle upon Tyne.

Phil Holdich is a Senior Lecturer in Adult Nursing, University of Huddersfield, Queensgate, Huddersfield.

Dr Andrew Inglis is a General Practitioner with an interest in the management of Diabetes at Tadcaster Medical Centre, North Yorkshire and a former Clinical Assistant in Diabetes at York Hospital.

Dr Paul Jennings is a Consultant Physician in Diabetes and Endocrinology, York Diabetes and Endocrine Centre, York Teaching Hospital NHS Foundation Trust, and co-leader of an MSc in Diabetes Care at the University of York.

Dr Ram Kela is a Specialist Registrar, Department of Diabetes, Leicester Royal Infirmary, Leicester.

Karen Khan is a lecturer in midwifery and is the lead midwife for education, at the University of York, Heslington, York.

Dr Paul Laboi is a Consultant Nephrologist with a special interest in Diabetes at York Teaching Hospital NHS Foundation Trust.

Clare MacArthur is a Lecturer/Practitioner in Diabetes Care at the University of York and a senior Diabetes Specialist Nurse at The Friarage Hospital, Northallerton, South Tees Hospitals NHS Foundation Trust.

Dr Ewan Masson is a consultant diabetologist and lead in the diabetic foot clinic, The Brocklehurst Centre, Hull Royal Infirmary.

Julie Oldroyd is the Diabetes and Renal Network Lead, NHS Kirklees, Bradley, Huddersfield.

Rebecca Owen is a Diabetes Specialist Nurse at York Diabetes and Endocrine Centre, York Teaching Hospital NHS Foundation Trust.

Anne Phillips is a Senior Lecturer in Diabetes Care and Long Terms Condition Team Lead at the University of York, Heslington, York.

Stephen Phillips is a Senior Lecturer in Primary Care, University of Huddersfield, Queensgate, Huddersfield.

Paul Pipe-Thomas is an Advanced Dietitian for Diabetes, The Robert Hague Centre for Diabetes & Endocrinology, Barnsley Hospital NHS Foundation Trust.

Dr Chinnadorai Rajeswaran is a Consultant Physician in Diabetes and Endocrinology, Kirklees Weight Management Service, Dewsbury & District Hospital, The Mid Yorks NHS Trust.

Dr Vicky Robins is presently a registrar in nephrology at St James University Hospital, Leeds Teaching Hospitals NHS Trust.

Maggie Shepherd is a honorary clinical senior lecturer at the Peninsula Medical School and Research Fellow at the Royal Devon and Exeter NHS Foundation Trust.

Theresa Smyth is a Consultant Nurse in Diabetes, University Hospitals Birmingham NHS Foundation Trust, Diabetes centre, Selly Oak Hospital, Birmingham.

Dion Smyth is a Lecturer-practitioner in cancer and palliative care, Birmingham City University.

Dr Balasubramanian Thiagarajan Srinivasan is a Locum Consultant Physician in Diabetes and Endocrinology, Kirklees Weight Management Service, Dewsbury & District Hospital, The Mid Yorks NHS Trust.

Lorna Storr is a lecturer in Leadership & Management at the University of York, Heslington, York.

Jerome Wright is a lecturer in Mental Health & International Health and at the University of York, Heslington, York.

Chapter 1

Diagnosis of diabetes

Clare MacArthur

Introduction

'Getting the right diagnosis of diabetes is the first step toward getting the right treatment, not just in terms of prescribing treatments but also in general advice.'
(Royal College of General Practitioners [RCGP], 2011:9)

Despite campaigns to raise awareness of diabetes, including World Diabetes Day (November 14th), and despite resources for effective diagnosis and treatment being widely available in the UK, diabetes often remains undiagnosed (Yorkshire and Humber Public Health Observatory [YHPHO], 2010). This chapter considers risk factors for developing diabetes and glucose intolerance, outlines diagnostic methods and considers the benefits of early diagnosis.

To illustrate presentations of and differential diagnoses for type 1 and type 2 diabetes, two case studies are presented. The person in *Case Study 1* (overleaf) has type 1 diabetes — while this scenario may seem clear cut, type 1 diabetes can go unrecognised and people who have it are sometimes misdiagnosed with other conditions. The common symptoms of diabetes (including thirst, tiredness, urinary frequency, weight loss and abdominal pain) can be confused with infection, abdominal problems, hyperventilation, depression, eating disorders and even cancer. See *Table 1* for a more comprehensive list of symptoms of diabetes.

Where diabetes is suspected, individuals must be assessed for ketoacidosis. This is potentially life threatening, so the presence of ketones indicates urgent referral — it may be necessary to admit the person to hospital for rehydration and insulin therapy. Although toxic ketones are excreted on the breath (as well as in the urine) unfortunately, not everyone can smell them. They are commonly tested for in urine samples and can be measured in the blood.

Late diagnosis can lead to severe illness, hospital admission and possibly an avoidable death. Early diagnosis can mean a smooth start to the person's journey with diabetes.

Diagnosis

For a formal diagnosis of diabetes mellitus, laboratory blood glucose testing is necessary. The diagnosis must be made accurately, as its implications are serious (World Health Organization [WHO], 2006) — as reliable and handy as blood glucose meters are, they are not as precise as laboratory-based tests.

Diagnosing diabetes by means of blood glucose tests can seem confusing, as several different categories of glucose intolerance exist. This means that people may fall in-between the states of having diabetes and not having diabetes. In 2006, the WHO and the International Diabetes Federation (IDF) published joint guidelines for the diagnosis of diabetes mellitus and intermediate hyperglycaemia (*Table 2*). de Lusignan *et al.*, (2010:203) reported that 'The WHO classifies diabetes into Type 1, Type 2 and four other types covering genetic forms, drug or chemical induced, gestational or unknown.' There are guidelines available to support and inform the management of all these types of diabetes.

When assessing the individual with possible diabetes, it is important to carefully assess their signs and symptoms, to distinguish between:

Table 1. Symptoms of undiagnosed diabetes
Indications of a high blood glucose level:
■ Dry mouth and unusual thirst
■ Frequent urination, including nocturia and possibly incontinence
■ Extreme tiredness or lethargy
■ Slow-healing wounds
■ Recurrent infections such as boils, thrush, urinary tract infections
■ Blurry vision
■ Sudden weight loss (usually in type 1 diabetes)
■ Abdominal pain, unusual breathing and lowered conscious level in ketoacidosis (usually type 1 diabetes)
It is common to have few or no symptoms at diagnosis, particularly for people with type 2 diabetes

- **Type 1 diabetes** — in which there is an absolute deficiency of insulin production, due to autoimmune destruction of the insulin-producing beta cells in the islets of Langerhans in the pancreas.
  Without insulin, ketoacidosis occurs
- **Type 2 diabetes** — in which there is a relative deficiency of insulin production and/or the insulin that is produced is not effective (insulin resistance).

Case study 1

Mrs Smith attends her GP surgery for travel immunisations and mentions that her 15-year-old son, Ben, has an appointment booked at the same practice for the following day. She is quite worried about him as he has wet the bed twice, and is extremely tired and moody, which isn't like him at all.

She asks you to test his urine as she thinks he may have an infection. You are happy to do so; bed-wetting is very unusual in this age group in a boy who has been dry since the preschool years. 'Are you thirsty much of the time?' you ask Ben; 'Yes, I always have to carry water around with me and I just don't feel right.'

Ben's urine sample has large amounts of glucose, and further testing reveals that ketones are present. You take a calming breath, knowing the likely implications of these findings. The practice nurse asks Ben if she can prick his finger to get a drop of blood for another test, to see how much glucose — sugar — is in his blood. 'I don't eat that many sweets,' he says, alarmed. You explain that if his blood glucose is too high it will make him feel tired, thirsty and pass a lot of urine, and that the test will help you all to understand what the problem may be — it's unlikely to be due to him eating too many sweets. His blood glucose reading on the practice meter is 26.5mmol/l.

Ben's treatment should not be delayed. The practice nurse asks Ben's GP to assess him and to refer him to the local paediatrician for diagnosis and organisation of the likely treatment options.

Ben goes to the local hospital and stays overnight on the paediatric ward. After 24 hours he comes home, as he is well and making good progress with injections and blood glucose testing. He is followed up by the paediatric diabetes team, which includes dietitian, diabetes specialist nurse and consultant (among others) and is proud of his new insulin pen.

Case Study 2

Mrs Fletcher arrives for her routine smear appointment. She is 38 years old and has been generally well, but mentions that she is a bit sore 'down below.' She has a body mass index (BMI) of 30 and has been trying to lose weight for years. Her vulval area looks reddened, and the practice nurse checks a urine sample for glucose as well as screening her for infection. A moderate amount of glucose is found, which suggests diabetes. Urgent referral is not necessary as Mrs Fletcher feels well.

She agrees to a fasting blood glucose test and the practice nurse advises her to fast for a minimum of 8 hours beforehand (Expert Committee on the Diagnosis and Classification of Diabetes Mellitus, 2002). Her fasting blood glucose is 7.5mmol/l, which indicates diabetes.

The individual in *Case Study 2* has signs of type 2 diabetes. If there is any doubt over the interpretation of the results of a fasting laboratory blood glucose test (for example, if Mrs Fletcher had no symptoms at all) a second test can be done, such as an oral glucose tolerance test on a different day (WHO, 2006) (*Table 3*). If Mrs Fletcher's fasting blood glucose was found to be less than 7mmol/l, then a full glucose tolerance test would be required, as she may have impaired glucose tolerance. It is relatively rare for glucose to be present in the urine without some form of diabetes, so this should always be investigated further.

Further testing will be necessary if the diagnosis remains unclear. The fasting blood glucose test fails to diagnose about 30% of cases of previously undiagnosed diabetes (WHO, 2006).

Had Mrs Fletcher suddenly lost weight, type 1 diabetes would be possible, and careful monitoring by the practice or the individual would be necessary. In any case, she should be advised to contact the practice should she become more unwell. A frailer person living on his or her own may need earlier follow-up.

Renal thresholds

The renal threshold describes the blood glucose level at which the kidneys filter glucose into the urine (glycosuria). This varies from person to person. Some older people have lower renal thresholds and excrete glucose into the urine without diabetes — in other words, glycosuria is not always linked with diabetes. This is

Table 2. Diagnosis of diabetes	
Diabetes	Fasting plasma glucose ≥7mmol/l **or** 2–hour plasma glucose ≥11.1mmol/l*
Impaired glucose tolerance (IGT)	Fasting plasma glucose <7mmol/l **and** 2-hour plasma glucose 7.8–11.1mmol/l*
Impaired fasting glucose (IFG)	Fasting plasma glucose 6.1–6.9mmol/l **and** 2-hour plasma glucose <7.8mmol/l (if measured)†

*Venous plasma glucose 2 hours after ingestion of 75g oral glucose load
† If 2-hour plasma glucose is not measured, status is uncertain as diabetes or IGT cannot be excluded
From: World Health Organization and International Diabetes Federation, 2006: 3

Additionally, where there are no conditions present that may interfere with accurate measurement, such as haemoglobinopathies, certain anaemias, and disorders such as malaria, an HbA_{1c} above 6.5% can be used for diagnosing diabetes. A value less than 6.5% does not exclude diabetes diagnosed using glucose tests (WHO, 2011).

Table 3. The oral glucose tolerance test
A fasting blood glucose is taken, then 75g glucose is taken orally, followed by another blood glucose measurement exactly 2 hours later (WHO, 2006)
To ensure accuracy, it is important that a normal diet is eaten before testing, as a reduction in dietary sugars and carbohydrates can affect the results
Exercise can also affect the results, so rest should be advised for the duration of the test — perhaps a book can be brought to the surgery?

one of the reasons why testing urine for glucose is an inappropriate method for diagnosing diabetes.

No completely infallible method of testing is available (Waugh *et al*, 2007). The WHO (2011) has formally accepted the use of the HbA_{1c} test for the diagnosis of diabetes, rather than the more common method of taking a blood sample for a blood glucose test (Table 2). However, Diabetes UK (2011) has advocated the use of clinical judgement when deciding which test is most appropriate, on an individual basis.

Benefits of diagnosis

Early diagnosis offers immediate benefits — not least of all, it leads to treatment and the relief of symptoms, which can be embarrassing and troublesome. Some people are relieved to know that it is diabetes causing their weight loss, rather than cancer or another debilitating condition. Furthermore, diagnosis can help avoid the development of serious illness or acute problems, such as ketoacidosis or hyperglycaemic hyperosmolar state (as occasionally seen in type 2 diabetes) — this benefits the individual and saves NHS expenditure.

Diabetes and its complications account for at least £9 billon of NHS funds — an estimated £1 million an hour, or 10% of the NHS budget for England & Wales (Diabetes UK, 2011). Diabetes currently accounts for 7.7% of prescription costs in England (YHPHO, 2011) but such costs should be considered part of a strategy to prevent complications. There are clear benefits to controlling this condition. Each year, 35.5 million items are prescribed in primary care, with a net ingredient cost of £649.2 million (NHS, 2010).

Diabetes is associated with significantly increased rates of premature mortality and microvascular and cardiovascular complications. Most practitioners are aware of these complications, which include myocardial infarction, stroke, blindness, kidney damage, limb amputation and complications during pregnancy. Generally, the complications of diabetes are associated with high HbA_{1c} levels over long periods of time, or a long duration of diabetes. Hypoglycaemia is the obvious exception to this and is an unfortunate side effect of treatment. In the long term, earlier diagnosis is always beneficial (Colaguri *et al*, 2002).

Diabetes prevention

A diagnosis of impaired glucose tolerance (IGT) or impaired fasting glucose (IFG) is associated with an increased risk of cardiovascular disease of about 1.5 times the normal rate (Levitan *et al*, 2005) and up to six times the risk of developing diabetes, although this varies in different studies (WHO, 2006). For these diagnoses, important lifestyle advice about preventing diabetes should be offered, such as taking regular or increased exercise, achieving a healthy weight and (if relevant) giving up smoking. An annual review should also be recommended (Reed, 2010).

Who gets diabetes?

Diabetes is one of the fastest-growing conditions and one of the most significant threats to public health, both in the UK and worldwide. In the UK, its prevalence in people aged 16 years and older (both diagnosed and undiagnosed) is currently estimated to be 7.4% (uncertainty range: 5.3–10.8%) (Association of Public Health Observatories [APHO], 2010). However, due to rising rates of obesity, ageing populations and changes in ethnicity, this is predicted to rise to 8.5% by 2020 and 9.5% by 2030 (APHO, 2010).

Diabetes UK (2009) proposed that about 7 million people in the UK are presently living with pre-diabetes, with IFG and/or IGT. Diabetes can be well hidden, yet as it is so common, it is good practice to maintain an awareness of the condition and to actively screen for it in those who are at risk.

Certain groups of people are at greater risk of developing diabetes and if they have not already been assessed for cardiovascular risk, they should be considered for screening (*Table 4*). For example, the risk of type 2 diabetes is almost 13 times higher in women with obesity (5 times higher for men) compared with those of normal weight (YHPHO, 2006). In areas of social deprivation, both the incidence and prevalence of diabetes are greater and outcomes are poorer (YHPHO, 2006). *Figure 1* demonstrates the RCGP (2011) classification of diabetes information.

Table 4. Risk factors for developing diabetes
Age and ethnicity is important:
• Being white and over 40 years old, or • Being black, Asian or from other minority ethnic groups and over 25 years old
Plus one or more of the following risk factors:
• A close family member with type 2 diabetes (parent, brother or sister) • Being overweight, or if the waist is ≥80cm (31.5 inches) for women; ≥90cm (35 inches) for Asian men; ≥94cm (37 inches) for white and black men • High blood pressure (>140/80mmHg) or history of heart attack or stroke • Female with polycystic ovary syndrome and overweight • Female, having had gestational diabetes • Impaired glucose tolerance or impaired fasting glycaemia • Severe mental health problems
Diabetes UK (2008) suggests that people matching the criteria above should contact their general practice for a test for diabetes. A 'two-minute test' is available online, to help people decide whether or not they need to do so. From: Diabetes UK (2008).

Other types of diabetes

Genetic or monogenic diabetes

People with a strong family history of diabetes may have one of the many different forms that are collectively known as 'monogenic diabetes' (which includes 'maturity-onset diabetes of the young' [MODY]). To be classified in this group, the criteria have traditionally been:

- Diagnosis before the age of 25 years
- At least one parent with diabetes
- Not requiring insulin after 3 years of diabetes.

Monogenic diabetes affects about 1% of people with diabetes (YHPHO, 2006). The effects of prescribed treatments can be different than for more common forms of diabetes, so it is important to get an accurate diagnosis. This is a developing field and emerging evidence points to many different types of monogenic diabetes. For more information, please see chapter 26 and the website www.diabetesgenes.org

Secondary diabetes

Secondary diabetes is commonly a result of drug treatment, often with steroids, for other conditions. While relatively small doses of steroids (such as those used in asthma inhalers) rarely lead to diabetes, people who are taking high doses (for instance, those being managed for rheumatoid conditions or severe pulmonary disease) can be considered to be at risk and should be screened. It is a particular skill to teach people with known diabetes how to alter their medications for hyperglycaemia, when required, due to fluctuating doses of steroids.

Drugs that are used in the management of severe mental illnesses, including schizophrenia, have also been implicated in the development of diabetes (Smith *et al*, 2008).

Diabetes can also occur following illness that causes damage to the pancreas, such as pancreatitis or cystic fibrosis.

Gestational diabetes

The age at which women develop diabetes increasingly involves the childbearing years. Gestational diabetes — that which develops during pregnancy — is

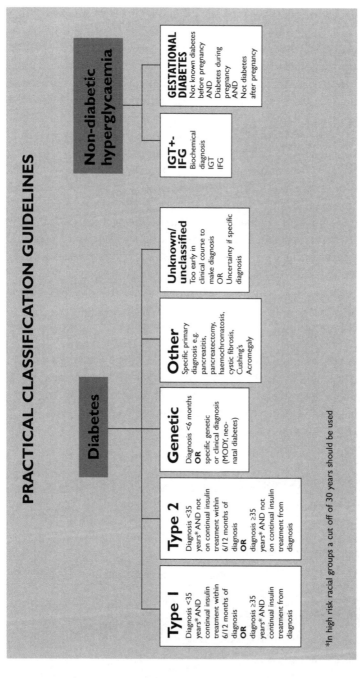

Figure 1. RCGP (2011) Diabetes classification guidelines

associated with risks to both the woman and the developing fetus and may or may not resolve after the pregnancy.

The National Institute for Health and Clinical Excellence (NICE) (2008) has produced updated guidelines for the detection and management of diabetes in pregnancy. These should be referred to by all who are involved in antenatal care, as well as by those who care for women of childbearing age with diabetes. Pre-pregnancy care may have been neglected in the UK in the past (Confidential Enquiry into Maternal and Child Health [CEMACH], 2005) and many women of childbearing age will need specific pre-pregnancy information.

Pregnant women can develop type 1 diabetes as a simultaneous event, although this is quite rare. However, it is important, as to ignore the effects can lead to fetal or maternal death.

A pregnant woman with any one risk factor for gestational diabetes (*Table 5*) should be offered screening. This entails a 2-hour, 75g oral glucose tolerance test at 24–28 weeks gestation, unless the woman has had previous gestational diabetes, in which case the first screening should be at 16–18 weeks. Women with a history of gestational diabetes also require a fasting plasma glucose measurement at the 6-week postnatal check and an annual fasting plasma glucose measurement thereafter, together with lifestyle advice as would be given for impaired glucose tolerance (NICE, 2008).

Hence, a recall system should be established for women with a history of gestational diabetes as well as for people with IGT or IFG, to enable them to be identified early. Those at particularly high risk of developing type 2 diabetes, due to a combination of risk factors, should be considered for regular annual appointments as part of cardiovascular screening.

Table 5. Risk factors for gestational diabetes
■ Body mass index above 30kg/m^2
■ Previous macrosomic baby weighing 4.5kg or above
■ Previous gestational diabetes
■ Family history of diabetes (first-degree relative with diabetes)
■ Family origin with a high prevalence of diabetes: South Asian, Black Caribbean, Middle Eastern
From: National Institute for Health and Clinical Excellence, 2004

Conclusions

A raised awareness of the symptoms, risk factors and recommended methods of diagnosing diabetes will lead to earlier diagnosis, which will benefit individuals with diabetes, their families and the healthcare system in general. For Ben Smith and Mrs Fletcher, a routine visit to the practice led to an unexpected diagnosis, yet both had some classic symptoms of undiagnosed diabetes. In general practice, this is a condition where vigilance is often repaid.

Key Points

- Many people with type 2 diabetes remain undiagnosed
- Benefits of diagnosis include relief of symptoms and the opportunity to prevent serious complications
- A recall system should be set up for women with a history of gestational diabetes and for people with impaired glucose tolerance (IGT) or impaired fasting glucose (IFG)
- Those at high risk of diabetes should be considered for annual review and intervention.

References

Association of Public Health Observatories, (2010) Diabetes Prevalence Model, http://www.apho.org.uk/resource/item.aspx?RID=49317

Bagust A et al (2002) The projected health care burden of type 2 diabetes in the UK from 2000 to 2060. *Diabet Med* **19**(Suppl 4): 1-5

Colagiuri S, Cull CA, Holman RR; UKPDS Group (2002) Are lower fasting plasma glucose levels at diagnosis of type 2 diabetes associated with improved outcomes? (UKPDS 61). *Diabetes Care* **25**(8): 1410-17

Confidential Enquiry into Maternal and Child Health (2005) Pregnancy in Women with Type 1 and Type 2 Diabetes in 2002– 03, England, Wales and Northern Ireland. CEMACH, London

Currie CJ et al (1997) NHS acute sector expenditure for diabetes: the present, the future and excess in-patient cost of care. *Diabet Med* **14**: 686-92

de Lusignan S et al (2010) A method of identifying and correcting miscoding, misclassification & misdiagnosis in diabetes: a pilot and validation study of routinely collected data. *Diabet Med* **27**(2): 203-9

Diabetes UK (2008) Causes and risk factors. http://tinyurl.com/54sjne

Diabetes UK (2009) 7 million predicted to have pre diabetes http://www.diabetes.org.uk/About_us/News_Landing_Page/7m-in-UK-have-prediabetes/

Expert Committee on the Diagnosis and Classification of Diabetes Mellitus (2002) Report of the Expert Committee. *Diabetes Care* **25**(Suppl 1): S5-S20

International Diabetes Federation (2008) World Diabetes Day, a campaign led by the International Diabetes Federation. www.worlddiabetesday.org (accessed 29 October 2008)

International Diabetes Federation (2008) Why should I care? www.idf.org/home/index.cfm?node=21 (accessed 29 October 2008)

Levitan E et al (2005) Is nondiabetic hyperglycemia a risk factor for cardiovascular disease? A meta-analysis of prospective studies. *JAMA* **293**: 194-202

National Institute for Health and Clinical Excellence (2008) Diabetes in pregnancy: management of diabetes and its complications from pre-conception to the postnatal period. Clinical guideline 63: www.nice.org.uk/cg063

NHS (2010) Prescribing for Diabetes in England:2004/5 to 2009/10. The Health & Social Care Information Centre

Reed A (2010) Diabetes Evidence-Based Management 15, Pre-Diabetes. *Practice Nursing* **21**(1): 28-32

Royal College of General Practitioners and NHS Diabetes (2011) Coding, Classification and Diagnosis of Diabetes, March, www.nhs.diabetes.uk

Smith M et al (2008) First- v. second-generation antipsychotics and risk for diabetes in schizophrenia: systematic review and meta-analysis. *Br J Psychiatry* **192**(6): 406-11

Waugh N et al (2007) Screening for type 2 diabetes: literature review and economic modelling. *Health Technol Assess* **11**(17): 1-125

Williams R et al (2002) The True Costs of Type 2 Diabetes in the UK - Findings from T2ARDIS and CODE-2 UK. Monograph of studies supported by GlaxoSmithKline. GSK, Uxbridge

World Health Organization (2011) HbA1c test accepted for use for diabetes diagnosis, http://www.diabetes.co.uk/news/2011/Jan/hba1c-test-accepted-for-use-for-diabetes-diagnosis-91069725.html

World Health Organization (2011) Use of glycated haemoglobin (HbA1c) in the diagnosis of diabetes mellitus. Abbreviated report of a WHO consultation, WHO/NMH/CHP/CPM/11.1. Geneva, WHO

World Health Organization, International Diabetes Federation (2006) Definition and diagnosis of diabetes mellitus and intermediate hyperglycaemia: report of a WHO/IDF consultation. Geneva, WHO. http://tinyurl.com/6r4qge (accessed 29 October 2008)

Yorkshire and Humber Public Health Observatory (2006) Diabetes key facts. YHPHO and National Diabetes Support Team, York

Yorkshire and Humber Public Health Observatory (2011) www.yhpho.org.uk

Chapter 2

Intensity of glycaemic management in type 2 diabetes mellitus

Dr Ram Kela and Professor Melanie Davies

Introduction

Diabetes mellitus is associated with hyperglycaemia and long-term microvascular and macrovascular complications, leading to end organ damage and an increased risk of cardiovascular disease. Nearly 3 million people in the UK have a diagnosis of diabetes (Holman, 2011), of which around 85–90% have type 2 diabetes. Perhaps more worryingly, a further 7 million people are estimated to have undiagnosed impaired glucose tolerance, and are in a 'pre diabetes' state (Diabetes UK, 2009).

The importance of early diagnosis and effective management is becoming increasingly recognised all over the world. Understanding of the management of this complex long-term condition has greatly increased because of studies such as those by the UK Prospective Diabetes Study (UKPDS) Group (1998) in relation to type 2 diabetes and the Diabetes Control and Complications Trial / Epidemiology of Diabetes Interventions and Complications (DCCT/EDIC) (Nathan *et al.*, 2005) in relation to people with type 1 diabetes. Due to these two landmark trials, it is well recognised that improved glycaemic control is associated with significant improvement in the microvascular complications in both type 1 and type 2 diabetes (UKPDS Group, 1998). Recent long-term data from the UKPDS have shown that this benefit also extends to macrovascular outcomes (Holman *et al.*, 2008).

This chapter reviews the evidence and explores the concept of glycaemic memory, alongside the implications this has for patient care.

The UK Prospective Diabetes Study (UKPDS)

The UKPDS study recruited 4209 newly diagnosed participants to receive either intensive glucose-lowering treatment or conventional treatment. The intensive group was treated with either a sulphonylurea or insulin and participants were additionally randomised to receive metformin. The study consisted of a

20-year intervention trial from 1977 to 1997 and a 10-year follow-up (post-trial monitoring) from 1997 to 2007 (UKPDS Group, 1998; Holman *et al.*, 2008a). This is the longest study to date in type 2 diabetes and as such provides unique insight into the management of this long-term disease.

The investigators studied the impact of intensive glycaemic control on microvascular and macrovascular complications and all cause mortality. Mean age of the study population was 54 years and mean baseline HbA_{1c} was 7.08% (54mmol/mol). All study participants had a fasting plasma glucose of 6.1–15mmol/l after a 3-month dietary run-in period, before randomisation.

Participants were treated for 6–20 years with a median follow-up period of 10 years. By the end of the intervention period, intensively treated participants had a lower HbA_{1c} by 0.9% and more weight gain (mean 3.1kg) as compared with the conventional group. There was no difference in HbA_{1c} between various agents used in the intensive group; however, weight gain was more with insulin (4kg) as compared with the sulphonylurea group (UKPDS Group, 1998).

Intensively-treated participants had a significant reduction (25%) in microvascular endpoints, including the need for photocoagulation.

Although there was a 16% reduction in myocardial infarction, including fatal, non-fatal myocardial infarction and sudden death, it did not quite reach statistical significance (p=0.052) (*Table 1*).

After the intervention period, 3277 participants were available for post-trial monitoring, which included annual visits to UKPDS clinics for 5 years followed by annual questionnaires for a further 5 years. No specific attempt was made to adhere to previously assigned interventions (Holman *et al.*, 2008b).

The difference in HbA_{1c} between the intensive and conventional arms had disappeared by 1 year in post-trial monitoring and both groups continued to have similar HbA_{1c} thereafter. This was because of improvement in the HbA_{1c} in participants with conventional treatment after the trial period. There was no

Table 1. Benefits of intensive glucose control		
Complication	**Reduced risk**	**p value**
Any diabetes-related endpoint	12%	p = 0.030
Microvascular endpoints	25%	p = 0.010
Myocardial infarction	16%	p = 0.052
From: UK Prospective Diabetes Study Group, 1998.		

significant difference in mean body weight, lipid levels, blood pressure, and renal function at baseline and during the 5 years of clinical follow-up.

Despite similar HbA_{1c} for 4 years during 10 years of post-trial monitoring, the microvascular benefits obtained with intensive therapy during the intervention period were sustained. These individuals continue to have a 24% reduction in microvascular events during follow-up. More strikingly, non-significant protection from myocardial infarction, which was noticed in intensively-treated participants during the intervention period emerged as a statistically significant benefit over this extended period of follow-up.

Death from any cause was significantly lower (13%) in intensively-treated participants and this was reflected during longer duration of follow-up. These benefits were not statistically significant during the initial intervention period.

In summary, the beneficial effect of earlier good glycaemic control over cardiovascular disease (CVD) outcomes and death emerged over a longer period of follow-up. Therefore, it is important to be proactive and adopt the strategies toward tight glycaemic control early in the course of diabetes.

However, in contrast to the findings on the effects of glycaemic control, the beneficial effects of earlier good blood pressure control were lost during the longer follow-up. Good blood pressure control was associated with significant improvement in microvascular as well as macrovascular outcomes after a median intervention period of 8.4 years in the UKPDS-embedded Hypertension in Diabetes Study (HDS, 1993).

A 10/5mmHg lower blood pressure in the tightly-controlled group was beneficial in reducing any diabetes-related endpoints by one quarter (24%), deaths related to diabetes by one third (32%), strokes by almost half (44%) and peripheral vascular disease by half (49%). The risk of myocardial infarction was reduced by 21% and microvascular complication (mainly retinopathy) was reduced by 37% (*Table 2*).

During the post-trial monitoring period of 10 years, the difference in blood pressure in both groups disappeared within the first 2 years. In contrast to the effect of blood glucose control, the above beneficial effects noted due to good blood pressure control did not persist during the subsequent follow-up (Holman *et al.*, 2008b).

In summary, the beneficial effects of good blood pressure control were seen only for as long as such control was maintained. Therefore, effective blood pressure control must be sustained throughout, to maintain these benefits.

Table 2. Benefits of tight blood pressure control		
Complication	**Reduced risk**	**p value**
Any diabetes-related endpoint	24%	p = 0.0046
Deaths related to diabetes	32%	p = 0.019
Stroke	44%	p = 0.013
Heart failure	56%	p = 0.0043
Myocardial infarction	21%	p = 0.13
Microvascular complication	37%	p = 0.0092
From: UK Prospective Diabetes Study Group, 1998.		

'Legacy effect' of good glycaemic control

The 'legacy effect' (also known as 'glycaemic memory') is a name given to the positive long-term effect (in terms of CVD outcomes and mortality rates) of good glycaemic control early on in the course of type 2 diabetes. By contrast, in advanced disease, tight glycaemic control can be harmful. To maintain the HbA_{1c} at below 6.5% (<48mmol/l) can have a negative outcome in established cases, especially if there is macrovascular disease (Action to Control Cardiovascular Risk in Diabetes [ACCORD] Study Group, 2008).

Researchers have observed a similar 'legacy' effect in people with type 1 diabetes, with intensive treatment for a mean duration of 6.5 years being shown to reduce the risk of cardiovascular events by almost half (DCCT, 2005). As before, the benefits of good, early glycaemic control did not gain statistical significance until the follow-up period, which lasted a mean duration of 17 years in this trial (Nathan *et al*, 2005).

Implications for glycaemic management

How does this evidence from UKPDS and other recent trials inform strategies for glycaemic management to improve CVD outcomes? The epidemiological analysis of the UKPDS cohort by Stratton *et al.*, (2000) suggested that a 1% reduction in updated HbA_{1c} was associated with reduction in myocardial infarction by 14%, stroke by 12% and peripheral vascular disease by 43%. Similarly, meta-analysis of ten prospective cohort studies by Selvin *et al.*, (2004) showed that each 1%

increase in HbA_{1c} was associated with a 13–28% increase in cardiovascular complications or mortality.

Although improvement in HbA_{1c} is associated with the significant benefits discussed above, it is important to look at whether these benefits remain the same for the whole population with type 2 diabetes. Further information is available from the recently presented ACCORD Study Group (2008) and ADVANCE Collaborative Group (2008) studies.

In the ACCORD trial, just over 5000 people with a mean age of 62 years and a median of 10 years of type 2 diabetes were intensively treated to lower HbA_{1c} from a baseline of 8.1% (65mmol/mol) to 6.4% (46mmol/mol) over a period of 1 year, and tight glycaemic control was sustained over 3.5 years. It is important to note that nearly 36% of the participants in this group had pre-existing cardiovascular disease. This study had to be terminated prematurely due to a relative increase in all-cause mortality (22%) in the intensively-treated participants. This clearly suggested that, in the older population (as compared with the UKPDS intervention group) with pre-existing cardiovascular disease, intensive glycaemic control to achieve an HbA_{1c} below 6.5% (<48mmol/mol) can be more harmful.

The reasons for increased mortality in this high-risk group were initially thought to be related to hypoglycaemia, due to the rapid decline in HbA_{1c} (1.4% over 4 months) in the intensively-treated participants. However, a recent post-hoc epidemiological analysis of the ACCORD data suggests that individuals who experience symptomatic, severe hypoglycaemia are at increased risk of death, but such risk of death from hypoglycaemia was less in intensively-treated individuals (Miller *et al.*, 2010).

The likelihood of developing such hypoglycaemic episodes was more in people with poor glycaemic control at baseline, irrespective of the treatment strategy (Miller *et al.*, 2010; Bonds *et al.*, 2010). In fact, people who were resistant to improvements in HbA_{1c} had more hypoglycaemia and a greater mortality. This suggests that if there is no improvement in HbA_{1c}, instead of intensifying the therapy and possibly increasing the risk of hypoglycaemia, attention should be directed toward supporting individuals' understanding and adherence to treatments. In the ADVANCE trial, participants had a similar mean age, level of pre-existing CVD and were treated to achieve target HbA_{1c} of 6.5% (48 mmol/mol). The investigators noted a significant reduction (14%) in microvascular outcomes but did not find any significant reductions in CVD and mortality during the study period of 5 years. There was no increase in all cause mortality (ADVANCE Study Group, 2008).

In the UKPDS intervention trial, the relative risk reduction in myocardial infarction was of greater proportion than observed in the ACCORD/ADVANCE trials. This could be due to the younger participant group, randomisation done at the time of diagnosis of type 2 diabetes, and fewer pre-existing macrovascular complications at baseline (7.5%) (58mmol/mol) in the UKPDS cohort.

Conclusions

Although the positive macrovascular effects of early glycaemic control may take decades to become apparent, tight glycaemic control — achieving HbA_{1c} of 6.5% (48mmol/mol) or below — must be instituted soon after diagnosis. Where macrovascular complications develop, the intensity of glycaemic control should be individualised, as tight control has been shown to be harmful in these cases. Efforts should be made to identify individuals with existing CVD, as well as those who are at risk of hypoglycaemia, and patient education should be tailored accordingly. Where there is a high baseline HbA_{1c} and the patient does not appear to respond to glycaemic therapy, caution must be practiced, as these people seem to have the highest risk of severe hypoglycaemia and mortality.

Key points

- The UK Prospective Diabetes Study (UKPDS) and the Diabetes Control and Complications Trial (DCCT) have improved understanding of diabetes mellitus
- Early, good glycaemic control is beneficial in type 2 diabetes, in terms of cardiovascular disease outcomes and mortality
- Caution must be practiced in people who have a high HbA_{1c} and who do not to respond to glucose-lowering therapy, as these individuals appear to be at high risk of severe hypoglycaemia and mortality.

Further information

ACCORD Trial: www.accordtrial.org

ADVANCE Trial: www.advance-trial.com

Diabetes Control and Complications Trial (DCCT):
http://diabetes.niddk.nih.gov/dm/ pubs/control/

UK Prospective Diabetes Study (UKPDS):
http://www.dtu.ox.ac.uk/index. php?maindoc=/ukpds/

References

Action to Control Cardiovascular Risk in Diabetes Study Group (2008) Effects of intensive glucose lowering in type 2 diabetes. *N Engl J Med* **358**(24): 2545-59

ADVANCE Collaborative Group (2008) Intensive blood glucose control and vascular outcomes in patients with type 2 diabetes. *N Engl J Med* **358**(24): 2560-72

Bonds D et al (2010) The association between symptomatic, severe hypoglycaemia and mortality in type 2 diabetes: retrospective epidemiological analysis of the ACCORD study. *BMJ* **340:** b4909

Diabetes UK (2009) Diabetes in the UK 2009: Key statistics on diabetes. http://tinyurl.com/ydocmlo (accessed 24 February 2010)

Diabetes UK (2009) 7 million predicted to have pre diabetes. http://www.diabetes.org.uk/About_us/News_Landing_Page/7m-in-UK-have-prediabetes/

Holman R et al (2008a) 10-year follow-up of intensive glucose control in type 2 diabetes. *N Engl J Med* **359**(15): 1577-89

Holman R et al (2008b) Long-term follow-up after tight control of blood pressure in type 2 diabetes. *N Engl J Med* **359**(15): 1565-76

Holman N (2011) Diabetes Evidence-Based Management 31, Using data to inform care needs planning for people with diabetes. *Practice Nursing* **22**(5): 258-63

Hypertension in Diabetes Study (1993) Hypertension in Diabetes Study (HDS) 1. Prevalence of hypertension in newly presenting type 2 diabetic patients and the association with risk factors for cardiovascular and diabetic complications. *J Hypertens* **11**(3): 309-17

Miller M et al (2010) The effects of baseline characteristics, glycaemia treatment approach, and glycated haemoglobin concentration on the risk of severe hypoglycaemia: post hoc epidemiological analysis of the ACCORD study. *BMJ* **340:** b5444

Nathan D et al, Diabetes Control and Complications Trial/ Epidemiology of Diabetes Interventions and Complications Study Research Group et al (2005) Intensive diabetes treatment and cardiovascular disease in patients with type 1 diabetes. *N Engl J Med* **353**(52): 2643-53

Selvin E et al (2004) Meta-analysis: glycosylated hemoglobin and cardiovascular disease in diabetes mellitus. *Ann Intern Med* **141**(6): 421-31

Stratton I et al (2000) Association of glycaemia with macrovascular and microvascular complications of type 2 diabetes (UKPDS 35): prospective observational study. *BMJ* **321**(7258): 405-12

UK Prospective Diabetes Study (UKPDS) Group (1998) Intensive blood-glucose control with sulphonylureas or insulin compared with conventional treatment and risk of complications in patients with type 2 diabetes (UKPDS 33). *Lancet* **352**(9131): 837-53

Chapter 3

Promoting healthy eating and weight loss

Paul Pipe-Thomas

Introduction

Rising obesity rates are strongly associated with an increase in the incidence of type 2 diabetes, which looks set to increase further — the Association of Public Health Observatories has forecast that by the year 2015, 8% of the UK population will have diabetes (APHO, 2010). This will have a significant impact on life expectancy, given that type 1 diabetes can reduce life expectancy by 15 years and type 2 diabetes by between 5 and 7 years (YHPHO, 2006).

The diagnosis of diabetes can be devastating, and many people are left in a state of shock, unsure of what to do next, often overwhelmed with a lot of information (Snoek and Skinner, 2005). Following diagnosis, people may be informed about what they can and cannot eat, and they may feel that they understand the risks of blindness, foot amputation, kidney problems and heart disease. As they attend many appointments to see nurses, specialist nurses, podiatrists, doctors, ophthalmologists and dietitians, psychological consequences such as learned powerlessness and reduced self-esteem can develop (Fitzgerald Miller, 2000; Snoek and Skinner, 2005).

Standard 3 of the national service framework (NSF) for diabetes (Department of Health [DoH], 2001; 2005) promotes the empowerment of individuals with diabetes to take an active role in their treatment. It recommends that this is achieved through referral to a structured education programme. This approach has also been recommended by the National Institute for Health and Clinical Excellence (NICE) (2003; 2008).

In line with standards 9 and 10 of the NSF for diabetes (DoH, 2001), people with diabetes should be referred for annual retinal screening and foot assessment. This is particularly important as a large proportion of people who are diagnosed with type 2 diabetes already have associated complications (United Kingdom Prospective Diabetes Study [UKPDS], 1990).

Waist circumference and body mass index

For some time, body mass index (BMI) has been used to classify obesity (*Table 1*). However, BMI does not take body composition, such as muscle bulk, and the different amounts of visceral and subcutaneous fat, into consideration — simply mass and height. Body composition is important when assessing obesity, as an athlete with a high muscle mass can have the same BMI as a person with central obesity.

Waist circumference can provide a clearer picture of a person's risk of obesity, particularly when used in conjunction with BMI (World Health Organization [WHO], 1998). Together with the BMI chart, there are criteria for classifying obesity according to waist circumference (*Table 2*).

Naser *et al* (2006: p.1093) argued that 'central obesity is strongly associated with development and worsening of type 2 diabetes' and that 'waist circumference has emerged as a more specific marker of metabolic risk'. This recommendation was taken up by Diabetes UK in its 'Measure up' campaign, which highlighted the importance of waist circumference.

Central obesity (visceral fat) is more than merely a marker of diabetes risk. It has a strong association with the development of diabetes and cardiovascular disease through insulin resistance and cardiometabolic effects (Grundy *et al*, 2004; Stumvoll *et al*, 2005).

Table 1. Classification of obesity in adults based on body mass index (BMI)	
Underweight	$\leq 18.5\text{kg/m}^2$
Healthy/normal weight	$18.5–24.9\text{kg/m}^2$
Overweight (pre-obese)	$25–29.9\text{kg/m}^2$
Moderate obesity (class 1 obesity)	$30–34.9\text{kg/m}^2$
Severe obesity (class 2 obesity)	$35–39.9\text{kg/m}^2$
Morbid obesity (class 3 obesity)	$\geq 40\text{kg/m}^2$

Table 2. Classification of risk of obesity based on waist circumference		
	Risk	**Waist circumference**
Men	Increased risk	94–102cm
	Substantially increased risk	>102cm
Women	Increased risk	80–88cm
	Substantially increased risk	>88cm

Achieving weight loss through dietary change

In simple terms, weight loss might be regarded as addressing an energy imbalance. If energy intake (from food consumed) is greater than energy expended (through physical activity), the result is an increase in weight. Likewise, if energy intake is less than energy expended, the net result is weight loss. However, the full picture is more complex — social factors must be taken into account. Weight loss has proven benefits for health (SIGN, 1996; 2010).

Diabetes UK has revised its evidence-based guidelines for the prevention of, and nutritional management in type 2 diabetes (Dyson *et al*, 2011). The new guidelines put greater emphasis on carbohydrate counting, a more flexible approach to weight loss and adherence to alcohol guidelines, in accordance with national recommendations.

It can be argued that the availability of affordable convenience foods (including 'ready meals') has reduced the population's cooking skills and led to an increase in the consumption of energy-dense foods. At the same time, labour-saving devices and cars have become widely available, resulting in an overall reduction in physical activity. Hence, the current population generally consumes higher-energy foods and uses less energy than in the past. Perhaps to counter this, an industry of health clubs and gyms has developed, which promotes exercise (BBC Online, 1998).

Dietary behaviour is shaped by a complex developmental process, from childhood and adolescence into adult life. Therefore, it is not surprising that many find it difficult to make dietary changes in adulthood. Lifestyle changes are crucial to the treatment of obesity (Bandura, 1997) and to be successful, individuals must have great motivation and a readiness to change (Prochaska and Velicer, 1998). Change is a difficult process to undertake, especially if the individual feels the actions are either unrelated to him/herself or have no value.

Achieving and maintaining weight loss is a complex task that requires support from health professionals and immediate family. No single approach suits everyone, so a variety of approaches must be made available. Different approaches can be used at different stages during an individual's attempts to lose weight.

The dietitian's role, which incorporates assessment, negotiation, encouragement and support, is illustrated by the case study below. Dietitians are increasingly trained in behaviour change techniques, including counselling skills, motivational interviewing and cognitive behavioural therapy, to help patients set realistic goals. These goals must be appropriate to the individual — it is unrealistic to set a target BMI within the normal range when the perso᠆ ᠄

grossly overweight. In such cases, a more realistic target might be 10% weight loss (Scottish Intercollegiate Guidelines Network [SIGN], 1996).

It can help to set smaller, more achievable targets. For instance, it has been proven that a 10kg reduction in weight has substantial benefits (SIGN, 1996) (*Table 3*). In patients with diabetes, losing weight can improve insulin sensitivity and may eventually lead to improved glycaemic control (SIGN, 1996).

Physical activity and weight loss in diabetes

Exercise has many benefits for people with diabetes (*Table 4*). A number of key reviews and guidelines have highlighted the importance of physical activity (SIGN, 1996; Shaw *et al*, 2002; DoH, 2004; Thomas *et al*, 2006).

In a Cochrane review, Thomas *et al* (2006) reported that 'exercise significantly improves glycaemic control and reduces visceral adipose tissue and plasma triglycerides, but not plasma cholesterol, in people with type 2 diabetes, even without weight loss.'

SIGN (1996: 13) reported that 'exercise training improves glucose tolerance and insulin sensitivity independent of weight loss.'

A Cochrane protocol on exercise for obesity warned that exercise encourages weight loss by bringing about a negative energy balance, but this negative balance can be easily lost through additional calorie intake (Shaw *et al*, 2002: 3). These authors recommended that 'exercise should be considered an adjunct to dietary intervention aimed at weight control'.

The Chief Medical Officer for England has recommended that 'adults should achieve at least 30 minutes moderate activity on five or more days of the week' (DoH, 2004: 24). This reaffirms previous recommendations by the DoH (1996a; 1996b).

Anti-obesity medications

Anti-obesity medications (such as orlistat) are effective in supporting short-term weight loss (Norris *et al*, 2005). However, to address an individual's long-term goals, dietary and other lifestyle changes must be made. Many people regard anti-obesity medications as 'miracle cures', so it is important to stress that their benefits are short-term, i.e. they can be a useful adjunct when introducing long-term dietary changes.

Table 3. The benefits of a 10 kg weight loss	
Mortality	>20% fall in total mortality
	>30% fall in diabetes-related deaths
	>40% fall in obesity-related cancer deaths
Blood pressure	Fall of 10mmHg systolic
	Fall of 20mmHg diastolic
Diabetes	Fall of 50% in fasting glucose
Lipids	Fall of 10% total cholesterol
	Fall of 15% low-density lipoprotein (LDL)
	Fall of 30% triglycerides (TG)
	Rise of 8% high-density lipoprotein (HDL)
(Scottish Intercollegiate Guidelines Network, 2010)	

Table 4. Benefits of regular exercise for patients with type 2 diabetes mellitus	
1	Lower blood glucose concentrations during and after exercise
2	Lower basal and post prandial insulin concentrations
3	Improved insulin sensitivity
4	Lower glycosylated haemoglobin levels
5	Improved lipid profile:
	- Decreased triglycerides (TG)
	- Slightly decreased low-density lipoprotein cholesterol (LDL)
	- Increased high-density lipoprotein cholesterol (HDL)
6	Improvement in mild-to-moderate hypertension
7	Increased energy expenditure:
	Adjunct to diet for weight reduction
	Increased fat loss
	Preservation of lean body mass
8	Cardiovascular conditioning
9	Increased strength and flexibility
10	Improved sense of wellbeing and enhanced quality of life
From: LeRoith *et al*, 2004: 1100	

Case study

Table C1. Nutritional recommendations	
Protein	No more than 1g per kg body weight
Total fat	Less than 35% of energy intake
Saturated + transunsaturated fat	Less than 10% of energy intake
Omega-6 polyunsaturated fat	Less than 10% of energy intake
Omega-3 polyunsaturated fat	Eat fish, especially oily fish, once or twice weekly Fish oil supplements are not recommended
Monounsaturated fat	Between 10–20% of energy intake
Total carbohydrate	Between 45–60% of energy intake
Sucrose	Up to 10% of daily energy intake
Fibre	No quantitative recommendation
Vitamins and anti-oxidants	Encourage foods naturally rich in vitamins and antioxidants
Salt	6g sodium chloride per day
From: Nutrition Subcommittee of the Diabetes Care Advisory Committee of Diabetes UK, 2003.	

Jane is a 55-year-old married woman who was diagnosed with type 2 diabetes following an oral glucose tolerance test. Within 2 weeks of diagnosis she was seen by a dietitian, who recorded her height (1.55m) and weight (111.5kg). Her body mass index (BMI) was 46.4kg/m^2 (morbidly obese) and her waist circumference was 129.5cm.

In line with national recommendations for people with diabetes (*Table C1*), Jane's initial appointment with the dietitian included a dietary assessment. Dietary goals were agreed (*Table C2*) and a follow-up appointment was arranged for 3 months later.

Review appointment

Jane's first review with the dietitian focused on her concerns about her weight and barriers to losing weight. Despite her efforts in the previous 10 weeks, she had achieved only minimal weight loss.

The dietitian suggested that she keep a food diary. This self-help tool was explained as a two-step process — she was to keep an accurate record of her daily intake of food and drink for 7 days, then she was

Table C2. Summary of agreed dietary changes for Jane
Include a starchy food at each meal
Reduce protein portion size and don't add cheese to salads
Limit shellfish, replace with oily fish
Increase milk to half a pint a day
Aim to reduce weight by 0.5–1kg per week

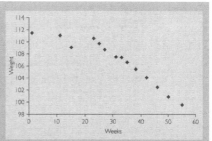

Figure C1. Weight loss recorded for Jane

to self-evaluate and make dietary changes, as appropriate.

With the primary aim of reducing her weight, Jane requested further professional support.

Further reviews

Jane found the food diary an excellent tool for reviewing her diet and found that she managed to lose weight as she increased her physical activity. After relaxing her diet her weight increased again, but she promptly used the food diary to help regain control.

Latest review

Over the following weeks, Jane's physical activity increased and she lost weight (*Figure C1*). She had long held an interest in swimming, which was the mainstay of her exercise regimen. She now swims three or four times a week.

At week 32, an anti-obesity medication (orlistat) was introduced. Its use was discussed and she agreed to try it, with regular dietetic review to monitor her weight and dietary intake, to ensure that her diet was nutritionally balanced.

As Jane maintained her weight loss and increased physical activity, she achieved improvements in her glycaemic control and serum lipids (*Table C3*).

Table C3. Improving Jane's glycaemic control						
Date	HbA1c (%)	Cholesterol	Serum lipids			
			HDL	LDL	Ratio	TG
Baseline	6.3	5.7	1.3	3.9	4.4	1.07
16 weeks	5.5					
32weeks	5.6	3.7	1.5	1.7	2.5 1	10
HDL = high-density lipoprotein; LDL = low-density lipoprotein; TG = triglycerides						

Conclusions

People with diabetes who are obese should be referred to a dietitian for specialist advice. Referral to a structured education programme, such as 'Diabetes Education and Self Management for Ongoing and Newly Diagnosed' (DESMOND) or the 'Expert Patients Programme' can also help, enabling people to take control of their diet and lifestyle changes. Further information on these is available online:

www.desmond-project.org.uk
www.expertpatients.co.uk

Healthy eating is a fundamental principle of diabetes treatment, and the Nutrition Subcommittee of the Diabetes Care Advisory Committee of Diabetes UK (2003; 2011) has published dietary guidelines, to help health professionals support people with diabetes to make informed choices about food.

People with diabetes often feel stressed and confused when faced with choices about which foods to buy and eat. Reviews with a dietitian, at diagnosis and at regular intervals thereafter, can help by translating dietary recommendations into practical, individualised advice on food choices, food shopping, and meal planning, which can ease this stress.

It is essential that people are given ongoing support. Healthy eating is more than simply choosing the right ingredients or isolated nutrients, or the mechanics of eating and digesting food. Eating behaviours are rooted in personal development from birth, throughout childhood and into adulthood, and comprise a complex interaction of feelings, economic and cultural factors, cooking skills, likes and dislikes. Furthermore, food choices and eating take place within the context of a person's family and social life, which can make dietary changes difficult to implement.

Dietitians have an important role within the multidisciplinary team that supports people with diabetes. To provide people such as Jane with effective, high-quality care, it is essential that there is effective communication with and other members of her health professional team is essential to providing effective care.

Key points

- Central obesity is strongly associated with the development of insulin resistance, diabetes, and cardiovascular disease
- People with diabetes should be referred to a dietitian for advice at diagnosis
- Dietitians can translate complex dietary recommendations into practical, individualised advice on food choices, food shopping, and meal planning.

References

Bandura A (1997) Self-Efficacy, The Exercise of Control. Freeman, New York

BBC News (1998) Business: the company file: healthy business. http://news.bbc.co.uk/1/hi/business/the_company_file/194804.stm (accessed 18 July 2011)

Department of Health (1996a) Strategy Statement on Physical Activity. DH, London

Department of Health (1996b) More People, More Active, More Often. DH, London

Department of Health (2001) National Service Framework: Diabetes: Standards. The Stationery Office, London

Department of Health (2004) At least five a week: Evidence on the impact of physical activity and its relationship to health. DH, London

Department of Health (2005) *Structured Education in Diabetes—Report from the Patient Education Working Group.* DH, London

Dyson P et al (2011) Diabetes UK evidence-based nutritional guidelines of the prevention and management of diabetes. Diabetes UK position statements and care recommendations. www.diabetesuk.org

Fitzgerald Miller J (2000) Coping with Chronic Illness, Overcoming Powerlessness. FA Davis Company, USA

Grundy S et al (2004) Definition of metabolic syndrome: Report of the National, Heart, Lung, and Blood Institute/American Heart Association conference on scientific issues related to definition. *Circulation* **109**: 433-38

LeRoith D et al (2004) Diabetes Mellitus: A Fundamental and Clinical Text. 3rd edn. Lippincott Williams and Wilkins, Philadelphia PA

Naser K et al (2006) The emerging pandemic of obesity and diabetes: Are we doing enough to prevent a disaster? *International Journal of Clinical Practice* **60**(9): 1093-97

National Institute for Health and Clinical Excellence (2003) Guidance on the Use of Patient- Education Models for Diabetes. NICE, London

National Institute for Clinical Excellence (2008) Type 2 Diabetes (Update). NICE, London

Norris S et al (2005) Pharmacotherapy for weight loss in adults with type 2 diabetes mellitus. *Cochrane Database Syst Rev* 2005(1): CD004096

Nutrition Subcommittee of the Diabetes Care Advisory Committee of Diabetes UK, (2003) The implementation of nutritional advice for people with diabetes. *Diabet Med* **20**: 786-807

Prochaska J, Velicer W (1998) Behaviour change: The transtheoretical model of health behavior change. *Am J Health Promot* **12**(1): 38-48

Scottish Intercollegiate Guidelines Network (1996) Obesity in Scotland: Integrating Prevention with Weight Management. SIGN, Edinburgh

Scottish Intercollegiate Guidelines Network (2010) Obesity. SIGN, Edinburgh

Shaw K, et al (2002) Exercise for obesity. (Protocol) *Cochrane Database Syst Rev* 2002(3): CD003817

Snoek F, Skinner C (2005) Psychology in Diabetes Care. John Wiley and Son

Stumvoll M et al (2005) Type 2 diabetes: principles of pathogenesis and therapy. *Lancet* **365**(9467): 1333-46

Thomas D et al (2006) Exercise for type 2 diabetes mellitus. *Cochrane Database Syst Rev* 2006(3): CD002968

United Kingdom Prospective Diabetes Study (UKPDS) Group (1990) Hypertension in type 2 diabetes. UKPDS 6. *Diabetes Research* 13: 1-11

World Health Organization (1998) Obesity: Preventing and Managing the Global Epidemic. Report of a WHO consultation on obesity. WHO, Geneva

Yorkshire and Humberside Public Health Observatory (2006) Diabetes—Key Facts. YHPHO, York University

Chapter 4

Physical activity and health

Francesca Annan

Introduction

Achieving a healthy, active lifestyle is considered an important part of diabetes management for people of all ages and with all types of diabetes. This chapter explains how healthcare practitioners can motivate people to achieve their recommended targets for physical activity, and explain the relationships between exercise, blood glucose control and diabetes management. To provide effective advice, practitioners must have a good knowledge of activities to recommend and also a clear understanding of the physiological effects of exercise on glucose homeostasis.

Definitions relating to exercise and physical activity

'Physical activity' can be described as any movement of skeletal muscle that results in energy expenditure. Examples of physical activity include household tasks such as gardening, walking the dog, carrying heavy loads and doing the weekly shopping. 'Exercise' is physical activity that is planned, structured and that involves repetitive body movements, done to improve or maintain one or more components of physical fitness (World Health Organization [WHO], 2010). Examples of exercise include swimming, gym classes and sports such as football and rugby.

Exercise is divided into 'aerobic' and 'anaerobic' subcategories. Aerobic exercise, characterised by relatively low levels of muscular contraction, is of prolonged duration and uses carbohydrates, fats and some proteins as fuel sources. Aerobic activities are often described as 'endurance sports' and include running, cycling, swimming and football. Anaerobic exercise is characterised by high levels of muscular contraction, for short periods of time. There are two anaerobic energy systems — phosphagen and anaerobic glycolysis (Powers and Howley, 2007). Anaerobic activities promote strength and power, and include sprinting, weight lifting and field athletic events. Because different energy systems are used to fuel these different types of exercise, there can be marked differences in blood glucose responses. Aerobic exercise generally lowers blood glucose levels, whereas anaerobic exercise often causes them to rise.

'Resistance' exercise involves the repetitive movement of specific muscle groups against opposing forces that are generated by resistance (e.g. to pushing or pulling). It is used to develop muscle strength.

Intensity of exercise

Together with recommendations for the type of exercise to be performed, advice on the intensity of exercise should also be given. This can be quantified by determining the ratio of a person's metabolic rate when performing a specific activity to their basal metabolic rate (resting energy expenditure) — this ratio is known as the metabolic equivalent of task (MET). Sitting quietly (resting) has a MET of 1, equivalent to an energy cost of 1 kilocalorie per kg of body weight per hour.

A compendium of physical activities together with MET values has been published by Ainsworth *et al.* (2000) (*Table 1*), who describe activities with MET values of between 3 and 6 as 'moderate intensity activities' and those with values of 6 and above as 'vigorous exercise'.

Exercise recommendations for the general population

The links between physical activity, exercise and health are well-recognised, and recommendations for the amount of physical activity necessary to promote good health in adults and children in the general population have been published by national bodies and the WHO.

The WHO (2010) recommends that adults participate in 150 minutes of physical activity and exercise per week, incorporating both moderate and vigorous exercise. The same publication advises that 300 minutes of exercise per week has even greater health benefits.

Table 1. Examples of moderate and vigorous activities	
Moderate intensity activities (3–6 METs)	**Vigorous exercise (≥6 METs)**
Low impact aerobics, Walking at 3mph Gardening Cycling (leisure) <10mph Ballroom dancing	High impact aerobics Walking uphill carrying a 10kg load Heavy digging Cycling (moderate effort) >12mph
From: Ainsworth *et al.*, 2000	

When considering an individual's exercise and physical activity targets, energy balance and weight maintenance must be accounted for. A review by the American College of Sports Medicine (Donnelly *et al.*, 2009) concluded that individuals who were striving to achieve weight loss often needed physical activity levels of 60 minutes a day in order to achieve a negative energy balance. The WHO target of 300 minutes of activity per week may be appropriate in this group.

Exercise recommendations include advice on the types of activity that should be undertaken — for instance, shorter bursts of more vigorous activity might be recommended together with resistance exercise, to improve muscle strength and tone (*Table 2*).

Exercise recommendations for people with diabetes

People with diabetes are encouraged to do the same amount of exercise as the general population. Increased levels of physical activity have been shown to be beneficial to the person with type 2 diabetes, particularly with regard to cardiovascular health (Marwick *et al.*, 2009). The evidence for the benefits of exercise in type 1 diabetes is less well described.

The American Diabetes Association (Sigal *et al.*, 2006) and the American College of Sports Medicine (Albright *et al.*, 2000) recommend that patients with type 2 diabetes undertake at least 150 minutes of physical activity or exercise a week, with no more than two consecutive non-exercise days. In a position paper published by the Association of British Clinical Diabetologists (ABCD), Nagi and Gallen (2010) discuss the benefits of increased physical activity in type 2 diabetes. Compared with rest, physical activity increases peripheral muscle glucose uptake by 7–20 times.

Table 2. Sources of physical activity guidelines
American College of Sports Medicine: www.acsm.org
At least five a week: Evidence on the impact of physical activity and its relationship to health (DoH, 2004): http://tinyurl.com/26jual
British Heart Foundation National Centre for Physical Activity and Health: www.bhfactive.org.uk
World Health Organization Global Strategy on Diet, Physical Activity and Health: www.who.int/dietphysicalactivity/en/

Table 3. Examples of resistance and moderate intensity exercise	
Resistance exercise	**Moderate intensity exercise**
Use of weight machines	Running (e.g. on treadmill)
Circuit training	Exercise bike
	Cross-training

The possible health benefits of increasing physical activity include weight loss or maintenance of lost weight, improvement in wellbeing, an improved lipid profile and improved glycaemic control. With regular activity, these benefits are sustained. In terms of glycaemic control, regular daily exercise is of greater benefit than exercise performed on two to three days per week. The American Diabetes Association (ADA) guidelines (2006) recommend leaving a gap of no more than two days between exercise sessions.

It should be noted that most exercise recommendations are for moderate intensity exercise. However, the DARE trial (Sigal *et al.*, 2007) showed that mixed exercise programmes (including moderate intensity and resistance exercise) are potentially of benefit (*Table 3*).

Energy balance

It is important to consider the energy costs of physical activity. For many people with type 2 diabetes, exercise is part of a programme aimed at lowering body weight, or at least preventing further weight gain. The advice given to these people must account for the energy costs of exercise/physical activity and also energy intake. If individuals are to lose weight, then a negative energy balance must be achieved. Hence, higher levels of physical activity may be required.

Knowing the MET values of different activities, health professionals can develop strategies for people to increase energy expenditure and promote weight loss. For some people, it is more achievable to increase the physical activities of daily living than to engage in exercise programmes. Some everyday tasks can provide moderate intensity activity (3–6 METs). For example, sweeping a floor has a MET of 4, and raking a lawn has a MET of 4.3. To get in the habit of performing such activities for just 10 minutes at a time can significantly increase an individual's energy expenditure.

In people with type 2 diabetes, where hypoglycaemia is a concern, care should be taken that low blood sugar prevention strategies do not promote positive energy balance. It is more appropriate to reduce medication than to advise an increase in the intake of carbohydrates (MacArthur, 2010). If increased carbohydrates are needed, their energy content should be considered.

It is worth noting that some people with type 2 diabetes who have an insulin deficiency and poor metabolic control may have similar hyperglycaemic responses to intense or strenuous anaerobic exercise as those with type 1 diabetes.

Type 1 diabetes

Evidence of the effects of exercise on glycaemic control in people with type 1 diabetes is conflicting. While the maintenance of high levels of activity does have health benefits, these are not always associated with improvements in HbA_{1c} levels. The glycaemic effects of exercise depend on the type, intensity and duration of activity, as well as circulating levels of insulin and glucose counter-regulatory hormones. These factors are described by Riddell and Perkins (2006).

Depending on the nature of the exercise being undertaken, hypo- or hyperglycaemia can develop. To predict the likely glycaemic response, and make appropriate changes, the intensity and the type of exercise must be identified. *Table 4* shows a list of common activities and their effects on blood glucose levels.

A key factor associated with poor blood glucose control during exercise is a lack of understanding that different types of exercise have different effects in type 1 diabetes. To better understand this, people with type 1 diabetes should be encouraged to check their blood glucose levels before, during (preferably every 30 minutes) and after exercise.

While the advice of different bodies varies, it is generally agreed that pre-exercise values should be near normal. If blood glucose levels are found to be greater than 12mmol/l before exercise, the person should also check for the presence of ketones and delay exercise if they are found. If blood glucose levels are less than 4mmol/l before exercise, then appropriate intervention is required. Where blood glucose levels are between 4 and 7mmol/l, additional carbohydrate is likely to be needed.

When assessing pre-exercise blood glucose levels, the type and duration of exercise to be performed must be considered. During anaerobic activities, blood glucose levels generally rise, and subsequently fall in the post-exercise period. Aerobic activities generally lower blood glucose levels and mixed activities may maintain them. Possible strategies that can be used to manage blood glucose levels include insulin dose adjustment, addition of carbohydrate and manipulation of the exercise programme to include short bursts of high intensity exercise (Bussau *et al.*, 2006). Adjustments for anaerobic activities must be timed, to prevent hyperglycaemia during exercise and late-onset hypoglycaemia afterwards.

Table 4. Types of exercise and blood glucose responses	
Exercise associated with hypoglycaemia	**Exercise associated with hyperglycaemia**
Aerobic activities	*Anaerobic activities*
Swimming	Sprinting
Running	Weight lifting
Cycling	Some movements in team sports
Team sports	(e.g. basketball)

Insulin adjustment

When exercise occurs within 1–2 hours of insulin administration, the person is faced with the problem of over-insulinisation (Riddell, 2006). An excess of insulin prevents liver glucose production and increases the uptake of glucose by skeletal muscle, which results in hypoglycaemia. At the beginning of exercise, insulin levels should drop, to allow the liver to release glucose into the bloodstream to match the increased uptake by skeletal muscle. Individuals with intensive insulin regimens can adjust their doses before exercise to reduce the risk of hypoglycaemia. The degree of adjustment will depend on the type, duration and intensity of exercise to be performed.

Post-exercise hypoglycaemia is usually due to increased glucose uptake by muscles and increased insulin sensitivity. Strategies to reduce this include the consumption of carbohydrate-rich foods within one hour of activity, a reduction in post-exercise bolus and basal insulin doses and adequate consumption of carbohydrate during exercise — especially when duration exceeds 60 minutes.

Food and fluid intake

It is important to ensure that individuals are well hydrated for all types of activity. To prevent hypoglycaemia during aerobic activities, additional carbohydrate should be consumed. This may also be needed to maintain energy levels during exercise.

People with diabetes who participate in sports have the same sports nutrition requirements as non-diabetic athletes. Where additional carbohydrate is necessary to maintain performance during an activity, this should be provided in a form that is immediately available to active muscle. Some examples of suitable exercise snacks are given in *Table 5*. Carbohydrate requirements vary

Table 5. Suitable exercise snacks	
Snack	**Energy and carbohydrate content**
Jaffa cakes (3–4)	140kcal, 30g carbohydrate
Raisins (40g)	120kcal, 30g carbohydrate
Isotonic sports drinks (500ml)	120kcal, 30g carbohydrate
Jelly sweets (40g)	130kcal, 30g carbohydrate

with body weight, duration of exercise, blood glucose levels and timing of the most recent insulin injection.

Exercise that lasts for more than 60 minutes is also associated with an increase in carbohydrate requirements post activity. Individuals who undertake regular training will benefit from the support of a registered dietitian, who can give advice on amounts and timing of carbohydrate foods for exercise.

Conclusions

As well as being part of a healthy lifestyle, physical activity and exercise are part of diabetes management. To successfully adopt exercise recommendations and achieve good glycaemic control, support is necessary and to provide this, health professionals must understand the issues related to exercise management and the promotion of physical activity.

Key points

- Exercise has general health benefits for all people, and specific benefits for those with type 2 diabetes
- Healthcare professionals can understand people and manage the glycaemic effects of different types of exercise
- Strategies include insulin dose adjustment, consumption of carbohydrate and informed choice of exercise programme
- Individuals should be encouraged to check blood glucose levels before, during and after exercise.

References

Ainsworth B et al (2000) Compendium of physical activities: an update of activity codes and MET intensities. *Med Sci Sports Exerc* **32**(9): S498-S504

Albright A et al (2000) American College of Sports Medicine position stand. Exercise and type 2 diabetes. *Med Sci Sports Exerc* 32: 1345-60

American Diabetes Association (2006) Standards of medical care in diabetes–2006. *Diabetes Care* **29**(Suppl 1): s4–s42

Bussau V et al (2006) The 10-s maximal sprint: A novel approach to counter an exercise-mediated fall in glycemia in individuals with type 1 diabetes. *Diabetes Care* 29: 601-6

Donnelly J et al (2009) American College of Sports Medicine. Appropriate physical activity intervention strategies for weight loss and prevention of weight regain for adults. *Med Sci Sports Exerc* 41: 459-71

MacArthur C (2010) Hypoglycaemia in type 2 diabetes. *Practice Nursing* **21**(14): 206-9

Marwick T et al (2009) Exercise training for type 2 diabetes mellitus. Impact on cardiovascular risk: a scientific statement from the American Heart Association. *Circulation* **119:** 3244-62

Nagi D, Gallen I (2010) ABCD position statement on physical activity and exercise in diabetes. *Practical Diabetes International* **27:** 158-63a

Powers S, Howley E (2007) In: *Exercise Physiology: Theory and Application to Fitness and Performance* 6th edn. McGraw Hill, New York

Riddell M, Perkins B (2006) Type 1 diabetes and vigorous exercise: Applications of exercise physiology to patient management. *Canadian Journal of Diabetes* 30: 63-71

Sigal R et al (2006) Physical activity/exercise and type 2 diabetes: a consensus statement from the American Diabetes Association. *Diabetes Care* **29:** 1433-38

Sigal R et al (2007) Effects of aerobic training, resistance training, or both on glycemic control in type 2 diabetes: a randomized trial. *Ann Intern Med* 147: 357-69

World Health Organization (2010) Global recommendations on physical activity for health. WHO, Geneva

Chapter 5

Assessing and communicating risk with people with diabetes

Dr Gillian Hawthorne

Introduction

Supporting and educating patients to take responsibility for the management of their own health is a key priority of the National Service Framework for Diabetes (Department of Health [DoH], 2001) and health professionals have an important role in empowering and helping individuals to do this. This chapter focuses on how to screen in a meaningful way and how to communicate risk with people with diabetes, using a case study to illustrate the main points.

Assessment

Brian has had diabetes for 5 years, and is an ex-smoker. The practice nurse has asked him to return to have his blood pressure measured following his last diabetes check up as his blood pressure is above the national target of 140/80mmHg (National Collaborating Centre for Chronic Conditions [NCC-CC], 2008).

At annual check up, Brian was screened for diabetes complications. Although he has no clinical evidence of diabetic microvascular disease (i.e. retinopathy, neuropathy or renal disease), it is clear that he is at increased risk of diabetic macrovascular complications because of his cardiovascular risk factors, namely:

- High blood pressure
- High total cholesterol.

Evidence base for treatment

Most people with type 2 diabetes (70–80%) are likely to die from cardiovascular disease (Meigs *et al.*, 1997). Coronary heart disease rates are 2–6 times higher than in the non-diabetic population (Stammler *et al.*, 1993) and there is robust evidence to show that effective treatment of cardiovascular risk factors is of benefit (Feher, 2004).

Table 1. Results of tight blood pressure control		
Complication	**Reduced risk**	**p value**
Stroke	44%	p=0.013
Heart failure	56%	p=0.0043
Microvascular endpoint	37%	p=0.0092
Any diabetes-related endpoint	24%	p=0.0046
From: United Kingdom Prospective Diabetes Study Group [UKPDS], 1998.		

Case study 1

Brian is a 55-year-old man who is married with three children. He has had type 2 diabetes for 5 years. He stopped smoking last year, with support from the smoking cessation service. His diabetes has been treated with dietary therapy alone but since he stopped smoking he has gained weight. He has always struggled with his weight and when it was measured at his annual checkup 6 weeks ago (*Table C1*) it was found that his BMI had increased from 30kg/m^2 to 32kg/m^2 in the past year.

At his annual review there was no evidence of either vascular or neuropathic problems. On retinal screening there was no reported diabetic retinopathy and a clinical examination showed that his feet were normal. He was not tested for microalbuminuria, as he forgot to take a urine sample.

At his annual review, he was asked to attend regular appointments for repeat blood pressure readings. Six weeks after his annual review, his blood pressure reading was 146/82mmHg.

Table C1. Brian's biometric data at his annual checkup	
HbA$_{1c}$	6.7%/50mmol/mol
Blood pressure	145/84mmHg
Total cholesterol	5.4mmol/l
eGFR	74ml/minute/1.73m^2
BMI	32kg/m^2
BMI = body mass index; eGFR = estimated glomerular filtration rate; HbA$_{1c}$ = haemoglobin A$_{1c}$	

Blood pressure

The United Kingdom Prospective Diabetes Study Group (UKPDS, 1998) demonstrated that better control of hypertension reduces the risk of death from the long-term complications of diabetes by a third and the risk of death from stroke by more than a third. In this landmark study, 1148 people with hypertension were randomised into one of two groups — a group with 'tight blood pressure control', which achieved a mean blood pressure of 144/82mmHg and a group with 'less tight blood pressure control', which achieved a mean of 154/87mmHg. Tighter blood pressure control was shown to be associated with significant reductions in the risk of stroke, heart failure, macrovascular endpoints and any diabetes-related endpoint (*Table 1*).

Since the UKPDS (1998), a number of trials have investigated the treatment of blood pressure in people with diabetes. Based on the results of these trials, the NCC-CC (2008) for the National Institute for Health and Clinical Excellence (NICE) has recommended a target blood pressure of <140/80mmHg for people with diabetes.

Cholesterol

Since the introduction of statin therapy it has been possible to significantly reduce plasma levels of total cholesterol. Large trials have demonstrated the benefits of statin therapy in reducing coronary heart disease (CHD) risk, many of which — including CARE (Goldberg *et al.*, 1998), 4S (Pyorala *et al.*, 1997) and HPS (Collins *et al.*, 2003) — have included diabetes subgroups. These trials have demonstrated that lowering total cholesterol reduces CHD risk by 25–55% in people with diabetes and by 22–32% in people who do not have diabetes. Hence, the benefit to people with diabetes is equal to or greater than that for non-diabetic individuals. At the time of writing, NICE guidelines (NCC-CC, 2008) recommend a target total cholesterol of <4mmol/l for people with type 2 diabetes.

Sharing goals

Although the practice nurse and general practitioner (GP) understand that Brian is at increased cardiovascular risk because of his elevated blood pressure and total cholesterol, Brian himself may not fully understand the risks. The challenge here is to effectively communicate this information to Brian, so that he can work with the multidisciplinary team to agree on his priorities of care and plan his management accordingly. The manner in which information is communicated to an individual is as important as the information itself (Travaline *et al.*, 2005); both verbal and non-verbal cues can influence a person's perception of the message being given. If Brian understands what the GP or nurse tells him, he is more likely to act on this information. There is increasing evidence to show that people are more adherent to treatment and achieve better outcomes when they are well-informed and engaged in decisions about their management.

Risk communication

Risk can be defined as the probability that a hazard will give rise to harm (Edwards *et al.*, 2002). The diabetes team must engage in risk communication with Brian, which is an open, two-way exchange of information and opinion about his risk of heart disease and stroke. Engaging Brian in this discussion will help him to reach a better understanding and make more informed decisions about his clinical management (Ahl *et al.*, 1993).

A person's understanding of their own risk will be influenced by their overall health, age and language preference. For example, Brian might prefer his risks to be presented numerically, whereas another person may prefer verbal communication. The practice nurse should be mindful of this.

Individuals' perceptions of risk

While doctors tend to overestimate patients' cardiovascular risk (Haussler *et al.*, 2007) people tend to underestimate their own. It is possible that Brian may not be aware of his cardiovascular risk. Furthermore, people recall as little as half of what their physicians tell them. A study by Bairey-Merz *et al.* (2002) found that 70% of individuals with diabetes were not aware that they had an increased risk of cardiovascular disease and stroke.

The practice nurse needs to take time to explain Brian's cardiovascular risk to him, and to check that he understands this explanation. Barriers to risk communication include a lack of time for discussion during the consultation, limited understanding of risk by the individual, a lack of information and poor health literacy (Thomson *et al.*, 2005).

Framing

Information can be presented to people in different ways. How the practice nurse presents information to Brian will influence how he responds. When giving information on risk, a balanced presentation is best. It is better to present data using absolute risk and avoid presenting data as a percentage or a relative risk reduction, particularly when the baseline is not clear (Edwards *et al.*, 2002). However, it should be noted that positive framing (chance of survival) is more effective than negative framing (chance of death) (Edwards *et al.*, 2001), and information on relative risk is can be persuasive (Edwards *et al.*, 2001).

Use of risk calculators

To help explain and demonstrate the effects of risk factors on Brian's cardiovascular risk, the practice nurse may use a risk calculator.

The QRisk is a risk calculator that works out the individual's chance of having heart disease or stroke if he or she is otherwise generally fit and healthy. However, this risk calculator is not helpful for people with diabetes, and it should not be used to explain risk to Brian.

Risk scoring tools are available on general practice computer systems such as EMIS. These calculate cardiovascular risk using data from the Framingham Heart Study (Dawber, 1980). They calculate adjusted risk for people with diabetes by taking actual risk and increasing it by a factor of 1.5 (Chauhan, 2007).

A more robust risk calculator is the UKPDS risk engine, which uses data from the long-term follow-up of 4050 patients in the UKPDS study (Guzder *et al.*, 2005); this is available as a free download from the Diabetes Trials Unit website: www.dtu.ox.ac.uk/riskengine/

Self-assessment tools are becoming available, which people with diabetes can use to estimate their own risk. The American Diabetes Association (ADA) has developed a particularly person-friendly self-assessment tool, which is available on their website: www.diabetes.org

Setting goals

The practice nurse explains that because Brian's cardiovascular risk factors are high blood pressure and high total cholesterol, his treatment goals are those recommended by national guidance (NCC-CC, 2008):

- Blood pressure <140/80mmHg
- Total cholesterol <4mmol/l.

Sharing these treatment goals enables Brian to identify his priorities for care, and increases his chance of achieving valued health outcomes.

Treatment

Brian has successfully reduced his cardiovascular risk by stopping smoking. The practice nurse congratulates him on continuing to maintain this. However, it is clear that since stopping smoking, he has gained weight. For various reasons, he did not attend a structured education course after he was diagnosed with diabetes.

An educated person who can take an active role in managing their disease is an empowered person. The practice nurse ascertains that Brian is keen to learn more about diabetes, and she arranges referral to a structured education course for people with type 2 diabetes (NCC-CC, 2008).

Brian's blood pressure is 145/84mmHg, which is above his target blood pressure of <140/80mmHg. Therefore, his GP and practice nurse arrange for him to start taking an antihypertensive agent, to reduce his blood pressure to target. The choice of antihypertensive is guided by local protocol and the individual's comorbidity (NCC-CC, 2008). Brian is started on an angiotensin-converting enzyme (ACE) inhibitor, which needs to be titrated until his blood pressure is well controlled.

His GP and practice nurse also recommend statin therapy to treat his raised cholesterol. They introduce simvastatin 10mg, which is titrated in a stepwise approach as needed to 40mg, and then reviewed according to local protocol.

Working in partnership

Through discussion, the practice diabetes team has developed a therapeutic alliance with Brian, and has counselled him on his recommended standard of care. The team has respected his individual values and maintained a person-centred approach — they have discussed his problems in implementing advice and tailored management strategies to suit his needs.

Review

At a review 8 weeks later, Brian has attended the structured education course, which he found helpful. He says that he now has a better understanding of the aims of his diabetes treatment, and because of this he is keen to maintain his blood pressure, cholesterol level and blood glucose levels at their agreed targets. He feels more in charge of his diabetes.

He has adjusted his diet, cutting out high-fat snacks and chocolate, and in the past 4 weeks he has lost 2kg in weight. To manage his cholesterol, he is taking simvastatin 20mg once daily and he is keen to have his cholesterol rechecked, to find out if it has fallen below 4mmol/l. He knows that his blood pressure is on target as this has been measured regularly — he has been attending the surgery for titration of his ACE inhibitor and is currently stabilised on lisinopril 10mg once daily. He keeps a record of his results and is glad when his blood pressure is recorded at 136/76mmHg.

Conclusions

Empowering people with diabetes is a core aim (Standard 3) of the national service framework (NSF) for diabetes (DoH, 2001). Empowered people are educated and involved in the planning of their care, so to achieve this aim, people with diabetes must receive adequate and appropriate information to actively participate in their care planning.

In Brian's case, the practice diabetes team has explained his cardiovascular risk to him and helped him to take steps to treat his elevated blood pressure and elevated cholesterol. The success of both of these treatments relies on Brian's understanding of the reasons for being prescribed certain medications and his commitment to continuing to take them.

By sharing the priorities of care with Brian, his GP and practice nurse have actively involved Brian in his care. They have shared and communicated his cardiovascular risk and together they have implemented an action plan with set evidence-based targets for Brian to achieve. The consultation has been supported by referral to evidence-based guidelines and decision aids.

Care planning and structured education facilitate active involvement of people in their treatment. This is how person-centred care works. When people are full partners in decision-making, visual aids which contextualise risk can be useful adjuncts. Successful care planning depends on the individual's engagement and provides an opportunity to discuss and communicate risk.

Key points

■ Care planning and structured education facilitate active involvement of people in their treatment
■ Empowered people are educated and involved in their care planning
■ Maintaining a person-centred consultation maintains a therapeutic alliance in diabetes care.

References

Ahl A et al (1993) Standardisation of nomenclature for animal health risk analysis. *Rev Sci Tech* **12:** 1045–53

Bairey-Merz C et al (2002) Physician attitudes and practices and patient awareness of the cardiovascular complications of diabetes. *J Am Coll Cardiol* **40:** 1877–81

Chauhan U (2007) Cardiovascular disease prevention in primary care. *Br Med Bull* **81–82:** 65–79

Collins R et al; for the Heart Protection Collaborative Group (2003) MRC/BHF heart protection study of cholesterol lowering with simvastatin in 5963 people with diabetes: A randomized placebo-controlled trial. *Lancet* **361:** 2005–16

Dawber T (1980) *The Framingham Study. The Epidemiology of Atherosclerotic Disease.* Harvard University Press, Cambridge, MA

Department of Health (2001) *National Service Framework for Diabetes: Standards.* 14 Dec. DH, London

Edwards A et al (2001) Presenting risk information: A review of the effects of 'framing' and other manipulations on patient outcomes. Review. *J Health Communication* **6:** 61–82

Edwards A et al (2002) Explaining risks: turning numerical data into meaningful pictures. *BMJ* **324:** 827–30

Feher M (2004) Diabetes: preventing coronary heart disease in a high risk group. *Heart* **90**(Suppl iv): iv18–iv21

Goldberg R et al; the CARE investigators (1998) Cardiovascular events and their reduction with pravastatin in diabetic and glucose-intolerant myocardial infarct survivors with average cholesterol levels: Subgroup analyses in the cholesterol and recurrent events trial (CARE). *Circulation* **98:** 2513–9

Guzder R et al (2005) Prognostic value of the Framingham cardiovascular risk equation and the UKPDS risk engine in newly diagnosed type 2 diabetes: Results from a United Kingdom study. *Diabet Med* **22:** 554–62

Haussler B et al (2007) Risk assessment in diabetes management: how do general practitioners estimate risks due to diabetes? *Qual Saf Health Care* **16:** 208–12

Meigs J et al (1997) Metabolic control and prevalent cardiovascular disease in non-insulin dependent diabetes mellitus (NIDDM): The NIDDM patient outcomes research team. *Am J Med* **102:** 38–47

National Collaborating Centre for Chronic Conditions (2008) Type 2 Diabetes: National Clinical Guideline for management in Primary and Secondry Care (Update). NICE guideline 66 (update). Royal College of Physicians, London

Pyorala K et al (1997) Cholesterol lowering with simvastatin improves prognosis of diabetic patients with coronary heart disease. A subgroup analysis of the Scandinavian simvastatin survival study (4S). *Diabetes Care* **20:** 614–20

Stammler J et al for the Multiple Risk Intervention Trial Group (1993) Diabetes other risk factors and twelve year cardiovascular mortality for men screened in the Multiple Risk Intervention Trial. *Diabetes Care* **16:** 443–4

Stewart M (1995) Effective physician-patient communication and health outcomes: A review. *CMAJ* **15:** 1423–33

Thomson R et al (2005) Risk communication in the clinical consultation. *Clin Med* **5:** 465–9

Travaline J et al (2005) Patient- physician communication: Why and How. *J Am Osteopath Assoc* **105:** 13–8

United Kingdom Prospective Diabetes Study (UKPDS) Group (1998b) Tight blood pressure control and risk of macrovascular and micro-vascular complications in type2 diabetes. UKPDS 38. *BMJ* **317:** 703–13

Chapter 6

Supporting individuals after a diagnosis of diabetes

Mandy Edwards

Introduction

Nearly 3 million people in the UK have a diagnosis of diabetes (Diabetes UK, 2010) and a further 7 million are estimated to be in a 'pre diabetes state', with impaired fasting glucose (IFG) levels and impaired glucose tolerance (IGT), (Diabetes UK, 2009). The majority of new cases will be diagnosed and managed in primary care, so practice diabetes teams' workloads can be expected to increase greatly as they support and educate these individuals.

Using a significant event analysis (*Figure 1*) to highlight key points, this chapter examines the education needs of newly-diagnosed individuals.

The newly-diagnosed individual

One should never underestimate the impact that a diagnosis will have on an individual. While some people may already have some knowledge of diabetes and its complications, other people may have no knowledge at all. The newly-diagnosed individual may be shocked and frightened, envisaging amputation and kidney failure within the next few months. The practitioner should establish a good rapport with the person, and explain that concordance with a drug and dietary regimen is associated with a good prognosis.

Although some people may appear to have a limited understanding, you should not assume that your explanations fall on deaf ears. It is important to understand people's experiences and find common goals. The individual's active involvement in self-management is central to improving their glycaemic control.

The focus of patient education has shifted from providing medical information by didactic teaching to empowering people to manage their conditions by strengthening and improving self-management skills, self-efficacy and motivation (Miller and Rollnick, 2002). Self-management techniques such as measuring blood glucose levels, accessing preventive services (including eye, dental and foot care), and making lifestyle changes have reportedly had discouraging results

51

in reducing diabetic complications (Hornsten *et al.*, 2005). Conversely, Hayes *et al.* (2008) cite studies that associate self-management with the maintenance of optimum blood glucose, lipid and blood pressure levels and improved patient outcomes. It should be noted that to sustain behavioural changes, frequent contact is needed between the person with diabetes and the education provider.

Good communication, supported by evidence-based information, is essential for patient-centred care (National Institute for Health and Clinical Excellence [NICE], 2008). At diagnosis, every person and/or their carer should be offered structured education, with annual reinforcement and review (*Table 1*). They should be informed that this is an integral part of diabetes care. Although NICE (2008) recommends that people attend group education sessions, one-to-one sessions are common in general practice, at the time of diagnosis, with ongoing reinforcements for the rest of the individual's life.

Structured education

Effective patient education can enable individuals to manage their diabetes on a day-to-day basis (Department of Health [DoH], 2005). Structured education can improve knowledge, glycaemic control, weight and dietary management, physical activity and psychological wellbeing — especially when tailored to the needs of the individual and when skills-based approaches are incorporated (NICE 2008) (see *Table 1*).

Education of the newly-diagnosed person with diabetes in general practice involves all of the elements of group structured education, but presented in a less formal way. Every person requires the same education, even if they profess to know about the condition. Second-hand information and 'scare stories' need to be clarified and refuted where appropriate. The minimum amount of structured education that an individual should receive from their practice is outlined in the first seven points presented in *Table 1*.

Early dietetic support

Support from a specialist diabetic dietetic team is best practice, but in reality it might be difficult to access. A practice nurse with diabetes training is expected to have the skills necessary to support most people with dietary advice and weight management, although specialist help will be required for complicated cases involving comorbidities. Given the number of issues involved (*Table 2*) and the amount of associated information that needs to be discussed following diagnosis, several visits will be necessary to enable the person and their partner (or carer) to

Table 1. Structured patient education Key Quality Statements
■ A structured curriculum
■ Concerned with all aspects of diabetes
■ Flexible in content
■ Relevant to the individual's psychological needs
■ Adaptable to a person's educational and cultural background
■ Evidence-based and meets the needs of the individual
■ Delivered by trained educators
■ Quality assured
■ Regularly audited
From: DoH 2005, Bannister 2008, NICE 2008

assimilate all of the important facts.

Goals should be realistic and achievable (Furze *et al.*, 2008). One should not assume that people receive all of the information they need in secondary care. In primary care, the practice diabetes team should reinforce the key messages and ensure that people have understood previous guidance.

Does education work?

The Dose Adjustment for Normal Eating (DAFNE, 2011) and the Diabetes Education and Self-Management for Ongoing and Newly-Diagnosed (DESMOND, 2011) and XPERT projects (2011) are national patient education courses for people with type 1 and type 2 diabetes respectively. These courses help people to identify their own health risks, set specific goals and meet the criteria for structured education. The DESMOND project is highly-valued by many of its participants, and examples of participant experiences are available on its website.

One such participant, Tim Taylor gives an account of his diagnosis, treatment and education programme (Taylor, 2009). Tim found that the scare stories he came across in books were dispelled during group sessions, where participants talked about the disease, its causes, implications, the mechanics of what was going wrong in the body, and how to adapt diet and lifestyle to reduce the dangers posed by diabetes.

Table 2. Issues to be covered at the initial and subsequent consultations
Topics for discussion with a person newly diagnosed with diabetes:
■ Diet and lifestyle
■ Exercise
■ Glucose control
■ Blood pressure control
■ Smoking
■ Insurance
■ Driving
■ Travel
■ Foot care
■ Managing illness
■ Vaccinations

Although not all localities have access to these projects, the person diagnosed with diabetes still requires education. A practice nurse with diabetes training can offer this on a one-to-one basis. As highlighted in Tim's story, people have many misconceptions about their diabetes — for example, that they are not allowed to eat biscuits or drink alcohol. Lack of education and misunderstanding are key factors in the development of diabetic complications.

Ethnic minorities

In the UK, the Bangladeshi community is the population that is most susceptible to diabetes (Rahul *et al.*, 2008). Delivering a structured education programme for hard-to-reach ethnic groups is a challenge for all health professionals, but many resources are available to ensure that people from minority ethnic backgrounds receive the recommended support, advice and education.

Interpreters can be used face-to-face and via the telephone, through services such as the Language Line. One should avoid using relatives and friends to interpret for a person whose first language is not English, as confidentiality might be breached and what is said might be misinterpreted (Dhami and Sheikh, 2008). Untrained lay interpreters may not convey the correct information from the person to the nurse and vice versa. It is worth remembering that, although some health promotion materials are available in different languages, not everybody is able to read in their first language.

The significant event report (*Figure 1*) gives an example of one person's management following diagnosis with diabetes. The wait between being informed of the diagnosis and receiving education can create unnecessary anxiety, which can be partially alleviated by reassuring the individual that the multidisciplinary team is there to educate and support them and that follow-up arrangements have been made.

Figure 1. An example of one person's management following diagnosis with diabetes

SIGNIFICANT EVENT REPORT

Date: *DD/MM/YYYY*	**Place where the incident occurred** *Practice P*
What happened?	Patient A was extremely anxious and it was up to nurse B to reassure her and to explain what a diagnosis of diabetes meant.
Why did it happen?	Patient A had recently been diagnosed with type 2 diabetes following two raised fasting blood glucose readings. She had a body mass index of 32kg/m^2, was normotensive and had no significant family history. Following diagnosis, she was naturally anxious, having trawled the internet for information.
What action was taken?	Nurse B introduced herself and explained that she managed all the patients with diabetes, which reassured patient A that the nurse was knowledgeable. She explained to patient A that she would need to be seen over several weeks for education and support, as there was too much to discuss in one visit. During this first visit, nurse B explained what the diagnosis meant, and discussed general lifestyle issues, such as healthy eating to lose weight and exercise to reduce the blood sugar. Nurse B offered patient A literature to support this visit and made another 30-minute appointment for the following week. Over the next 5 weeks, nurse B discussed the importance of blood glucose control, relating it to complications as the weeks progressed.
How could it have been prevented?	At time of diagnosis, patient A could have been forewarned against potentially worrying information available on the internet or at the library. Patient A should be reassured at diagnosis that her first appointment would explain everything clearly.
Positive outcomes	A realistic action plan was negotiated, which empowered patient A to make behavioural changed that suited her lifestyle. She decided to modify the family diet to reduce convenience food and include more fruits and vegetables, and to take evening walks. The repeat blood glucose reading after three months was lower and the haemoglobin A$_{1c}$ (HbA$_{1c}$) was within the recommended parameters. Patient A's BMI had fallen to 31.2kg/m^2. Nurse B continued to review patient A every 4 months for the first year, then twice yearly. Patient A knew she could make an appointment or telephone nurse B at any time if she had any concerns.

Patient satisfaction

It has been reported that, despite efforts to individualise care and find ways to communicate with people in healthcare situations, many people report dissatisfying clinical encounters (Hornsten *et al.*, 2005). People like to be talked 'with', and not 'to'. Diabetes teams must accept that they can please some people some of the time, but they cannot please every person all of the time.

Conclusion

Two major challenges of diabetes education are imparting knowledge to the individual and their significant others as soon as possible after diagnosis, and incorporating changes into the person's life (Kiely and Crestodina, 2006). The third greatest challenge for diabetes teams must be to motivate people to change behaviour, which in turn will reduce the risk of developing complications from diabetes. Education must be timely, have realistic goals, and be spread over a period of time, with frequent reinforcement.

Key points

- Care planning and structured education facilitate active involvement of people in their treatment
- Empowered people are educated and involved in their care planning
- Maintaining a person-centred consultation maintains a therapeutic alliance in diabetes care.

References

Bannister M (2008) Management of type 2 diabetes: updated NICE guidelines. *Primary Health Care* **18**(8): 32-34

DAFNE (2011) Dose adjustment for normal eating DAFNE Programme for Type 1 Diabetes. http://www.dafne.uk.com/

Department of Health (2001) National Service Framework for Diabetes: Standards. http://www.dh.gov.uk (accessed 1 April 2011)

Department of Health (2005) Structured patient education in diabetes: Report from the Patient Education Working Group. http://www.dh.gov.uk (accessed 1 April 2011)

DESMOND (2011) Diabetes Education for Type 2 Diabetes. http://www.desmond-project.org.uk/

Dhami S, Sheikh A (2008) Health promotion: reaching ethnic minorities. *Practice Nurse* **36**(8): 21-25

Diabetes-help (2010) Diabetes statistics. http://www.diabets-help.co.uk. (accessed 1 April 2011)

Diabetes UK (2008) Undiagnosed Diabetes: a big problem in the UK. 25Feb 2008. http://www.diabetes.co.uk (accessed 1 April 2011)

Diabetes UK (2010) Diabetes prevalence 2010. http://www.diabetes.org.uk (accessed 1 April 2011)

Furze G, Donnison J, Lewin R (2008) The Clinician's Guide to Chronic Disease Management for Long Term Conditions: A Cognitive Behavioural Approach, M&K Update Ltd, UK

Hayes E et al (2008) Alliance not compliance: coaching strategies to improve type 2 diabetes outcomes. *J Am Acad Nurse Pract* **20**(3): 155-62

Hornsten A et al (2005) Patient satisfaction with diabetes care. *J Adv Nurs* **51**(6): 609-17

Kiely C, Crestodina L (2006) Diabetic foot care education: it's not just about the foot. *J Wound Ostomy Continence Nurs* **33**(4): 416-21

Miller W, Rollnick S (2002) *Motivational Interviewing: Preparing People to Change.* Guildford Press, New York

National Institute for Health and Clinical Excellence (2008) Patient education programme for people with type 2 diabetes. Commissioning Guide. Implementing NICE guidance. http://www.nice.org.uk (accessed 1 April 2011)

Rahul A et al (2008) Strategies and effectiveness of diabetes self-management education interventions for Bangladeshis. *Diversity in Health and Social Care* **5**(4): 269-79

Taylor T (2009) Does education work when you are newly diagnosed? Desmond Project. http://www.desmond-project.org.uk (accessed 1 April 2011)

X-PERT (2011) The XPERT Programme: taking control. http://www.xperthealth.org.uk/

Further resources

Diabetes Australia Multilingual Internet Resource
Leaflets on various diabetes topics are available in Arabic, Chinese, Croatian, English, Greek, Hindi, Indonesian, Italian, Serbian, Spanish, Thai, Turkish, Ukrainian, and Vietnamese
http://diabetesaustralia.com.au/About-Diabetes-Australia/Multilingual

Diabetes Education and Self Management for Ongoing and Newly Diagnosed (DESMOND) (type 2 diabetes)
www.desmond-project.org.uk

Diabetes UK
Information materials in English plus nine other languages
www.diabetes.org.uk

Dose Adjustment for Normal Eating (DAFNE) (type 1 diabetes)
www.dafne.uk.com

Electronic Quality Information for the Public (EQUIP)
Links to electronic booklets www.equip.nhs.uk

Language Line
www.languageline.co.uk

Multicultural Health Communication Service on Diabetes
An Australian Government site giving information on diabetes written by doctors in many different languages
www.health.qld.gov.au/multicultural/public/diabetes.asp

You Have Diabetes (Learning Disabilities Booklet)
www.diabetes.org.uk

Chapter 7

Person-centred planning

Phil Holdich

Introduction

This chapter reviews the so-called diabetes 'annual review', which is an opportunity to check that a person with diabetes has received elements of care such as screening for complications and a review and revision of their diabetes knowledge (Diabetes UK, 2005a). The aim of review is to delay, detect or prevent acute and longer-term complications of diabetes by considering metabolic control and associated risk factors. The elements of care which are recommended for inclusion in an annual review are identified in *Figure 1* (overleaf). Targets for carrying out many of the measures necessary to fulfil these recommendations appear in the Quality and Outcomes Framework of the GMS Contract (British Medical Association [BMA], 2011).

It is important that all people with diabetes consent to be included on a practice diabetes register, so they can be monitored regularly (Crumbie, 2002). Anonymised data can then be aggregated for a district-wide register, which may be used for epidemiological purposes (Haynes *et al.*, 2007), such as monitoring the prevalence of diabetic complications to plan future services.

Structuring a diabetes review

A useful guide to ensuring that key aspects of diabetes care are carried out is the alphabet strategy — advice, blood pressure, cholesterol, diabetes control, eyes, feet, guardian drugs (Patel and Morrissey, 2002). While this strategy can be perceived as somewhat prescriptive rather than person-centred, and some parameters have been changed since it was first introduced, the mnemonic focuses attention on key interventions to reduce cardiovascular, renal, retinal and foot complications. Guidelines published by the National Institute for Health and Clinical Excellence (NICE, 2008) recommend a target systolic blood pressure of <130mmHg where there are signs of end organ damage and a target total cholesterol of <4.0mmol/l. However, advising people to reach such targets can be considered out of step with a person-centred approach, and it may be more appropriate and effective to 'agree' a plan of care.

Care planning is part of a person-centred approach that facilitates people to take a more active role in the management of their diabetes. It allows the person

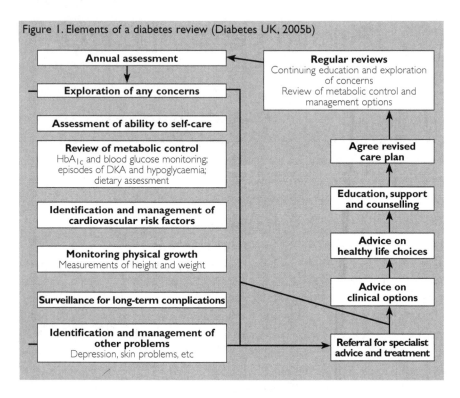

Figure 1. Elements of a diabetes review (Diabetes UK, 2005b)

with diabetes to make more decisions regarding their care, in collaboration with a health professional who is practising a partnership approach (Department of Health [DoH], 2006; National Diabetes Support Team [NDST], 2008). Some core principles of this approach require that clinicians set aside the 'professional expert' persona and become facilitators who use a more behavioural approach to consultation (Tomkins and Collins, 2006). Using such an approach, people like John (see *case study*) would be encouraged to share and discuss information and to negotiate goals and agendas with the practice diabetes team (DoH, 2006).

A simple strategy for helping people with diabetes to prepare for and gain more from their review, is to send them their results in advance. It can also be useful to send a leaflet that lists the parameters of each metabolic measure, that explains what they mean and that provides space for the person to write down why their results might not meet preset goals (NDST, 2008) (*Figure 2*). This approach may encourage John to consider why his blood glucose and blood pressure are higher than ideal, before the consultation. The practice nurse and practice diabetes team can then offer their support, helping identify which lifestyle factors they might want to address, to improve his metabolic results. It is encouraging that John has had some previous success in stopping smoking — the team can help John build on this to make further changes that he feels he can achieve.

Case study

John Sykes, a 62-year-old plumber, is visiting the practice nurse for a review of his diabetes care. John was diagnosed with type 2 diabetes 7 years ago and has missed his last two appointments owing to work commitments. His biometric data are presented in *Table C1*.

He is being treated with metformin 500mg three times daily, gliclazide 80mg twice daily, and lisinopril 10mg daily (for high blood pressure).

John has recently had his annual retinal screen, which revealed some background retinopathy, and he is concerned about losing his sight. He has forgotten to bring his blood glucose testing diary and meter with him today and he admits that he doesn't often use them — he usually only remembers to test his blood glucose just before an appointment.

Since his last visit, his weight has increased. John says that he now has to wear a belt to keep his trousers up below his stomach. He thinks this is probably because he stopped smoking 6 months ago.

Table C1. John's biometric data	
■ Haemoglobin A_{1c} (HbA_{1c})	70mmol/mol/8.6%
■ Blood pressure	152/90mmHg
■ Lipids:	
• Total cholesterol	5.5mmol/l
• Low-density lipoprotein (LDL)	2.8mmol/l
• High-density lipoprotein (HDL)	0.8mmol/l
• Triglycerides (TG)	2.3mmol/l
■ Microalbuminuria (albumin creatinine ratio)	8.3mg/mmol
■ Estimated glomerular filtration rate (eGFR)	N/A
■ Body mass index (BMI)	32kg/m^2

Figure 2. A sample results sharing sheet for care planning (National Diabetes Support Team, 2008).

	Your result	Comment
Diabetes control Your HbA$_{1c}$ is an overall measure of glucose control over the past 8–10 weeks. A level of 42–53mmol/mol (6–7%) is associated with the lowest risk of complications.	HbA$_{1c}$ 49mmol/mol /6.6%	While this shows good control, your sugars are frequently below 4 in the morning. We have agreed to reduce your evening glicazide to 40mg (half a tablet), and may even stop it
Blood pressure (BP) A target blood pressure of below 130/80 lowers the risk of complications (a target of below 125/75 is used if you have kidney disease).	BP 125/72	Excellent
Cholesterol and blood fats Lowering your cholesterol can reduce the risk of complications such as heart attacks and strokes. Whether or not you need treatment depends on your overall risk. If you are on treatment the target cholesterol is less than 5.	Cholesterol 4.2	Excellent
Kidney tests Your kidneys are tested by looking at a blood test (creatinine) and the leak of protein in your urine.	Creatine 146 Urine: Normal	Your creatinine is slightly high (eGFR 45) but this has been stable since at least 2001. I explained this does demonstrate some damage to the kidneys but suggested I was not too worried about this at the moment

Figure 2. [continued]

	Your result	Comment
Weight and body mass index (BMI) Being overweight increases the risk of many medical conditions including heart disease, arthritis and premature death. It can also make your diabetes and blood pressure more difficult to control. The body mass index (BMI) is another way to look at your weight, adjusting for your height. A BMI of between 19 and 25 is associated with the lowest risk to your health	Weight 104.6kg BMI 34.95	We discussed this in some detail today and used the action-planning approach sheet. You have already made some changes such as cutting down portion sizes and avoiding fatty foods, and these seem to be working (you have lost some weight since the last appointment). You are confident that you will be able to keep this up.
Smoking Smoking causes problems with your health in many ways, and is particularly damaging in people with diabetes.	You are an ex-smoker	Excellent

Name: .... Date of Birth: .... Date sheet completed: ....

63

Cardiovascular risk

Cardiovascular disease is responsible for 65% of all deaths in people with diabetes (Garg and Bakris, 2002) and microalbuminuria is regarded as a marker for this. Together with microalbuminuria, John also has hypertension and dyslipidaemia, which puts him in a higher-risk category. A key strategy for reducing cardiovascular risk is to make lifestyle changes (Centers for Disease Control and Prevention [CDC], 2005), and John may consider altering his diet and/or increasing his level of physical activity. In addition, his angiotensin-converting enzyme (ACE) inhibitor medication needs to be optimised. The MICRO-HOPE study, which included over 3500 people with diabetes, found that cardiovascular risk was reduced by 25–30% in those who were treated with an ACE inhibitor (ramipril) (HOPE Investigators, 2000). Furthermore, an ACE inhibitor was found to be renoprotective and to reduce the need for laser therapy for diabetic retinopathy (HOPE Investigators, 2000).

For people with type 2 diabetes and persistent microalbuminuria, target blood pressure is <130/70mmHg (NICE, 2008a). In people with chronic kidney disease (CKD) and diabetes, the aim is to keep the systolic blood pressure below 130mmHg (target range: 120–129mmHg) and the diastolic blood pressure below 80mmHg' (NICE, 2008b). Consequently, it is worth discussing the potential benefits of increasing John's lisinopril to a maintenance dose of 20–40mg (Joint Formulary Committee, 2008). Any increase in ACE inhibitor should be followed by an assessment of renal function (NICE, 2006).

Microvascular risk

Diabetes is the most common cause of blindness in people of working age in England and Wales (Bunce and Wormald, 2006), so John's concerns about his vision are justified. Moreover, retinal changes have already been seen during screening. Although John does not require photocoagulation at this stage, it is important to treat his hypertension and hyperglycaemia, which will accelerate eye disease. The United Kingdom Prospective Diabetes Study (UKPDS) (1998a, 2000) reported improved outcomes in those who maintained good control of both blood pressure and blood glucose.

If John's blood pressure and albumin-creatinine ratio (ACR) improve with titration of his lisinopril, then his risks of eye, kidney and heart disease will all be reduced. Kidney function can be monitored more accurately with a blood test for serum creatinine, which can be used to estimate the glomerular filtration rate (eGFR).

Communicating risk

Usher (2008a) proposes that cultural and personal beliefs play a significant role in the perception of risk. People often attribute health risks to things that are beyond their control, yet factors which they can influence may be far more significant, particularly where it is possible to provide 'clear' information and stimulate greater awareness.

John is concerned about losing his sight, so an understanding of the mechanisms by which diabetic eye disease can develop and the ways in which he can reduce his longer-term risks of vision loss may help motivate him to improve his blood glucose and blood pressure control. Explanations of cardiovascular risk can be complex and do not always lead to changes in lifestyle. Quantifiable measures of behavioural change may be useful (Hawthorne, 2009); for more information, please refer to *Chapter 5*.

It can be helpful to present information in different ways (using a cardiovascular risk calculator, for instance), particularly if accompanied by simple explanations (Goldman *et al.*, 2006). The UKPDS Risk Engine (Diabetes Trials Unit, 2001) can be used to calculate cardiovascular risk in people with type 2 diabetes (Stevens *et al.*, 2001), and is available as a free download (www.dtu.ox.ac.uk/riskengine/). Indeed, NICE (2008) advocates the annual calculation of cardiovascular risk using the UKPDS Risk Engine. Although a crude measure of risk reduction, this may appeal to John if his diabetes care team can recalculate reductions in risk, for example, by entering a target for lowering his cholesterol or blood pressure.

Considering John's age, history of diabetes and his risk of vascular disease, he may experience erectile dysfunction. This can have a profound effect on self-esteem, mood and relationships. About 50% of men with diabetes experience some problems with erectile dysfunction and many do not volunteer this unless asked (McCoid, 2007). Sensitive questioning may provide an opportunity for John to respond so that he can be assessed and receive appropriate treatment, which is likely to be an oral medication such as sildenafil (NICE, 2008). *Chapter 18* deals with sexual dysfunction in diabetes.

It is important to ask John if he has any problems with his feet, and he should be asked to remove his shoes and socks so that the nurse, GP or podaitrist can carry out a neurovascular assessment (NICE, 2004). The practitioner may require further training in foot assessment, the use of a monofilament and the use of a simple clinical algorithm such as the Tayside Clinical Risk Tool to stratify risk (Leese *et al.*, 2006). The practitioner should also ask John to talk through how he might examine his own feet and what he would do if he thought he had any problems (NICE, 2004). For more information on foot complications, please refer to *Chapter 15*.

The onset of diabetic complications can be linked with low mood. Depression can disrupt glycaemic control and it is twice as common in people with diabetes as it is in those without, often going undiagnosed or being under-treated (Snoek and Skinner, 2006). A simple screen for depression may help identify individuals who require further support or services, and is part of the Quality and Outcomes Framework (BMA, 2008) (see *Chapter 12* and *Chapter 25*).

The value of self-monitoring

John has indicated a reluctance to test his blood glucose and he may have good reasons for this, particularly if his readings are higher than he would prefer, if he receives no feedback on results when attending clinic, of if he does not know how to use his results to help self-manage his diabetes (Davidson, 2005; Peel *et al.*, 2007). He may also be reluctant to self-test due to pain, inconvenience (especially when at work) or feelings of self-consciousness (Peel *et al.*, 2004; Hadley-Brown *et al.*, 2008). While guidance suggests that self-monitoring blood glucose levels is of benefit to some people with diabetes (Owens *et al.*, 2004), Simon *et al.* (2008) concluded that in type 2 diabetes, self-monitoring may increase anxiety, have a negative impact on quality of life and may not be sufficiently cost-effective for routine use.

It might be more acceptable to ask John to test his blood glucose for short periods, for example, while his HbA_{1c} remains above target, and teach him to self-monitor when there are any changes to his treatment or lifestyle. It might also be useful for him to test his blood glucose level if he is experiencing any unusual symptoms, such as dizziness or shaking, which could relate to a low blood glucose level with a sulphonylurea (Hadley-Brown *et al.*, 2008). While self-monitoring of his blood pressure may be an additional burden, this could be very useful for John to see the effects of any changes in medication, enabling him to have some control and to work in partnership with his diabetes team. For people with diabetes like John, self-monitoring of blood pressure can be empowering and can help people to see the importance of their prescribed medications.

Medication review

Raynor (1998) advises that people who take prescribed medicines require sufficient information to:

* Enable them to take and use medicines effectively
* Understand the relative risks and benefits, to allow them to make an informed decision about taking them.

However, Raynor (1998) also points out that providing information does not always result in a transfer of knowledge, nor does knowledge transfer necessarily result in changes in behaviour or attitude. Before making any changes to doses or adding in any additional therapies, it is important to ensure that a person is taking their current medications. The practitioner should open a dialogue and discuss how and when medicines are taken.

Adherence to prescribed medications, particularly anti-hypertensives, can be suboptimal — after a year, as many as 50% of people abandon treatment altogether, or take 'drug holidays' for single doses or for several days (Vrijens *et al.*, 2008). A study by Diabetes UK (2008) found that one in five people with diabetes did not take their medication and lacked knowledge about the cardiovascular risks associated with type 2 diabetes; encouraging people to home monitor their blood pressure can be helpful in such circumstances.

To reduce blood pressure and help prevent end organ damage, many people will require more than one antihypertensive, together with lifestyle changes (NICE, 2008). The mechanisms of hypertension are complex and a single agent is rarely sufficient to manage the blood pressure, even when the dose is optimised (Ritz, 2011). Hence, the addition of a second antihypertensive agent (possibly a calcium channel blocker in John's case) may be indicated (SIGN, 2010; NICE, 2008). John should be asked about his understanding of his medication, the timing of his doses, whether he forgets or omits tablets and if he ever has any problems taking them. He should also be asked about his knowledge of the potential risks of diabetes and hypertension.

Beliefs have a key role in adherence. A study by Farmer *et al.* (2006) found that negatively-perceived side effects (for example, weight gain with sulphonylureas) were significant predictors of non-adherence, as were changes to daily routine, which made taking medications more difficult. Measures which might help people to take their medications appropriately include once-daily doses, combination therapies and the use of tablet dispensers (Goldie, 2006).

Guardian drugs

Metformin has been shown to have a positive effect in cardiovascular disease. In the UKPDS (1998b), when compared with intensive treatment with other agents, it was found to reduce the risk of myocardial infarction by 39% and stroke by 41%. John could try a modified-release form, so that he would have fewer tablets to take and he would not have to take them at work, which might encourage him to take his medication (Usher, 2008b). If he is able to change his diet or increase his level of physical activity, then his blood glucose level might be kept under control by increasing the dose of metformin (which has a neutral effect on weight) and stopping the sulphonylurea (which causes weight gain).

Due to concerns about the risk of bleeding, guidance on the use of low-dose aspirin in primary prevention of cardiovascular disease has been revised (Regional Drug and Therapeutics Centre, 2010; MRHA, 2009); now only people with an identified risk should be prescribed low-dose aspirin (75mg daily) (SIGN, 2010; MRHA, 2009). John's individual risk of cardiovascular disease should be assessed, and he should be asked about any history of gastric problems before considering the use of aspirin or any anti-platelet therapy.

John's cholesterol is elevated, and while he should consider improvements to his diet, such as reducing saturated fats or taking plant sterols in dairy products (such as spreads and yoghurts) it is likely he will benefit from a statin, taken in the evening — statins work most effectively overnight (NICE, 2008).

Conclusions

While the National Service Framework for Diabetes (DoH, 2001) recommends regular surveillance for complications, the consultation should be an opportunity for the person with diabetes to discuss any areas of concern, including their psychological, emotional and social wellbeing (Jerreat, 2003). It should culminate in a care plan with jointly-negotiated goals, which may be reviewed at 3–6 months or more frequently, depending on the individual's needs and the regularity of monitoring for other purposes, such as blood pressure checks for hypertension (NICE, 2008). Nurse-led risk reduction services for people with type 2 diabetes have been evaluated positively (Denver *et al.*, 2003; Woodward *et al.*, 2005) and are good examples of strategies that help to engage with people in risk management. Furthermore, primary care diabetes clinics provide continuity of care. There is accumulating evidence to support continuity of care, which has been shown to increase patient satisfaction, be a better use of resources and, most importantly, improve adherence to treatment (van Servellen *et al.*, 2006).

Key points
- The diabetes review is an opportunity to monitor diabetes care and to share and discuss information and results with the person with diabetes
- The aim of review is to support people in the prevention of acute and longer-term complications
- Information relating to risk is part of the review and can be communicated in a way that enables people with diabetes to make decisions and choices about their diabetes care.

References

British Medical Association (2011) Quality and Outcomes Framework (QOF) guidance, 4th revision 2011-2012. Available at www.bma.org.uk

Bunce C, Wormald R (2006) Leading causes of certification for blindness and partial sight in England and Wales. BMC Public Health. www.pubmedcentral.nih

Centers for Disease Control and Prevention (2005) National diabetes fact sheet. US Department of Health and Human Services, Atlanta, GA

Crumbie A (2002) Diabetes. In: Crumbie A, Lawrence J, eds. Living with a Chronic Condition. Butterworth Heinemann, Oxford

Davidson M (2005) Counterpoint: Self-monitoring of blood glucose in type 2 diabetic patients not receiving insulin. A waste of money. *Diabetes Care* 28: 1531-33

Department of Health (2006) Care Planning in Diabetes. DH, London

Department of Health (2001)National Service Framework for Diabetes: Standards. DH, London

Denver E et al (2003) Management of uncontrolled hypertension in a nurse-led clinic compared with conventional care for patients with type 2 diabetes. *Diabetes Care* 26: 2256-60

Devereux R et al (2000) Impact of diabetes on cardiac structure and function: the strong heart study. *Circulation* 101: 2271-76

Diabetes Trials Unit (2001) The UKPDS Risk Engine. www.dtu. ox.ac.uk/index. php?maindoc=/riskengine/download.php

Diabetes UK (2005a) Management of diabetes in primary care. Diabetes UK, London

Diabetes UK (2005b) Recommendations for the provision of services in primary care for people with diabetes. www.diabetes.org.uk/Documents/Professionals/primary_recs.pdf

Diabetes UK (2008) 650,000 people with diabetes putting their lives at risk by not taking tablets. Press release, 27 May. Diabetes UK, London

Farmer A et al (2006) Measuring beliefs about taking hypoglycaemic medication among people with type 2 diabetes. *Diabet Med* **23**(3): 265-70

Garg J, Bakris G (2002) Microalbuminuria: marker of vascular dysfunction, risk factor for cardiovascular disease. *Vascular Medicine* **7**(1): 35-43

Goldie L (2006) Keep taking the tablets: achieving adherence in type 2 diabetes. The British Journal of Primary Care Nursing: Cardiovascular Disease and Diabetes 3: 3

Goldman R et al (2006) Patients' perceptions of cholesterol, cardiovascular disease risk, and risk communication strategies. *Ann Fam Med* **4**(3): 205-12

Hadley-Brown M et al (2008) Structured episodic monitoring: A novel approach to SMBG in type 2 diabetes. *Diabetes and Primary Care* **10**(3): 165-72

Hawthorne G (2009) A risk management partnership. *Practice Nursing* **20**(2): 86-90

Haynes C et al (2007) Legal and ethical considerations in processing patient-identifiable data without patient consent: lessons learnt from developing a disease register. *J Med Ethics* 33: 302-7

HOPE—Heart Outcomes Prevention Evaluation Study Investigators (2000) Effects of ramipril on cardiovascular and microvascular outcomes in people with diabetes mellitus: results of the HOPE study and MICRO- HOPE substudy. *Lancet* **355**(9200): 253-59

Jerreat L (2003) Diabetes for Nurses. 2nd edn. Whurr Publishers Ltd, London

Joint Formulary Committee (2008) British National Formulary 56. September. *BMJ* Publishing Group Ltd and RPS Publishing, London: 2.5.5

Leese G et al (2006) Stratification of foot ulcer risk in patients with diabetes: a population-based study. *Int J Clin Pract* **60**(5): 541-45

McCoid J (2007) Therapeutic management of erectile dysfunction. *Nurse Prescribing* **5**(4): 143-47

MRHA (2009) Safety Update. October 2009. Volume 3 Issue 3

National Diabetes Support Team (2008) Partners in care: A guide to implementing care planning. NDST, London

National Institute for Health and Clinical Excellence (2008a) Type 2 diabetes: The management of type 2 diabetes (update). Clinical guideline 66. NICE, London

National Institute for Health and Clinical Excellence (2008b) Chronic kidney disease: early identification and management of chronic kidney disease in adults in primary and secondary care. Clinical Guideline 73. NICE, London

National Institute for Health and Clinical Excellence (2006) Hypertension: management of hypertension in adults in primary care. Clinical guideline 34. NICE, London

National Institute for Health and Clinical Excellence (2004) Management of type 2 diabetes: prevention and management of foot problems. Clinical guideline 10. NICE, London

Owens D et al (2004) Blood glucose self- monitoring in type 1 and type 2 diabetes: reaching a multi-disciplinary consensus. *Diabetes and Primary Care* 6: 398-402

Patel V, Morrissey J (2002) The alphabet strategy: The ABC of reducing diabetes complications. *British Journal of Vascular Disease* **2**(1): 58-59

Peel E et al (2007) Self monitoring of blood glucose in type 2 diabetes: longitudinal qualitative study of patients' perspectives. *BMJ* **335**(7618): 493

Peel E et al (2004) Blood glucose self- monitoring in non-insulin-treated type 2 diabetes: a qualitative study of patients' perspectives. *Br J Gen Pract* 54: 183-88

Raynor D (1998) The influence of written information on patient knowledge and adherence to treatment. In: Myers LB, Midence K (eds.) Adherence to Treatment in Medical Conditions. Harwood Academic, London

Simon J et al (2008) Diabetes Glycaemic Education and Monitoring Trial Group. Cost effectiveness of self monitoring of blood glucose in patients with non-insulin treated type 2 diabetes: economic evaluation of data from the DiGEM trial. *BMJ* 336: 1177-80

Regional Drug and Therapeutics Centre RDTC (2010) No. 65 Drug Update. Aspirin for primary prevention of cardiovascular disease. Newcastle, RDTC

Ritz, E (2011) Drug of Choice in the Management of Hypertension in Diabetes and Diabetic Nephropathy: Angiotensin-Converting Enzyme Inhibitors. *The Journal of Clinical Hypertension* **13**(4): 285-89

Scottish Intercollegiate Guidelines Network (SIGN) (2010) 116 Management of Diabetes. A National Clinical Guideline. Edinburgh, SIGN.

Snoek F, Skinner T (2006) Psychological aspects of diabetes management. *Medicine* **34**(2): 61-62

Stevens R et al (2001) UKPDS 56: The UKPDS Risk Engine: a model for the risk of coronary heart disease in type 2 diabetes. *Clin Sci* 101: 671-79

Tomkins S, Collins A (2006) Promoting Optimal Self Care. Consultation techniques that improve quality of life for patients and clinicicans. Dorset and Somerset Strategic Health Authority

UK Prospective Diabetes Study Group (1998a) Tight blood pressure control and risk of macrovascular and microvascular complications in type 2 diabetes: UKPDS 38. *BMJ* 317: 703-13

UK Prospective Diabetes Study Group (1998b) Effect of intensive blood-glucose control with metformin on complications in overweight patients with type 2 diabetes (UKPDS 34). *Lancet* 352: 854-65

UK Prospective Diabetes Study Group (2000) Association of glycaemia with macro-vascular and microvascular complications of type 2 diabetes (UKPDS 35). *BMJ* 321: 405-12

Usher A (2008a) Mind your language. Diabetes Update Spring

Usher A (2008b) Mind your language. Diabetes Update Summer

Van Servellen G et al (2006) Continuity of care and quality care outcomes for people experiencing chronic conditions: A literature review. *Nursing and Health Sciences* 8: 85-195

Vrijens B et al (2008) Adherence to prescribed antihypertensive drug treatments: longitu-dinal study of electronically compiled dosing histories. *BMJ* 336: 1114-17

Woodward A et al (2005) Improved glycaemic control—an unintended benefit of a nurse-led cardiovascular risk reduction clinic. *Diabet Med* 22: 1272-74

Chapter 8

Diabesity: aims of treatment and a multidisciplinary practice team approach

Dr Chinnadori Rajeswaran, Jo Bissell, Dr Ravi Bachuwar and Dr Balasubramanian Thiagarajan Srinivasan

Introduction

The term 'diabesity' describes the strong link between type 2 diabetes mellitus and obesity (Sims *et al.*, 1973; Haslam and James, 2005). Diabesity is a twin metabolic problem and its aetiology and management are complex, combining many aspects of healthcare. Effective management of diabesity requires that many complex interrelated issues are addressed, not just glycaemia.

To effectively manage people with diabesity, a specialist and holistic approach should be adopted. The diabesity team should include an endocrinologist, clinical psychologist, specialist dietitian, specialist diabesity nurse and physiotherapist. The team is required to work together to address weight, glycaemic control, obesity and diabetes-related complications (*Table 1*).

Managing this twin epidemic in a diabesity clinic has several advantages, including improved compliance, a reduction in complications, and cost savings in drug use and time. This chapter will discuss the importance of specialist diabesity clinics, outline why people with diabesity need referral for management, and also discuss how diabesity clinics have been established to meet the challenges faced by healthcare services in managing these patients.

Prevalence

The prevalence of type 2 diabetes is increasing, and it is predicted that there will be a further rise in the incidence and prevalence of this disease in the future (World Health Organization [WHO], 2010; Yorkshire and Humber Public Health Observatory [YHPHO], 2011).

Table 1. Common health problems related to obesity	
System	**Health problems**
■ Cardiovascular	• Hypertension • Dyslipidaemia • Coronary heart disease • Cerebrovascular disease • Deep vein thrombosis • Varicose veins
■ Endocrine	• Type 2 diabetes • Insulin resistance • Polycystic ovary syndrome • Amenorrhoea, infertility • Hirsuitism • Breast cancer
■ Respiratory	• Breathlessness • Obstructive sleep apnoea • Sleep-related hypoventilation
■ Gastrointestinal	• Gastro-oesophageal reflux disease • Gallstones • Hiatus hernia • Fatty liver and non-alcoholic steatohepatitis • Colon cancer
■ Musculoskeletal	• Immobility • Osteoarthritis • Back pain
■ Genitourinary	• Stress incontinence • Endometrial cancer
■ Psychological	• Depression and low self-esteem • Binge eating disorder • Night eating syndrome
From: National Audit Office, 2001	

Between 2003 and 2011, the number of people diagnosed with type 2 diabetes in the UK rose from an estimated 1.3 million cases to more than 3 million (Department of Health [DoH], 2008; YHPHO, 2011). Obesity has been identified as the largest risk factor in the development of type 2 diabetes, and it has been predicted that the prevalence of obesity in the UK will treble between 2005 and 2013 (The National Heart Forum, 2007).

Table 2. Causes of weight gain with improved glycaemic control
■ Decreased glycosuria
■ Increased anabolic effect (insulin)
■ Hypoglycaemia leading to raised calorie consumption
■ Inappropriate and excess insulin administration
■ Fluid retention
■ Sarcopenic obesity, less muscle mass so fewer calories used
From: Haslam and James, 2005

Most people with type 2 diabetes present with obesity at diagnosis, and oral hypoglycaemic agents and insulin are invariably accompanied by weight gain. The restoration of glycaemic control offers a partial explanation for this initial weight gain (Haslam and James, 2005). Some other causes are given in *Table 2*.

Increased weight results in increased insulin resistance and a greater risk of developing obesity-related complications (National Audit Office, 2001), which need to be considered as well as the typical macro- and microvascular complications associated with type 2 diabetes, such as cardiovascular disease and diabetic retinopathy.

Treatment aims

For people with diabesity, the aims of treatment are to reduce cardiovascular risk, regain normoglycaemia and reduce the risks of related complications and comorbidities (DoH, 2001; Krentz and Bailey, 2005). Recent studies have shown that quality of life is twice as poor for individuals living with type 2 diabetes and obesity, when compared with people living with just one of these conditions (Gough *et al.*, 2009). Hence, another aim of treatment should be to improve quality of life.

Why 'diabesity'?

For several years, 'diabesity' has been a popular term for describing the association of type 2 diabetes and obesity, or the tendency towards type 2 diabetes in obesity, and it is now emerging as a speciality within diabetes care (Haslam and James, 2005). This provides structure for the management of metabolic syndrome and its associated complications and an approach that is patient-centred and holistic. It should be noted that although type 2 diabetes is related to obesity, a number of other factors can cause weight gain and impact on diabesity.

In addition to its strong association with type 2 diabetes, obesity carries its own risks. For example, a 5kg increase in body weight increases a person's cardiovascular risk by 30%. Conversely, a 10% reduction in body weight is associated with clear health benefits, including a 15% reduction in haemoglobin A_{1c} (HbA$_{1c}$) (Jung, 1997) (*Table 3*).

A study by Oldridge *et al.* (2001) found that for people aged 51–60 years, the adjusted odds ratio for death by metabolic category for those with type 2 diabetes was 2.63%, for those with obesity it was 0.78%, and for those with both conditions it was 6.81%, demonstrating an increase in risk of death when type 2 diabetes and obesity were combined. Specific management of both conditions will result in a significant reduction in cardiovascular risk.

Specialist diabesity service

Diabesity is now recognised as a specialist discipline within medical and endocrinology departments, and the complex healthcare needs of people with diabesity should be addressed by a specialist team, including:

- Consultant endocrinologist (lead)
- Clinical psychologist
- Specialist dietitian
- Diabesity specialist nurse
- Occupational therapist
- Physiotherapist

The diabesity team aims to empower people, to improve their understanding of diabesity, enable them to manage their diabetes and establish safe weight loss. The person with diabesity is put at the centre of care, and interventions are individualised. The focus of the diabesity clinic is not glucocentric; instead, emphasis is put on body weight, hunger patterns, psychological issues, and the investigation and treatment of underlying endocrine abnormalities.

Referrals

In light of increasing referrals, the referral criteria for patients to be accepted by a diabesity service are:

- HbA$_{1c}$ >8% (64mmol/mol)
- Body mass index (BMI) >27.5kg/m^2.

Following referral to the diabesity service, an initial assessment of each patient is carried out by the consultant endocrinologist. A full medical and social history is taken, including childhood, menstrual, family, personal, drug and previous weight loss history. People are also required to have full body composition analysis, including height, weight, BMI, basal metabolic rate, body fat percentage and muscle mass estimations.

Glycaemic excursion

An assessment of the effect of food on glycaemia should be performed, investigating blood glucose levels before and after meals. The difference in fasting and postprandial blood glucose levels is known as 'glycaemic excursion'. The effect of physical activity on glycaemia should also be assessed (Annan, 2011).

It is necessary to ascertain when the person feels hunger, and by determining

Table 3. Benefits of a 10% weight loss	
Outcome	**Benefit**
■ Mortality	• >20% decrease in total mortality • >30% decrease in diabetes-related deaths • >40% decrease in obesity-related cancers
■ Blood pressure	• Fall of 10mmHg systolic pressure • Fall of 20mmHg diastolic pressure
■ Diabetes	• 30–50% fall in fasting glucose • 50% fall in risk of developing diabetes • 15% reduction in haemoglobin A$_{1c}$ (HbA$_{1c}$)
■ Lipids	• 10% reduction in total cholesterol • 15% reduction in LDL cholesterol • 30% reduction in triglycerides • 8% increase in HDL cholesterol
LDL = low density lipoprotein; HDL = high-density lipoprotein From: Jung, 1997	

hunger patterns, causes of hunger can be identified. Hunger is classified into physical (physiologically driven) and hedonic (pleasure driven) subtypes (Lowe and Butryn, 2007; Schultes *et al.*, 2010). At assessment, the health professional should look for any mismatch between the person's blood glucose levels and their hunger patterns.

This is important for people with type 2 diabetes with suboptimal control of blood glucose, as a relative lowering of glucose, even to within the normal range, can precipitate symptoms of hypoglycaemia, which leads to further food intake and weight gain.

Sleep deprivation

Sleep patterns and daytime sleepiness are assessed using the Epworth sleepiness scale, and if a person scores more than 10, they should be referred for a sleep study to rule out obstructive sleep apnoea (Johns, 1991; Sweeting, 2011). Assessment for sleep deprivation is vital.

Erectile dysfunction

A history of erectile dysfunction should be ascertained and relevant investigations requested (Fisken, 2010). Obesity is associated with low levels of testosterone in men. A substantial number of obese men with type 2 diabetes have a biochemical picture of hypogonadotrophic hypogonadism.

Psychological wellbeing

Psychological wellbeing is assessed in relation to weight management. A history should be elicited to determine if there was a life-changing event which may have contributed to weight gain. Some events can trigger the use of food for comfort or security (Seng *et al.*, 2004). Additionally, it is important to assess individuals' perception of their body weight. The practitioner can ask, for example, do they see their body weight as a problem? What do they think the cause of their increased body weight might be?

Reasons for wanting to lose weight are often significant, and motivation should also be assessed. Motivated individuals are more likely to achieve successful outcomes, both in terms of weight loss and glycaemic control.

Mobility assessment

A mobility assessment should be performed by the team physiotherapist, to assess the effects of obesity on mobility. Obesity-related mobility issues are thought to be mechanical rather than metabolic, so they may not be improved by weight loss (The National Heart Forum, 2007).

Detailed drug history

A detailed drug history should be taken to establish whether or not any medications are contributing to diabetes or obesity, such as norethisterone.

Investigations

Initial investigations include full blood count, baseline kidney and liver function tests and HbA_{1c}. Endocrine abnormality is established as a cause of weight gain in around 10% of patients who attend the diabesity clinic, thus blood tests looking for thyroid dysfunction, hypogonadism and hypercortisolism should also be performed.

If reactive hypoglycaemia is suspected, an extended glucose tolerance test should be arranged. Patients are also asked to complete food diaries, blood glucose diaries and hunger pattern diaries, and bring these to appointments for discussion.

Multidisciplinary approach

Each member of the diabesity team provides specialist support. The diabesity specialist nurse plays a vital role in a successful diabesity service, and provides specialist expertise in delivering nurse-led clinics to ensure:

*   Appropriate initiation of pharmacotherapy
*   Monitoring and evaluation of treatment plans
*   Management of people with diabetes, before and after bariatric surgery
*   Protocol, guideline and service development.

The specialist dietitian can offer behavioural therapy and low calorie diets to aid weight loss (Oliver, 2010). Individuals are educated about carbohydrates and the effect they have on blood glucose.

The physician and the diabesity specialist nurse also work closely with the clinical psychologist, and people who are identified to benefit from a psychologist's review after basic cognitive behavioural therapies are referred to psychology services. Individuals are encouraged to identify the differences between cravings and hunger, and hunger scores are used to empower people.

The physiotherapist can help improve physical activity, and create exercises tailored to a person's ability. The physiotherapist's role is to provide individualised exercise programmes according to a person's associated comorbidities. The physiotherapist also works together with the nurse to empower individuals to alter their doses of insulin and oral hypoglycaemic agents, based on activity and glucose levels. The team should also include a moving and handling specialist, who is familiar with bariatric equipment.

Insulin management

Traditionally, management of the person with diabesity has been glucocentric, but titration of insulin and oral hypoglycaemic agents causes inevitable weight gain, owing to the anabolic effect of insulin and the return to normoglycaemia (Makimattila *et al.*, 1999). It is apparent that larger doses of insulin result in increased hunger, weight gain and insulin resistance. This is compounded by insulin stacking, glycaemic deviation and complications associated with poor glycaemic control (Russell-Jones and Khan, 2007).

Regaining and maintaining glycaemic control reduces insulin requirements, which in turn reduces hypoglycaemia and hunger. Individuals are encouraged to identify their hunger patterns, and support is provided so they can understand and reset them. To provide this support, practitioners require specialist knowledge of diabetes and obesity management and skills in motivational interviewing (Miller and Rollnick, 2002).

Pharmacological interventions

Pharmacological interventions should be tailored to the individual, choosing the right medication for the right person. Specialist and up-to-date knowledge is vital in this area, as many new drug therapies are now available for the treatment of diabesity (National Institute for Health and Clinical Excellence, 2009). The supported use of these agents is beneficial, and practitioners should support people in the use of medications such as orlistat, gliptins and GLP-1 analogues (Phelan and Wadden, 2002).

Insulin regimen

Insulin regimens should be tailored to each person, rather than using a standard insulin regimen. This optimises glycaemic control and prevents hypoglycaemia and abnormal hunger.

Self-management

Education is paramount. People need to understand that to have a positive effect on weight loss and glycaemic control, drug therapy alone will not suffice. Any medications should be used in conjunction with lifestyle and dietary changes. When medications are prescribed, advice should be given on potential side effects.

Self-management is a vital concept. The Expert Patients Programme and the Diabetes Education and Self Management for Ongoing and Newly Diagnosed (DESMOND) programme both offer people information and skills to effectively self-manage their diabetes (DoH, 2005; Diabetes UK and DoH, 2005); it is recommended that individuals attend one of these programmes, or an equivalent, locally-available type 2 diabetes education programme.

Coping strategies

Coping strategies for stress and techniques for distraction should be discussed to conquer cravings, as they usually only last for about 30 minutes (Kohsaka and Bass, 2007). This method helps to reduce portion size and comfort eating.

Food diaries

Glucose, food and mood diaries should be evaluated during each visit. This enables the health professional and person to set specific and appropriate glycaemic control and weight management goals (Radimer *et al.*, 1990).

Some practical tips

- **Psychological issues** — It is vital that these are identified and addressed before starting any intervention for weight loss and glycaemic control (Polivy and Herman, 1999)

- **Sleep apnoea** — People with proven obstructive sleep apnoea should be offered continuous positive airway pressure (CPAP) equipment, as sleep deprivation caused by lack of oxygen increases a person's cardiovascular risk and compounds metabolic problems related to obesity (Johns, 1991)
- **Testosterone replacement** — This has been shown to increase insulin sensitivity, improve glycaemic control and have a positive effect on cholesterol levels in men who have low levels of testosterone and type 2 diabetes. Testosterone replacement therapy causes an increase in skeletal muscle mass and improves glycaemic control. It has also been shown to result in weight loss (Andersson *et al.*, 1994; Kapoor *et al.*, 2006)
- **Motivational interviewing** — A patient-centred method for enhancing intrinsic motivation to change, by exploring and resolving ambivalence (Silverman *et al.*, 1998; Miller and Rollnick, 2002). This method should be considered for all people living with diabesity.

Conclusions

The link between type 2 diabetes and obesity is firmly established, and diabesity is becoming increasingly prevalent worldwide. There are many factors that contribute to the development and progression of diabesity, and for management to be effective it is vital that any underlying issues are addressed.

To effectively manage the person with diabesity, a specialist and holistic approach should be adopted. Multidisciplinary teamwork has a growing role to play in person-centered, collaborative diabesity management.

Key points

- Diabesity is a recognised long-term condition and its care requires specialist, multidisciplinary and person-centred teamwork
- To effectively manage the person with diabesity, a specialist and holistic approach should be adopted
- There are many factors that contribute to the development and progression of diabesity — to effectively manage these people it is vital that any underlying issues are addressed.

References

Andersson B et al (1994) Testosterone concentrations in women and men with NIDDM. *Diabetes Care* **17**(5): 405-11

Annan F (2011) The connection between better health and exercise in diabetes. *Practice Nursing* **22**(1): 17-20

Department of Health (2001) The National Service Framework for Diabetes. The Stationery Office, London

Department of Health (2005) Improving Care, Improving Lives. Self care: A Real Choice http://tiny.cc/0y2zh (accessed 28 March 2011)

Department of Health (2008) Five Years On: Delivering the National Service Framework. The Stationery Office, London

Diabetes UK, Department of Health (2005) Structured patient education: Report from the working group. COI for the Department of Health, London

Fisken R (2010) Assessment and treatments for erectile dysfunction in diabetes. *Practice Nursing* **21**(8): 416-20

Gough S et al (2009) Impact of obesity and type 2 diabetes mellitus on health related quality of life in the general population of England. *Diabetes Metab Syndr Obes* 2: 179-84

Haslam D, James WP (2005) Obesity. *Lancet* **366**(9492): 1197-209

Johns M (1999) A new method for measuring daytime sleepiness: the Epworth sleepiness scale. *Sleep* **14**(6): 540-45

Jung R (1997) Obesity as a disease. *Br Med Bull* **53**(2): 307-21

Kapoor D et al (2006) Testosterone replacement therapy improves insulin resistance, glycaemic control, visceral adiposity and hypercholesterolaemia in hypogonadal men with type 2 diabetes. *Eur J Endocrinol* **154**(6): 899-906

Kohsaka A, Bass J (2007) A sense of time: how molecular clocks organize metabolism. *Trends Endocrinol Metab* **18**(1): 4-11

Krentz A, Bailey C (2005) Type 2 Diabetes. 2nd edn. The Royal Society of Medicine Press, London

Lowe, M, Butryn M (2007) Hedonic hunger: a new dimension of appetite? *Physiol Behav* **91**(4): 432-39

Makimattila S et al (1999) Causes of weight gain during insulin therapy with and without metformin in patients with type II diabetes mellitus. *Diabetologia* **42**(4): 406-12

Miller W, Rollnick (2002) Motivational Interviewing: Preparing People to Change. Guildford Press, New York

National Audit Office (2001) Tackling Obesity in England. The Stationery Office, Norwich

The National Heart Forum (2007) Lightening the Load: Tackling Overweight and Obesity. http://tiny.cc/72o3g (accessed 16 May 2011)

National Institute for Health and Clinical Excellence (2009) Type 2 diabetes: Newer agents. http:// www.nice.org.uk/cg87 (accessed 28 March 2011)

Oldridge N et al (2001) Prevalence and outcomes of comorbid metabolic and cardio-vascular conditions in middle- and older-age adults. *J Clin Epidemiol* **54**(9): 928-34

Phelan S, Wadden T (2002) Combining behavioral and pharmacological treatments for obesity. *Obes Res.* **10**(6): 560-74

Polivy J, Herman C (1999) Distress and eating: why do dieters overeat? *Int J Eat Disord* **26**(2): 153-64

Radimer K et al (1990) Development of indicators to assess hunger. *J Nutr* **120**(Suppl 11): 1544-48

Russell-Jones D, Khan R (2007) Insulin-associated weight gain in diabetes--causes, effects and coping strategies. *Diabetes Obes. Metab* **9**(6): 799-812

Schultes B et al (2010) Hedonic hunger is increased in severely obese patients and is reduced after gastric bypass surgery. *Am J Clin Nutr* **92**(2): 277-83

Seng J et al (2004) Abuse-related post-traumatic stress during the childbearing year. *J Adv Nurs* **46**(6): 604-13

Silverman et al (1998) Skills for Communicating with Patients. Radcliffe Medical Press, Oxford

Sims EA, Danforth E, Jr Horton ES, Bray GA, Glennon JA, Salans LB (1973) Endocrine and metabolic effects of experimental obesity in man. *Recent Prog Horm Res* 29: 457-96

Sweeting H (2011) Assessing and treating obstructive sleep apnoea in diabetes patients. *Practice Nursing* **22**(3): 150-53

World Health Organization (2011) Diabetes. Fact sheet 312. http://tiny.cc/tod3j (accessed 28 March 2011)

Chapter 9

Anti-diabetic treatment options

Dr Paul Jennings and Dr Myint Myint Aye

Introduction

The prevalence of diabetes is increasing due to population growth, ageing, urbanisation, the increasing prevalence of obesity and reduced physical activity. While there are many types and sub-types of diabetes, type 2 diabetes is the most common and has associated micro- and macrovascular complications that can substantially reduce quality of life and increase morbidity and mortality. For this reason, prevention, early diagnosis and management of diabetes poses a global challenge for health professionals. Lifestyle modification and control of hyperglycaemia, blood pressure and cholesterol are essential in the management of diabetes. This chapter, with the help of two case studies, will discuss the use of oral anti-diabetic agents — particularly sulphonylureas, biguanides and the more recently introduced incretin agents — in managing type 2 diabetes mellitus.

Diagnosis

In non-diabetic individuals, glucose homeostasis is mediated by the stimulation of insulin secretion from the beta cells in the pancreas. Insulin suppresses the endogenous production of glucose by the liver and promotes glucose utilisation in the peripheral tissues. Type 2 diabetes mellitus develops as a result of progressive deterioration of beta cell function coupled with increasing insulin resistance, for which the beta cells cannot compensate. By the time of diagnosis, beta cell function is already reduced by about 50% and will continue to decline, regardless of therapy (*Table 1*).

Table 1. Diagnosis of type 2 diabetes
1 Osmotic symptoms + random plasma glucose ≥11.1mmol/l
2 Fasting plasma glucose >7mmol/l
3 75g oral glucose tolerance test 2-hour plasma glucose ≥11.1mmol/l
Note: If the person is asymptomatic, diagnosis by one method should be confirmed on a subsequent day using either of the other methods From: World Health Organization, 1999.

Case study 1

Mr Smith, a 46-year-old businessman, went for a medical check-up for his insurance. He had a random plasma glucose level of 14mmol/l and reported nocturia, constant dry mouth, thirst and tiredness in the last few months. He had no history of any significant illness. He is a non-smoker but drank about 30 units of alcohol per week. His elder brother has diabetes and is on metformin 1g twice daily and gliclazide 160mg twice daily. Mr Smith's BMI was 32kg/m^2, waist circumference 110cm and blood pressure 131/72mmHg. His urine test showed 3+ glucose but no ketones or nitrates. His biochemical data are shown in *Table C1*.

Mr Smith's practice nurse diagnosed him with type 2 diabetes mellitus. After discussion with his GP, she devised a management plan for him. He was entered into the diabetes register, provided with basic education about type 2 diabetes and booked in for a diabetes education session. He was also advised on lifestyle changes such as weight reduction, cutting his alcohol intake to a safe level (i.e. 14 units per week), and increasing physical activity. It was also arranged for him to see a dietitian for diabetic dietary advice. Metformin 500mg daily was initiated with a plan to gradually increase the dose. He was given information about the possible adverse effects of metformin. Mary reassured him that his symptoms would be improved by these measures. A follow-up appointment was arranged for 3 months' time to check his HbA$_{1c}$ and fasting plasma glucose levels and to review his therapy.

Table C1. Mr Smith's biochemical data		
	Mr Smith	**Normal value**
Fasting plasma glucose	11.2mmol/l	4-6mmol/l
HbA$_{1c}$	65mmol/mol	21-43mmol/mol
Urine albumin-creatinine ratio	1.9mg/mmol	<2.5mg/mmol
Total cholesterol	5.2mmol/l	<4.0mmol/l
Low density lipoprotein cholesterol	2.5mmol/l	<1.5mmol/l
Triglyceride	2.1mmol/l	<1.7mmol/l
High density lipoprotein cholesterol	0.7mmol/l	>0.9mmol/l
Creatinine	83μmol/l	59-104μmol/l
Estimated glomerular filtration rate	95ml/min/1.73m^2	
Liver function test	Normal	N/A

Importance of control

Glycaemic control is fundamental to the management of diabetes. The epidemiological analyses of the Diabetes Control and Complications Trial (DCCT, 1993) and the UK Prospective Diabetes Study (UKPDS, 1998a; 2000) showed a continuous relationship between the risks of microvascular complications and glycaemia. They also demonstrated a continuous association between the risk of cardiovascular complications and glycaemia. For every percentage point decrease in haemoglobin A_{1c} (HbA_{1c}), there was a 35% reduction in the risk of microvascular complications, a 25% reduction in diabetes-related deaths, a 7% reduction in all-cause mortality, and an 18% reduction in combined fatal and non-fatal myocardial infarction (DCCT, 1993; UKPDS, 1998a). The UKPDS conclusively demonstrated that the intensive use of pharmacological therapy to lower blood glucose levels in people with type 2 diabetes significantly reduced the risks of microvascular complications and possibly macrovascular complications (UKPDS, 2000).

Unfortunately, it is a challenge to achieve and maintain good glycaemic control. Diabetes is a complex and progressive disease and secondary drug failure can develop over time. Intensification of treatment is often required and newer anti-diabetic drugs such as incretin agents are being recommended as a means to improve glycaemic control.

Glycaemic target

In the UKPDS and the DCCT, microvascular complications were significantly reduced with intensive therapy. People with type 2 diabetes who received 10 years of conventional treatment had a median HbA_{1c} of 7.9% (63mmol/mol), whereas those who were treated with intensive therapy achieved a median HbA_{1c} of 7% (53mmol/mol) (DCCT, 1993; UKPDS, 1998a). Epidemiological analysis suggests an incremental benefit, such that the HbA_{1c} can be lowered even further, achieving a normal level of 6.2% (44mmol/mol) (DCCT, 1993; DeFronzo and Goodman, 1995; UKPDS, 1998a).

The American Diabetes Association (ADA, 2008) generally recommends a target HbA_{1c} of <7% (53mmol/mol) for non-pregnant adults (*Table 2*). It also suggests that a person's HbA_{1c} goal should be as close to normal as can be achieved without significant hypoglycaemia. The National Institute for Health and Clinical Excellence (NICE, 2008) recommends that for each individual, the target HbA_{1c} level should be set somewhere between 6.5% and 7.5% (48–58mmol/mol). HbA_{1c} targets should be determined on an individual basis, considering the duration of diabetes, pregnancy, life expectancy, comorbid conditions and hypoglycaemic awareness (*Case Study 1*).

Table 2 Recommended glycaemic targets for people with diabetes			
Organisation	HbA$_{1c}$	Fasting PG mmol/l	Post-prandial PG mmol/l
ADA, 2008	<7 53mmol/mol	<6.7	None
NICE, 2008	6.5–7.5 48–58mmol/mol		
IDF-Europe, 2005	<6.5 48mmol/mol	<6	<7.5
ADA = American Diabetes Association; HbA1c = haemoglobin A1c; IDF = International Diabetes Federation; NICE = National Institute for Health and Clinical Excellence; PG = plasma glucose. From: IDF, 2005; ADA, 2008; NICE, 2008			

Anti-diabetic agents

There are five major classes of oral diabetes medication, which are: biguanides, sulphonylureas, meglitinides, thiazolidinediones, and alpha-glucosidase inhibitors. Other available anti-diabetic agents are insulin and two recently-introduced agents: glucagon-like peptide-1 (GLP-1) receptor agonists and gliptins (dipeptidylpeptidase-4 [DPP-4] inhibitors).

Biguanides (metformin)

The mechanism of action of metformin is not entirely understood, but its main effects are to suppress hepatic glucose production and enhance insulin sensitivity in peripheral tissues (primarily muscle). It is not metabolised but simply excreted in the urine. Metformin decreases the HbA$_{1c}$ level by 1–2% (Bailey and Turner, 1996; Chitre and Burke, 2006). The fasting plasma glucose level begins to fall within 3–5 days of initiation of therapy but it takes 1–2 weeks to achieve its maximal effect.

The UKPDS trial demonstrated that participants who were initially assigned to intensive therapy with metformin had decreased risks of combined diabetes-related endpoints, diabetes-related deaths, all-cause deaths, and myocardial infarction, compared with conventionally-treated participants. These risks were significantly reduced by about one third (p<0.0023–0.017) (UKPDS, 1998b). In another study, Garber *et al.* (1997) proved that the maximal effect of metformin is achieved at a dose of 2000mg per day, but it still has a strong effect if only 500mg is taken once or twice daily (DCCT, 1993). Metformin, unlike other anti-diabetic agents, does not lead to an increase in weight; it may help in weight loss.

The most common adverse effect of metformin — which sometimes limits its use — is gastrointestinal upset, including diarrhoea, cramps, and nausea and vomiting. This is more common when metformin is first administered and when its dose is increased. To improve tolerability, metformin should be started at a dose of 500mg a day with main meals, which can then be gradually increased over a period of weeks up to a maximum dose of 2000mg daily.

Potentially the most serious adverse effect of metformin is lactic acidosis but fortunately, this is rare and seems to be limited to individuals with impaired liver or kidney function. According to NICE (2008), metformin should not be initiated (or its dose should be reviewed) where serum creatinine is >130mmol/l, or estimated glomerular filtration rate (eGFR) is <45ml/min/1.73m^2. NICE (2008) also recommends stopping metformin if serum creatinine is >150mmol/l or eGFR is <30ml/min/1.73m^2. Where serum creatinine is raised, the use of metformin requires specialist advice and support.

Metformin should be withheld if the individual has a condition that provokes dehydration and acute renal failure. It should also be withheld two days before conducting any radiographic study involving iodinated contrast, but it can be resumed two days afterwards if kidney function is normal (Joint Formulary Committee, 2008).

Sulphonylureas

Sulphonylureas stimulate the secretion of insulin from beta cells in the pancreas (so long as functioning pancreatic beta cell mass remains) and can reduce the HbA$_{1c}$ level by 1.5–2% from baseline (Groop, 1992) (*Table 3*). In the UK, the commonly-used sulphonylureas are second-generation drugs, such as gliclazide, glimepiride and glipizide. Their clearance depends very little on renal excretion, so they are relatively safe to use if kidney function is impaired. Common adverse effects are hypoglycaemia and weight gain.

Meglitinides

Meglitinides (such as repaglinide and nateglinide) lower plasma glucose levels, especially after eating, by stimulating the release of endogenous insulin in response to the glucose obtained from food. Therefore, to achieve maximal effects, these medications should be taken immediately before meals; they can improve HbA$_{1c}$ by 0.5–1% (Rosenstock *et al.*, 2004). Like sulphonylureas, they carry a risk of hypoglycaemia and weight gain. They should be avoided in cases of severe liver disease.

Table 3. Efficacy of monotherapy with oral anti-diabetic drugs		
Drug class	**Fasting PG reduction (mmol/l)**	**HbA$_{1c}$ reduction (%)**
Thiazolidinediones	1.9–2.2	0.5–1
Sulphonylureas	3.3–3.9	1–2
Biguanides	3.3–3.9	1–2
Meglitinides	3.3–3.9	0.5–1
Alpha-glucose inhibitors	1.4–1.7	0.5–1
PG = plasma glucose; HbA$_{1c}$ = Haemoglobin A$_{1c}$ From: DeFronzo, 1999.		

Thiazolidinediones

Thiazolidinediones enhance the insulin sensitivity of muscle and fat tissues and promote the effective utilisation of glucose (i.e. they are 'insulin sensitisers'). They also reduce glucose production by the liver. The fasting plasma glucose level starts to decrease 5–7 days after starting on thiazolidinediones, and their full effect is achieved by 3–4 weeks. They can cause weight gain and fluid retention, which can lead to, or exacerbate, congestive heart failure. They are contraindicated in acute coronary syndrome, congestive heart failure and abnormal liver function.

The incretin effect

In normal individuals, the ingestion of food stimulates two phases of insulin secretion — early and late. Early insulin secretion is important as it suppresses the production of endogenous glucose after a meal and initiates insulin-mediated glucose use (Pratley and Weyer, 2001); late insulin secretion enhances insulin-mediated glucose disposal by skeletal muscle and adipose tissue. Loss of early insulin secretion initially leads to impaired glucose tolerance and eventually progresses to diabetes mellitus (Pratley and Weyer, 2001).

In 1964, a study by Elrick *et al.* showed a considerably larger and sustained insulin response to oral glucose when compared with intravenously-administered glucose (Elrick *et al.*, 1964). This led to the suggestion by Nauck *et al.* (1986) that substances within the gastrointestinal tract stimulate insulin secretion. This is now known as the 'incretin effect'.

Two incretin hormones, glucagon-like peptide-1 (GLP-1) and glucose-dependent insulinotropic peptide (GIP), have since been identified. GLP-1, which is produced by L cells of the small intestine in response to ingested food, stimulates the release of insulin by beta cells in the pancreas. It also inhibits the release of glucagon, which is inappropriately raised in people with type 2 diabetes, contributing to hyperglycaemia. Furthermore, GLP-1 improves gastric emptying and promotes satiety, which reduces food intake (*Figure 1*).

The secretion and action of GLP-1 is glucose-dependent and self-limiting (when the plasma glucose level normalises after a meal). GLP-1 has a biological half-life of less than 3 minutes as it is inactivated by an enzyme called dipeptidylpeptidase-4 (DPP-4). The physiological actions of GLP-1 are listed in *Table 4*.

Figure 1. The physiological effects of glucagon-like peptide-1 (GLP-1) and dipeptidylpeptidase-4 (DPP-4) and the sites of action of the incretin agents

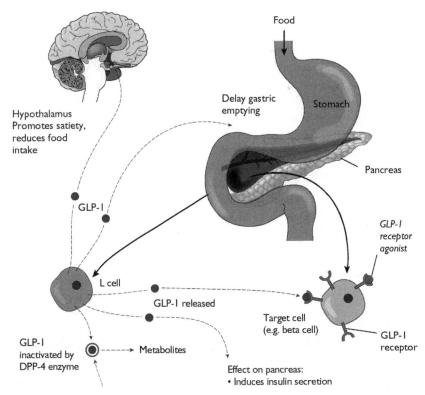

Evidence suggests that early insulin secretion is blunted or absent in people with type 2 diabetes, as a result of reduced GLP-1 secretion (Toft-Nielsen *et al.*, 2001) and is restored by the intravenous infusion of exogenous GLP-1 (Vilsboll *et al.*, 2003).

Incretin agents

There are two types of incretin agent — GLP-1 receptor agonists (incretin mimetic) and DPP-4 inhibitors (incretin enhancers). GLP-1 receptor agonists act like naturally-occurring GLP-1, by binding directly to receptors. DPP-4 inhibitors prevent the inactivation of GLP-1, which enhances and prolongs the effects of endogenous GLP-1 (Charbonnel *et al.*, 2006) (*Tables 5* and *6*).

Incretin mimetics (GLP-1 receptor agonists)

Exenatide is a first generation, twice-daily or once-weekly (Bydureon 2mg prolonged-release suspension) injectable drug that mimics the physiological actions of GLP-1. It is derived from exendin-4, which was originally isolated from the saliva of the Gila monster (a venomous lizard). Buse *et al.* (2007) demonstrated that people with type 2 diabetes (n=283) completing 2 years of treatment with exenatide had a sustained mean reduction of HbA$_{1c}$ of 1.1% (range: -1 to -1.3%) (CI 95%, p<0.001). There was a mean weight reduction of 4.7kg (range: -4 to -5.4kg) (CI 95%, p<0.001).

A meta-analysis by Amori *et al.* (2007) found the most common adverse effects of exenatide to be nausea and vomiting. Severe hypoglycaemia is rare. However, hypoglycaemia is more common when exenatide is used in combination with a sulphonylurea. It is not recommended in people with severe renal impairment.

Exenatide should be commenced as subcutaneous injections of 5g twice daily, one hour before main meals. It should not be used after a meal (Eli Lilly Ltd, 2008). Side effects are common initially but these usually settle. After 6–12 weeks, according to individual tolerance, the dose should be increased to 10g twice daily. However, if intolerable nausea and vomiting occur at higher doses, it should be reduced back to 5g twice daily. A prolonged-release suspension (marketed as Bydureon) is available for once-weekly administration.

Liraglutide is a longer-acting GLP-1 agonist, with 97% sequence homology to human GLP-1. Its physiological actions are mediated via specific GLP-1 receptors (*Table 6*). In a 26-week, double-dummy, multicenter, multinational study by Marre *et al.* (2009), adding liraglutide (either 1.2mg or 1.8mg) to glimepiride was found to significantly reduce HBA_{1c} by 1.1% (from a baseline of 8.5% [69mmol/mol]), fasting blood glucose by 1.6mmol/l (baseline 9.8mmol/l) and postprandial glucose by 2.5mmol/l (baseline 12.9mmol/l). Liraglutide is administered subcutaneously at an initial dose of 0.6mg once daily, which should be increased after at least a week to 1.2mg once daily. As with exenatide, it can be used as a part of dual or triple therapy, in combination with metformin, a sulphonylurea and/or a thiazolidinedione. It should be avoided in renal impairment (eGFR <60ml/min/$1.73m^2$) and hepatic impairment.

Table 4. Actions of glucagon-like peptide-1	
Induces glucose-stimulated insulin secretion	Delays gastric emptying
Reduces glucagon secretion during hyperglycaemia	Improves satiety and reduces food intake
May improve beta cell mass and function	Reduces systolic blood pressure
From: Ducker, 2006.	

Table 5. Incretin agents		
	Available in the UK	**Investigational**
GLP-1 receptor agonists	Exenatide (Byetta) Liraglutide (Victoza, Novo Nordisk) Exenatide LAR	
DPP-4 Inhibitors	Sitagliptin (Januvia) Vildagliptin (Galvus) Vildagliptin plus metformin (Eucreas) Saxagliptin (Onglyza) Sitagliptin with metformin (Janumet)	Alogliptin
GLP-1 = glucagon-like peptide-1, DPP-4 = dipeptidylpeptidase-4		

93

Table 6. Differences between incretin agents		
	GLP-1 receptor agonists	**DPP-4 inhibitors**
Effect on GLP-1 receptors	Direct	Indirect
HbA_{1c} reduction	0.5–1.5%	0.5–0.8%
Effect on weight	Reduction	Neutral
Safety and tolerability	Low incidence of hypo-glycaemia, nausea, vomiting	Low incidence of hypo-glycaemia, nausea, vomiting
Route of administration	Subcutaneous	Oral
Frequency of administration	Exenatide: 5–10µg twice daily Liraglutide: once a day Exenatide LAR: once a week	Sitagliptin: 100mg once daily Vildagliptin: 50-100mg daily

GLP-1 = glucagon-like peptide-1; DPP-4 = dipeptidylpeptidase-4; HbA_{1c} = haemoglobin A_{1c}
From: Brunton *et al*, 2008.

Incretin enhancers (DPP-4 inhibitors)

Sitagliptin and vildagliptin are both DPP-4 inhibitors, which available as tablets. These drugs are rapidly absorbed and mainly excreted by the kidneys, thus renal function should be assessed before their use and they should be avoided in people with moderate to severe renal impairment. Vildagliptin is contraindicated in people with pre-treatment values of alanine aminotransferase (ALT) and aspartate aminotransferase (AST) of more than three times of the upper limits of normal (5–45iu/l [ALT]; 3–45iu/l [AST]).

According to a meta-analysis by Richter *et al.* (2008), DPP-4 inhibitors are well-tolerated and improve HbA_{1c} by 0.7% compared with placebo. The overall risk of hypoglycaemia, nausea and vomiting was found to be low. However, in those treated with sitagliptin, an increased relative risk of 34% for all-cause infections was observed. Compared with placebo, a small increase in weight (0.7–0.8kg) was found. Data on long-term efficacy and safety are not available.

The recommended dose of sitagliptin is 100mg once daily. For vildagliptin, the recommended dose is 50mg twice daily when used with metformin or a thiazolidinedione, and 50mg once daily when used in conjunction with a sulphonylurea (Joint Formulary Committee, 2009).

Use of incretin agents

In practice, GLP-1 agonists are considered for use in people with type 2 diabetes who are obese, on oral anti-diabetic medications and who are unable to achieve glycaemic targets. Evidence suggests that exenatide can be used as a part of dual therapy or triple therapy in combination with metformin, sulphonylureas or thiazolidinediones (Kendall *et al.*, 2005; Zinman *et al.*, 2007). Exenatide is not currently licensed for use in conjunction with insulin therapy.

The DPP-4 inhibitors sitagliptin and vildagliptin are well-tolerated, available as tablets and they do not cause significant weight gain. Therefore, they are an option for people with type 2 diabetes who are overweight, who need adjuvant therapy to achieve glycaemic target and who are not keen on injections. Both drugs are licensed for use in type 2 diabetes in combination with metformin and/or a sulphonylurea and/ or a thiazolidinedione, when dual therapy with these drugs cannot achieve adequate glycaemic control. NICE did not provide a recommendation for the use of sitagliptin and vildagliptin in type 2 diabetes in its 2008 guidance. However, the Scottish Medicines Consortium (2008), offering local guidance within NHS Scotland, recommended the use of vildagliptin in combination with metformin for treatment of type 2 diabetes when adjuvant treatment with a sulphonylurea is inappropriate.

Initiation of oral anti-diabetic agents

Pharmacotherapy is routinely initiated when dietary measures and exercise fail to achieve a target HbA_{1c} of 6.5% (48mmol/mol) (NICE, 2008). In the UKPDS, only 15% of people with newly-diagnosed diabetes were able to achieve this target with lifestyle changes alone; 85% of cases required pharmacotherapy (Turner *et al*, 1999). Pharmacological treatment of type 2 diabetes should be initiated when the person has a fasting blood glucose greater than 11.1mmol/l and/or they fail to respond effectively to lifestyle management (see Chitre and Burke's algorithm, 2006).

The ADA (2008) recommends starting metformin, as well as making lifestyle changes, at the time of diagnosis. It also advises continual and timely augmentation of drug therapy with additional agents to achieve and maintain the recommended level of glycaemic control (Nathan *et al.*, 2006).

Choice of agent

■ **Metformin** — The first-line oral anti-diabetic agent, according to guidance from ADA (2008) and NICE (2008). If a person is intolerant to metformin, then a modified-release form should be considered.

- **Sulphonylureas** — NICE guidelines (2008) recommend sulphonylureas as first-line treatment if the person is not overweight, metformin is contra-indicated or not tolerated, and a rapid therapeutic response is required due to hyperglycaemic symptoms.
- **Thiazolidinediones** — These can be substituted for sulphonylureas if hypoglycaemia is a potential problem, and for metformin if it is not tolerated (NICE, 2008).
- **Combination therapies** — If monotherapy fails to achieve target control, a combination therapy should be considered. NICE (2008) recommends adding sulphonylureas to metformin where monotherapy fails. Other combination therapies are metformin plus a thiazolidinedione, or a sulphonylurea plus a thiazolidinedione. In some people, triple therapy with metformin, a sulphonyl-urea and a thiazolidinedione is required. Anti-diabetic agents should be chosen specifically for the individual, based on factors such as risk of weight gain, risk of hypoglycaemia, risk of fluid retention, liver and kidney function, expense, and most importantly, tolerability.

Follow-up

Until the individual's target control has been achieved, HbA_{1c} and fasting plasma glucose should be checked every 2–6 months, according to individual need (NICE, 2008). Once the blood glucose level and blood glucose-lowering therapy are stable, they should be reviewed every 6 months (Nathan *et al.*, 2006; ADA, 2008; NICE, 2008).

Referral

People should be referred to diabetes specialists for consideration of insulin therapy in the following cases:

- Newly-diagnosed type 2 diabetes mellitus with a significantly-elevated blood glucose level
- Newly-diagnosed diabetes mellitus with any suspicion of possible type 1 diabetes
- People no longer achieving therapeutic goals on maximal tolerable oral anti-diabetes therapy
- Pregnancy
- High-dose glucocorticoid therapy.

Conclusions

The overall objective of diabetes treatment is to achieve and maintain glycaemic levels as close to the non-diabetic range as possible (Nathan *et al.*, 2006). Improving blood glucose levels significantly reduces morbidity and mortality from the micro- and macrovascular complications of diabetes, and improves quality of life. Diabetes is a progressive disease and secondary drug failure develops over time (DCCT, 1993). Therefore, frequent review, continual augmentation of therapy and timely and appropriate referral to a diabetes specialist is essential.

GLP-1 receptor agonists improve blood glucose levels and HbA_{1c} as well as body weight. Aside from metformin, these are the only anti-diabetic agents that are associated with both glycaemic control and weight loss. However, pancreatic beta cell failure can occur in chronic diabetes, which would hinder their effect, so it is essential to regularly monitor HbA_{1c} during their use. DPP-4 inhibitors reduce HbA_{1c} and do not cause significant weight gain. These appear to be well-tolerated, are available orally and are very easy to use. They work well in combination with metformin, pioglitazone or sulphonylureas. However, the long-term effects of DPP-4 inhibition are not yet known. Therefore, they should only be used in individuals who are being monitored closely.

Although oral hypoglycaemic agents are not a substitute for insulin therapy, they have an important role in the management of diabetes. After initiating therapy, blood glucose and HbA_{1c} must be reviewed regularly to ensure that glycaemic control improves. It should be noted that despite encouraging results, the long-term safety and efficacy of some newer therapies still needs to be observed and studied in wider population groups.

Key points

- Achieving glycaemic target is fundamental to the management of diabetes
- Metformin is the first-line oral anti-diabetic agent for type 2 diabetes
- Frequent review and continual augmentation of therapy is of paramount importance to achieve glycaemic target
- Appropriate and timely referral to a diabetes specialist is essential.

References

American Diabetes Association (2008) Executive summary: standards of medical care in diabetes. *Diabetes Care* **31**(1): S5

Amori R et al (2007) Efficacy and safety of incretin therapy in type 2 diabetes: systematic review and meta-analysis. *JAMA* **298**(2):194-206

Bailey C, Turner R (1996) Metformin. *N Engl J Med* **334**(9): 574-79

Buse J et al (2007) Metabolic effects of two years of exenatide treatment on diabetes, obesity, and hepatic biomarkers in patients with type 2 diabetes: an interim analysis of data from the open-label, uncontrolled extension of three double-blind, placebo-controlled trials. *Clin Ther* **29**(1):139-53

Charbonnel B et al Study 020 Group (2006) Efficacy and safety of the dipeptidyl peptidase-4 inhibitor sitagliptin added to ongoing metformin therapy in patients with type 2 diabetes inadequately controlled with metformin alone. *Diabetes Care* **29:** 2638-43

Chitre M, Burke S (2006) Treatment algorithms and pharmacological management of type 2 diabetes. *Diabetes Spectrum* **19**(4): 249-55

DeFronzo R, Goodman A (1995) Efficacy of metformin in patients with non-insulin dependent diabetes mellitus. The Multicenter Metformin Study Group. *N Engl J Med* **333**(9): 541-49

DeFronzo R (1999) Pharmacologic therapy for type 2 diabetes mellitus. *Ann Intern Med* **131**(4): 281-303

Diabetes Control and Complications Trial Research Group (1993) The effect of intensive treatment of diabetes on the development and progression of long-term complications in insulin-dependent diabetes mellitus. *N Engl J Med* 329: 977-86

Eli Lilly (2008) Byetta (exenatide) injection. Summary of product characteristics. Eli Lilly Ltd, Indiana

Elrick H et al (1964) Plasma insulin response to oral and intravenous glucose administration. *J Clin Endocrinol Metab* 24: 1076-82

Groop L (1992) Sulfonylureas in non-insulin-dependent diabetes mellitus (NIDDM). *Diabetes Care* **15**(6): 737-54

Information Centre for Health and Social Care (2008) Quality and Outcomes Framework 2007/2008. http://www.ic.nhs.uk/qof

Joint Formulary Committee (2008) British National Formulary 56. September. BMJ and RPS Publishing, London

Joint Formulary Committee (2009) British National Formulary 57. March. BMJ group and RPS publishing, London

Kendall D et al (2005) Effects of exenatide (exendin-4) on glycemic control over 30 weeks in patients with type 2 diabetes treated with metformin and a sulfonylurea. *Diabetes Care* 28: 1083-91

Marre M et al. LEAD-1 SU study group (2009) Liraglutide, a once-daily human GLP-1 analogue, added to a sulphonylurea over 26 weeks produces greater improvement in glycaemic and weight control compared with adding rosiglitazone or placebo in subjects with Type 2 diabetes (LEAD-1 SU). *Diabet Med* 26: 268-78

Nathan D et al (2006) Management of hyperglycemia in type 2 diabetes: A consensus algorithm for the initiation and adjustment of therapy. *Diabetes Care* **29**(8): 1963-72

National Institute for Health and Clinical Excellence (2008) Type 2 diabetes: the management of type 2 diabetes. Clinical guideline 66. http://tinyurl.com/db8dfg

National Institute for Health and Clinical Excellence (2009) Type 2 diabetes: newer agents for blood glucose control in type 2 diabetes. clinical guideline 87.

National Institute for Health and Clinical Excellence (2010) Liraglutide for the treatment of type diabetes mellitus, NICE technology appraisal guidance 203

Nauck et al (1986) Incretin effects of increasing glucose loads in man calculated from venous insulin and C-peptide responses. *J Clin Endocrinol Metab* 63: 492-98

Pratley R, Weyer C (2001) The role of impaired early insulin secretion in the pathogenesis of type II diabetes mellitus. *Diabetologia* 44: 929-45

Richter B et al (2008) Emerging role of dipeptidyl peptidase-4 inhibitors in the management of type 2 diabetes. *Vasc Health Risk Manag* **4**(4): 753-68

Rosenstock J et al (2004) Repaglinide versus nateglinide monotherapy: A randomised, multicenter study. *Diabetes Care* 27: 1265-70

Scottish Medicines Consortium. (2008) Vildagliptin 50 mg tablets (Galvus), http://tinyurl.com/cyjglh (accessed 24 March 2009)

Toft-Nielsen M et al (2001) Determinants of the impaired secretion of glucagon-like peptide-1 in type 2 diabetic patients. *J Clin Endocrinol Metab* 86: 3717-23

Turner R et al (1999) Glycemic control with diet, sulfonylurea, metformin, or insulin in patients with type 2 diabetes mellitus: progressive requirement for multiple therapies (United Kingdom Prospective Diabetes Study 49). *JAMA* **281**(21): 2005-12

United Kingdom Prospective Diabetes Study Group (1998a) Intensive blood-glucose control with sulphonylureas or insulin compared with conventional treatment and risk of complications in patients with type 2 diabetes (UKPDS 33). *Lancet* **352**(9131): 837-53

United Kingdom Prospective Diabetes Study Group (1998b) Effect of intensive blood-glucose control with metformin on complications in overweight patients with type 2 diabetes (UKPDS 34). *Lancet* **352**(9131): 854-65

United Kingdom Prospective Diabetes Study Group (2000) Association of glycaemia with macrovascular and microvascular complications in type 2 diabetes (UKPDS 35). *BMJ* 321: 405-12

Vilsboll T et al (2003) The pathophysiology of diabetes involves a defective amplification of the late-phase insulin response to glucose by glucose-dependent insulinotropic polypeptide—regardless of etiology and phenotype. *J Clin Endocrinol Metab* 88: 4897-903

World Health Organization (WHO) (1999) Definition, Diagnosis and Classification of Diabetes Mellitus and its Complications, Part 1: Diagnosis and Classification of Diabetes Mellitus. A report of a WHO consultation, Geneva. http://tinyurl.com/anezhq

Zinman B et al (2007) The effect of adding exenatide to a thiazolidinedione in suboptimally controlled type 2 diabetes: a randomized trial. *Ann Intern Med* **146**(7): 477-85

Chapter 10

Optimising insulin therapy to individual need

Kim Hamson

Introduction

Good glycaemic control is known to reduce the risk of microvascular complications in people with type 2 diabetes and may also result in fewer macrovascular events (UKPDS, 1998; Holman *et al.*, 2008). Insulin is the most effective treatment in reducing hyperglycaemia (Nathan *et al.*, 2006). Type 2 diabetes is progressive and leads to beta cell dysfunction, which causes diminished insulin secretion. Hence, a large proportion of people with type 2 diabetes will inevitably go on to require insulin therapy. The United Kingdom Prospective Diabetes Study (UKPDS, 1999) demonstrated that within 6 years, approximately 53% of patients treated with sulphonylureas required additional treatment with insulin. This chapter sets out how to explain how good glycaemic control can be achieved with the commencement of timely and efficacious insulin therapy.

The National Institute of Health and Clinical Excellence guidelines on type 2 diabetes (NICE, 2009) recommend the addition of insulin for people with poorly-controlled type 2 diabetes who are already on the maximum tolerated doses of metformin and a sulphonylurea. NICE recognises this as the preferred management plan for those with marked hyperglycaemia. Historically, the management of diabetes, in particular insulin therapy, has been within secondary care. However, due to rising patient numbers and other challenges faced by policy makers, insulin initiation in type 2 diabetes has shifted from secondary to primary care (Meneghinia *et al.*, 2010). This has been made possible with the introduction of training programmes to enable healthcare professionals to initiate insulin confidently and competently.

In primary care, a commonly used regimen for starting insulin in type 2 diabetes is the addition of basal insulin alongside current oral hypoglycaemic agents. This is supported by NICE (2009) recommendations to use neutral protamine Hagedorn (NPH) insulin as a first-line approach to insulin therapy, although alternatives (such as long-acting analogues) are advocated in particular cases (NICE, 2009). As the disease progresses, insulin intensification and the addition of other insulins, such as twice-daily mixtures or basal bolus regimes will likely be required to address postprandial hyperglycaemia. Despite increasing recognition of the importance of insulin therapy, add-ons and intensification of therapy do not often occur in a

---

Case study

John, a 58-year-old man, was diagnosed with type 2 diabetes 6 years ago. His initial management was lifestyle changes and oral therapy with metformin and glimeperide, but for the past three years he has been treated with once-daily NPH (neutral protamine Hagedorn) insulin.

John initially responded well to insulin therapy, his HbA$_{1c}$ reducing by 1.5% (8.5 to 7% [69 to 53mmol/mol]). However, owing to work pressures, he did not attend regularly for his appointments. At his annual review, the practice nurse notes that his HBA$_{1c}$ has risen again and is now 9.4% (79mmol/mol). John reports not feeling his usual self and that he has started to feel increasingly tired, often falling asleep during the day. He thinks this is probably due to the erratic shifts he has been working. He also reports episodes of low blood glucose, although he does not monitor this regularly — usually just a few times a week, first thing in the morning.

The practice nurse asks John to monitor his blood glucose levels at least four times a day over the next week (both pre- and post-meal) and to record his results in a diary, together with comments relating to diet and activity where possible. An appointment is made to discuss further treatment options. John is a little reluctant to increase the number of daily injections, but he realises that this is almost inevitable to improve his diabetes control and his wellbeing.

---

timely, proactive fashion; instead, they are often discussed late and then commenced reactively (Baxter *et al.*, 2006). Indeed, Ziemer *et al.* (2005) suggested that within primary care, poor diabetes control can be attributed to clinical inertia — inadequate intensification of therapy due to clinicians being unfamiliar with the need for, or the process of treatment intensification.

Management options

Many national and international documents offer guidance on achieving glycaemic targets (Owens *et al.*, 2009). However, practice nurses, community nurses and GPs must attempt to strike a balance between the best glycaemic management for each individual, based on national and international recommendations, and any potentially-conflicting needs and concerns that the individual may have.

Some issues that primary care practitioners are faced with when optimising diabetes treatment regimens are illustrated in the case of John (*case study*).

Assessment

John has had type 2 diabetes for 6 years. He works shifts in a local factory. During a routine diabetes review, his wife informs the practice nurse that despite eating a fairly balanced diet, he has gained weight since starting insulin therapy 3 years previously. Over the past 2 years, his BMI has increased from $27kg/m^2$ to $29kg/m^2$. He currently injects 68 units of NPH insulin in an evening, and on average, he monitors his fasting blood glucose levels twice a week. He initially titrated his insulin with guidance from his practice nurse, although when seen at annual review, he had not altered his doses for over a year.

Persuading people to take responsibility for their insulin injection therapy is a confidence-building exercise, which needs to overcome deeply-ingrained psychological barriers, while enabling the primary care provider to efficiently and confidently implement insulin management strategies (Brod *et al.*, 2009). The practice nurse will have to spend some time with John exploring his current understanding of his diabetes control and his ability to self-titrate his insulin.

The treatment regimens of people with diabetes are frequently complex, and adherence to the self-care aspects of any regimen are typically low (Nelson *et al.*, 2007). Reasons for non-adherence include poor comprehension of the treatment regimen, a lack of confidence, poor diabetes self-efficacy and a lack of belief in the benefits of medication (Peyrot *et al.*, 2005).

Issues

- John works long shifts, often working overtime and may sometimes miss meals
- His mealtimes are unpredictable, and several times a week he eats takeaway foods for convenience
- John finds himself eating extra food to prevent feelings of hypoglycaemia, as he has recently had a few episodes while on night shifts. This may be contributing to his weight gain, which in turn could increase his insulin resistance and ultimately cause an increase in his HbA_{1c}
- John feels he has little opportunity to exercise or otherwise increase his level of physical activity, due to long working hours.

Evidence base for treatment

Many people with type 2 diabetes eventually require insulin (Wright *et al.*, 2002). Although basal insulin supplementation alone can lower HbA_{1c} to guideline targets (Bretzel *et al.*, 2008), it is common practice to commence a basal insulin in combination with oral hypoglycaemic agents when making the initial switch to insulin therapy. NICE (2009) recommends NPH insulin as first-line insulin therapy in type 2 diabetes, which is what John was prescribed 3 years previously. However, it should be noted that in particular cases alternatives are advocated, such as long-acting analogues, or a twice-daily fixed mixture regime with metformin. The main limitation on insulin dosing is its potential to cause hypoglycaemia. NPH insulins also have pharmacokinetic and pharmacodynamic limitations, which prevent them from matching the body's natural absorption of, and response to insulin (Russell *et al.*, 2007). The absorption rates of human insulin can vary from day to day in the same individual, and there can be fluctuations in the glucose-lowering action of insulin (Gin and Hanaire-Broutin, 2005).

It is important that NPH insulin injections are timed carefully, as the nocturnal peak after a bedtime injection can lead to hypoglycaemia, which can then be followed by a high fasting glucose, due to its short duration of action (less than 24 hours) (Rosenstock *et al.*, 2005). John has experienced some nocturnal hypoglycaemic episodes while working night shifts, as well as weight gain. Therefore, the practice nurse may wish to discuss switching him to a newer basal insulin analogue, as these reportedly give a less peaked action profile when compared with NPH insulin and carry a lower risk of hypoglycaemia, particularly during the night (Riddle *et al.*, 2003). They have further been shown to achieve glycaemic control with less weight gain (Hermansen *et al.*, 2006). John's weight gain may be due to his hypoglycaemia and his treatment of the same, so the practice nurse should take the opportunity to give advice regarding the roles of hypoglycaemia and its treatment in avoiding unnecessary weight gain (MacArthur, 2010).

John's basal insulin can be titrated until his blood glucose profile is smooth, with very little variation throughout the day. Once the practice nurse and John have discussed his individual targets for glycaemic control, they can then discuss further treatment options. It is important that John is involved in his care and understands the rationale behind setting and reaching targets. While the practice nurse is aware of the potential harm that a raised HBA_{1c} can have, this risk must be effectively communicated to John if they are to jointly plan and agree his best treatment options (Hawthorne, 2009; Holdich, 2009). Allowing people with diabetes to participate fully in decisions regarding their management is an important way of improving adherence to drug treatments and self-care (Kenny, 2010). If John understands why his insulin regimen needs intensifying and is informed and engaged in decisions about his treatment, he is more likely to adhere to the treatment and achieve better outcomes.

When John returns to see his practice nurse a week later, she examines his blood glucose readings and notes that his fasting blood glucose levels are within the target range (5–7mmol/l) but his postprandial glucose excursions range from 10.8mmol/l to 15.9mmol/l. There is much debate over the implications of excessive glucose excursions in response to meals and how these might contribute to the progression of diabetic complications. The DECODE study (2001) demonstrated that a 2-hour raised blood glucose level was associated with an increased risk of death, independent of fasting blood glucose levels.

John reached his target HBA_{1c} of ≤7% (53mmol/mol) after he commenced insulin three years ago. However, type 2 diabetes is a progressive disease and it is natural that his treatment will need intensification over time. John's HBA_{1c} is now raised, and the practice nurse needs to discuss the further treatment options that are available with him. These include switching to a twice-daily premixed insulin regimen — consisting of a short or rapid-acting insulin analogue plus an intermediate acting insulin in a fixed ratio — or changing to a 'basal plus bolus' insulin regimen, where prandial insulin is taken prior to one meal, two meals or all meals in addition to a once-daily injection of basal insulin.

Treatment considerations

A number of factors are important when choosing between the addition of prandial insulin or switching to premixed insulin at the point of insulin intensification (Barnett *et al.*, 2008). To opt for premixed insulin would ultimately mean fewer injections and less self-monitoring of blood glucose levels. However, due to the fixed ratio of short- or rapid-acting insulin and intermediate-acting insulin, John would have to ensure that he ate regularly and did not skip meals. In contrast, factors favouring intensification to a basal plus, or basal bolus approach include a variable meal pattern and a variable daily routine, despite the potential for more injections and self-monitoring of blood glucose levels. John and the practice nurse need to take some time to consider these factors before changing his regimen. Given his current lifestyle (working long and varied shifts), a basal plus regimen may be preferred.

John is already using basal insulin — the next step would be to target his greatest blood glucose peak of the day. The practice nurse has asked John to test his blood glucose four times a day for a week, before meals and 2 hours postprandially, to find out where the greatest increase is. This is revealed to be with his evening meal, although the time of this meal varies by several hours due to his shift pattern.

John's best option would be to start a rapid-acting insulin analogue at this mealtime, which would work immediately and be of relatively short duration, reducing the risk of subsequent hypoglycaemia. This bolus dose would then be titrated until his blood glucose level before the meal is similar to that 2–3 hours after the meal, thereby smoothing out the peak. A recommended starting dose is ≥4 units or 50% of the 2-hour post-prandial blood glucose concentration (Owens *et al.*, 2009). The practice nurse should also recommend that John continue to monitor his blood glucose level postprandially for the week following initiation and if the average of the last 3 days' readings is in excess of target, then John should increase his prandial insulin by 2 units, with further dose titration taking place weekly as necessary.

John should also be informed that his basal insulin may have to be reduced as his blood glucose levels smooth out. As his post evening meal blood glucose levels reduce and his blood glucose levels continue to fall overnight, he is likely to become hypoglycaemic, unless his basal insulin is reduced. If his HbA_{1c} remains above target once the desired postprandial blood glucose level has been achieved, a second or third injection of prandial insulin may be required to achieve near-normal levels of glycaemia. Should John require just one injection of prandial insulin, then he may be able to continue at his original dose, or a reduced dose of glimeperide. However, when more than one injection of prandial insulin is required, insulin secretagogues such as glimepiride can be discontinued, although metformin should be sustained (Owens *et al.*, 2009).

Conclusion

John's case highlights some of the issues that need to be addressed when considering different types of insulin and dose intensification in trying to achieve good glycaemic control without hypoglycaemia. It demonstrates how a basal plus regimen can be a suitable option and how, due to the progressive nature of type 2 diabetes, this can evolve into other regimens for maintaining glycaemic control. Some people will benefit from shorter-acting human insulins, which have a longer action than rapid-acting analogues, and a short-acting basal insulin that has a peak of action (as opposed to a 24-hour basal analogue) may be useful in some cases. Therefore, it is extremely important to make a full and thorough assessment of the individual's needs, ability and motivation to self-manage before introducing new regimens, particularly those which may be more complex.

Key points

■ The progressive nature of type 2 diabetes, which leads to diminished insulin secretion due to beta cell dysfunction, means that a large proportion of people with the disease inevitably go on to require insulin therapy

■ A number of factors are important when choosing between adding prandial insulin or switching to a premixed insulin

■ Before introducing a new regimen, especially a more complex one, it is extremely important to make a full and thorough assessment of the person's needs, understanding, and their ability and motivation to self-manage.

References

Barnett A et al (2008) Insulin for type 2 diabetes: Choosing a second line insulin regimen. *The International Journal of Clinical Practice* **62**(11): 1647-53

Baxter M et al (2006) Editorial-empowering primary care practitioners to meet the growing challenge of diabetes care in the community. *British Journal of Diabetes and Vascular Disease* 6: 245-48

Bretzel R et al (2008) Once-daily insulin glargine versus thrice-daily prandial insulin lispro in people with type 2 diabetes on oral hypoglycaemic agents (APOLLO); an open randomised controlled trial. *Lancet* **371**(9618): 1073-84

Brod M et al (2009) Psychological insulin resistance: patient's beliefs and implications for diabetes management. *Quality of Life Research* **18**(1): 23-32

Decode Study group (2001). Glucose tolerance and all-cause mortality. *Cardiology Review* **18**(2): 28-32

Diabetes UK (2011) http://www.diabetes.org.uk/About_us/News_landing_Page/2887/ [last accessed: 19/1/12]

Diabetes UK (2010) http://www.diabetes.org.uk/professionals/publications-reports-and-resources/Reports-statistics-and-case-studies/Reports/diabetes-prevalence-2010/ [last accessed: 19/1/12]

Gin H, Hanaire-Broutin H (2005) Reproducibility and variability in the action of injected insulin. *Diabetic Metabolism* 31: 7-13

Hawthorne G (2009) Diabetes: Evidence Based Management 4 A risk-management partnership. *Practice Nursing* **20**(2): 86-90

Hermansen K et al. (2006). A 26 week, randomised, parallel, treat-to –target trial comparing insulin detemir with NPH insulin as add-on therapy to oral glucose-lowering drugs in insulin naïve people with type 2 diabetes. *Diabetes Care* 29: 1269-74

Holdich P (2009) Diabetes: Evidence Based Management 3 Patient-centred care planning. *Practice Nursing* **20**(1): 18-23

Holman R et al (2008) 10 year follow up of intensive glucose control in type 2 diabetes. *The New England Journal of Medicine* 359: 1577-89

Kenny C (2010) Analysing Adherence: controlling prescribing costs. *Diabetes and Primary Care* **12**(1): 7-8

MacArthur C (2010) Diabetes Evidence based management 18: Hypoglycaemia in type 2 diabetes. *Practice Nursing* **21**(4): 206-9

Meneghinia L et al. (2010). Practical Guidance to Insulin Management. *Primary Care Diabetes* **4**(Suppl 1): S43-S46

Monnier L et al (2003). Contributions of fasting and postprandial plasma glucose increments to the overall diurnal hyperglycaemia of type 2 diabetes patients. *Diabetes Care* 26: 881-85

Nelson K et al (2007). Factors influencing disease self management among veterans with diabetes and poor glycaemic control. *Journal of General internal Medicine* 22: 442-47

National Institute for Health and Clinical Excellence (NICE) (2009) Type 2 diabetes. The Management of Type 2 Diabetes. *NICE Clinical Guideline 87.*

Owens D et al (2009) Algorithm for the introduction of rapid-acting insulin analogues in patients with type 2 diabetes on basal insulin therapy. *Practical Diabetes International* **26**(2): 70-77

Peyrot M et al (2005). Psychological problems and barriers to improved diabetes management; results of the Cross- National Diabetes Attitudes, Wishes and Needs (DAWN) Study *Diabetic Medicine* 22: 1379-85

Riddle M et al (2003). The treat-to-target-trial:randomised addition of glargine or human NPH insulin to oral therapy of type 2 diabetic patients. *Diabetes Care* **26**(11): 3080-86

Rosenstock J et al (2005). Reduced hypoglycaemia risk with insulin Glargine: a meta-analysis comparing insulin glargine with Human NPH insulin in type 2 diabetes. *Diabetes Care* **28**(4): 950-55

Russell D, White M (2007). The Treat-to-Target A1C Approach to Control Type 2 Diabetes and Prevent Complications. *Advances in Therapy,* **24**(3): 545-59

UK Prospective Diabetes Study (UKPDS) Group (1998). Intensive blood-glucose control with sulphonyureas or insulin compared with conventional treatment and risk of complications in patients with type 2 diabetes (UKPDS 33) *Lancet* 352: 837-53

Wright A et al (2002). Sulphonylurea inadequacy:efficacy of addition of insulin over 6 years in patients with type 2 diabetes in the U.K. Prospective Diabetes Study (UKPDS 57) *Diabetes Care* 25: 330-36

Chapter 11

Blood pressure and lipid management: a primary care approach

Dr Andrew Inglis

Introduction

The short and long-term complications of diabetes mellitus make it a major public health problem. In type 2 diabetes, the overall cardiovascular risk (including myocardial infarction and stroke) is more than doubled, and the risk of myocardial infarction is increased by 2–4 times (Folsom *et al.*, 1997).

As the vast majority of people with diabetes are treated in primary care, this chapter outlines the management of blood pressure and lipids in people with type 2 diabetes, and reviews the aims of treatment for people with type 1 diabetes. An individual interpretation of the guidance is illustrated by the case of Peter, a gentleman with type 2 diabetes who presents at his general practice for management.

Type 2 diabetes mellitus
Management of blood pressure

As many as 50–80% of people with type 2 diabetes also have hypertension (Internatonal Diabetes Federation, 2011). The Hypertension In Diabetes study (UKPDS, 1998) has confirmed the adverse effect of hypertension in people with type 2 diabetes; tight control of blood pressure was found to reduce diabetes-related endpoints by 24%, diabetes-related deaths by 32% and microvascular disease by 37%.

Regular monitoring of blood pressure is very important. NICE Clinical Guideline 87 (NICE, 2008) recommends a target blood pressure (BP) of <140/80mmHg (or <130/80mmHg in people with kidney, eye, or cerebrovascular damage). NICE (2008) further recommends that all people with diabetes without hypertension or renal disease have annual BP measurements.

Once the person with diabetes is detected to have hypertension, given treatment, and their blood pressure reaches target, it should be routinely checked every 4–6 months. The person should also be assessed regularly for any side-effects, including any that may be due to over-treatment, and antihypertensive medications should be adjusted accordingly.

Case study

A 51-year-old man, called Peter, presenting with a history of anxiety, hypertension and gout was diagnosed with type 2 diabetes on the basis of two abnormal fasting plasma glucose results. He had a history of ramipril intolerance and so at diagnosis he was started on candesartan 4mg, atorvastatin 10mg, aspirin 75mg and metformin 500mg daily. A resting electrocardiogram was normal. His biometric data are presented in *Table C1*.

He was reviewed at 3 months. After his 9-month review his candesartan was increased to 8mg. However, 1 month later, because of symptoms of postural hypotension, his candesartan was stopped. Repeat blood measurements were taken and after analysis of the results and in cooperation with Peter, his candesartan 4mg was restarted. His blood pressure was 136/76mmHg a week later and his retinal screening was normal.

During the following 8 months, his blood pressure was recorded at: 138/84, 144/86 and 134/88mmHg.

After an annual review followed by a 6-monthly review, Peter's blood pressure was 138/72mmHg. A practice review of statin prescribing resulted in a change from atorvastatin to simvastatin 80mg.

At the next annual review, he was noted to have bilateral background retinopathy on retinal screening. His HbA$_{1c}$ had increased and his candesartan was increased to 6mg.

Table C1. Peter's biometric results

	At diagnosis	At 3 months	At 9 months	At 10 months
Body mass Index (BMI)	32.3kg/m^2			
Total cholesterol	5mmol/l			4mmol/l
HDL	1mmol/l			1mmol/l
Serum creatinine	88ml/min	91ml/min	91ml/min	90ml/min
ACR	3.1mg/mol			1.4mg/mol
Blood pressure	152/102mmHg	142/86mmHg	148/92mmHg (post surgery)	138/86mmHg
HbA$_{1c}$		54mmol/mol (7.1%)	50mmol/mol (6.7%)	49mmol/mol (6.6%)

At review 2 months after this dose increase, his blood pressure was 144/80mmHg and he was prescribed amlodipine 5mg daily. This was stopped shortly afterwards owing to side effects. However, 8 weeks later, Peter presented complaining of lower urinary tract symptoms. Urinalysis was negative and rectal examination revealed some prostatic enlargement but his prostate-specific antigen (PSA) levels were normal. Doxazosin 1mg daily was started. At review 8 weeks later, his blood pressure was 142/80mmHg.

At his latest annual review Peter remains on metformin, candesartan 6mg, doxazosin 1mg and simvastatin 80mg daily.

Table C1. [cont.]

	First annual review	Second annual review	Third annual review
Body mass Index (BMI)	30.7kg/m^2		31.3kg/m^2
Total cholesterol	4mmol/l	4mmol/l	4mmol/l
HDL	1mmol/l	1mmol/l	1mmol/l
Serum creatinine		88ml/min	86ml/min
ACR	1.4mg/mol	2.2mg/mol	1.2mg/mol
Blood pressure	142/82mmHg	140/70mmHg	136/78mmHg
HbA$_{1c}$		58mmol/mol (7.5%)	55mmol/mol (7.2%)

HDL=high-density lipoprotein

ACR=albumin-creatinine ratio

HbA$_{1c}$=haemoglobin A$_{1c}$

Lifestyle changes

Obesity is associated with increased blood pressure (Carlson, 2011). People should be encouraged to achieve as close to their ideal body weight as possible, to reduce dietary salt (Taylor *et al.*, 2011), and to do regular aerobic exercise (Annan, 2011). If their blood pressure remains above target, then NICE (2008) recommends starting drug therapy.

Drug management of blood pressure

1. Renin-aldosterone system blocker

NICE (2008) recommends initial treatment with an angiotensin-converting enzyme inhibitor (ACE inhibitor), unless there is a possibility that the person might become pregnant, in which case a calcium channel blocker should be used instead. ACE inhibitors block the conversion of angiotensin-I to angiotensin-II and a number of landmark studies (SYST-EUR, 1997; HOPE, 2000; MICRO-HOPE, 2000; ALLHAT, 2002) have demonstrated significant reductions in cardiovascular events when people with diabetes are prescribed ACE inhibitors.

Blocking the conversion of angiotensin-I to angiotensin-II blocks the production of aldosterone — a hormone which causes the kidneys to retain salt and water. To bring the blood pressure down, the ACE inhibitor's dose should be titrated up. Renal function should be measured before treatment is initiated, after 1–2 weeks of treatment, and again at 1–2 weeks following any dose increase. The commonest side effect is a dry cough, present in about 15% of those taking an ACE inhibitor. If the individual is intolerant of the ACE inhibitor, this should be changed to an angiotensin-II receptor blocker (ARB).

2. Calcium channel blocker (or diuretic)

Second-line treatment of hypertension in people with type 2 diabetes should be with a calcium channel blocker (CCB) (HOT study, 1998; SYST-EUR, 1997). Long-acting preparations should be used, and short-acting preparations (including dihydropyridine preparations such as nifedipine) should be avoided, as they may impair insulin activity and may be associated with an increase in cardiovascular events. NICE (2008) recommends CCBs as first-line drug treatment where there is a possibility that the patient might become pregnant. The side-effects of CCBs include headaches and ankle swelling. If a CCB is contraindicated, or not tolerated, a diuretic can be used in its place.

3. Diuretic (or calcium channel blocker)

Third-line treatment of hypertension should be with a diuretic (typically bendroflumethiazide 2.5mg once daily). Thiazide diuretics increase the urinary excretion of sodium and are associated with hyponatraemia and dehydration, particularly when used in combination with ACE inhibitors, or in older adults (Pandya, 2011; Milta and Little, 2011). Renal function should be carefully monitored in at-risk groups. The use of diuretics increases the risk of gout in at-risk patients, which is a relative contraindication (Cea Soriano *et al.*, 2011).

If a diuretic has been used as second-line treatment for hypertension, then a CCB should be considered as third-line treatment (NICE, 2008). The SHEP (1996), SYST-EUR (1997) and ALLHAT (2002) studies all demonstrated a reduction in cardiovascular events in people with diabetes who were prescribed thiazide diuretics.

4. Alpha-blocker, beta-blocker, or potassium-sparing diuretic

Other pharmacological management options include alpha-blockers, beta-blockers and potassium-sparing diuretics. Alpha-blockers (e.g. doxazosin) are potent antihypertensives, although they can worsen heart failure (in which they are contraindicated) and cause postural hypotension (Chapman *et al.*, 2011).

Beta-blockers (e.g. propranolol) can be particularly useful in people with ischaemic heart disease, as in addition to their antihypertensive effect, they also help to control angina. However, they are contraindicated in asthma.

Potassium-sparing diuretics (e.g. spironolactone) can be a useful adjunct when managing hypertension in people with heart failure. When used alongside an ACE inhibitor or ARB, spironolactone can reduce albuminuria (Gorriz, 2011). However, potassium-sparing diuretics should be used with care (and with careful monitoring of renal function) in people who are taking ACE inhibitors or ARBs, as hyperkalaemia can develop.

The direct renin inhibitor aliskiren has also been shown to reduce albuminuria and blood pressure when used together with an ARB (Siragy and Carey, 2010). However, there is no research data to demonstrate that either treatment has a significant effect on cardiovascular or renal morbidity or mortality in type 2 diabetes.

The aim of all these treatments is to lower the blood pressure. The ALLHAT study (2002) compared groups that were treated with a thiazide diuretic (chlorthalidone), a calcium channel blocker (amlodipine), an ACE inhibitor (lisinopril) and an alpha-blocker (doxazosin). During this trial, the doxazosin arm had to be stopped as an increased risk of heart failure was detected, but no major differences were found in the primary end-points of fatal coronary heart disease or non-fatal myocardial infarction in the other groups, which has been interpreted as meaning that the choice of agent is not so important, so long as blood pressure is lowered. All antihypertensive treatments should be used with care in people with autonomic neuropathy, as this can increase the risk of postural hypotension.

Management of lipids

The link between total cholesterol level and cardiovascular mortality was first identified in the Multiple Risk Factor Intervention Trial (MRFIT) (Stamler *et al*, 1993), in which people with diabetes were shown to have a 3–4 times higher risk of cardiovascular disease for any given level of total cholesterol.

Other studies have since looked at the use of statins in people with diabetes. The Collaborative AtoRvastatin Diabetes Study (CARDS, 2004) and the Heart Protection Study (HPS, 2003) both demonstrated significant reductions in cardiovascular morbidity and mortality in individuals with diabetes mellitus, even at low initial levels of cholesterol.

NICE (2008) recommends annual assessment of cardiovascular risk in all people with diabetes mellitus (*Box 1*), which should include a full lipid profile. A fasting sample should be considered in individuals with a history of high triglycerides, although one should be mindful of the risk of hypoglycaemia if the person in taking an oral hypoglycaemic agent (e.g. a sulphonylurea) or insulin.

Statins

Statins work by inhibiting HMG-CoA reductase, an enzyme that is involved in one of the early stages of cholesterol synthesis in the liver. They also promote the removal of low density lipoproteins (LDL) and very low density lipoproteins (VLDL) from the blood.

Statins are generally well-tolerated, although they can cause generalised muscular aching in some people. A mild increase in alanine transaminase (ALT) is common with statins, but they should not be stopped unless the ALT level reaches three times the upper limit of the laboratory's normal range (see *Box 2*).

Very rarely, serious side-effects can manifest, including myositis (muscle inflammation) and rhabdomyolitis (muscle breakdown, leading to renal failure). Myositis seems to be more common in people who also take a fibrate or nicotinic acid (Wagner *et al.*, 2011).

Age <40: NICE (2008) recommends that a person aged under 40 with a poor cardiovascular risk profile should be considered for treatment with a statin. It is vital that the person concerned is enabled to make an informed choice. All statins are contraindicated in pregnancy — if there is any doubt about pregnancy in a woman of child-bearing age, a statin should not be prescribed.

Age 40+: A person with type 2 diabetes but low cardiovascular risk should be assessed using the UKPDS risk engine (van Dieren *et al.*, 2011) and if found to have a cardiovascular risk of >20%, should be offered treatment with a statin.

Box 1

The person with type 2 diabetes should be considered to be at high cardiovascular risk, unless <u>all</u> of the following apply:

- Not overweight
- Normotensive (BP <140/80 and not on antihypertensive therapy)
- No microalbuminuria
- Non-smoker
- No high-risk lipid profile
- No history of cardiovascular disease
- No family history of cardiovascular disease.

If the person is assessed as not being at high risk of cardiovascular disease, using the above criteria, the UKPDS risk engine (van Dieren *et al.*, 2010) should be used annually to assess risk.

Box 2: choice of statin

NICE (2008) recommends a total cholesterol (TC) of <4.0mmol/l (HDL ≤1.4mmol/l or LDL <2 mmol/l). In order to achieve this:

- Offer generic simvastatin 40mg daily, initially (or a statin of similar efficacy and cost, e.g. pravastatin 40mg)
- Assess lipid profile and other modifiable risk factors 1–3 months after starting therapy and annually thereafter
- If there is high cardiovascular risk and triglycerides (TG) of 2.3–4.5mmol/l despite the statin, consider adding a fibrate
- If TC/HDL/LDL targets are not reached, then consider increasing simvastatin to 80mg, or intensifying therapy with a more powerful statin. This would usually be atorvastatin (titrated depending on effect and side-effects) followed by rosuvastatin. In addition, ezetimibe can be added
- Other agents, such as nicotinic acid preparations or omega-3 fish oils, should not be used routinely; it is recommended that these are used only by health professionals with specialist expertise (McEwen *et al.*, 2011).

Indeed, all people with normal or high cardiovascular risk with type 2 diabetes should be offered a statin. Once again, the risk of pregnancy must be taken into account and discussed with the person.

High serum triglycerides

People with high serum triglycerides (TG) should be assessed for secondary causes (including poor glycaemic control) and then appropriate action should be taken, such as lifestyle and dietary advice. If TG levels remain above 4.5mmol/l, then a fibrate should be offered. If these measures prove ineffective, consider a trial of highly-concentrated omega-3 fish oils (Reaven, 2011).

Fibrates

Fibrates activate PPAR-alpha receptors, which leads to the increased breakdown of TGs and raised levels of HDL. Several studies, including the FIELD study (2005), have shown that fibrates reduce the incidence of cardiovascular events in people with diabetes. More recently, the ACCORD study (2010) looked at combined therapy with a fibrate (fenofibrate) and a statin (simvastatin) and compared this with treatment with simvastatin alone. No significant difference ($p=0.33$) in cardiovascular mortality was found between the two groups. The only significant beneficial effect ($p=0.057$) was noted in individuals with high TG levels and low HbA_{1c}.

Type I diabetes mellitus

Assessment of arterial risk

NICE guidance on the management of type 1 diabetes in adults (Clinical Guideline 15, 2010) recommends annual assessment of arterial risk factors. This should include:

- Albumin excretion rate (through measuring urine albumin-creatinine ratio [ACR])
- Smoking status
- Blood glucose control
- Blood pressure
- Full lipid profile, including HDL, LDL and TG
- Age
- Family history of arterial disease
- Abdominal adiposity.

Risk calculators are not recommended as they underestimate cardiovascular risk in type 1 diabetes mellitus.

People who have microalbuminuria or two or more features of the metabolic syndrome should be managed as high risk (as per persons with type 2 diabetes or established arterial disease). Those who are not in the highest risk category, but who have other risk factors (such as age >35, family history of premature heart disease, high-risk ethnic group, deranged lipids or hypertension) should be considered 'moderately high risk'. Individuals with type 1 diabetes who are not found to be at any additional arterial risk should be managed in the same way as the non-diabetic population.

Management of blood pressure
Lifestyle changes
As previously mentioned, when managing blood pressure in type 2 diabetes, lifestyle factors (including smoking, high alcohol intake, obesity and lack of exercise) should be checked, and appropriate support should be offered.

If blood pressure remains persistently at or above 135/85mmHg (or 130/80mmHg in the high arterial risk individual, assessed as above), NICE (2010) recommends starting treatment to lower the blood pressure. The person should be enabled to make an informed decision about the choice of agents used, taking into account individual factors, such as risk of pregnancy, as discussed in the section on management of blood pressure in type 2 diabetes.

Drug management of blood pressure in type 1 diabetes
NICE (2010) recommends a trial of a low dose of a thiazide diuretic (such as Bendroflumethiazide 2.5mg once daily), unless the person is already taking a renin-aldosterone system blocking drug. Multiple drugs will often be needed to achieve adequate control of blood pressure. If a CCB is used, it should be a long acting preparation, as in type 2 diabetes.

Management of lipids
Arterial risk should be assessed, and a standard dose of a statin should be offered to adults with type 1 diabetes who are at high or moderately high risk of arterial disease. If statins are not tolerated, a fibrate can be used instead. Fibrates should also be used to treat hypertriglyceridaemia. Adults with type 1 diabetes who have experienced a myocardial infarction or stroke should be managed intensively in line with relevant vascular disease management guidelines.

Conclusions

The management of diabetes mellitus in primary care is complex. In addition to therapies to control blood glucose, it is highly likely that people will need to take several drugs to control their blood pressure, and a statin to lower their cholesterol. Concordance with treatment can therefore be more difficult to achieve, and it is vital that clinicians use a person-centred approach, taking account of each individual's needs and preferences, to agree the management plan together. Peter's case study demonstrates the need to interpret the guidelines taking the individual patient's circumstances and wishes into account.

Key points

- Hypertension and dyslipidaemia are both common in people with diabetes, particularly as part of the metabolic syndrome
- Extensive evidence supports the use of anti-hypertensives and lipid-lowering drugs to reduce macrovascular and microvascular risk in diabetes
- NICE guidelines provide useful treatment algorithms
- A person-centred approach with good communication and structured education is vital.

References

ACCORD study group (2010) Effects of combination lipid therapy in type 2 diabetes mellitus. *N Engl J Med* 362: 1563-74

ALLHAT collaborative research group (2002) Major outcomes in high-risk hypertensive patients randomized to angiotensin-converting enzyme inhibitor or calcium channel blocker vs diuretic. *JAMA* 288: 2891-97

Annan F (2011) Diabetes Evidence based management 27, The connection between better health and exercise in diabetes. *Practice Nursing* 22(1): 17-22

Carlson Y (2011) Mechanisms underlying hypertension and obesity. *Hypertension* 57(3): 375

Cea Soriano L et al (2011) Contemporary epidemiology of gout in the UK general population. *Arthritis Res Ther* 13(2): R39

Chapman N et al (2010) Time to re-appraise the role of alpha-1 adrenoceptor antagonists in the management of hypertension? *Journal of Hypertension* 28(9): 1796-803

Collins R et al (2003) MRC/BHF Heart Protection Study of cholesterol-lowering with simvastatin in 5963 people with diabetes: a randomised placebo controlled-trial. *Lancet* 361: 2005-16

Colquhoun H et al (2004) Primary prevention of cardiovascular disease with atorvastatin in type 2 diabetes in the Collaborative AtoRvastatin Diabetes Study (CARDS): multicentre randomised placebo-controlled trial. *Lancet* 364: 685-96

Curb J et al (1996) Effect of diuretic-based antihypertensive treatment on cardiovascular disease risk in older diabetic patients with isolated systolic hypertension (SHEP cooperative research group). *JAMA* 276: 1886-992

FIELD study investigators (2005) Effects of longterm fenofibrate therapy on cardio-vascular events in 9795 people with type 2 diabetes mellitus (the FIELD study): randomised controlled trial. *Lancet* 366: 1849-61

Folsom A et al (1997) A prospective study of coronary heart disease in relation to fasting insulin, glucose and diabetes: the Atherosclerosis Risk In Communities (ARIC) Study. *Diabetes Care* 20: 935-42

Gerstein H et al (2000) Effects of ramipril on cardiovascular and microvascular outcomes in people with diabetes mellitus: results of the HOPE study and the MICRO-HOPE sub-study. *Lancet* 355: 253-59

Gorriz J (2011) New developments in diabetic nephropathy. *Port J Nephrol Hypert* **25**(2): 127-36

Hansson L et al (The HOT study group) (1998) Effects of intensive blood-pressure lowering and low-dose aspirin in patients with hypertension: principle results of the Hypertension Optimal Treatment (HOT) randomized trial. *Lancet* 351: 1755-62

Jensen B et al (2010) Alpha-1-adrenergic receptors: Targets for agonist drugs to treat heart failure. *Journal of Molecular & Cellular Cardiology* (published online: 29/11/10)

International Diabetes Federation Diabetes Atlas (2011) http://da3.diabetesatlas.org/index2983.html [last accessed: 19/1/12]

McEwen B et al (2010) Effect of Omega-3 Fish Oil on Cardiovascular Risk in Diabetes, *The Diabetes Educator* **36**(4): 565-84

Milta O and Little D (2011) Hypertension: How does management change with aging? *Geriatric Medicine* **95**(3): 525-37

Pandya N (2011) Common clinical conditions in long term care, Long term care medicine, Current Clinical Practice, Chapter 5, Springer science business media:UK.

Reaven G (2011) Relationships among insulin resistance, type 2 diabetes, essential hypertension & cardiovascular disease: similarities & differences. *Journal of Clinical Hypertension* **13**(4): 238-43

Siragy H, Carey R (2010) Role of the Intrarenal Renin-Angiotensin-Aldosterone System in Chronic Kidney Disease. *American Journal of Nephrology* **31**(6): 541-50

Stamler J et al (1993) Diabetes, other risk factors, and 12-year cardiovascular mortality for men screened in the Multiple Risk Factor Intervention Trial. *Diabetes Care* 16: 434-444

Staessen J et al (1997) Randomised double-blind comparison of placebo and active treatment for older patients with isolated systolic hypertension. The Systolic Hypertension in Europe (SYST-EUR) investigators. *Lancet* 350: 757-64

Taylor et al (2011) Reduced dietary salt for the prevention of cardiovascular disease: a meta-analysis of randomized controlled trials (Cochrane Review), *American Journal of Hypertension* 24: 843-53

Type 1 diabetes: diagnosis and management of type 1 diabetes in children, young people, and adults (2010) (NICE Clinical Guideline 15). www.nice.org.uk/ CG015NICEguideline

Type 2 diabetes (2008): national clinical guideline for management in primary and secondary care (NICE Clinical Guideline 87). www.nice.org.uk/CG66fullguideline

UK prospective diabetes study group (UKPDS) (1998) Tight blood pressure control and risk of macrovascular and microvascular complications in type 2 diabetes: UKPDS 38. *BMJ* 7160: 703-13

UK prospective diabetes study group (UKPDS) (1998) Efficacy of atenolol and captopril in reducing risk of macrovascular and microvascular complications in type 2 diabetes: UKPDS 39. *BMJ* 7160: 713-20

Van Dieren et al (2011) External validation of the UK Prospective Diabetes Study (UKPDS) Risk engine in patients with type 2 diabetes. *Diabetologia* **54**(2): 264-70

Wagner M et al (2010) Statin-induced focal myositis of the upper extremity. A report of two cases. *European Journal of Radiology Extra* **76**(2): e61-e63

Chapter 12

Psychosocial support for people with diabetes

Anne Phillips and Jerome Wright

Introduction

For decades, non-adherence to treatment regimens has been perceived as a major barrier to the successful treatment of many long-term illnesses (Vermeire *et al.*, 2005). Although the word 'adherence' implies following an imposed regimen, this chapter recognises it as an umbrella term for concordance, cooperation and partnership. Adherence to a treatment regimen is driven by the individual as a decision maker, alongside professional empathy.

Research suggests that in long-term conditions, rates of adherence to treatments and lifestyle recommendations remain low (Vermeire *et al.*, 2005, Phillips and Wright, 2010). In light of this, the need for holistic management is being increasingly recognised. To improve outcomes, health professionals need to understand people who live with long-term conditions, such as diabetes; especially in terms of psychosocial and behavioural barriers to effective self-management and decision making (Stumvoll *et al.*, 2005).

Practice nurses, GPs, community nurses, podiatrists and dietitians all have valuable roles in primary care diabetes clinics, which should not be underestimated. Nurses in particular are in an ideal position to form enduring relationships with the people who attend these clinics. Health professionals who work with people who are facing psychological challenges in the management of their diabetes have a unique role, and this chapter will consider this role, using the example of a practice nurse's interaction with a client, which is presented in the case study below.

Case study

Mr Keith Jones is a 66-year-old retired warehouseman who was diagnosed with type 2 diabetes 15 months ago. He visits his practice nurse for monitoring and to receive diabetes-related education — a routine part of care for all newly-diagnosed individuals (Diabetes UK and Department of Health [DoH], 2005). Although Mr Jones is experiencing difficulties with dietary changes and his oral hypoglycaemic regimen, he has previously failed to attend several appointments. A blood test has shown that Mr Jones has an HbA_{1c} of 9.6% (81.4mmol/mol) and his cholesterol is 6.1mmol/l.

Listening to the story

Noting Mr Jones' previous non-attendance and possible non-adherence to medication, his nurse is immediately aware that any number of factors may be influencing his reluctance to engage with the service or self-manage his diabetes. A diagnosis of diabetes requires adjustment to the realities of living with a serious and lifelong health problem, and changes need to be made to diet, physical activity and smoking habits. A person's optimum physical health is predicated on following the prescribed medication regimen (Woodcock and Kinmonth, 2001). In general, people find it more difficult to be concordant with regimens that are complex, that need to be followed for long periods of time, that involve lifestyle changes and that are designed to prevent rather than cure illness (Sarafino and Smith, 2011).

Opening the consultation

The nurse begins the consultation with a greeting and asks Mr Jones 'open' questions to establish what he understands as the reason for his attending the consultation and what issues (if any) concern him.

Williams *et al.* (2005) suggested that common open questions, such as 'How does diabetes make you feel?', prompt a particular answer and also imply that the person cannot act alone. However, truly open-ended questions allow a person to explore a situation and reach conclusions from their own perspective.

When questioned, Mr Jones replies with slow, quiet speech and makes very little eye contact. He says that he knows the nurse is worried about his diabetes and that's why he's here, but he is not really sure what else he can do.

The nurse then asks Mr Jones if there are any specific aspects of his illness that he is having difficulty with. She is met with a vague response that seems to indicate a limited knowledge of what is required in self-management, that he has limited interest, or that something else is concerning him. The nurse is keen to find out more. She is aware that Mr Jones does not appear to have an active health-seeking manner or behaviour, and despite an elevated HbA_{1c} he makes no mention of any problems.

It is healthy for a person's emotional reactions to change over time and to fluctuate in intensity depending on their perspective and circumstances. However, it is vital that the practitioner explores these issues in situations where the psychological component of a person's health problem appears to have reached a level of distress, and where emotional aspects are highly evident in interaction — either through vented feelings, an apparent absence of interest or a lack of expression of feelings.

To explore an individual's psychological state at a routine review risks losing track of the content and direction of the consultation. Additionally, either party may feel there is insufficient time or fear being overwhelmed by feelings during the consultation — in one study, a third of health professionals reported that they felt ill-equipped to offer psychological support to people with diabetes (Peyrot *et al.*, 2005). A 'consultation map' is suggested (Phillips and Wright, 2009; 2010) to help the nurse and the person concerned reach a shared appraisal of issues and difficulties, and begin to establish a collaborative, therapeutic and purposeful relationship that can be 'contained' within the consultation (*Figure 1*).

An alternative would be for the nurse to focus solely on the physical health demands and adopt a prescriptive approach. Not only would this approach be likely to have limited success in terms of self-management, but it also risks alienating the individual, who may not be physically or emotionally ready to meet the practitioner's expectations.

Recognising diabetes as a long-term condition that requires ongoing attention and application, the nurse sets about establishing a relationship of trust and

Figure 1. The consultation map

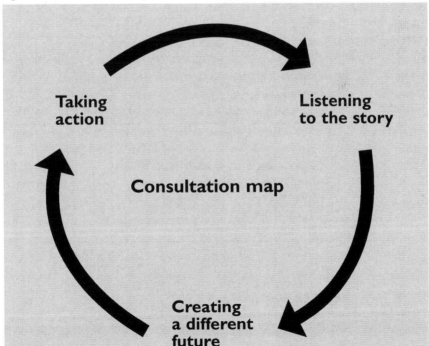

purposefulness by outlining the time-frame and agenda for the appointment — she and Mr Jones have 20 minutes in which she is keen to learn more about his health concerns.

Hearing the individual

The first stage of the consultation map involves listening to issues from the person's perspective, so that the health practitioner and person can establish a joint understanding of the problems (Stewart *et al.*, 2003) (*Table 1*). While Mr Jones is initially reluctant to disclose his concerns, the nurse explains that in her experience a diagnosis of diabetes can often cause people to experience a significant emotional shock and can lead to a sense of feeling overwhelmed, and she wonders if he might be feeling anything like this. Such an empathic question, asked tentatively (as the person might have no such concerns), can help by giving the person 'permission' to divulge difficult feelings. Also, it is not uncommon for people to assume that health professionals are interested only in the functional (rather than emotional) aspects of their illness; an invitation to discuss difficult emotions makes this opportunity clear.

Table 1. Skills and desired outcomes of a staged consultation		
Stage	**Skills**	**Outcomes**
'Listening to the story'	• Demonstrate listening • Follow the person's concerns • Demonstrate empathy • Initiate discussion of the person's concerns	• To establish a joint understanding of the problems
'Creating a different future'	• Demonstrate empathy and identify strengths • Demonstrate confidence in a potential for change • Encourage critical thinking and goal-setting • Provide health information	• To establish partnership to achieve goals
'Taking action'	• Encourage and support action • Demonstrate commitment to the plan(s) • Review, monitor and evaluate progress • Encourage reflection on action	• To support action towards achieving and sustaining goals

Mr Jones acknowledges that he feels overwhelmed by his diabetes and explains that the diagnosis was made just one year after the sudden death of his wife, who died of a heart attack. As he attempted to cope, he ignored symptoms of fatigue, poor concentration and overeating, generally feeling that 'everything was a haze' during this time. However, after performing routine blood and urine tests, his GP diagnosed him with diabetes mellitus, and he now has to deal with this on top of his grief and his adjustment to his wife's death.

Following Mr Jones's disclosure of his concerns, the nurse asks if he still feels 'in a haze' and he replies that he still does a lot of the time. He goes on to describe everyday struggles in managing his finances, shopping and cooking, all of which his wife used to deal with. The nurse enquires about the feelings that accompany these difficulties and Mr Jones describes himself as feeling 'miserable'. He cannot think of one occasion where he has felt happy or content, since the death of his wife. He seldom leaves the house and only occasionally speaks to his sister on the telephone. While he is grateful that the diagnosis has been made, and he accepts that diabetes is a serious health condition, he is fairly resigned to the situation and unconvinced that anything he or anyone else can do will make a difference to the way he is feeling.

Creating a different future

Concerned that Mr Jones's outlook and experiences might indicate a low mood or depression, the nurse explains that she would like to understand more about how he is feeling and invites him to complete a PHQ-9 depression screening tool (Rubin *et al.*, 2004). The nurse is aware that poor psychological wellbeing has been found in 41% of people with diabetes and that this has been found to severely affect regimen adherence (Peyrot *et al.*, 2005). With an estimated 30% of people with diabetes experiencing depression at any one time (Egede, 2005; Katon *et al.*, 2010) the PHQ-9, or alternatively the Beck II and Hospital Anxiety and Depression Scale (HADS), is recommended as part of good practice in the assessment and management of depression in primary care (Clinical Services Improvement Partnership [CSIP], National Institute for Mental Health in England [NIMHE], 2006; National Institute for Clinical Excellence [NICE] CG90, 2010).

It is important to remember that while depression in diabetes care is under-diagnosed and under-treated (Kahn *et al.*, 2008, Katon *et al.*, 2010), it is not the only common mental health problem affecting people living with diabetes. Many people with diabetes experience generalised anxiety or anxiety that relates to specific aspects of their diabetes, such as glucose monitoring or administering injections (Das-Munshi *et al.*, 2007). In each instance, careful 'listening to the story' — recognising the thoughts and feelings behind behaviours — is the basis from which a shared understanding of the person's problems can be reached. Different psychological assessment scales may also be used to increase an awareness of the person's story (*Table 2*).

Mr Jones's story, together with a PHQ-9 score of 9, indicates a probable mild depressive illness. His low mood may be caused by a complicated grief reaction. Tools such as the NHS Norfolk Heron 'Grief Wheel' can help Mr Jones to make sense of his symptoms and the 'tasks of grieving', which include accepting loss, experiencing the pain of grief and adjusting to a new environment without his wife and 'moving on' (NHS Norfolk Heron, 2001). Mr Jones can then start to return to his previous level of functioning. In addition to the loss of his wife, other factors may also be contributing to his low mood, including his retirement from work and diagnosis of diabetes. His low mood is currently the most pressing issue, as it is severely affecting his ability to care for himself and self-manage his diabetes. There is unlikely to be much progress in establishing a self-management approach until his mood improves (Snoek and Skinner, 2005).

It is important to remember that listening to a person's story is a joint assessment of the issues raised and is 'therapeutic' in itself. The 15 minutes spent discussing Mr Jones's concerns may well be the first opportunity he has had to speak about his feelings and to have them acknowledged and accepted. The National Institute for Health and Clinical Excellence (NICE) guidelines for the management of mild depression in primary care (NICE, 2009) emphasise talking therapies over the use of antidepressant medications, so the first stage of the consultation map is an appropriate first step. The benefits of a 'psychologically-minded' health practitioner's approach — incorporating emotional aspects into routine care — have been described in detail by Nichols (1993) and Phillips and Wright (2010).

Further exploration of the person's perspective, by asking a question such as 'how do you see things for yourself in the future?', links to the second stage of the consultation map, which is 'creating a different future'.This enables further insight into Mr Jones's mood and provides an opportunity for the practice nurse to express the optimistic view that, while difficult, positive change is possible.

In the first session, a therapeutic working relationship is established and the nurse summarises that Mr Jones's low mood is the priority issue. This is met with agreement and full eye contact for the first time from Mr Jones. The nurse adopts an optimistic approach, emphasising that the majority of people recover from an episode of depression (NICE, 2009) and that she expects that his case will be no different. In terms of 'taking action' (the third stage of the consultation map) they arrange to meet in one week and he is asked to monitor his mood level each day

Patient questionnaire	Assessment
Table 2. Assessing psychological and psychosocial adjustment to diabetes: a selection of patient questionnaires for use in practice	
Hypoglycaemia Fear Survey	Assess people who are experiencing hypos and are fearful of hypos
Diabetes Treatment Satisfaction Questionnaire	Monitors satisfaction with treatment regimens and detects changes in patients' satisfaction which may affect their feelings about their diabetes and self-management
Perceived Control of Diabetes Questionnaire	Measures individuals' perceptions of the impact of diabetes on their quality of life
Diabetes Obstacles Questionnaire	Validated questionnaire to identify obstacles in the self-management of type 2 diabetes
Hospital Anxiety and Depression Scale	Self-assessment scale for detecting depression and anxiety in the setting of an outpatient clinic
Beck II Depression Scale	Assesses levels of depression
PHQ-9 Depression Scale	Self-administered diagnostic instrument for common mental health disorders such as depression
From: Zigmond and Snaith, 1983; Cox et al, 1987; Beck et al, 1988; Bradley et al, 1999; Kroenke et al, 2001; Bradley et al, 2007; Hearnshaw et al, 2007	

in the meantime, to observe for any fluctuations. Finally, the nurse arranges to discuss their appointment with the GP, so they can plan appropriate care for his next appointment

Taking action

At the second consultation, continuity of care is ensured as Mr Jones is greeted by the same nurse, who asks him if he has any comments or concerns from their previous appointment. She then asks how things have been during the past week.

He reports that he was surprised that he had been able to speak about his wife without becoming overwhelmed with sadness and that although his mood has generally remained at a similar level, he did feel slightly better following his discussion with the nurse. He goes on to describe a telephone conversation that he had with his sister in the week, during which she asked about his diabetes and told him not to ignore his medical condition.

The nurse acknowledges Mr Jones's account of the last appointment and that his low mood did appear to be a significant factor in terms of his taking care of himself. She notes that his mood has not fallen further and asks if they might repeat the PHQ-9 to monitor his mood at his next appointment. The nurse also reports that his GP has requested to be updated about his level of mood.

The nurse then uses Mr Jones's account of the telephone conversation with his sister as a key to further investigate his attitude towards diagnosis and to explore 'creating a different future'. First, she offers praise — despite his low mood and tendency to isolate himself, he has been able to talk to his sister about his health. The nurse acknowledges how difficult this must have been. She then asks Mr Jones why he thinks his sister is concerned. This is an example of helping people to 'shift their perspective' of their diagnosis and its impact.

It can be helpful to ask if he has ever had any similar worries for his sister. This type of approach, to challenge 'ambivalence', is a major aspect of motivational interviewing and encourages Mr Jones to take a more empowered approach in the management of his diabetes (Jones *et al.*, 2001; Vallis *et al.*, 2003; Katon *et al.*, 2010).

When discussing his sister's comments, his own negative outlook regarding his self-caring ability resurfaces, which indicates a need to return to the 'listening to the story' stage in order to find out the origins of such thinking. The stages of the consultation map should not be rigid and formulaic, as it is frequently necessary to move backwards and forwards as more information is uncovered. However, this general structure can help individuals understand where they have come from (in terms of self-management), where they are now and where they might be in the future.

At this point in the consultation, the nurse extends her questioning about his low mood to ask whether or not he ever feels that life is not worth living. This is an essential question to ask any person with low mood, to ascertain the likelihood (or otherwise) of suicide (CSIP/NIMHE, 2006). Mr Jones replies that he occasionally wishes that he didn't wake up in the mornings, but also says that he has never actively considered taking his life. Any intentional suicidal thoughts and planning would represent a psychiatric emergency, demanding planning for immediate safety and care (Millar and Walsh, 2000).

While acknowledging Mr Jones's low mood and ambivalence regarding the possibility of change, it is still appropriate to move on to the 'taking action' stage in order to promote Mr Jones's self-efficacy, however minimal this may be at the present time.

Since Mr Jones previously derived some benefit from discussing his grief over his wife's death, the nurse offers a further opportunity to speak about his feelings and encourages him to identify a person who he trusts and feels that he could speak with in this way. Mr Jones identifies his wife's sister and plans to meet with her at the weekend to test this out. The nurse is aware that if required, counselling resources are available at the practice and through the local branch of Cruse Bereavement Care.

The nurse is also aware that the successful completion of small tasks can have a positive effect on those who are experiencing depression and she asks Mr Jones to pick one intervention that he considers would contribute to his self-care abilities. This gives her an opportunity to assess Mr Jones's level of knowledge about his diabetes, and provides a basis for planning his diabetes education (Diabetes UK and DoH, 2005; Katon *et al.*, 2010).

Mr Jones suggests that a valuable first step would be to create a manageable yet appropriate menu of foods that he would be able to purchase locally. The practice nurse and Mr Jones discuss his food preferences and their suitability within the context of his diabetes and by the time he leaves the consultation, there is a clear, meaningful and realistic plan. The nurse is aware that specific dietetic support will likely be required at some point in the future, but she feels that it is important to focus on developing trust and that Mr Jones needs to achieve successes within the current relationship.

For a nurse who is cognisant of the multi-system health problems that a condition such as diabetes can provoke, it is tempting to immediately refer people to specialists. However, premature referral risks fragmenting care, especially when a psychologically fragile individual is entering a healthcare relationship for the first time. In time, when Mr Jones is feeling more able, it may be of benefit for him to enter a structured group education programme. However, at the current time, the one-to-one approach is the preferred option, as trust and confidence building are occurring.

Cruse Bereavement Care	
Helpline:	0844 477 9400
Email:	helpline@cruse.org.uk
Web:	www.crusebereavementcare.org.uk.

Conclusions

Diabetes mellitus is a serious and lifelong health condition, which makes significant demands of an individual's resources and ability to cope. People adjust to the stress of this diagnosis and the demands of self-management in different ways. The development of mental illness (especially depression) is a common reaction to these demands, or it can be a separate but concurrent problem. Whatever its cause, depression severely restricts a person's self-management abilities. It is important for the practitioner to respond in a holistic way — in particular by recognising how an individual's thinking influences their coping styles and strategies. If a person does have problems with coping and self-management, their psychological issues need to be addressed first. Interpersonal skills (especially professional empathy) can help transform otherwise dislocated relationships, and encourage engagement and the development of a helping alliance.

The consultation map is a simple guide that gives structure to the psychological journey within the care relationship — it helps the practitioner and the individual involved to be transparent, to plan and to not be overwhelmed. It is important to acknowledge that each stage has therapeutic elements in itself.

Maintaining a hopeful and optimistic attitude (even when people are struggling) and taking action will reduce people's fears and help motivate them to become more successful in their self-care.

Anderson *et al.* (2002) emphasised that rather than being responsible *for* their patients, health professionals should be responsible *to* their patients, by collaborating with them to develop self-management programmes that help them to meet their goals.

Key points

- Health professionals are likely to meet clients with diabetes who have low mood, which can affect self-management
- A clear consultation style can be created using person-centred approaches
- Acknowledging small changes and difficulties can help shift a client's perspective
- Recognising low mood and creating an atmosphere of mindfulness can help healing.

References

Anderson R et al (2002) 101 Tips for Behaviour Change in Diabetes Education. American Diabetes Association, Alexandria, VA

Beck A et al (1988) Psychometric properties of the Beck Depression Inventory: Twenty-five years of evaluation, *Clin Psychol Rev* **8**(1): 77-100

Bradley C et al (1999) The development of an individualized questionnaire measure of perceived impact of diabetes on quality of life: the ADDQoL. *Qual Life Res* **8**(1-2): 79-91

Bradley C et al (2007) The Diabetes Treatment Satisfaction Questionnaire change version (DTSQc) evaluated in insulin glargine trials shows greater responsiveness to improvements than the original DTSQ. *Health Qual Life Outcomes* 5: 57

Clinical Services Improvement Partnership, National Institute for Mental Health in England (2006) Best practice guidance for primary care staff: Using the mental health domains in the Quality and Outcomes Framework. http:// tinyurl.com/lm8xb4

Cox D et al (1987) Fear of hypoglycaemia: quantification, validation, and utilization. *Diabetes Care* **10**(5): 617-21

Diabetes UK, Department of Health (2005) Structured patient education in diabetes: Report from the Patient Education Working Group. http://tinyurl.com/lh7ohc

Das-Munshi J et al (2007) Diabetes, common mental disorders, and disability: findings from the UK National Psychiatric Morbidity Survey. *Psychosom Med* **69**(6): 543-50

Egede L (2005) Effect of depression on self-management behaviors and health outcomes in adults with type 2 diabetes. *Curr Diabetes Rev* **1**(3): 235-43

Hearnshaw H et al (2007) Development and validation of the Diabetes Obstacles Questionnaire (DOQ) to assess obstacles in living with Type 2 diabetes. *Diabet Med* **24**(8): 878-82

Jones H et al (2001) Diabetes Stages of Change (DiSC): Evaluation methodology for a new approach to diabetes management. *Canadian Journal of Diabetes Care* 25: 97-107

Kahn L et al (2008) Assessing the prevalence of depression among individuals with diabetes in a Medicaid managed- care program. *Int J Psychiatry Med* **38**(1): 13-29

Katon W, Maj M, Sartorius N (2010) Depression and Diabetes, Wiley Blackwell, UK

Kroenke K et al (2001) The PHQ-9: validity of a brief depression severity measure. *J Gen Intern Med* **16**(9): 606-13

National Institute for Health and Clinical Excellence (2009) Depression: the treatment and management of depression in adults, Clinical guidelines C90.

NHS Norfolk Heron (2001) The Grief Wheel. http://www.heron.nhs.uk/specialist_directory/bereavement/grief_wheel.htm (accessed 1/2/12)

Nichols K (1993) Psychological Care in Physical Illness. 2nd edn. Chapman and Hall, London, UK

Peyrot M et al (2005) Psychosocial problems and barriers to improved diabetes management: results of the cross- national Diabetes, Attitudes, Wishes and Needs (DAWN) Study. *Diabet Med* 22: 1379-85

Phillips A, Wright J (2009) Diabetes, evidence based management 9, Achieving treatment concordance. *Practice Nursing* **20**(7): 353-57

Phillips A, Wright J (2010) Recognising the impact of mental well being on self management of physical conditions. *British Journal of Wellbeing* **1**(6): 30-35

Millar E, Walsh M (2000) Mental Health Matters in Primary Care. Stanley Thornes, Cheltenham, UK

Sarafino E, SmithT (2011) Health Psychology: Biopsychosocial Interactions. 7th edn. Wiley, London, UK

Snoek F, Skinner T (eds) (2005) Psychology in Diabetes Care. 2nd Edn. Wiley, Chichester

Stewart M et al (2003) Patient-Centred Medicine: Transforming the Clinical Method (2nd edn). Radcliffe Medical Press, Oxford, UK

Stumvoll M et al (2005) Type 2 diabetes: principles of pathogenesis and therapy. *Lancet* **365**(9467): 1333-46

Rubin R et al (2004) Recognizing and treating depression in patients with diabetes. *Curr Diab Rep* **4**(2): 119-25

Vallis M et al (2003) Stages of change for healthy eating in diabetes. *Diabetes Care* **26**(5): 1468-74

Vermeire E et al (2005) Interventions for improving adherence to treatment recommendations in people with type 2 diabetes mellitus. *Cochrane Database Syst Rev* 2005(2): CD003638

Williams K et al (2005) Enhancing communication with older adults overcoming elderspeak. *J Psychosoc Nurs Ment Health Serv* **43**(5): 12-16

Woodcock A, Kinmonth A (2001) Patient concerns in their first year with type 2 diabetes: patient and practice nurse views. *Patient Educ Couns* **42**(3): 257-70

Zigmond A, Snaith R (1983) The hospital anxiety and depression scale. *ACTA Psychiatr Scand* **67**(6): 361-70

Chapter 13

Have diabetes, can and will travel

Rebecca Owen

Introduction

For people living with the demands of diabetes, travel can pose additional challenges. A UK survey reported that 10% of people with diabetes experienced problems while travelling (Burnett, 2006). This chapter offers help and advice for practitioners to help people with diabetes wishing to travel.

The key to a safe and enjoyable trip is careful planning, and the person with diabetes may approach their practice nurse, GP or diabetes specialist nurse for advice. A summary of the points to consider when planning travel is presented in *Table 1*. It is recommended that all travellers purchase travel insurance and declare pre-existing medical conditions, such as diabetes. Policies should be checked to ensure they cover events that relate to diabetes, as well as planned activities or sports; it is worth shopping around, as prices can vary greatly — Diabetes UK may be a useful starting point. In the UK, many insurance companies and supermarket chains offer competitive rates for travel insurance. However, travellers over 70 may find that they have more difficulty when seeking travel insurance, especially when they have diabetes.

The European Health Insurance Card (EHIC) is free of charge to UK residents, and allows access to healthcare in all countries of the European Economic Area (EEA) at a reduced price — in some cases, free of charge. However, this is not an alternative to travel insurance, and people with diabetes should be warned of this.

While people with diabetes should still have all the usual recommended travel vaccinations and malaria prophylaxis, they need to be aware that blood glucose levels can be affected in the days following vaccine injections (Bilous and Donnelly, 2010). Insulin users may temporarily increase their doses if they

Table 1. Travel checklist
■ Obtain travel insurance/European Health Insurance Card
■ Recommended vaccinations and malaria prophylaxis
■ Order prescription medications and diabetes supplies
■ Obtain travel cover letter for carrying supplies

experience elevated blood glucose levels.

It is recommended that a full list of prescription medications (generic names) is taken, as well as an adequate supply of oral medications and other diabetes supplies. Information on the availability of insulin in the country or countries being visited is available through pharmaceutical companies.

Insulin strengths can vary in different countries, so dose adjustment may be required. It should also be noted that the same type of insulin may have a different name in a different country.

Travelling by air

Security controls have tightened in recent years, and there are restrictions on certain items. The practitioner can help to minimise difficulties that the person with diabetes may face by providing a covering letter explaining the individual's need to carry medications, syringes/needles and blood glucose testing supplies (see *Table 2*). People may not be able to take their usual hypoglycemia treatments through airport security (especially when in liquid form, like Lucozade) and the practitioner should discuss alternatives that may be available to purchase before boarding the plane. People with insulin pumps should be advised that security alarms are likely to sound when they pass through scanners, and that when this happens they will have to be searched. This should be highlighted as it can be a shock to the individual if they are not prepared. They should be allowed to proceed if they show the insulin pump to the airport security personnel.

Table 2. Essentials for safe travel
■ Oral medications
■ Copy of prescription
■ Insulin supplies
■ Insulin pen/needles/syringes
■ Wallet/bag for insulin storage
■ Blood glucose meter, lancets, strips and a spare battery
■ Sharps container/needle clip device
■ Urine/blood ketone strips
■ Medical ID card and/or jewellery
■ Emergency contact numbers
■ Hypoglycaemia treatments
■ First aid kit (including over the counter remedies)

Insulin and other injectable diabetes medications, such as exenatide and liraglutide, should be carried in the person's hand luggage as the low temperatures in an aircraft's hold can cause them to freeze. Blood glucose meters and test strips should also be kept in the hand luggage. A useful tip is to split medications and diabetes supplies with a companion, in case luggage is lost.

On long journeys, people on glucose-lowering medications should be encouraged to have snacks and drinks to hand, in case there are long periods between meals. In-flight 'diabetic' meals can be requested, which are often low in carbohydrates, but these are not specifically recommended.

There is little or no need to adjust insulin regimens on shorter flights, so people can inject in accordance with their usual schedules. However, some people who are on multiple-injection regimens may use carbohydrate-counting skills to adjust their doses, and others may opt to make minor adjustments based on the type and amount of food eaten. It is recommended that people wait until the in-flight meal has arrived before injecting, to avoid hypoglycaemia that could be caused by any delays. People who take oral medications or exenatide or liraglutide should keep to their usual schedules during travel, and any readjustments due to time zone differences should be made upon arrival.

Longer journeys, particularly those crossing several time zones, require a bit more planning. The practitioner should discuss the flight schedule and travel itinerary with the person, to determine an alternative insulin schedule. Westbound travel extends the day, so extra insulin may be needed, particularly by people with type 1 diabetes. This is more easily managed with a multiple-injection regimen or where the person uses an insulin pump, as rapid-acting insulin can be given every 3–4 hours as needed (Bilous and Donnelly, 2010). Eastbound travel shortens the day and reduces the time between injections, so it may be necessary to reduce the dose of long-acting or pre-mixed insulin on these journeys. The person may find it helpful to keep their watch set to their 'home' time, so they can keep track of insulin doses. Where travel schedules are complicated, diabetes specialist nurses can usually provide specific, individually-tailored advice.

All people with diabetes should be advised to prepare for delays and have adequate supplies of medication, food and drink for the journey.

At the destination

Hot climates appeal to many people choosing a holiday destination, but there are some special considerations for those on insulin. One issue is that warm weather increases the absorption of insulin at injection sites and can potentially cause hypoglycaemia (Westphal *et al.*, 2010). It is recommended that people monitor their blood glucose levels carefully and more frequently as they adjust to warmer temperatures; this enables them to adjust insulin doses accordingly and maintain good glycaemic control. For people on a twice-daily insulin regimen this can be fairly straightforward but those on multiple-injection regimens may require specialist dietetic input for carbohydrate counting and dose adjustment, if they are not already doing this. In warmer climates, a reduction in dosage of 20–30% may be needed. For those visiting colder climates, for instance on skiing trips, insulin absorption can be slower. However, if the person is engaged in physical activity, such as skiing, the risk of delayed hypoglycaemia increases as the body warms up. Again, regular blood glucose testing is recommended, with insulin dose adjustments as needed.

Carrying and storing supplies is also an issue. Insulin is unstable at temperatures above 25°C and it should not be stored in direct sunlight. Additionally, if a cool bag (a lunch bag, for instance) is being used to keep it below this temperature, the insulin should not come into direct contact with the frozen packs, as they may cause it to freeze. Cooling insulin wallets are available in different sizes; further information is available from Diabetes UK and Frio UK (see *Table 3*).

Blood glucose meters and strips can also be affected by extremes of temperature and may give inaccurate readings, so it is advisable to carry a spare kit.

People using insulin or glucose-lowering medications may need a plan for

Table 3. Resources
■ **Information for travellers**
• Department of Health. Health Information for Overseas Travel (the 'Yellow Book'). London: TSO; 2001.
• Diabetes UK: http://www.diabetes.org.uk/
• Foreign and Commonwealth Office Travel Advice: http://www.fco.gov.uk/en/travel-and-living-abroad/
• Frio UK: http://www.friouk.com/
• Fit for travel NHS website: http://www.fitfortravel.nhs.uk/
• MedicAlert: http://search.myway.com
■ **Insulin manufacturers**
• Lilly UK (www.lilly.co.uk)
• Novo Nordisk (www.novonordisk.co.uk)
• Sanofi-aventis (www.sanofi-aventis.co.uk)
• Wockhardt (www.wockhardt.co.uk)

dealing with different activities or sports. This generally requires careful meal planning and more frequent blood glucose testing, as hypoglycaemia can occur with increased exercise, often several hours after activity (Perry and Gallen, 2009). It may be necessary to reduce insulin doses before and after the activity by 20–30%.

Holidays provide the opportunity to enjoy different foods, and having diabetes should not prevent this. Rather than restricting food choices, people should be encouraged to consider the effects of different foods on their blood glucose levels. This is more of an issue for people on insulin, who may need to make dose adjustments according to a change in diet.

Alcohol can cause high blood glucose readings, but for those on glucose-lowering medications, such as sulphonylureas and insulin, there is also a risk of hypoglycaemia (Heller, 2010). This can occur overnight or even the day after drinking alcohol, so it is crucially important that blood glucose levels are monitored closely, that the symptoms of hypoglycaemia are recognised and that appropriate and timely treatment is given where necessary.

Some people may decide to reduce their insulin doses if they are planning to have several alcoholic drinks. In addition to advice on alcohol limits (DoH, 2007), people with or without diabetes should be warned against drinking on an empty stomach and encouraged to maintain good hydration with water and sugar-free mixers.

It is recommended that a 'sick-day' plan is agreed, which will generally include increased fluid intake and more frequent blood glucose testing. People with type 1 diabetes should be able to test for ketones with urine sticks or a blood ketone monitoring device, and should know how to respond to elevated readings and when and how to seek help. During illness, individuals who are treated with insulin will likely need to increase their doses, which is essential if ketones are present (Farmer *et al.*, 2008; Heller, 2010). If further education is needed, the individual should be referred to a diabetes specialist nurse.

A supply of 'over the counter' (OTC) preparations should be taken, including simple analgesia and anti-diarrhoea agents. Also, upon arrival at the destination the person should find out where the local pharmacies, medical centres and hospitals are. They should also be reminded to keep receipts for any medical costs as these may be useful when making an insurance claim. Individuals with insulin pumps (continuous subcutaneous insulin infusion therapy) should contact their specialist team for specific advice on travelling with a pump.

When planning extended and specialised trips, the recommendations for travel insurance cover, vaccinations, air travel, lifestyle changes, storing and carrying supplies, managing insulin and dealing with illness can be more complex. Diabetes should not stop people from going on long trips, but careful planning will be necessary. Diabetes UK can be a useful resource.

People need to think about how they will access medical facilities and obtain medications and other diabetes supplies, particularly in rural areas. Those considering voluntary work through an agency may be required to undergo a medical assessment.

Conclusion

With so much to consider, it is perhaps not surprising that people with diabetes can feel anxious when planning a trip. However, with the right preparation and the support of the healthcare team, having diabetes need not be a barrier to travel.

Key points

- The key to a safe and enjoyable trip is careful planning
- It is recommended that all travellers purchase travel insurance and declare any pre-existing medical conditions such as diabetes
- With the right preparation and the support of the healthcare team, having diabetes need not be a barrier to travel.

References

Bilous R, Donnelly R (Eds) (2010) Handbook of diabetes, 3rd Ed. Blackwell Publishing Ltd, Oxford, UK

Burnett J (2006) Long and short-haul travel by air: issues for people with diabetes on insulin. *J Travel Med* **13**(5): 255-60

Department of Health (2007) Safe. Sensible. Social. The next steps in the National Alcohol Strategy. Department of Health, London, UK

Farmer P et al (2008) Monitoring diabetes across the lifetime of illness, in: Evidence based medical monitoring, from principles to practice. Blackwell publishing online http://onlinelibrary.wiley.com/doi/10.1002/9780470696323.ch16/summary (accessed 31-1-12)

Heller S (2010) Hypoglycaemia in diabetes, Medicine **38**(12): 671-75

Levene L (2003) Management of type 2 diabetes mellitus in primary care: a practical guide. Elsevier Science Ltd.

Perry E and Gallen I (2009) Guidelines on the current best practice for the management of type 1 diabetes, sport and exercise. *Practical Diabetes International* **26**(3): 116-23

Westphal et al (2010) Managing diabetes in the heat. *Endocrine Practice* **16**(3): 506-11

Hypoglycaemia in type 1 and type 2 diabetes and recognising hypoglycaemic unawareness

Clare MacArthur and Helen Gibson

Introduction

When considering diabetes care, most health professionals immediately think of blood glucose control. Treatments are prescribed to reduce blood glucose to near-normal levels and this is intended to prevent or postpone the long-term complications of diabetes. Yet hypoglycaemia — a level of blood glucose that has dropped too low — is a common, costly, troublesome and hazardous side effect of several treatments for diabetes mellitus, in particular sulphonylurea and insulin treatment (*Table 1*).

Viewing hypoglycaemia as a side effect of treatment is helpful as it encourages both health professionals and people with diabetes to regard it as an undesired effect of treatment, rather than something that might be 'expected' when living with diabetes (Phillips, 2009).

This chapter discusses the incidence and impact of hypoglycaemia in type 1 and type 2 diabetes, giving consideration to causes, risk factors, consequences, recognition, management and prevention.

Definitions

Hypoglycaemia is an acute complication of diabetes and occurs when the blood glucose level drops too low to provide enough energy for the body's activities. It is an unwanted side effect of several glucose-lowering therapies used in diabetes.

In people with diabetes, hypoglycaemia is defined as any episode of abnormally low plasma glucose concentration (self-monitored result below 4mmol/l, with or without symptoms) that exposes the individual to harm (Cryer, 2011).

Table 1. Drugs that commonly cause hypoglycaemia
■ **All insulins and insulin secretagogues especially sulphonylureas such as:**
• Glibenclamide (avoid in older people, very long-acting)
• Gliclazide
• Glipizide
• Glimepiride
• Tolbutamide
■ **Drugs that potentially increase the risk of hypoglycaemia in combination with those above:**
• Alcohol (interferes with glucose production from the liver)
• Aspirin
• Allopurinol
• Warfarin
• Sulphonamides
• Trimethoprim
• Fibrates
• Non-steroidal anti-inflammatory agents (NSAIDs)
Adapted from Amiel et al. (2008).

Three features are usually expected in order to formally identify hypoglycaemia (Amiel *et al.*, 2008):

• Typical symptoms or signs (*Table 2*)
• Decreased blood glucose concentration, if measured
• Improvement of these signs and symptoms when the glucose level is raised.

Severe hypoglycaemia is where the individual requires the assistance of a third party to administer treatment, regardless of blood glucose level (Schopman *et al.*, 2011); this could be anyone from a relative or member of the public to a paramedic.

Prevalence

Hypoglycaemia occurs more frequently in type 1 than type 2 diabetes (Cryer, 2009). However, its incidence increases in people with type 2 diabetes on intensive insulin regimes and with increased duration of insulin treatment, to

Table 2. Signs and symptoms of hypoglycaemia and main origin of effects
■ **Autonomic nervous system (neuroendocrine; includes adrenalin response)**
• Tremor
• Sweating
• Feeling hot/cold
• Hunger
• Palpitations
• Pallor
• Paraesthesia and numb mouth/lips
• Feeling anxious or nervous
■ **Neuroglycopenia (insufficient glucose to the brain)**
• Difficulty concentrating
• Weakness/fatigue
• Mood/behavioural change
• Lack of coordination
• Feeling faint or dizzy
• Visual disturbance
• Confusion
• Seizure
• Coma
• Headache
• General malaise, nausea
• Other: related to either process above and/or possibly glucagon production
From: Frier and Fisher (2007).

similar levels as seen in type 1 diabetes (Heller, 2011). It is estimated that a person with type 1 diabetes experiences countless episodes of asymptomatic hypoglycaemia, approximately two episodes of symptomatic hypoglycaemia per week and one episode of temporarily disabling hypoglycaemia per year, on average (Cryer, 2011).

Those with impaired awareness of hypoglycaemia bear the burden of this average figure, with twice the rate of hypos of those with normal awareness, and half of them experience one severe hypo per year, compared with around 1 in 20 with normal hypo awareness (Schopman *et al.*, 2011).

Hypoglycaemia in type 1 diabetes

Type 1 diabetes is a complex disease that demands multidisciplinary management by highly specialised services (Department of Health [DoH], 2006). Routine care of people with stable type 1 diabetes can be managed successfully in primary care with access to support and training. However, when complications such as hypoglycaemia occur, failure to refer to a specialist in a timely manner can have disastrous consequences.

Excellent communication and clear pathways of care are essential to successful multidisciplinary planning (DoH, 2006). As pressure increases to deliver more diabetes services in primary care, the educational requirements of GPs, practice nurses and community nurses must be evaluated, acknowledged and met.

Hypoglycaemia in type 2 diabetes

This is arguably a neglected subject for people living with diabetes, as it is a notable omission in primary care targets for diabetes. The drive is towards avoiding the long-term complications caused by raised blood glucose levels in diabetes, without measuring the potentially adverse effects of forcing levels too low.

Impaired awareness of hypoglycaemia

Impaired awareness of hypoglycaemia means a diminished ability to perceive the onset of hypoglycaemia, thus self-treatment may not occur or it may be delayed. This affects one in five adults with type 1 diabetes and around one in ten people with type 2 diabetes taking insulin (Schopman *et al.*, 2009). This can lead to hypoglycaemic unawareness — a dangerous situation in which severe hypoglycaemia is more likely to occur.

The exact point at which blood glucose is low enough to be deemed hypoglycaemia is controversial, as symptoms vary from person to person and from day to day, depending on customary glucose levels. This explains why a person whose levels have been running high for some time may have hypoglycaemic symptoms at 5mmol/l, while another person who has an HbA_{1c} close to 5% (31mmol/mol), or who has a long duration of diabetes, may not notice symptoms at all — even when at 2.5mmol/l. However, the cognitive impairment is present even if the individual does not 'feel hypo,' so harm can still occur.

Additionally, people usually find that over time their symptoms change and become less apparent; correspondingly they will be more prone to hypos. This is because after just five years of diabetes, the natural glucagon response is blunted and after 15 years, both the glucagon and adrenaline responses to hypoglycaemia are severely reduced (Heller, 2011). The average 30-year-old in a diabetes clinic is likely to have had type 1 diabetes for 15–20 years, so it is not surprising that hypos are a problem. Around 20% of adults with type 1 diabetes have impaired awareness. Compared to those with normal awareness, this is associated with twice the usual frequency of mild hypoglycaemia and six times the incidence of severe hypoglycaemia (Schopman *et al.*, 2011).

Schopman *et al.* (2009) also found that around 10% of people with type 2 diabetes taking insulin had impaired awareness of hypos, and this made them 17 times more likely to experience severe hypoglycaemia in one year.

Targets for blood glucose

While many people with or without diabetes will feel fine with a blood glucose level of 3.9mmol/l, in order to avoid hypoglycaemia it is worth reiterating the target capillary blood glucose measurements for type 1 and type 2 diabetes (National Institute for Health and Clinical Excellence [NICE], 2004; 2008). After all, avoiding levels that are too low is one of the aims of diabetes treatment. The recommended targets are:

- Before meals: 4–7 mmol/l for both types of diabetes
- 2 hours after meals:
  - less than 9.0 mmol/l in type 1 diabetes
  - less than 8.5 mmol/l in type 2 diabetes.

The target HbA_{1c} for many people with type 2 diabetes is 6.5% (48mmol/mol), which is considered likely to achieve the right balance between the risks of low blood glucose and the risks of long-term high levels in most people. However, those at risk of severe hypoglycaemia are more likely to agree a target of 7.5% (58mmol/mol) or higher, for safety. The ACCORD study (2008) demonstrated increased mortality in the participants with the lowest HbA_{1c} results.

In type 1 diabetes, the usual target is below 7.5% (58mmol/mol) but for those at increased arterial risk, it is below 6.5% (48mmol/mol) (NICE, 2004). Payment thresholds for primary care are currently set at 7.5% (58mmol/mol), to allow for individual targets.

According to NICE (2008):

- An HbA$_{1c}$ target should be set in agreement with the individual
- Intensive therapy to achieve levels lower than 6.5% (48mmol/mol) is not required. In fact, a higher target may be set if side effects impair quality of life.

Occasionally in practice this means that people with type 2 diabetes who may have originally needed treatment with a sulphonylurea — but who have made substantial lifestyle changes — may be able to reduce or stop these tablets if their HbA$_{1c}$ is below target.

Advice given in the NICE (2011) pathway for type 1 diabetes is to 'avoid inappropriately pursuing tight blood glucose control if quality of life is compromised despite otherwise optimal care, or the risk of hypoglycaemia is significant to the individual. With lower HbA$_{1c}$ levels, beware of undetected hypoglycaemia, risk of disabling hypoglycaemia and the risk of hypoglycaemia unawareness.' Thus, 'the lower the better' does not apply to targets set for HbA$_{1c}$ or blood glucose levels.

Consequences of hypoglycaemia

'Fear of hypoglycaemia can be a major obstacle to the achievement of the blood glucose levels required to prevent the long-term complications of diabetes. Repeated episodes of hypoglycaemia may seriously impair quality of life.'

DoH (2001: 31)

Hypoglycaemia and subsequent fear of hypoglycaemia have a profound effect on everyday life (Davis *et al.*, 2005; Phillips, 2009), and its potential effects include disruption to the progress of a normal day, embarrassment and social stigma. Yet these would be considered minor effects. As the body releases counter-regulatory hormones, symptoms range from tremor, sweating, and extreme hunger in mild hypos, to cognitive impairment, requiring the help of another person in severe hypoglycaemia (Amiel *et al.*, 2008). Confusion and weakness follows as the brain suffers cognitive impairment due to neuroglycopenia, leading eventually to coma or seizures and rarely death if untreated (Cryer, 2011).

Hypoglycaemia can be fatal, with mortality estimates in type 1 diabetes ranging from 6 to 10% (Cryer, 2011). Recurrent hypoglycaemia has been associated with cognitive impairment (McCulloch, 2011), particularly in older adults and young children, and severe hypoglycaemia requiring hospitalisation has been associated with an increased risk of dementia (Whitmer, 2009). Severe hypoglycaemia can also contribute to depression, which is more common in people with diabetes than in the general population. Therefore, every effort should be made to avoid severe hypoglycaemia (Scottish Intercollegiate Guidelines Network [SIGN], 2010).

These effects should not be underestimated — they are alarming and costly, both to the individual and to the healthcare system. Hypoglycaemia unawareness and severe hypoglycaemia have adverse effects on self-confidence, self-esteem and quality of life. In a survey conducted by Diabetes UK (2006), a person with diabetes described the impact of hypoglycaemia on his life, saying that 'simple day-to-day things that most people take for granted, like driving or looking after your children, sometimes even going out for a walk, can be difficult for me and mean I've always got this nagging fear at the back of my mind.'

Despite this, hypoglycaemia often goes unreported. People may be reluctant to disclose information due to embarrassment, wanting to maintain independence, or for fear of losing their driving licence or their job, and it may require sensitive questioning to uncover the true extent of the problem.

Intensive management of blood glucose leads to a significant increase in the number of episodes of hypoglycaemia and severe hypoglycaemia (DCCT, 1993, UKPDS, 1998, ACCORD, 2008, ADVANCE, 2008, VADT, 1997). Severe hypoglycaemia in type 2 diabetes is strongly associated with an increased risk of major micro- and macrovascular events and death but as yet, hypoglycaemia has not been shown to be a direct cause (De Galan *et al.*, 2010). In the ACCORD study (2008) the intensive treatment arm was terminated early due to an increase in mortality from cardiovascular disease — possibly related to cardiac arrhythmias caused by hypoglycaemia — and a lower HbA_{1c} was significantly correlated with an increase in new cardiovascular events in the Veterans Affairs Cooperative Study of Diabetes Mellitus (VACSMD 1997).

Hypoglycaemia and symptoms

The common symptoms of hypoglycaemia are numerous and vary from person to person and even from hypo to hypo. Therefore, it is not always easy to recognise, or to teach people about hypoglycaemia. If neuroendocrine symptoms do not occur early (*Table 2*) then blood glucose can drop to a level so low that the person has advanced cognitive impairment before they realise they are having a hypoglycaemic episode, thus they may not be able to take action.

When dealing with severe hypoglycaemia, oral glucose treatments must never be given to an unconscious person. Glucagon can be given by a friend or relative who has been trained to administer it, but it is worth bearing in mind that it may not be effective if their glycogen stores are depleted (such as after sustained exercise, vomiting or starvation) or if gluconeogenesis is impaired (such as following alcohol).

Good links with the ambulance service can enable health professionals to communicate about individuals with diabetes who are regularly attended by paramedics for hypoglycaemia treatment but who are not often admitted to hospital. GPs, practice nurses and community nurses can also refer people for structured education. According to the National Service Framework for Diabetes (DoH, 2001), 'people who take on greater responsibility for the management of their diabetes have been shown to have reduced blood glucose levels, with no increase in severe hypoglycaemic attacks', as well as a marked improvement in quality of life (NICE, 2003; Diabetes UK, 2006).

Financial costs of hypoglycaemia

Hypoglycaemia can lead to the use of ambulance services, attendance at accident and emergency departments and even hospital admission. The average cost to health services of a severe hypoglycaemic event has been estimated at around £480 for a person with type 2 diabetes (Hammer *et al.*, 2009) — this is more expensive than in type 1 diabetes, which is probably due to age, concurrent illness and frailty. Although severe hypos are relatively less frequent in people with type 2 diabetes, given the large numbers of people affected in the UK, the total cost is very high.

Alarmingly, in 2008–2009, in England alone, around 50,000 hospital bed days were due to hypoglycaemic emergencies — a fifth of all the diabetes-related bed days during this period (Health and Social Care Information Centre, 2009). While this figure includes all types of diabetes, Amiel *et al.* (2008) estimate that each year a minimum of 5000 people with type 2 diabetes will experience a severe event that requires emergency assistance, with numerous follow-on contacts in primary care.

Mortality from hypoglycaemia

In those admitted to hospital with type 2 diabetes and severe hypoglycaemia the mortality rate is estimated at 5–9% (Amiel *et al.*, 2008). In type 1 diabetes, severe episodes of nocturnal hypoglycaemia can lead to death, which is thought to be due to cardiac arrhythmias — the 'dead in bed' syndrome. This is in addition

Table 3. Risk markers for severe hypoglycaemia
■ **Non-modifiable**
• Previous severe hypoglycaemia
• Long duration of diabetes (>10 years)
• Older age group
• Type 1 diabetes (greater incidence)
• Lower socioeconomic status
■ **Potentially modifiable**
• Hypoglycaemia unawareness
• HbA$_{1c}$ at lower end of range
• High total daily dose of insulin (units/kg body weight)
• Abrupt lowering of HbA$_{1c}$ from high previous level
• Impaired renal function
• Possible drug interaction
Individual factors may also include alcohol and substance abuse, suicide attempt, any form of inadequate nutrition, communication difficulty, poor understanding, gastroparesis, malabsorption and auto-immune conditions such as Addison's disease and coeliac disease.
Adapted from: Frier and Fisher, 2007; Amiel et al, 2008

to death of or injury to the individual or other people due to accidents while hypoglycaemic (Frier and Fisher, 2007). In type 2 diabetes, the exact cause of death may be a comorbidity such as stroke, myocardial infarction or trauma. Hypoglycaemia is particularly dangerous in older people, and often causes falls and injuries. Therefore, identifying and preventing hypoglycaemia is of the utmost importance in the day-to-day management of diabetes. Risk markers for severe hypoglycaemia are presented in *Table 3*.

Driving guidelines

Hypos are particularly dangerous if they occur when performing certain everyday tasks, such as driving. This was demonstrated in study by Cox *et al.* (2000), using driving simulators. Worryingly, the individual with hypoglycaemia may believe that he or she is still safe to drive (Stork *et al.*, 2007). Personal and public safety concerns have led to the current Driver Vehicle Licensing Authority (DVLA) guidelines (Drivers Medical Group, 2010).

By law, people who are taking insulin for their diabetes must notify the DVLA. If on insulin, a licence will be issued only for one, two or three years. Until October 2011, drivers of buses and large lorries (category 2 drivers) who were on insulin would automatically lose their HGV/PSV licences — and sometimes their careers — due to a blanket ban in the UK. This has now changed to a more individualised approach, which includes the need for full awareness of hypos and proof of regular blood glucose monitoring. At the time of writing, people taking diabetes therapies other than insulin are not automatically required to inform the DVLA, but some reasons why people with diabetes might need to inform them are given in *Table 4*.

Whether on tablets or insulin for diabetes, drivers must recognise the warning symptoms of hypoglycaemia and meet the required visual standards. In certain cases where people have problems with the circulation or sensation in their lower limbs, only certain kinds of vehicles can be driven, such as automatics, and the DVLA must be informed.

It is important that health professionals record when they have advised a person to contact the DVLA, to ensure that comprehensive advice is given within their practice.

Drivers are sent information about licensing rules and guidance on safe driving with diabetes, which is also available on the internet (Drivers Medical Group, 2010). The most up-to-date information can be found online:

www.direct.gov.uk/en/Motoring/index.htm

Table 4. Advice for drivers with diabetes
People must inform the Driver and Vehicle Licensing Authority (DVLA) if:
• They are taking or starting insulin
• They have suffered more than one episode of disabling hypoglycaemia within 12 months, or if they or their carer feels they are at high risk of developing disabling hypoglycaemia
• They develop impaired awareness of hypoglycaemia (difficulty in recognising the warning symptoms of low blood sugar)
• They suffer disabling hypoglycaemia while driving
• An existing medical condition gets worse or they develop any other condition that may affect driving safely
In the interests of road safety people must be sure that they can safely control a motor vehicle at all times.
From: Drivers Medical Group, 2010

The role of blood glucose monitoring

Can blood glucose monitoring prevent episodes of severe hypoglycaemia? Farmer *et al.* (2009) found an increased rate of reported hypoglycaemia with self-monitoring, which suggests that hypoglycaemia may be undiscovered without it. In this study, participants used blood glucose monitoring to check whether or not their symptoms related to their diabetes. However, the researchers found no evidence to recommend the routine use of self-monitoring of blood glucose by reasonably well-controlled, non-insulin-treated people with type 2 diabetes.

The appropriate course of management will be determined, as ever, through working in partnership. For most people, like Jeff in *case study 1*, blood glucose monitoring might prevent a recurrence of the problem by warning when levels are below target. However, others may find it an unnecessary burden, and it may not be useful if they are unable to act on the results (Farmer *et al.*, 2009). In cases such as Jeff's, people should be given the choice — it can be part of their self-management education at diagnosis and it should be discussed when starting on medication that is known to cause hypos. In people with type 1 diabetes who are dependent on insulin, and people with type 2 diabetes who are starting insulin, self-monitoring is an expected part of management (NICE, 2008).

Type 1 diabetes

Historically, all people with type 1 diabetes have been looked after in secondary care. As the burden of diabetes increases (Yorkshire and Humber Public Health Observatory [YHPHO], 2011), secondary care facilities are becoming more highly specialised. As a result, the management of less complex individuals, including those with insulin-treated type 2 diabetes and 'stable' type 1 diabetes, has shifted to primary care.

A large number of primary care diabetes clinics are run by nurses alone. Although many practice nurses are highly-skilled and experienced at delivering services for and with people with type 2 diabetes, and are keen to develop their knowledge and skills, they also frequently acknowledge that they can lack the confidence and skills required to recognise and manage all of the clinical issues facing people with type 1 diabetes.

Most practice nurses see few individuals with type 1 diabetes. It is estimated that 4–5% of the UK population has diabetes, of which 5–10% have type 1 diabetes (Diabetes UK, 2011). This means that a practice list of 5000 patients can be expected to have just 10–25 patients with type 1 diabetes (compared with around 230 with type 2 diabetes). As some empowered people may choose not to access care regularly and most people with diabetes are seen in specialist services, practice nurses can have little opportunity to develop their expertise. Furthermore, it is acknowledged that caring for people with diabetes is becoming more, not less, specialised. Therefore, it is essential that GPs, practice nurses and community nurses identify the level of their diabetes skills and practice within their capabilities (DoH, 2006a).

Case Study I

Jeff was brought to accident and emergency by his wife Sally, who described him as being almost unresponsive when she returned to their holiday caravan from a sightseeing trip. Jeff had been hillwalking that day. On examination, he was pale, clammy, disorientated, semi-conscious and weak. Hypoglycaemia was diagnosed and he responded well to treatment. Following observation for a few hours, he was discharged as he was otherwise well and his wife intended to take him back home. It was suggested that he seek advice from his practice diabetes team regarding a potential adjustment to his medication.

Jeff's GP recommended a reduction in the dose of his gliclazide and asked the practice nurse to review him. She asked Jeff and Sally to describe the events leading up to the problem. That day Jeff had been out walking in the hills with a friend. This friend had not noticed any problems during the day, and they had walked about 8 miles before parting company an hour or so after lunch.

On further questioning it transpired that over the last few weeks Sally had noticed Jeff appearing distant, uninterested and very quiet at times, particularly in the afternoons. She had put this down to difficulties at work and had hoped that a holiday would help. Previously, Jeff had been advised to take more exercise, as his blood pressure was elevated. He had been very attentive to his plan of walking for at least 30 minutes every day, usually taking a walk at lunchtime, and he had also reduced his food intake in an attempt to lose some weight. A recent HbA1c was 6.0% (42mmol/mol).

The actual cause of Jeff's hypo was gliclazide treatment, and the underlying modifiable risk factors likely included increased exercise and decreased food intake, resulting in a slightly low HbA_{1c}. A change in his routine while on holiday may also have contributed. It is important that causes, symptoms and treatments for hypoglycaemia are revised with him and his wife, as it seems he may have been having unrecognised hypos before the event occurred. Jeff should also be advised to take extra care over the next 2–3 days, as repeat severe hypoglycaemia occurs in 2–7% of cases where the individual is not admitted to hospital (Fitzpatrick and Duncan, 2009).

Case Study 2

John is a farmer with type I diabetes on multiple injection therapy. He has had diabetes for 30 years and during this time his HbA_{1c} has rarely been above target. He has no evidence of diabetes-related complications and denies any diabetes-related problems when attending for annual review. However, John's wife reports that he often seems unaware that he is having a 'hypo' and that he can sometimes become aggressive during these episodes. As a result, she can no longer leave their young children in his sole care.

John also has epilepsy; his epileptic seizures have recently increased in severity and he has lost his driving licence, which has severely compromised his work. His seizures seem to be precipitated by hypoglycaemia.

Discussion with John and his wife allowed their concerns to be aired, and a mutually-agreed management plan was put in place, which included review by a diabetes physician/endocrinologist. The aims of treatment were to reduce the frequency of hypoglycaemia, reverse unawareness, prevent severe hypoglycaemia and eliminate hypoglycaemia-precipitated epileptic seizures. Hypoglycaemia unawareness may be reversible by avoiding hypoglycaemia, or any blood glucose result under 4mmol/l, for 2–3 weeks (Cryer and Childs, 2002).

Initial treatment involving splitting basal insulin, structured education, better hypoglycaemia management and intensive telephone support. This was ultimately unsuccessful and he was started on insulin pump therapy combined with intensive education (NICE, 2008). Although glycaemic control improved, warning signs of hypoglycaemia were not restored, as it was not possible to prevent 'hypos'. To achieve this, real-time continuous blood-glucose monitoring was then considered. By sounding an alarm at a predetermined blood glucose level, this enables individuals to intervene and treat low blood glucose levels, potentially preventing severe hypoglycaemia. Funding was secured and treatment instigated.

This strategy has been effective in preventing further episodes of severe hypoglycaemia and seizure. John's driving licence was restored, he can work safely on the farm again and quality of life has improved for him and his family. For John, a combination of insulin pump therapy and continuous blood-glucose monitoring has prevented severe hypoglycaemia, in line with NICE guidance (2010). This required access to a specialist pump service and intensive education in self-management. Without the intervention of his wife, the outcome may have been very different.

Uncovering hypoglycaemia and hypoglycaemic unawareness

As illustrated by John's case (*case study* 2), severe hypoglycaemia and hypoglycaemia unawareness can be overlooked if health professionals do not address them. Despite a reasonable HbA_{1c} many problems may remain hidden until disaster strikes, when they can be difficult to resolve. Identification of hypoglycaemia relies on detective work and access to blood glucose monitoring results. Some factors suggesting impaired hypoglycaemia awareness are given in *Table 5*.

Regular home blood-glucose monitoring, identifying trends and changing or adapting insulin regimens in response may help, but accurate interpretation of the results is vital. In addition, home blood-glucose monitoring results are

Table 5. Factors suggesting impaired hypoglycaemia awareness
■ Recurrent, asymptomatic hypoglycaemia (≤3.9mmol/l) on home blood glucose testing
■ Previous hypoglycaemia including severe and/or night hypoglycaemia
■ Onset perceived only when external factors occur, such as relative's concern, or mistakes during tasks
■ HbA_{1c} towards lower levels
From: Frier and Fisher, 2007; Amiel et al, 2008.

Table 6. Common misconceptions in diabetes clinics
• *I'm not hypoglycaemic until my blood sugar gets below 2; I can function perfectly normally at 2.3*
• *I know you told me to have Lucozade, but my neighbour's husband has diabetes and he says that Mars Bars work best*
• *I don't need to check my blood sugar — I can tell exactly what it is by how I feel*
• *I can't test my blood sugar at work — it takes ages and my colleagues wouldn't like it*
• *I don't get hypoglycaemia. If I feel a bit shaky I have some dextrose tablets and then I'm fine. I haven't collapsed for ages*
• *I hate it when my blood sugar gets really high. Anything above 10 and I give some extra insulin, even after a hypo*
• *I just take one glucose tablet and I can carry on*
• *I usually have a can of coke and some crisps, because I get really hungry*

of limited use as they provide an incomplete picture, and the gaps between test results can only be filled by 'best guessing'. They can also be insufficient or unreliable due to user error, antiquated equipment, or falsification.

In the absence of warning signs, a period of continuous blood-glucose monitoring is often the only way to identify hypoglycaemia (Ng *et al.*, 2008) but the tools with which to do this are not usually available in general practice. Therefore, referral to specialist care for full assessment and review of the treatment options is required, which should not be delayed. Insulin pump therapy has been shown to reduce hypoglycaemia in people with type 1 diabetes (NICE, 2008) and may need to be considered (*case study 2*).

Table 7. A structured 'hypo' questionnaire
■ What symptoms do you get when your blood sugars are low?
■ What is your blood sugar when you get these symptoms?
■ Do other people notice it before you do?
■ What blood sugar level do you think would indicate that you are hypo?
■ How often do you get a result under 4mmol/l?
■ Is there a particular time of day that this happens?
■ Do you know which insulins are working at these times? Does this match your food intake or need for insulin?
■ Have you noticed any particular activities that are likely to make your blood sugar drop?
■ What exercise do you do?
■ What about alcohol?
■ What would you do if you thought you were hypoglycaemic?
■ What do you use to treat hypoglycaemia?
■ How do you know if the treatment has worked?
■ Do you do anything to try to prevent hypos?
■ Do you experience unexpected or unpredictable swings in your blood sugars?
■ Have you noticed any changes at your injection sites? Do you mind if I take a look?
■ What would you consider to be a high blood sugar? (Is it perceived or real?)
■ What would you do if your blood sugar reached this level?

Identifying and addressing hypoglycaemia

Practitioners need to dispel myths and misconceptions of hypoglycaemia (*Table 6*). A structured questionnaire can be used as a prompt to help gain as much information as possible and make sure that consistent care is offered to all people who may be experiencing hypoglycaemia (*Table 7*). If blood glucose levels are erratic, fasting blood glucose levels are low or there are suggestions that other people recognise hypoglycaemia in the individual before they are aware of it, alarm bells should ring. To address hypoglycaemia, the underlying cause must be identified (*Table 8*).

Table 8. Addressing hypoglycaemia and meeting educational needs
■ Clarify what hypoglycaemia is (blood glucose <4mmol/l is clinical hypoglycaemia) and encourage prompt treatment with 15–20g high glycaemic index (GI) carbohydrates, followed by 20g medium GI carbohydrates when blood glucose is over 4mmol/l
■ Advise re-checking blood glucose after 10–15 minutes to make sure the treatment has worked, rather than just relying on symptom relief; repeat treatment if necessary
■ Examine injection sites for evidence of lipodystrophy. Advise the individual to avoid damaged areas and make an initial insulin dose reduction of 25%
■ Encourage the person to use a specific insulin sensitivity ratio at a pre-agreed blood glucose level to treat hyperglycaemia, but avoid over-correction
■ Check if insulin is being given at the correct times
■ Check injection technique
■ Identify which activities predispose to hypoglycaemia and agree prevention strategies (less insulin or extra carbohydrates)
■ Give advice about the effects of alcohol, especially how long this may affect results
■ Give advice about avoiding hypoglycaemia when driving and refer to the Driver and Vehicle Licensing Agency (DVLA) for further information
■ Advise the person not to drive if you suspect loss of hypoglycaemia awareness and advise that he/she is obliged to inform the DVLA
■ Refer for structured education
■ Ask the individual to check blood glucose levels overnight (usually 3am) in the presence of low or high fasting glucose results to eliminate nocturnal hypoglycaemia and assess background or 'basal' insulin dose
■ Remember that physical activity may mask hypoglycaemic symptoms

In the absence of warning signs, even empowered, self-managing individuals will be unable to detect episodes of hypoglycaemia; erratic blood glucose readings should alert the practitioner. Apart from the obvious difficulty of identifying asymptomatic hypoglycaemia, many people have been bombarded with messages about target blood glucose levels and are afraid to let glycaemic control deteriorate even for a short time, especially in the presence of complications.

At every appointment, the person should be asked about hypoglycaemia 'or any low results'. They may have very fixed ideas about hypoglycaemia management and be resistant to change. Successful treatment may require a period of intense support from a diabetes specialist nurse or a psychologist (NICE, 2011).

How can secondary care offer support?

Clear pathways of care enable practice diabetes teams to deliver care within their level of expertise and support timely referral to appropriate specialists as necessary. Gaps in knowledge need to be identified and appropriate, accessible education should be provided. Diabetes specialist nurses (either hospital or community-based) can support practice and community nurses and GPs by offering telephone support, case reviews and mentoring. Managing and preventing severe hypoglycaemia and reversing hypoglycaemia unawareness is difficult and requires skill (Hicks *et al.*, 2005). The review of insulin-to-carbohydrate ratios, insulin sensitivity ratios, basal insulin requirements and self-management skills often needs referral to the multidisciplinary team with a structured education programme. The successful diagnosis and treatment of hypoglycaemia may require review by a physician, continuous blood glucose monitoring and insulin pump therapy and should be done by specialists.

Practice diabetes teams play a pivotal role. While empowered individuals may only attend for their annual diabetes review, not all people with diabetes have the capacity or desire to develop advanced self-management skills, and these people need ongoing support. In both cases, practice teams may identify problems and should refer for specialist intervention as necessary.

Practice development

As hypoglycaemia is such a burden on resources and has such a high impact on individuals, it might be expected that its rate would be carefully monitored along with those of other costly problems due to diabetes. In fact, the only routinely kept national records for hypoglycaemia are inpatient stays; researchers have had to conduct specific studies to reveal the relevant figures.

Standard 7 of the National Service Framework for Diabetes (DoH, 2001) explicitly refers to prevention of hypoglycaemia, stating that procedures should be in place to reduce the risks of repetition of emergencies, such as severe hypoglycaemia. However, prevention of hypoglycaemia does not fall under the Quality and Outcomes Framework (QOF) in England (NHS Employers and British Medical Association, 2009), so there are no targets for prevention and remuneration within general practice. Commentators have noted that health policy affects practice — that 'what is measured gets done' (Glasgow *et al.*, 2008). Thus, while everyone who runs a diabetes clinic knows that hypoglycaemia is a significant problem, there is the possibility that its omission as a measure of delivered care may lead to a lack of focus on the issue.

In practice, given the numerous issues to be covered in the management of this complex condition, it may be necessary for the person with diabetes to have a separate appointment from the usual diabetes reviews for patient education about hypoglycaemia and the various issues presented in this chapter. In particular, driving safely with any type of diabetes is an issue which cannot be ignored.

Conclusions

Health professionals should use their skills, knowledge and experience to help people with diabetes to minimise this indirect effect of the condition. They have an important role in providing individuals with up-to-date information, particularly as new therapies emerge that are intended to improve such outcomes. To deliver care effectively, professionals need to work together in multidisciplinary teams (NICE, 2004; DoH, 2007). It should not matter whether the expertise is located in primary or secondary care, so long as it is easily accessible when needed by people with diabetes (Diabetes UK, 2004).

Key points

- Hypoglycaemia is a common, costly, troublesome and hazardous side effect of several treatments for diabetes mellitus, in particular sulphonylureas and insulin
- Viewing hypoglycaemia as a side effect of treatment is helpful as people with diabetes and health professionals are dissuaded from regarding it as something that might be 'expected' when living with diabetes
- Hypoglycaemia is a serious side effect of diabetes treatment and should be considered seriously by people with diabetes and practitioners alike.

References

Action to Control Cardiovascular Risk in Diabetes Study Group, Gerstein H et al (2008) Effects of intensive glucose lowering in type 2 diabetes. *N Engl J Med* 358: 2545

ADVANCE Collaborative Group, Patel A et al (2008) Intensive blood glucose control and vascular outcomes in patients with type 2 diabetes. *N Engl J Med* 358: 2560

Abraira C et al (1997) Cardiovascular events and correlates in the Veterans Affairs Diabetes Feasibility Trial. Veterans Affairs Cooperative Study on Glycaemic Control and Complications in Type 2 Diabetes. *Arch Intern Med* 157: 81

Amiel S et al (2008) Hypoglycaemia in Type 2 diabetes. *Diabet Med* 25(3): 245-54

Cox D et al (2000) Progressive hypoglycaemia's impact on driving simulation performance. Occurrence, awareness and correction. *Diabetes Care* 23(2): 163-70

Cryer P, Childs B (2002) Negotiating the barrier of hypoglycaemia in diabetes, *Diabetes Spectrum* 15(1): 20-27

Cryer P (2011) Management of hypoglycaemia during treatment of diabetes mellitus. Official reprint from UpToDate, http://www.uptodate.com/contents/management-of-hypoglycemia-during

Cryer P (2009) Hypoglycaemia in Diabetes. Pathophysiology, Prevalence and Prevention. American Diabetes Association, Alexandria, VA,

Davis R et al (2005) Impact of hypoglycaemia on quality of life and productivity in type 1 and type 2 diabetes. *Curr Med Res Opin* 21(9): 1477-79

De Galan B et al (2010) Nature of association between severe hypoglycaemia and risks of vascular events and death in ADVANCE. *Diabetologia* 53(S238): 12-186X

Department of Health (2001) National Service Framework for Diabetes: Standards. London, Department of Health.

Department of Health (2006) Turning the corner: improving diabetes care. http://www.dh.gov.uk/en/Publicationsandstatistics/Publications/PublicationsPolicyAndGuidance/DH_4136141

Department of Health (2007) Working together for better diabetes care: clinical case for change, http://www.dh.gov.uk/en/Publicationsandstatistics/Publications/PublicationsPolicyAndGuidance/DH_074702

Diabetes UK (2004) Structured care: delivering better diabetes care part 3. Diabetes UK, London.

Diabetes UK (2006) Position statement: structured education for people with diabetes, Diabetes UK, London.

Diabetes UK (2011) Diabetes UK and NHS Diabetes Workforce Audits 2010 (Apr 2011). Diabetes UK, London.

Drivers Medical Group (2010) At a glance guide to the current medical standards of fitness to drive. www.dft.gov.uk/dvla/medical/ataglance.aspx

Farmer A et al (2009) Blood glucose self monitoring in type 2 diabetes: a randomised controlled trial. *Health Technol Assess* **13**(15): 1-50

Fitzpatrick D, Duncan E (2009) Improving post-hypoglycaemic patient safety in the pre-hospital environment: a systematic review. *Emerg Med J* **26**(7): 472-78

Frier B, Fisher B (2007) Hypoglycaemia in Clinical Diabetes. 2nd edn. John Wiley & Sons Ltd, Chichester

Glasgow R et al (2008) Where is the patient in diabetes performance measures? The case for including patient-centered and self-management measures. *Diabetes Care* **31**(5): 1046-50

Hammer M et al (2009) Costs of managing severe hypoglycaemia in three European countries. *J Med Econ* **12**(4): 281-90

Health and Social Care Information Centre (2009) Hospital episode statistics: health resource groupsK11–17 2007–2008. http://tinyurl.com/yhle2h3

Heller S (2011) Impaired hypoglycemia awareness. *Diabetic Hypoglycemia* **4**(1): 1-2

Hicks D et al (2005) A professional toolkit for nurses working in diabetes care, Wiley interface limited. Chichester.

Ismail-Beigi F et al (2010) Effect of intensive treatment of hyperglycaemia on microvascular outcomes in type 2 diabetes: an analysis of the ACCORD randomized trial. *Lancet* 376: 419

McCulloch, D et al (2011) Glycaemic control and vascular complications in type 2 diabetes mellitus. UpToDate. http://wwwuptodate.com

National Institute for Health and Clinical Excellence TA60 (2003) Guidance on the use of patient education models for diabetes, NICE, London

National Institute for Health and Clinical Excellence CG14. (2004) Diagnosis and management of type 1 diabetes in children, young people and adults, NICE, London

National Institute for Health and Clinical Excellence (review of TA57) (2008) Final appraisal determination: continuous subcuteanous insulin infusion for the treatment of diabetes mellitus, NICE, London

National Institute for Health and Clinical Excellence, CG66 (2008) Type 2 diabetes: National clinical guideline for management in primary and secondary care (update). NICE, London

National Institute for Health and Clinical Excellence, CG87 (2009) Type 2 diabetes: newer agents for blood glucose control in type 2 diabetes, May.

National Institute for Health and Clinical Excellence, CG15 (2010) Type 1 diabetes: diagnosis and management of type 1 diabetes in children, young people and adults. www.nice.org.uk/guidance/CG15/NICEGuidance/changesApr.

National Institute for Health and Clinical Excellence (2011) Diabetes in adults quality standard. http://www.nice.org.uk/guidance/qualitystandards/diabetesinadults/diabetesinadultsqualitystandard.jsp

Ng J et al (2008) Continous blood glucose monitoring: does it really affect diabetic control? *Practical Diabetes International* 25: 239-40

NHS Employers, British Medical Association (2009) Quality and Outcomes Framework Guidance for GMS contract 2009/2010. NHS Confederation, British Medical Association, London

Phillips A (2009) Diabetes evidence-based management, revisiting hypoglycaemia, *Practice Nursing* **20**(10): 516-18

Schopman J et al (2009) Prevalence of impaired awareness of hypoglycaemia and frequency of hypoglycaemia in insulin-treated type 2 diabetes. *Diabetes Res Clin Pract* **87**(1): 64-68

Schopman J et al (2011) Frequency of symptomatic and asymptomatic hypoglycaemia in Type 1 diabetes: effect of impaired awareness of hypoglycaemia. *Diabet Med* **28**(3): 352-55

Scottish Intercollegiate Guidelines Network (2010) 116 Management of diabetes, a national clinical guideline, March.

Stork A et al (2007) The decision not to drive during hypoglycaemia in patients with type 1 and type 2 diabetes according to hypoglycaemia awareness. *Diabetes Care* **30**(11): 2822-26

The Diabetes Control and Complications Trial Research Group (1993) The effect of intensive treatment of diabetes on the development and progression of long-term complications in insulin-dependent diabetes mellitus. *N Engl J Med* 329: 997

UK Prospective Diabetes Study (UKPDS) Group (1998) Intensive blood-glucose control with sulphonylureas or insulin compared with conventional treatment and risk of complications in patients with type 2 diabetes (UKPDS 33). *Lancet* 352: 837

Whitmer, R et al (2009) Hypoglycaemic episodes and risk of dementia in older patients with type 2 diabetes mellitus. *JAMA* 301: 1565

Yorkshire & Humber Public Health Observatory (2011) APHO Diabetes Prevalence Model. http://www.yhpho.org.uk/resource/view.aspx?RID=81090

Chapter 15

Managing foot complications in people with diabetes

Dawn Bowness

Introduction

Bakker (2005) suggested that the most feared disabling complication that can affect people with diabetes mellitus is loss of a limb. Although avoidance of major amputation is crucial, living longer without foot ulceration is also important (Pound *et al.*, 2005). Indeed, Boulton (2005) argued that the development of foot problems is not an inevitable consequence of diabetes, believing most foot lesions to be avoidable with robust screening, optimal multidisciplinary management and appropriate education. A continuing question for all health professionals involved in diabetes care is how best to help people make lifestyle changes that are necessary for the prevention of foot ulceration and amputation.

This chapter will explore the complex management of feet in diabetes, outlining how diabetes affects the feet, how to screen for the risk factors that predispose a person to complications and the care pathways that will optimise a person's care. This reinforces the pivotal role of diabetes teams and practice nurses in the prevention and early detection of foot complications.

The foot and diabetes

The word 'risk' is synonymous with diabetes and its complications. In the context of the foot in diabetes, health practitioners must predict which patients out of their clinic populations are at risk of developing foot ulceration. Boulton, (2005) highlighted that foot ulcerations do not occur spontaneously, but are a consequence of an interaction of known risk factors (*Table 1*).

Diabetes and foot complications are a fine example of prevention being better than cure. When a person with diabetes suffers their first foot ulceration, a decline in health status is often triggered. A history of foot ulceration increases the risk of future incidences (Peters *et al.*, 2001) and, sadly, it has been estimated that 70% of healed foot ulcerations will recur within 5 years (Apelqvist *et al.*, 1993).

Table 1. Risk factors for ulceration
■ Peripheral neuropathy
■ Peripheral vascular disease
■ Biomechanical abnormality or malfunction
■ Infection
■ Duration of diabetes
■ Poor-fitting footwear
■ Callosities
■ Previous ulceration
■ Smoking
■ Old age
■ Poor vision
■ Social deprivation and isolation
From: National Institute for Health and Clinical Excellence, 2004.

Screening and prevention

Health practitioners should be fully aware of the pivotal role they play in the prevention and early detection of foot complications. The recent shift brought about by the publication of *Our Health, Our Care, Our Say* (Department of Health [DoH], 2006) means that primary care is now the locus for foot screening, and there is evidence to support the effectiveness of the surveillance and management of people with diabetes mellitus in primary care (Edelman *et al.*, 1998; Lavery *et al.*, 2005; Lawton *et al.*, 2005).

Although lacking in evidence, a careful, systematic inspection of the feet, together with the taking of a background history is still thought to be the easiest, least expensive and most effective measure in the prevention of foot complications (Young *et al.*, 2006) (See *case study*). The National Institute for Health and Clinical Excellence (NICE) (2004) recommends that as part of annual review, trained personnel should examine patients' feet to detect risk factors for ulceration.

NICE also recommends that the examination of patients reporting foot-related symptoms should include:

• Testing of foot sensation using a 10g monofilament or vibration
• Palpation of foot pulses
• Inspection of any foot deformity and footwear.

Case study

Mr Brown has recently been diagnosed with type 2 diabetes. He presented to his practice nurse complaining of a strange sensation in his feet, similar to pins and needles, and of certain parts of his feet feeling numb. On both feet, he has noticeable calluses over the first metatarsophalangeal joint, and these are speckled with blood. He admits to drinking alcohol daily, averaging 4–5 pints of lager a day and he smokes anything up to 25 cigarettes a day. He is still cutting his own toenails, but does catch the surrounding skin on occasion, making him bleed, which does not seem to concern him. He continues to walk around his home barefoot, as he does not like to wear slippers. He has just booked a holiday to Spain and will leave in 4 weeks.

Peripheral neuropathy

Mr Brown is describing classic neuropathic symptoms of pins and needles and numbness to certain areas of the feet (Edmonds *et al.*, 2008). The practice nurse confirms the presence of sensory peripheral neuropathy in Mr Brown with the use of a 10g monofilament. As neuropathy is related to the tightness of a person's blood glucose control (DCCT, 1993) and lifestyle factors can influence the development of peripheral neuropathy, the practice nurse advises Mr Brown on his diet, smoking and high alcohol intake.

Ischaemia or peripheral vascular disease?

The practice nurse checks Mr Brown for signs of peripheral vascular disease, by palpation of his foot pulses (NICE, 2004). As all of his foot pulses are palpable, the practice nurse determines that there are no significant vascular changes at this time. However, the fact that Mr Brown is regularly smoking up to 25 cigarettes a day is a very significant risk factor for peripheral vascular disease (Edmonds *et al.*, 2008).

Deformity and callus

The practice nurse is concerned about the presentation of blood-speckled calluses on Mr Brown's big toes. She is aware that this is indicative of damaged capillaries that are beginning to leak, and that an ulcer is imminent (Edmonds *et al.*, 2008). Mr Brown needs referral to a podiatrist for sharp debridement of these calluses without delay.

Care pathway

The practice nurse concludes that Mr Brown is at high risk of foot ulceration. The majority of Mr Brown's foot management will be delivered by a multidisciplinary team, but the practice nurse advises Mr Brown on self-care and daily self-monitoring. The practice nurse attributes Mr Brown's indifference to cutting his skin during nail care to a loss of protective pain function rather than dismissiveness of his diabetes.

In light of Mr Brown's impending holiday, the practice nurse is aware that extra advice is required — there is a strong association between holidays, particularly in hot climates, and foot ulceration (Stanaway *et al.*, 2001; Morbach *et al.*, 2001).

Outcomes

The practice nurse has appropriately classified Mr Brown as being at high risk of ulceration and ensured his timely referral to the specialist multidisciplinary services, so that intensive preventive measures can be implemented. This, in conjunction with the aggressive management of modifiable cardiovascular risk factors, will ensure that Mr Brown remains ulcer-free. However, his lifestyle and behavioural choices will ultimately determine the outcomes.

By undertaking the assessment in accordance with NICE (2004), health practitioners will also satisfy the Quality and Outcomes Framework (QOF) of the General Medical Services contract. The 2011/2012 QOF indicator, DM29 states that a practice should be able report the percentage of patients with diabetes with a record of a foot examination and risk classification as follows:

1) Low risk (normal sensation, palpable pulses)
2) Increased risk (neuropathy or absent pulses)
3) High risk (neuropathy or absent pulses plus deformity or skin changes or previous ulcer)
4) Ulcerated foot (within the preceding 15 months).

An assessment for the risk factors for foot ulceration leads to risk classification for the person with diabetes. The practitioner is then enabled to follow the appropriate care pathway.

Peripheral neuropathy

The classic neuropathic symptoms of 'pins and needles' and numbness to certain areas of the feet can indicate peripheral neuropathy (Edmonds *et al.*, 2008). The United Kingdom Prospective Diabetes Study (UKPDS, 1990) demonstrated that 50% of newly-presenting people with type 2 diabetes already had one or more complications at diagnosis. The presence of sensory peripheral neuropathy can be confirmed with the use of a 10g monofilament. The monofilament is recommended by NICE (2004) as it provides an easy, reliable and reproducible method for identifying people who are at increased risk of developing foot ulceration (Baker *et al.*, 2005). However, it is worth noting that a monofilament is only as reliable as the person who is using it. It is the responsibility of the practitioner to ensure that the test is carried out in a standardised, reproducible manner. It is presumed that nearly all foot ulcerations are secondary to some degree of peripheral neuropathy (Crawford *et al.*, 2007).

According to the Diabetes Control and Complications Trial Research Group (DCCT, 1993), neuropathy is related to the tightness of a person's blood glucose control. This study demonstrated a 57% reduction in clinical neuropathy in people with type 1 diabetes, who achieved near normal glycaemic control for the duration of the study.

Practitioners should also be aware that lifestyle factors can influence the development of peripheral neuropathy. Smoking and high alcohol intake have both been associated with the increased incidence of peripheral neuropathy (Edmonds *et al.*, 2008).

Ischaemia or peripheral vascular disease

The signs of ischaemia or peripheral vascular disease are identified by palpation of the patient's foot pulses (NICE, 2004). The absence of two or more pedal pulses is suggestive of peripheral vascular disease (Apelqvist *et al.*, 1990).

Dorsalis pedis can be palpated laterally to the extensor hallucis longus tendon (*Figure 1*), and the posterior tibial artery can be palpated posterior and inferior to the medial malleolus (*Figure 2*). If the person's foot pulses are palpable, it can be determined that there are no significant vascular changes.

Deformity and callus

Any presentation of a blood-speckled callus is indicative of damaged capillaries that are beginning to leak, and suggests that an ulcer is imminent (Edmonds *et al.*, 2008).

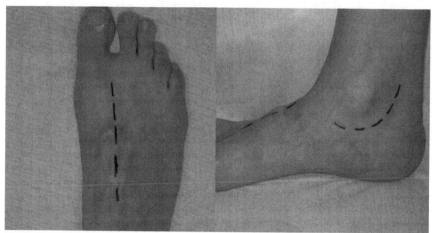

Figure 1. Dorsalis pedis pulse   Figure 2. Posterior tibial pulse

According to Murray *et al.* (1996), callus build-up is a characteristic of the neuropathic foot and is usually found over areas of deformity. Murray *et al.* (1996) noted a seventy-fold increase in ulceration at callused sites. Practice nurses, community nurses and GPs should always be suspicious of a callus as it could be masking an underlying problem — the person should be referred to a podiatrist for sharp debridement without delay.

Care pathway

Boulton (2005) recognised that most foot lesions are avoidable with robust screening, optimal multidisciplinary management and appropriate education. However, in reality, despite this knowledge, rates of foot ulceration and amputation remain unacceptably high (Vileikyte *et al.*, 2004). Furthermore, Akbari *et al.* (2005) have suggested that there is strong evidence that suboptimal referral processes between general and specialist care could be contributing to unfavourable outcomes in a number of conditions, diabetes being no exception. Therefore, it is imperative that a clear referral pathway is implemented locally and followed to the utmost, a sentiment which is supported by standard 11 of the National Service Framework for Diabetes (DoH, 2001), which stipulates that 'The NHS will develop, implement and monitor agreed protocols and systems of care to ensure that all people who develop long-term complications of diabetes receive timely, appropriate and effective investigation and treatment to reduce their risk of disability and premature death.'

In accordance with NICE (2004), the foot is classified into four distinct

Table 2. Risk classification for the foot for people with diabetes	
Risk status	**Definition**
Low current risk	Normal sensation, palpable pulses
Increased risk	Neuropathy or absent pulses or other risk factor
High risk	Neuropathy or absent pulses plus deformity or skin changes or previous ulcer
Ulceration, emergency	New ulceration, swelling, discoloration

From: National Institute for Health and Clinical Excellence, 2004.

Table 3. Care pathway for foot management for people with diabetes	
Ulceration (emergency)	**High risk**
■ Refer to multidisciplinary foot care team within 24 hours	■ Arrange 1–3-monthly review by foot protection team
■ Expect team, as a minimum, to: • Investigate and treat vascular insufficiency • Initiate and supervise wound management • Ensure redistribution of foot pressures • Optimise blood glucose control and control cardiovascular risk factors	■ At each review the team should: • Inspect the individual's feet • Consider the need for vascular assessment • Evaluate and ensure the appropriate provision of: 　- Intensive foot care education 　- Specialist footwear and insoles 　- Skin and nail care ■ Ensure special arrangements for those with disabilities or immobility
Increased risk	**Low current risk**
■ Arrange a 3–6-monthly review by a foot protection team ■ At each review the team should: • Inspect the individual's feet • Consider vascular review • Evaluate footwear • Enhance foot care education	■ Agree a management plan with each person ■ Provide basic foot care advice ■ Encourage self-care objectives

From: National Institute for Health and Clinical Excellence, 2004.

categories for assessment: low current risk, increased risk, high risk and ulcerated (see *Table 2*). The level at which intervention should be offered is determined by the risk classification reached during the assessment. The aim of any intervention offered must be to maintain ulcer-free survival, which has been suggested as a useful marker of the effectiveness of a person's management (Pound *et al.*, 2004) (*Table 3*).

Table 4. Advice for people with diabetes at high risk of developing a foot ulcer
■ **Encourage the individual:** • To practise self-care and daily self-monitoring of feet • To practise good hygiene • Not to walk around barefooted • To seek help for corns and callus management • To moisturise dry skin • To regularly check footwear for foreign objects and for areas that may cause friction • To seek help from a health professional if footwear causes injury or problems • To use prescribed therapeutic footwear
■ **Inform the individual:** • When urgent advice should be sought from a professional, i.e. foot emergency • Of the possible consequences of neglecting the feet • That every break in the skin is potentially serious • Of the dangers of over-the-counter preparations i.e. corn cures • Of the potentials for burning numb feet. They should check bathwater before entering, and avoid hot water bottles, microwavable wheat bags, electric blankets, foot spas and sitting too close to open fires • Of the need for the individual and the nurse to be extra vigilant if neuropathic and ensure additional precautions
■ **Give additional advice about foot care on holiday. Encourage the person to:** • Avoid wearing new shoes • Have adequate rest periods to avoid excess stress on feet • Walk up and down the aisle when travelling by air • Use sun block and socks to avoid sunburn • Use footwear on the beach and in the sea • Take a first aid kit • Seek help locally if any problems arise or telephone the foot care services at home for advice if necessary • Take out health insurance that covers diabetes
From: National Institute for Health and Clinical Excellence, 2004.

Risk factor management

Under the directives of NICE (2004), the majority of a patient's foot management will be delivered by a multidisciplinary team. However, practice nurses, GPs and community nurses must still be aware that certain risk factors can be addressed at the initial consultation. Practitioners should check that interventions are in place to ensure tight glycaemic control, blood pressure, blood cholesterol and triglyceride levels, and that anti-platelet therapy in is place if indicated (Edmonds *et al.*, 2008). If applicable, smoking cessation and the consequences of failing to reduce excessive alcohol should also be discussed with the patient, as quitting smoking and reducing alcohol intake can help delay further deterioration of neurological and cardiovascular function (Edmonds *et al.*, 2008).

Behaviour modification

As highlighted by Baker *et al.* (2005), informing the individual of the outcome of their foot examination is essential, providing a window of opportunity for foot health education. Incorporation of foot care education into the foot screening process can reinforce the individual's knowledge of self-care (Yetzer, 2004). Prevention of foot ulceration requires full behavioural cooperation by the person affected (Vileikyte, 2004). The education that should be offered is outlined in *Table 4*.

Sullivan (1953) describes pain as a potent modifier of behaviour, even in small quantities. However, most cases of foot pathology in the presence of peripheral sensory neuropathy are not painful.

Conclusions

Health practitioners working with people with diabetes or people who are at risk of diabetes need to appropriately classify people that are at high risk of ulceration and ensure timely referral to the specialist multidisciplinary services, so that intensive preventive measures can be implemented. This, in conjunction with the aggressive management of modifiable cardiovascular risk factors will ensure that people can remain ulcer-free. Ultimately, however, it is the lifestyle and behavioural choices of people that will determine their outcomes.

Key points

- The National Institute for Health and Clinical Excellence recommends a review of all patients' feet by trained personnel, to detect risk factors for ulceration
- Practice nurses and community nurses can play a pivotal role in prevention and early detection of foot complications
- The intensity of interventions offered to people with diabetes depends on the risk of developing foot ulceration
- Prevention of foot ulceration requires full behavioural cooperation by the person with diabetes.

References

Akbari A et al (2005) Interventions to improve outpatient referrals from primary care to secondary care. *Cochrane Database Syst Rev* 2005(3): CD005471

Apelqvist J et al (1990) The importance of peripheral pulses, peripheral oedema and local pain for the outcome of diabetic foot ulcers. *Diabet Med* **7**(7): 590-94

Apelqvist J et al (1993) Long-term prognosis for diabetic patients with foot ulcers. *J Intern Med* **233**(6): 485-91

Baker N et al (2005) A user's guide to foot screening, part 1: Peripheral neuropathy. *Diabetic Foot* **8**(1): 28-37

Bakker K (2005) Keeping people's feet perfect. *Diabetes Voice* 50: 5-7

Boulton A (2005) The diabetic foot: Epidemiology, risk factors and the status of care. *Diabetes Voice* 50: 5-7

British Medical Association, NHS Employers (2009) Quality and Outcomes Framework: Guidance for GMS contract 2009/10. http://tinyurl.com/d7gjp6 (accessed 6 May 2009)

Crawford F et al (2007) Predicting foot ulcers in patients with diabetes: A systematic review and meta analysis. QJM **100**(2): 65-86

Department of Health (2001) National Service Framework for Diabetes: Standards. http://tinyurl.com/39rf8g

Department of Health (2006) Our Health, Our Care, Our Say: A New Direction for Community Services. http://tinyurl.com/2zfw79

Diabetes Control and Complications Trial Research Group (1993) The effect of intensive treatment of diabetes on the development and progression of long-term complications in insulin- dependent diabetes mellitus. *N Engl J Med* **329**(14): 977-86

Edelman D et al (1998) Reproducibility and accuracy among primary care providers of a screening examination for foot ulcer risk among diabetic patients. *Prev Med* **27**(2): 274-78

Edmonds M et al (2008) A Practical Manual of Diabetic Foot Care. 2nd edn. Blackwell Publishing, Oxford

Lavery L et al (2005) Disease management for the diabetic foot: Effectiveness of a diabetic foot prevention program to reduce amputations and hospitalizations. *Diabetes Res Clin Pract* 70: 31-37

Lawton J et al (2005) Diabetes service provision: A qualitative study of newly diagnosed Type 2 diabetes patients' experiences and views. *Diabet Med* **22**(9): 1246-51

Morbach S et al (2001) Diabetic holiday foot syndrome': The dimension of the problem and patients' characteristics. *Practical Diabetes International* 18: 48-50

Murray H et al (1996) The association between callus formation, high pressures and neuropathy in diabetic foot ulceration. *Diabet Med* **13**(11): 979-82

National Institute for Health and Clinical Excellence (2004) Type 2 diabetes: Prevention and management of foot problems. Clinical guideline 10. NICE, London

Peters E, Lavery L, International Working Group on the Diabetic Foot (2001) Effectiveness of the diabetic foot risk classification system of the International Working Group on the Diabetic Foot. *Diabetes Care* **24**(8): 1442-47

Pound N et al (2005) Ulcer-free survival following management of foot ulcers in diabetes. *Diabet Med* **22**(10): 1306-9

Stanaway S et al (2001) Diabetic holiday foot syndrome: A preventable complication. *Practical Diabetes International* **18**(2): 45-47

Sullivan H (1953) The Collected Works of Harry Stack Sullivan, Vol. 1: The Interpersonal Theory of Psychiatry. Perry HS, Gawel ML, eds. Norton, New York

United Kingdom Prospective Diabetes Study (UKPDS) Group (1990) Complications in newly-diagnosed type 2 diabetic patients. UKPDS 6. *Diabetes Research* 13: 1-11

Vileikyte L et al (2004) Psychological aspects of diabetic neuropathic foot complications: An overview. *Diabetes Metab Res Rev* **20**(Suppl 1): S13-18

Yetzer E (2004) Incorporating foot care education into diabetic foot screening. *Rehabil Nurs* **29**(3): 80-84

Young M et al (2006) Best practice pathway of care for people with diabetic foot problem. Part 1: The 'at risk' foot. *Diabetic Foot* **9**(3): 148-52

Chapter 16

Assessment of retinopathy

Dr Warren Gillibrand and Phil Holdich

Introduction

This chapter concerns diabetic retinopathy — a serious complication of diabetes, which can have severe debilitating effects on lifestyle, work and relationships. In the UK, diabetic retinopathy remains the main cause of visual impairment and registered blindness in people under 65 years of age (Bunce and Wormald, 2006; Kumar *et al.*, 2006). This is despite evidence to show that 60–80% of visual loss is preventable by laser treatment (Dineen *et al.*, 2008).

To be effective, treatment for retinopathy needs to be given at the appropriate stage of the disease; usually before symptoms have developed. Hence, it is important to screen for the signs of retinopathy before they progress (see *case study*) (Arun *et al.* 2005).

The prevalence and incidence of type 1 and type 2 diabetes continues to rise, although type 2 diabetes may be preventable in many cases (Amos *et al.*, 1997; Yorkshire and Humberside Public Health Observatory, [YHPHO], 2009; Tuomilehto *et al.*, 2001). Data from large studies of the microvascular complications of diabetes demonstrate that good management can prevent diabetic retinopathy, or manage it effectively where it has already developed (Diabetes Control and Complications Trial [DCCT] 1993; United Kingdom Prospective Diabetes Study [UKPDS], 1999). Results from the UKPDS show that a reduction in HbA_{1c} reduces the risk of microvascular complications by up to 21% (p<0.0001) (Stratton *et al.*, 2000) (*Figure 1*).

Progression of retinopathy

Considerable fluctuations in blood glucose levels and hyperglycaemia affect the capillaries of the eyes, kidneys and those supplying the nerves, such that the capillary walls become thickened in small areas, forming micro-aneursyms. This leads to haemorrhages when they eventually burst.

If enough of this abnormal physiology occurs, the blood supply to these organs will not be sufficient for them to function properly, and ischaemic and scarring responses will be triggered.

Diabetic retinopathy is a progressive disease, which is classified into four main stages — background, pre-proliferative, proliferative, and advanced retinopathy.

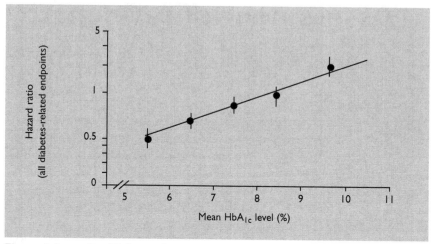

Figure 1. Lowering HbA₁c reduces the risk of diabetes complications in people with type 2 diabetes (UKPDS 35) (Stratton et al., 2000)

Background retinopathy

The term 'background retinopathy' is used when microanuerysms and haemorrhages (commonly termed 'dot and blot haemorrhages') are seen on fundoscopy (looking inside the eye with an ophthalmoscope).

It is important to consider what having background retinopathy means to the person with diabetes. It does not cause visual symptoms. When background retinopathy is detected, the effectiveness of the person's diabetes management should be checked, with monitoring of HbA_{1c} and blood pressure levels. To improve glycaemic control, lifestyle or treatment changes may be needed.

Practice indicators:
* Ensure that the individual is under an annual photographic screening programme for diabetic eye disease. People with background retinopathy only need to be re-screened once a year, and they do not require referral to an ophthalmology service
* Agree on changes to a shared care plan for improved diabetes management
* Check that the individual's level of retinopathy is recorded on the patient record database.

Case study

Michael is a 56-year-old married man with two children. He was diagnosed with type 2 diabetes 8 years ago after visiting his GP with symptoms of polyuria and fatigue. His diagnosis was confirmed by a fasting blood glucose test. For a short time he managed well on a diet and exercise regimen, but owing to weight gain and a rise in HbA_{1c} to 8.6% (70mmol/mol), he started on metformin. His blood pressure is 152/86mmHg (it was 150/88mmHg at the last recording) and he is not currently receiving any treatment for this.

Michael recently attended for an annual retinopathy screening examination. He was sent a letter by his local screening service, informing him about the screening and advising that he should not drive to or from the appointment. At the examination, the retinal screener explained the procedure to Michael and invited him to ask questions. The screening assessment began with a check of visual acuity, as some forms of retinopathy can affect vision in their early stages. His pupils were then dilated using tropicamide 1% eye drops, which the National Screening Programme for Diabetic Retinopathy (2008) recommends as being the most effective for pupil dilatation for fundoscopy and the least likely to cause adverse reactions. Once his pupils were dilated, a number of digital images were then taken of each fundus and stored on the computer for later grading of retinopathy by the screener.

Two weeks later, Michael received a letter from his GP stating that pre-proliferative retinopathy had been detected. He was referred to the ophthalmology department at his local hospital. When seen, a detailed examination was carried out, and the consultant ophthalmologist recommended 6-month follow-up to monitor his progress.

Michael also attended a consultation with his practice nurse. They devised an agreed shared care plan with the main goals being to help him do more exercise, reduce his weight and improve his glycaemic control. The nurse recommended a blood pressure target of 130/80mmHg. Following NICE guidance (2008), after checking his renal function and electrolytes she recommended an ACE inhibitor (enalapril 5mg). With follow up checks, his dose was titrated to 20mg daily. His HbA_{1c} fell to 7.8% (62mmol/mol) and his blood pressure to 136/82mmHg. When seen for review by the ophthalmologist, the pre-proliferative signs had reduced, with no progression to the proliferative stage.

Pre-proliferative retinopathy

'Pre-proliferative retinopathy' indicates signs of ischaemia (i.e. tissue death), resulting from the loss of blood supply to those affected areas of the retina. Features include 'cotton wool spots' (small areas of ischaemia comprising venous beading and reduplication or looping of blood vessels, which appear abnormal) and intraretinal microvascular abnormalities, which present as tortuous dilated blood vessels caused by retinal ischaemia.

Pre-proliferative retinopathy presents with no visual symptoms, but is considered hazardous and a precursor to more severe sight-threatening eye disease. Pre-proliferative retinopathy is divided into 'mild', 'moderate' and 'severe' subcategories, indicating a progression toward proliferation.

Practice indicators:

- Review individual diabetes management and shared care plan; consider changes to improve control
- The person needs to be under regular review (every 3–6 months) by the ophthalmology service
- Check that the level of retinopathy is recorded on the patient record database.

Proliferative retinopathy

'Proliferative retinopathy' is the manifestation of neovascular growth either in the peripheral fundus or at the optic disc. This occurs when retinal blood supply is no longer sufficient. However, these new vessels are fragile and they do not follow normal anatomical routes. They are prone to bleed, which causes pre-retinal haemorrhage or vitreous haemorrhage. Visual loss in the affected eye may be complete or partial. However, the person may not experience any visual symptoms before this occurs. Until the blood vessels bleed, the person may be unaware that they have sight-threatening eye disease.

Practice indicators:

- If proliferative retinopathy is picked up by screening, the person should be urgently referred for laser treatment by ophthalmology services. This prevents the development of partial sight and blindness in diabetes by burning and destroying the peripheral parts of the retina, which stops the proliferation of new vessels and concentrates the blood supply to the macula (the important, central area of the retina). It is highly effective and works in up to 90% of people (Dineen *et al.*, 2008).

176

- If the vessels bleed, laser treatment and possibly surgery may be required to clear the blood. Continued new vessel bleeding has an adverse effect on visual prognosis and can lead to 'end stage' severe advanced retinopathy.

Advanced retinopathy

'Advanced retinopathy' describes the late complications of neovascular growth. New vessels are eventually accompanied by fibrous proliferations, which contract, causing traction and retinal detachment. The visual prognosis for advanced retinopathy is poor and it usually results in blindness or partial sight registration. The person may only be able to see vague shapes, light and dark or nothing at all. However, most people retain some sight, despite being registered as blind.

Practice indicators:
- Appropriate referral to support services (such as social services, guide dogs for the blind, RNIB)
- Reorganisation of a shared-care plan and review of diabetes management
- Appropriate psychological monitoring and support
- Specialist ophthalmic services
- Referral to a low visual aids clinic, via either the local ophthalmology department or RNIB.

Maculopathy

The macula is an important area of the retina, which is responsible for detailed, central vision. 'Maculopathy' describes the manifestation of diabetic retinopathy in this area. The signs of maculopathy are exudates and clinically-significant macular oedema. Oedema is sight-threatening and will usually present as blurred vision. It can only be detected by stereoscopic examination of the fundus.

Health education

Health education is a vital strategy in diabetes management, which can empower people to seek annual eye checks and give them the encouragement and knowledge needed to take control of their diabetes by following a healthy lifestyle.

However, it must be tailored to each individual, considering different lifestyles and coping and cognitive mechanisms — a psycho-educational approach should be taken (Duke *et al.*, 2009). Health information is available from each of the devolved diabetic retinopathy screening services (*Table 1*).

Strategies for health education include individual education sessions, group talks and use of local health promotion services.

Practice indicators:
- Inform people with diabetes that they should be screened annually, using digital photography, for signs of eye disease (unless they are already under the care of a consultant specialist ophthalmic service)
- To aid improved diabetes control (including blood pressure), continue to instigate lifestyle change motivators and agreed shared care plans based on the individual's quality of life indicators
- People should know that diabetes can cause blindness and that if detected early enough, this is preventable.

NHS policy

The National Screening Programme for Diabetic Retinopathy (NSPDR, 2008) recommended that local health authorities and primary care trusts coordinate and fund a fully validated and tested digital photography-based diabetic retinopathy screening programme, to annually screen all people with diabetes. Current NHS reporting recommends that all people with diabetes have the opportunity for screening, although the target uptake of 90% is not always achieved (NSPDR, 2008).

The individual's experience

It is important to consider the person with diabetes' experience of screening and the benefits of attendance. Previously reported reasons for non-attendance at screening appointments include fear, lack of knowledge, economic constraints, poor access; social deprivation; duration of diabetes; and equity (Gillibrand *et al.*, 2000a; 2001; Hartnett *et al.*, 2005; Millett and Dodhia, 2006; Leese *et al.*, 2008).

Methods to improve attendance have focused on group education sessions using local networks, culturally-sensitive education, accessibility, and conducting regular equity audits (Livingston *et al.*, 1998; Gillibrand *et al.*, 2000b; Millett and Dodhia, 2006). The NSPDR (2008) has published guidelines and educational material for practitioners in England to use in supporting and maintaining an acceptable level of attendance. Further resources are presented in *Table 1*.

Table 1. Diabetic retinopathy screening resources in the UK	
England	National Screening Programme for Diabetic Retinopathy www.retinalscreening.nhs.uk/pages
Northern Ireland	Diabetic Retinopathy Screening www.dhsspsni.gov.uk/public_health_diabetic_retinopathy
Scotland	National Diabetes Retinopathy Screening Collaborative www.ndrs.scot.nhs.uk
Wales	Diabetic Retinopathy Screening Service for Wales http://tinyurl.com/3a2423w

Conclusions

There is a good evidence base to support the early detection and treatment of diabetic retinopathy via screening (National Institute for Health and Clinical Excellence [NICE], 2008). The implementation of a validated digital photography-based annual screening programme will, for most people, prevent the progression to advanced retinopathy and visual impairment. In addition, robust clinical trials have demonstrated that strict glycaemic control reduces the incidence and severity of complications in both type 1 and type 2 diabetes (DCCT, 1993; UKPDS, 1998). Therefore, to avoid progression of retinopathy, people with diabetes need to maintain stable blood glucose levels, as well as attending screening. Practitioners have an important educational role, and must ensure that people with diabetes understand the importance of annual diabetic retinopathy screening in the prevention of visual problems.

Key points

- All people with diabetes should be screened annually for diabetic retinopathy using a validated digital photography method
- Individuals should be supported by the diabetes practice team in managing their diabetes to prevent diabetic retinopathy
- There is good evidence that the majority of diabetic retinopathy can be effectively treated to maintain visual function, if detected early enough.

References

Amos A et al (1997) The rising global burden of diabetes and its complications: estimates and projections to the year 2010. *Diabetic Medicine* 14: S7-S85

Arun C et al (2003) Effectiveness of screening in preventing blindness due to diabetic retinopathy. *Diabetic Medicine* **20**(3): 186-90

Bunce C, Wormald R (2006) Leading cause of certification for blindness and partial sight in England and Wales. *BMC Public Health* 6: 58

Department of Health (2002) National Service Framework for Diabetes: Standards. Department of Health, The Stationery Office, London

Diabetes Control and Complications Trial Research Group (1993) The effect of intensive treatment of diabetes on the development and progression of long-term complications in insulin dependent diabetes mellitus. *N Engl J Med* **329**(14): 977-86

Dineen B et al (2008) Laser photocoagulation for diabetic retinopathy. *Cochrane Database Syst Rev* 2008(3): CD

Duke S et al (2009) Individual patient education for people with type 2 diabetes mellitus. *Cochrane Database Syst Rev* 2009(1): CD

Gillibrand W et al (2000a) Knowledge levels of diabetic eye disease in people with diabetes: results of a descriptive survey. *International Journal of Health Promotion & Education* **38**(4): 141-44

Gillibrand W (2000b) Users' perceptions of mobile eye screening. *Journal of Diabetes Nursing* 4: 82-85

Gillibrand W et al (2001) Why do people not attend diabetes eye screening services? *Diabetic Medicine* **18**(Suppl 2)(67): 108

Gillibrand W et al (2004) The English national risk reduction programme for the preservation of sight in diabetes. *Molecular and Cellular Biochemistry* **261**(1): 183-85

Hartnett E et al (2005) Perceived barriers to diabetic eye care: qualitative study of patients and physicians. *Archives of Ophthalmology* **123**(3): 387-91

Kumar N et al (2006) The incidence of visual impairment due to diabetic retinopathy in Leeds. *Eye* **20**(4): 455-59

Leese G et al (2008) Screening uptake in a well-established diabetic retinopathy screening program: the role of geographical access and deprivation. *Diabetes Care* **31**(11): 2131-35

Livingston P et al (1998) Use of focus groups to identify health promotion strategies for the early detection of diabetic retinopathy. *Australian & New Zealand Journal of Public Health* **22**(2): 220-22

Millett C, Dodhia H (2006) Diabetes retinopathy screening: audit of equity in participation and selected outcomes in South East London. *Journal of Medical Screening* **13**(3): 152-55

National Diabetes Retinopathy Screening (2010) Manual for the Diabetic Retinopathy Screening Programme for Scotland. www. ndrs.scot.nhs.uk/Manual/index.htm (accessed 24 May 2010)

National Institute for Health and Clinical Excellence (2008) Type 2 diabetes: the management of type 2 diabetes (update). Clinical guideline 66. NICE, London

National Screening Programme for Diabetic Retinopathy (2008) Essential Elements in Developing a Diabetic Retinopathy Screening Programme. Workbook 4.3. www.retinalscreening.nhs.uk/pages/ (accessed 24 May 2010)

National Screening Programme for Diabetic Retinopathy (2009) The English Diabetic Retinopathy Screening Programme. Annual report 1 April 2007 to 31 March 2008 annual report. http://www.retinalscreening.nhs.uk/pages (accessed 24 May 2010)

Stratton I et al (2000) Association of glycaemia with macrovascular and microvascular complications of type 2 diabetes (UKPDS 35): prospective observational study. *BMJ* **321**: 405-12

Tuomilehto J et al (2001) Prevention of type 2 diabetes mellitus by changes in lifestyle among subjects with impaired glucose tolerance. *N Engl J Med* **344**(18): 1343-50

United Kingdom Prospective Diabetes Study (1999) Quality of life in type 2 diabetic patients is affected by complications but not by intensive policies to improve blood glucose or blood pressure control (UKPDS 37). *Diabetes Care* **22**: 1125-36

UK Prospective Diabetes Study Group (1998). Intensive blood glucose control with sulphonylureas or insulin compared with conventional treatment and risk of complications in patients with type 2 diabetes (UKPDS 33). *Lancet* **352**: 837-53

Yorkshire and Humberside Public Health Observatory (2009) Inequalities in diabetes and obesity prevalence in England. November. www.yhpho.org.uk/resource/item. aspx?RID=73474 (accessed 24 May 2010)

Chapter 17

Diabetic nephropathy

Dr Victoria Robins and Dr Paul Laboi

Introduction

The World Health Organization (WHO) has defined diabetes as sustained elevated plasma glucose levels, sufficient to put the individual at risk of microvascular complications (WHO, 2006). Such microvascular complications include damage to the nerves (neuropathy), the eyes (retinopathy) and the kidneys (nephropathy). The focus of this chapter is diabetes-related kidney damage, which is termed 'diabetic nephropathy'. It occurs in both type 1 and type 2 diabetes.

Impact of diabetic nephropathy

Diabetes is the leading cause of kidney failure worldwide. However, not all people with diabetes will develop kidney failure. Nephropathy occurs in 30–40% of all people with diabetes after 25–40 years. Approximately one third of those with diabetic nephropathy will progress to end stage renal failure (ESRF) — that is, requiring some form of renal replacement therapy (Stippoli *et al.*, 2006).

Longstanding diabetes increases the risk of developing diabetic nephropathy. Other risk factors are poor glycaemic control, male gender and ethnicity — its incidence is higher in Native American (Pima), South Asian and Afro-Caribbean populations than in Caucasians (Vora and Ibrahim, 2003). Diabetes is associated with macrovascular complications, including ischaemic heart disease, stroke and peripheral vascular disease. Together, the micro- and macrovascular complications of diabetes result in reduced life expectancy and significant morbidity. People with kidney problems are independently more at risk of cardiovascular disease than the general population, so those with both kidney problems and diabetes are at even greater cardiovascular risk. More people with diabetic nephropathy succumb to cardiovascular disease than progress to ESRF (Vora and Ibrahim 2003).

The increasing prevalence of diabetes means that diabetic nephropathy is becoming an ever greater burden to the health service. Early detection, vigilant monitoring and appropriate interventions can slow its progression to end stage renal failure, and reduce cardiovascular mortality.

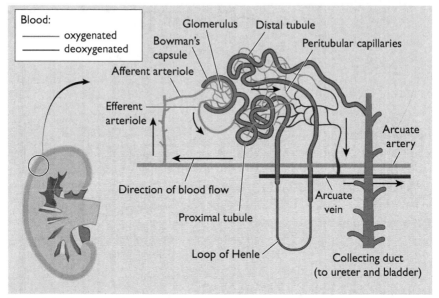

Figure 1. A schematic representation of the kidney

Functions of the kidney

The kidney is made up of roughly a million little filters called 'nephrons'. Each nephron consists of a glomerulus (the 'head' part) and a tube that leads out to the collecting duct (which collects urine). (*Figure 1*) Nephrons filter the blood and remove waste products (such as urea), which are excreted into the urine. The kidney has many other functions. It regulates acid-base balance by controlling how much acid and alkali (in the form of hydrogen ions and sodium bicarbonate, respectively) are excreted. When functioning normally, it also generates sodium bicarbonate when needed. The kidney controls the blood levels of various electrolytes by regulating their urinary excretion.

Hormonal functions of the kidney

The kidney produces calcitriol, a hormone that activates vitamin D. It also regulates the excretion of phosphate. Failure of these processes results in secondary or sometimes tertiary hyperparathyroidism, which are collectively termed 'metabolic bone disease' (primary hyperparathyroidism is not related to kidney problems). Therefore, patients with chronic kidney disease (CKD) can have low blood calcium levels requiring supplements, and high phosphate

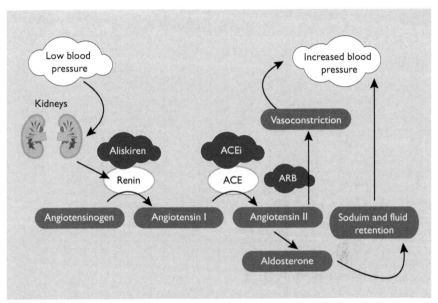

Figure 2. The renin-angiotensin-aldosterone-system. The sites of action of Aliskiren, angiotensin converting enzyme inhibitor (ACEi) and angiotensin II receptor blockage (ARB) are demonstrated.

levels requiring dietary restriction and phosphate-lowering tablets.

Another hormone produced by the kidney, erythropoietin (EPO), stimulates the production of red blood cells. EPO deficiency results in anaemia, so people with CKD may sometimes need to have iron infusions or an injection of artificial EPO.

Renin, a hormone which plays a key role in fluid balance and the control of blood pressure via the renin-angiotensin-aldosterone-system (RAAS), is also produced by the kidney. Manipulation of the RAAS is a key element in the management of diabetic nephropathy (see *Figure 2*). In response to low blood pressure, the kidney produces renin which converts angiotensinogen (an inactive protein) to angiotensin I. Angiotensin-converting enzyme (ACE) then converts angiotensin I to angiotensin II, which stimulates the release of aldosterone from the adrenals, causing sodium and fluid retention. Angiotensin II also causes vasoconstriction — together, these effects cause the blood pressure to rise.

Table I. The five stages of chronic kidney disease (CKD)		
CKD Stage	**Description**	**eGFR (ml/min/1.73m^2)**
I	Kidney damage with normal or increased GFR	>90
2	Kidney damage with mild reduction in GFR	60–89
3A	Moderate reduction in GFR	45–59
3B	Moderate reduction in GFR	30–44
4	Severe reduction in GFR	15–29
5	Kidney failure	<15
CKD = chronic kidney disease; GFR = glomerular filtration rate; eGFR = estimated glomerular filtration rate From: National Institute for Health and Clinical Excellence, 2008.		

Measuring renal function

To accurately measure renal function is a complicated, lengthy and expensive process. A more practical approach for use in day to day practice is to measure the serum creatinine (a protein produced by muscle breakdown), which can be used to approximate kidney function. Creatinine is excreted by the kidneys, and it is normally produced at a steady rate. Put simply, the higher the creatinine, the worse the kidney function.

Using a formula, the creatinine level can then be converted to an estimated glomerular filtration rate (eGFR), which can be particularly relevant and useful when serum creatinine is above the normal range. A normal eGFR is roughly 100ml/min/1.73m^2 — as creatinine rises, this falls. If we think of 100ml as representing 100%, then we can think of any reduction of eGFR in terms of percentage of renal function. For instance, an eGFR of 60ml/min/1.73m^2 would represent approximately 60% of normal kidney function. When explaining kidney function to people and carers, percentage of normal renal function is a more readily understandable concept than eGFR (NICE, 2008).

Chronic kidney disease (CKD) can be divided into five stages using eGFR (see *Table 1*).

Symptoms of kidney failure

People may have little in the way of symptoms until there has been a significant deterioration in eGFR. Occasionally an individual may incidentally be found to have a very low eGFR (e.g. 5ml/min/1.73m^2). People may complain of altered taste, nausea, decreased appetite or hiccups, which can all be caused by a build up of toxins. Fluid overload may develop, manifesting as peripheral oedema or shortness of breath, which can be indications to start dialysis. General lethargy is commonly reported, and this can be exacerbated by concurrent anaemia.

Impotence and decreased libido can also occur. Depression is not uncommon and psychological support is important — many dialysis units have an in-house specialist psychologist. It is vital that individuals are given the opportunity to manage their condition through education programmes.

How does diabetes affect the kidney?

Diabetes damages the kidney in 3 main ways:

- Increased predisposition to urinary tract infections
- Ischaemia as a result of damage to the blood vessels
- Glomerular damage.

Glomerular damage causes localised scarring, which results in a progressive leak of protein into the urine. The first sign of kidney damage is generally albuminuria (presence of albumin in the urine) (Baker, 1998). This is termed 'microalbuminuria' when between 30–300mg/day and 'proteinuria' or overt nephropathy when greater than 300mg/day. Progressive protein leak from the kidneys causes progressive damage (Steddon *et al.*, 2006).

Diagnosis

Proteinuria

Reagent dipsticks are commonly used to detect proteinuria and haematuria. Using a single sample, laboratory testing can formally quantify the albumin and protein present in the urine as an albumin-creatinine ratio (ACR) or a protein-creatinine ratio (PCR). ACR should be used rather than PCR, as it is more sensitive for detecting the onset of diabetic nephropathy (NICE, 2008). An early morning sample provides the most sensitive results but in practice any sample can be used for testing. Normal ACR is <2.5mg/l for males and <3.5mg/l for females (Steddon *et al.*, 2006).

Following the detection of albuminuria in the absence of a urinary tract infection, two early morning specimens should be collected over the next 3–6 months to provide confirmation (NFK-KDOQI, 2007).

187

People with type 1 diabetes should be assessed for proteinuria from 5 years after diagnosis. People with type 2 diabetes should be monitored routinely as part of annual review from diagnosis, as low-level hyperglycaemia often goes undetected; early morning ACR and concurrent serum creatinine should be checked. In people with a new finding of reduced eGFR, a repeat eGFR should be done within 2 weeks, to exclude acute kidney injury (NICE, 2008). If the initial eGFR reading is very low, the urgent advice of a nephrologist should be sought.

Confirming diabetic nephropathy

Proteinuria is a feature of many different kidney conditions. However, if there is evidence of microvascular change, such as retinopathy, it is highly likely that the person's renal failure is attributable to diabetes. If there is doubt as to the cause of proteinuria (or renal failure), a nephrologist may recommend a biopsy. Kidney biopsy is a relatively straightforward procedure, and is normally done as a day case.

Diabetes is one of many conditions that can cause nephrotic syndrome — a condition in which very heavy proteinuria develops, resulting in low levels of serum albumin and peripheral oedema. The presence of very heavy proteinuria or haematuria on dipstick testing warrants specialist referral.

Treatment

Proteinuria is the hallmark of diabetic nephropathy, and controlling the leak of protein decreases the rate of decline of kidney function. Inhibitors of the RAAS, have been shown to decrease proteinuria and reduce scarring (Stippoli *et al.*, 2006). There are three main classes of drug which do this: angiotensin-converting enzyme inhibitors (ACEi), angiotensin-II receptor blockers (ARB) and the relatively new class, direct renin inhibitors (e.g. aliskiren) (Pinto and Gradman, 2009).

The Heart Outcomes Prevention Evaluation (HOPE, 1996) study evaluated the effects of ramipril (an ACEi) on 3577 participants with diabetes. The trial was stopped early, after finding that cardiovascular mortality and nephropathy were greatly reduced. The observed cardiovascular benefit was greater than that attributable to the decrease in blood pressure.

To offer maximum benefit, drugs that block the RAAS should be titrated up to their maximum doses (Stippoli *et al.*, 2006). Combination therapy may be beneficial (Noris and Remuzzi, 2002; Pinto and Gradman, 2009) but it should

Case Study

Matthew is a 39-year-old bank worker who has a keen interest in the amateur theatre and a hectic schedule. He was diagnosed with type 1 diabetes aged 15. Like many young people he found it difficult to keep up with his diabetes, and his glycaemic control was poor.

Matthew was first referred to the renal service 5 years ago. He already had evidence of significant microvascular complications including retinopathy and proteinuria, and his kidneys were found to be functioning at around 40%. Matthew attended clinics on a regular basis in an attempt to achieve optimum BP and glucose control. Unfortunately, when an ACEi was commenced his creatinine deteriorated to unacceptable levels, and the ACEi had to be stopped.

As his kidney function progressively worsened, he developed anaemia and required intravenous iron and EPO therapy. Sodium bicarbonate was also required, to correct acidosis. Calcium acetate and 1-alfacalcidol were started to lower phosphate levels, increase calcium levels and control hyperparathyroidism. Other medications included simvastatin and aspirin for cardiovascular protection and insulin.

Matthews's renal function continued to deteriorate. He was visited by the pre-dialysis nurses who counselled him about the need for renal replacement therapy and the different options available to him, including peritoneal dialysis, haemodialysis and transplantation. Matthew was fortunate enough to receive a pre-emptive kidney-pancreas transplant. He made a good recovery and is now independent of insulin, with excellent kidney function.

be started under the supervision of a renal physician. It is important to monitor potassium levels closely, as hyperkalaemia (high potassium) can develop, which can be life-threatening. The On Target study (Mann *et al.*, 2008) found that combination therapy can have a deleterious effect on renal function; it should be discontinued if this develops. People are especially at danger of hyperkalaemia and deterioration of kidney function when they are ill. It is reasonable and perhaps prudent to discontinue therapy with ACEi and ARB for short periods during intercurrent illness, particularly diarrhoea and vomiting.

Serum creatinine should be checked within 2 weeks of initiating RAAS inhibitors, and with each dose increase. Chronic cough is a commonly-reported side effect, especially with an ACEi — an ARB or aliskiren may be better tolerated (Pinto and Gradman, 2009).

NICE guidelines (NICE, 2008) recommend that regardless of hypertensive status, all people with diabetes with proteinuria should be treated with an ACEi or ARB, where tolerated.

Blood pressure control

Hypertension can cause kidney damage irrespective of diabetic status, and the reduction of blood pressure (BP) slows the progression of renal failure (Lazarus *et al.*, 1997). BP should be measured regularly in people with diabetes, aiming for a target of less than 130/80mmHg (Bakris *et al.*, 2000).

Restricting salt intake to less than 5g/day can aid BP reduction (Steddon *et al.*, 2006). The advice of a trained dietitian can be helpful, as salt can be 'hidden' in many foods, such as breakfast cereals.

Home BP monitors are relatively inexpensive, and self-monitoring of BP can be a useful way to involve people in their management. Writing down or printing off serial BP measurements taken at home and at the GP surgery can be extremely useful to practitioners who are involved in BP management, as one-off readings taken in clinic may not truly reflect a person's BP control. Twenty four-hour monitoring can also be useful, especially if 'white coat' hypertension is suspected.

Glycaemic control

Good blood glucose control, aiming for an HbA_{1c} of <7.5% (58mmol/mol), has been shown to reduce diabetic nephropathy (Cassidy *et al.*, 2007). The first-line treatment for people with type 2 diabetes and obesity is usually metformin (NICE, 2008). Metformin is not advised in individuals with advanced kidney failure as it can precipitate lactic acidosis — a rare but serious complication. However, in people with milder kidney dysfunction, the benefits can outweigh the risks. If creatinine exceeds 150–200mmol/l, the advice of a nephrologist/diabetologist is advised. A useful way to provide consistent, relevant advice and forego the need for multiple hospital visits is to run a joint diabetic and renal clinic (with a diabetologist and a nephrologist both present).

Other cardiovascular factors

Statins have been shown to reduce cholesterol levels, cardiovascular mortality and proteinuria in people with stage 2–4 CKD, although they have not been shown to have an effect on creatinine levels. The mechanism by which they reduce proteinuria is not entirely clear but it has been suggested that they reduce inflammation and vascular calcification (Navaneethan *et al.*, 2009).

General healthy lifestyle changes, including weight control and smoking cessation, have not been proven to reduce the decline in kidney function. However, they are known to reduce cardiovascular mortality and should therefore be actively encouraged. Low dose aspirin may also provide cardiovascular protection (NICE, 2008).

The nephrologist's role

Nephrologists work within a multidisciplinary team, which includes dietitians, psychologists, specialist nurses and social workers. Together, the team manages any complications arising from renal impairment, such as anaemia, metabolic bone disease, biochemical imbalances and psychological and social issues.

To combat anaemia, synthetic EPO can be given (as a subcutaneous injection) and intravenous iron may be used. Blood pressure must be closely monitored when using synthetic EPO, as it can cause hypertension — over-correction has been associated with increased risk of stroke and cancer (Mix *et al.*, 2005).

Nephrologists attempt to slow the progression of renal failure. They have a role in BP management and investigate secondary causes of hypertension. Progressive renal failure can be plotted on a graph, which can be used to try and predict when the need for renal replacement therapy will occur, to make sure the individual affected is adequately prepared (*Figure 3*).

Figure 3. Kidney function can be plotted on a graph at each clinic visit and a line can then be drawn through the points to predict the rate of decline. This enables the nephrologist to estimate when the patient is likely to need renal replacement therapy (the shaded area) and to ensure that the person is physically and mentally prepared.

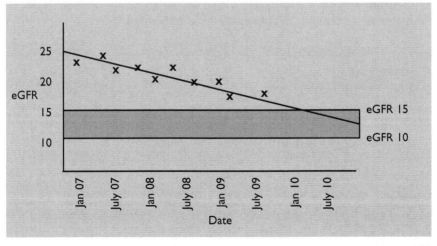

Who should be referred to a nephrologist?

NICE guidelines recommend that anybody with stage 4 or 5 CKD should be referred to a nephrologist, regardless of the presence of diabetes (NICE, 2008). However, people with diabetes may get complications of renal failure at an earlier stage, and require an earlier referral.

Other indications for referral include: poor BP control on 4 agents; a decline in eGFR of more than 5% in one year, or 10% over 5 years; or anybody whose kidney function is declining at a rate that may result in ESRF within their lifetime. Additionally, anyone with a rapid decline in eGFR, or who is suspected of having another kidney disorder (such as a person in whom haematoproteinuria is detected) should also be referred (NICE, 2008).

Renal replacement therapy

Renal replacement therapy falls into 3 categories:

* **Haemodialysis** — generally undertaken 3 times a week for four hours in an outpatient setting, haemodialysis involves extracting blood from a person, filtering it with a machine and then returning it to the individual
* **Peritoneal dialysis** — the person introduces a large volume of fluid into their abdomen via a long-term surgically placed catheter. This fluid is allowed to dwell in the abdomen and the peritoneal membrane acts in the same way as the filter in a haemodialysis machine. Depending on the individual's requirements, this is done several times a day, or overnight using an automated machine in the person's home
* **Transplantation** — this confers the highest survival rate. Combined kidney-pancreas transplant is an option for people with type 1 diabetes.

Conclusion

Diabetes is the leading cause of kidney failure worldwide. Coupled with cardiovascular risk factors it causes significant mortality and morbidity, as well as posing an increasing burden to the health service. Good control of proteinuria, blood pressure, glucose and cholesterol can slow the progression of renal failure and may delay or even prevent the need for renal replacement therapy. Working as part of a multidisciplinary team, nephrologists manage the complications of renal disease and prepare individuals for renal replacement therapy, should the need arise. Further research is needed into optimum combinations of medications and more accessible renal replacement therapies, such as portable dialysis machines.

Further resources

NICE guideline 66 Type 2 diabetes. The management of type 2 diabetes.
http://www.nice.org.uk/nicemedia/pdf/CG66NICEGuideline.pdf

NICE guideline 73 Chronic kidney disease. National clinical guideline for
early identification and management in adults in primary and secondary care.
http://www.nice.org.uk/nicemedia/pdf/CG073FullGuideline.pdf

Renal Association Guidelines.
http://www.renal.org/pages/pages/guidelines/current

Cochrane reviews.
http://www.cochrane.org/reviews/en/topics/index.html

Key points

- Diabetes is the leading cause of kidney failure worldwide and is associated with high cardiovascular mortality
- The urinary albumin-creatinine ratio and serum creatinine should be checked on a yearly basis
- Tight control of blood pressure, blood glucose and proteinuria slows the progression of renal failure and decreases cardiovascular risk. To keep a record of regular blood pressure measurements aids nephrologists in managing hypertension
- People with stage 4 or 5 CKD or complications of nephropathy should be referred to a nephrologist. Referral is also recommended where renal disease is progressive or where an alternative diagnosis is suspected
- Recognise that depression and social issues are major issues.

References

Baker L (1998) Renal Disease. In: Kumar P, Clark M, eds. Clinical Medicine. W B Saunders, London. 519-95

Bakris G et al (2000) Preserving renal function in adults with hypertension and diabetes: a consensus approach. *AJD.* **36**(3): 646-61

Cassidy M et al (2007) Renal Association Guidelines — Complications of CKD http:// www.renal.org/pages/pages/guidelines/current/complications.php [accessed: November 2009]

Lazarus J et al (1997) Achievement and safety of a low BP goal in chronic renal disease. *Hypertension.* **29**: 641-50

Mann J et al (2008) Renal outcomes with telmisartan, ramipril, or both, in people at high vascular risk (the ONTARGET study): a multicentre, randomised, double-blind, controlled trial. *Lancet.* **372**(9638): 547-53

Mix T et al (2005) Trial to Reduce cardiovascular events with Aranesp Therapy (TREAT): Evolving the management of cardiovascular risk in people with chronic kidney disease. *AHJ.* **149**(3): 408-13

National Kidney Foundation Kidney Disease Quality Outcomes Initiative (NFK-KDOQI) (2007) Clinical Practice Guidelines and Clinical Practice Recommendations for Diabetes and Chronic Kidney Disease http://www.kidney.org/professionals/KDOQI/guidelines_commentaries.cfm [accessed November 2009]

NICE (2008) Chronic kidney disease. National clinical guideline for early identification and management in adults in primary and secondary care. http://www.nice.org.uk/nicemedia/pdf/CG073FullGuideline.pdf [accessed November 2009]

Navaneethan S et al (2009) HMG CoA reductase inhibitors (statins) for dialysis patients. *Cochrane Database Syst Rev.* **8**(3): CD004289

Navaneethan S et al (2009). HMG CoA reductase inhibitors (statins) for people with chronic kidney disease not requiring dialysis. *Cochrane Database Syst Rev.* **15**(2): CD007784

Noris M, Remuzzi G (2002). ACE inhibitors and AT1 receptor antagonists: is two better than one? Kidney Int. **61**(4): 1545-47

Pinto R, Gradman A (2009) Direct renin inhibition: an update. *Curr Hypertens Rep.* **11**(6): 456-62

Steddon S et al (Eds) (2006) Oxford Handbook of Nephrology and hypertension. Oxford University Press. Oxford.

Strippoli G et al (2006) Angiotensin converting enzyme inhibitors and angiotensin II receptor antagonists for preventing the progression of diabetic kidney disease. *Cochrane Database Syst Rev.* **18**(4): CD006257

The HOPE study Investigators (1996) The HOPE (Heart Outcomes Prevention Evaluation) Study, the design of a large, simple randomised trial of an angiotensin converting enzyme inhibitor (ramipril) and vitamin E in patients at high risk of cardiovascular events. *Can J Cardiol.* **12**: 127-37

Vora J, Ibrahim H (2003) Clinical manifestations and Natural History of Diabetic Nephropathy. In: Johnson R, Feehally J. (Eds) Comprehensive Clinical Nephrology. Mosby, London: 425-37

World Health Organization (2006) Definition and diagnosis of diabetes mellitus and intermediate hyperglycemia. http://whqlibdoc.who.int/publictions/2006/9241594934_eng.pdf [accessed November 2009]

Chapter 18

Recognising sexual dysfunction in people with diabetes

Anne Phillips, Karen Khan and Dr Roger Fisken

Introduction

Sex is an important part of relationships for adults of all ages. According to the Sexual Dysfunction Association (2009) sexual problems can affect about 50% of women and tend to become more common with increasing age. Erectile dysfunction (ED) also affects many men in the general population. It is increasingly common with advancing age and in association with a number of medical conditions, including diabetes. However, the true prevalence of ED is difficult to determine, as many men are reluctant to report a problem (Fisken, 2010).

There is a growing awareness of the difficulties that female and male sexual dysfunction can cause. Lack of a fulfilling sex life can lead to feelings of guilt and rejection, which can affect relationships. It can also lead to depression, which is known to be much more common in people with diabetes (Rubin *et al.*, 2004; Phillips and Wright, 2009).

Exploring sexuality and sexual wellbeing is part of the holistic nature of care and cannot be separated from other care issues (Nelson, 2009). Therefore, the complexities of sex, sexual identity and sexual dysfunction need recognition when caring for the person with diabetes. Using the experiences of Ruth, a woman with type 1 diabetes (*case study 1*) and Frank, a man with type 2 diabetes (*case study 2*), we can examine such issues.

Diabetes and sexual dysfunction

Diabetes has long been considered a major cause of impaired sexual function in men (Enzlin *et al.*, 2009). As well as comorbidities that are usually associated with diabetes — older age group, use of antihypertensive medication, smoking and possibly having a high body mass index (BMI) — the severity and duration of diabetes can affect sexual function. The cardiovascular and/or neuropathic complications of diabetes can cause abnormalities in the endothelium, which can lead to sexual dysfunction in men; it could be expected that sexual dysfunction

Table 1. Physical causes of female sexual dysfunction with diabetes and their effects	
Physical cause	**Effects**
Blood vessel damage caused by atherosclerosis	Vaginal dryness and lack of blood flow to the clitoris affecting orgasm
Neuropathic damage	Reduced sensation, making arousal and orgasm more difficult
Associated endocrine disorders of the pituitary or thyroid gland	Problems with production of hormones which play an important role in normal sex drive. Low levels of these hormones can lead to a loss of sexual interest, desire and function
Low oestrogen levels	Disorders in the production of hormones which affect the amount of lubrication produced during sexual arousal
Smoking, recreational drugs and alcohol	All of these can affect blood flow to the clitoris and disturb messages between the clitoris, vagina and brain before and during sex. This can make orgasm very difficult to achieve
From: Diabetes UK, 2010.	

would occur in women with diabetes at a similar rate (Enzlin *et al.*, 2009).

Diabetes is thought to double the risk of sexual problems in men and women (Diabetes UK, 2009). In people with diabetes, sexual dysfunction is more common due to physical causes (*Table 1*) and psychological causes. *Sex and Diabetes* is a useful booklet available for both men and women (Diabetes UK, 2009).

Identifying the risks of having a sexual problem in diabetes can be more complex in women than in men, where ED is correlated with high HbA$_{1c}$ levels, cardiovascular problems and neuropathic difficulties (Fedele *et al.*, 2000; Enzlin *et al.*, 2003). In women with diabetes, sexual dysfunction is more strongly related to psychosocial and psychological factors than the typical pattern of cardiovascular and metabolic factors observed in men (Enzlin *et al.*, 2009). However the metabolic effects of diabetes do still have an influence.

Male sexual dysfunction

Erectile dysfunction (ED) is defined by the National Institutes of Health (1993) as 'the inability to achieve or maintain an erection sufficient for satisfactory sexual intercourse'. The term ED is preferred to 'impotence', as the latter

Case study 1

Ruth is 46 years old. She has had type 1 diabetes, which has been controlled by a multiple dose injection regime for the past sixteen years. In the past year, Ruth was also prescribed metformin 1g twice daily, when her HbA_{1c} reached 8.6% (70mmol/mol).

Ruth has a body mass index of $28kg/m^2$. She has high blood pressure, which is treated with ramipril 5mg and her total cholesterol is 4.2mmol/l. She has reduced sensation in her feet but no history of ulceration. She does not have microalbuminuria.

At Ruth's annual review, her practice nurse asks her about her contraception, as Ruth has a Mirena coil *in situ*, following the birth of her last child 7 years previously. Ruth comments that she has recently been experiencing pain during intercourse and that she has difficulty becoming aroused. She comments that she has not had an orgasm for at least a year.

Ruth has also been experiencing persistent thrush, which has caused tension in her relationship. Since starting her multiple dose injection regime and metformin, her HbA_{1c} has reduced to 7.5% (58mmol/mol). She has been prescribed treatment with antifungal agents.

The practice nurse senses that Ruth wants to say more and gives her the opportunity to do so. Ruth mentions that her husband's job is at risk and that he has been stressed and irritable at home. She says this has been making things difficult in their relationship and acknowledges that this may be contributing to her loss of libido.

Two weeks later, Ruth contacts her practice nurse and requests referral to counselling for herself and her husband. She also consents to screening for her difficulty in achieving orgasm and loss of libido, as she feels that her diabetes is implicated. Ruth's oestrogen levels are checked and found to be normal. Low oestrogen levels can inhibit libido, and are easily treated. Ruth is investigated further for neuropathy.

At her next review, Ruth reports that counselling is going well. She has begun to use a water-based gel lubricant before sex, and has agreed with her husband that their experience of sex is gradually improving.

The investigations prove that she has neuropathy, which has affected sexual arousal. Ruth values that she has the opportunity to discuss her sexual problems in a safe environment with her practice nurse.

Case study 2

Frank is a 58-year-old man who was diagnosed with type 2 diabetes 7 years ago. He works for a local printer's firm as the office manager, which is a fairly sedentary job. He is married with two grown children. He weighs 110kg (17st 5lb) and is 1.75m (5' 9") tall, giving him a body mass index (BMI) of 35.9kg/m^2.

Two years ago, Frank was admitted to hospital because of an acute coronary syndrome but without heart muscle damage — following this, he was started on treatment with aspirin, atenolol, simvastatin and ramipril. His diabetes is managed with a combination of metformin 1g, twice daily, and gliclazide 80mg, twice daily.

His last HbA$_{1c}$ result was not very good at 8.9% (74mmol/mol), so he has come to see his practice nurse, to discuss his diabetes in general — his blood glucose control in particular.

The practice nurse knows Frank quite well and notices that he seems rather low in spirits and withdrawn. She asks if there is anything wrong and he says no. After a little more (tactful) probing, she asks Frank if he has ever had any problems with his sexual function; Frank admits that, yes, there is a problem in that he and his wife have not been able to have sex for several months as he either cannot achieve an erection or, if he does, he loses it within a short time.

Frank is worried about his erectile dysfunction (ED) in general, and also wonders whether it may be caused by any of his medications. His practice nurse explains that atenolol can increase the risk of ED, but that he has been on it for longer than he has had the problem. She also points out that having diabetes is itself a strong risk factor for ED, as is being overweight and inactive.

The practice nurse advises Frank to see the doctor to discuss his problem in more detail and to have some blood tests taken — notably, to measure his testosterone level. She also reassures him that his condition can be treated in a variety of ways.

Frank sees his GP who reviews the problem with him, confirms that his condition is treatable and advises Frank on weight loss and increased physical activity. He also arranges some blood tests. With Frank's agreement, the GP issues a prescription for sildenafil (Viagra) 50mg, and advises Frank on its use.

implies a sharp distinction between completely normal sexual function and a total lack of erections; in many men with ED, a full or partial erection can be achieved, but this is either insufficient for penetration or fades away before satisfactory intercourse is complete (Fisken, 2010).

Estimates of the prevalence of ED in men with diabetes vary, with authors reporting prevalence rates of 35–71% (Bacon *et al.*, 2002; Giuliano *et al.*, 2004). Men with ED often expect a health professional to ask them about the problem; they will not mention a concern about ED unless specifically asked about it.

Increasing age and longer duration of diabetes increase the chances that a man will experience ED. A sedentary lifestyle, hypertension and hyperlipidaemia (conditions commonly found in men with diabetes) are independent predictors of ED risk. Perhaps surprisingly, it is not clear whether or not poor glycaemic control increases the risk of ED.

There is an association between ED and coronary heart disease (CHD), which works in two ways:

• Men with known vascular disease are more likely to develop ED
• ED is often a sign that CHD is present, even if the person has no previous history of this condition.

In any discussion of ED it is important to be aware of psychological and personal factors as causes and amplifiers of risk. Men with depression are much more likely to experience ED than those who are not depressed, and diabetes is well known to increase the risk of depression (Katon *et al.*, 2010). This leads to a vicious circle, as the development of ED can worsen the individual's feelings of low self-esteem, which in turn worsens his depression.

Female sexual dysfunction

The Diabetes Control and Complications Trial (DCCT, 1993) and the Epidemiology of Diabetes Interventions and Complications Trial (EDIC, 2009) show that the paucity of investigation into female sexual dysfunction has been influenced by small study sample size, social taboos regarding female sexuality (Rosen and Rosen, 2006; Althof *et al.*, 2005) and lack of characterisation of diabetes. This lack of attention has been made worse by difficulties in characterising glycaemic control, neurovascular complications and women's psychological adjustment to life with diabetes.

Sexual dysfunction is influenced by a number of causes, including physical, emotional, lifestyle and relationship factors and the effects of medication (Enzlin *et al.*, 2009). The four main areas of sexuality that women may have difficulty with are: desire, arousal, dyspareunia (pain with intercourse) and orgasm. Women may not discuss these issues with their partners, due to feelings of embarrassment, frustration and guilt if the cause is unknown. These are normal responses, which can make the problem worse (Phillips and Kahn, 2010).

Female sexual dysfunction refers to having problems with vaginal lubrication and sensation. Health practitioners can include discussion about sexual wellbeing in a holistic care approach, as this helps in broaching such issues.

Decreased blood flow to the vagina and clitoris may result from a number of factors, including cardiovascular disease, atherosclerosis (coronary artery disease, hypertension, diabetes and/or dyslipidemia), prior pelvic trauma or surgery (pelvic fracture, straddle injury, hysterectomy, birth trauma), cigarette smoking, and iatrogenic effects of medication (Basson, 2006).

Psychological factors

Several factors have been associated with reduced or absent subjective arousal. These include expectations of a negative experience (especially if dyspareunia is present), a partner's sexual dysfunction, negative past experiences (Basson, 2006), fatigue and depression. Medications for depression, for example selective serotonin-reuptake inhibitors (SSRIs), can affect and inhibit arousal and orgasm in both men and women (Clayton *et al.*, 2002), and depression can cause fatigue and reduce sexual desire in both sexes, with or without diabetes.

Depression is twice as common in people with diabetes as in those without; as many as one in three people with diabetes suffer a significant loss of quality of life due to depression (Katon *et al.*, 2010). The risk is higher for women than for men (Diabetes UK, 2010).

It is important to reassure the person that their problem is not 'all in the mind' (thus dispelling the idea that it is not important, or that he/she should just 'pull him/herself together'), and it is important to explain that for most men who experience ED and women who experience sexual dysfunction, there are both physical and psychological causes and help is available.

The practical difficulties of living with diabetes can cause stress, which may inhibit sexual desire. To worry about diabetes or a diabetes-related condition (such as the seemingly unsightly appearance of lipohypertrophy at an injection site) can be inhibiting when engaging in sexual activity.

A common worry for both men and women who use insulin is an unexpected hypoglycaemic episode (hypo) during or after sex, or having hypo unawareness (Gibson, 2009). These kinds of anxieties and emotions are more common than might be assumed, and they are well-founded.

Enzlin *et al.* found that women with diabetes who experienced sexual dysfunction reported a more negative experience of their diabetes, and had more problems emotionally adjusting to it. These women were also found to be less

Table 2. Investigative guide for asking women with diabetes about sexual dysfunction

Question (diabetes specific)	Rationale
What medications are you currently taking?	To establish whether there are any possible iatrogenic-related influences that can be addressed
Are you experiencing any stress or depressive symptoms?	To review if depression is present and to enable discussion if this is the case. Review of treatment if depression is already diagnosed
Have you recently had a baby?	To find out whether the woman has experienced a difficult delivery or birth injuries, and whether she is getting enough sleep and has sufficient support to help her
Do you feel tired all the time?	To establish whether this is due to hyperglycaemia or hypoglycaemic unawareness, which can both cause fatigue. If the woman's sleep pattern is disturbed, she may be experiencing anxiety, stress or depression
Do you have vaginal dryness?	To find out whether this is related to diabetes control, neuropathy, medication, hormones or the menopause, and whether the woman would like to have treatment for this
Do you feel uncomfortable or experience pain during sex?	To explore whether this may be causing sexual anxiety
Do you have recurrent infections, especially thrush or urine infections?	To investigate whether this is due to sub-optimal control of the diabetes. Fungal infection is easily treatable and advice regarding blood glucose control can be given

Table continues overleaf

Table 2. [continued]	
Question (general)	**Rationale**
Do you feel there is a problem with your relationship with your partner?	To explore whether the woman is experiencing marital tension or guilt about relationships, each of which can inhibit sexual experience
Do you feel embarrassed by the sex act?	To discover whether or not a past negative experience or previous abuse may be influencing the present situation
Do you have a poor self-image?	To give the woman an opportunity to discuss any feelings of depression or low self-esteem, for example due to obesity, which can have a negative effect on sexual function
Have you experienced sexual or physical abuse?	To discover whether the woman has had a past negative experience (see above)
From: Diabetes UK, 2008.	

satisfied with their diabetes treatments. The study compared women who reported both sexual dysfunction and other diabetes-related complications with those who were complication free. The main difference between the two groups was treatment satisfaction — women who had no complications believed that their treatment could keep them complication free, whereas those with complications besides sexual dysfunction had a high degree of dissatisfaction with treatment; their psychological response to sexual dysfunction was to view it as 'another complication' of the disease (Enzlin *et al.*, 2009).

In both sexes, the problems relating to sexual dysfunction are often complex and multifaceted, and may be connected to emotional or relationship difficulties, poor self image, embarrassment and guilt. Stress and tiredness play a role, and financial or job-related stress can influence coping mechanisms as well as stress levels. Some coping strategies — such as alcohol, cigarettes and recreational drugs — can inhibit sexual success, whether or not the individual has diabetes.

What do health practitioners need to ask?

Sexual health is very personal and both men and women may feel embarrassed when asked about it. They may feel that it is appropriate to see a professional of the same sex, and they may or may not want to have their partner in the room with them. When discussing sexual health and wellbeing, health practitioners need to be especially aware of cultural and religious sensitivities (Nelson, 2009). A simple way for the practitioner to broach the subject of sexual health is to ask: 'Some people with diabetes have problems with their sex lives; have you ever had a problem like that?'

If the person agrees that there is a problem, the practitioner should try to determine whether he or she is referring to a loss of libido or sexual dysfunction (or both) and also try to gain an idea of the problem's severity. *Table 2* presents an investigative guide for enquiring about sexual dysfunction in women during a diabetes review (Diabetes UK, 2008).

Practitioners need to be aware of some of the links between the causes and symptoms of sexual dysfunction, so that men and women can be understood and enabled to make the most appropriate treatment choices.

Assessment and treatments: male

The mechanisms leading to ED in diabetes are complex — as well as psychological factors, diabetes can cause macrovascular, microvascular and neuropathic complications, and it also increases the risk of testosterone deficiency. Some additional factors to consider are:

- Men with diabetes are at substantially greater risk of atherosclerosis than men without diabetes (Tuomilehto and Rastenyte, 1997). Such men are likely to have arterial narrowing in many parts of the body, including the small arteries that supply the penis
- The endothelial lining of blood vessels is almost always abnormal in people with established diabetes (Dandona *et al.*, 2006). Healthy endothelium responds to autonomic nerve fibre stimulation by releasing nitric oxide (an important chemical transmitter), which causes vasodilation and therefore increases the blood flow. If there is endothelial dysfunction, the penile arteries and their branches will not relax as well with sexual arousal, so the spongy vascular tissue in the penis that produces penile rigidity (the corpus cavernosa) will not fill adequately
- In sexual arousal, the brain sends a stream of nerve impulses to the genitals via the parasympathetic nervous system; in men, these signals lead to the development of an erection. This process is amplified by nerve impulses from the penis itself, when the man's partner touches the penis or when penetration occurs. Peripheral neuropathy, which is common in diabetes, has an adverse affect both of these processes
- Men who are deficient in testosterone often have decreased libido and reduced erectile function. Testosterone deficiency, like ED and diabetes, is associated with increasing age and obesity. It has been estimated that around 20% of men with diabetes and ED have testosterone deficiency (Kapoor *et al.*, 2007).

If the man agrees that there is a problem, it is important to gain an idea of the extent of the problem — is he never able to have intercourse or does his ED only happen sometimes? Does he have nighttime or early morning erections? If the man's performance is variable (normal intercourse sometimes but no success at other times), if he has regular early morning erections or if he can regularly achieve erections with masturbation, there is likely to be a significant psychological component to his ED.

It is worth reviewing the individual's medication, as many commonly used drugs, especially those used in the management of hypertension, can either cause or exacerbate ED (see *Table 3*). A physical examination is important to check blood pressure and to confirm that his femoral pulses, foot pulses and genitalia are normal.

Useful blood tests include HbA_{1c}, lipids, kidney and liver function and serum testosterone (preferably early in the morning as there is a diurnal rhythm in blood testosterone levels). If the person is known to have CHD, its severity should be assessed in relation to the physical demands of sexual intercourse; if the man cannot walk comfortably for 20 minutes on the flat without stopping, he is unlikely to be fit enough for sexual activity (Fisken, 2010). A related issue is peripheral vascular disease; if the person has claudication at short distances, it is likely that the vascular supply to the penis is reduced, so some commonly used ED treatments will not work.

Treatments

As with many complications of diabetes, initial treatment should be advice about weight reduction and increasing physical activity; combining these lifestyle changes together with drug treatments has been shown to be beneficial in the management of ED (Fonseca and Jawa, 2005). Where possible, the withdrawal of any drugs that may be causing or exacerbating the problem may be helpful. Stopping smoking and reducing excessive alcohol consumption is also likely to be of benefit.

Table 3. Medications likely to increase the risk of erectile dysfunction		
Drug group	**Examples**	**Usual indication**
Beta-blockers	atenolol, metoprolol, bisoprolol	Angina, acute coronary syndrome, hypertension
Thiazide diuretics	bendroflumethiazide, chlortalidone	Hypertension, oedema
Anti-androgens	finasteride	Prostatic disease
Major tranquillizers	chlorpromazine, flupentixol	Major psychiatric illness
Antidepressants	fluoxetine	Depression

Oral treatments

Three orally-active phosphodiesterase type-5 (PDE-5) inhibitors are widely available:

- Sildenafil (Viagra)
- Tadalafil (Cialis)
- Vardenafil (Levitra).

These drugs enhance the natural mechanisms for maintaining an erection by preventing the breakdown of an intermediate compound in the erection pathway, thus strengthening the response to parasympathetic nerve activity. They will only work in the presence of sexual arousal. There is no definite evidence that any single agent is better than the others in the management of ED in diabetes. Sildenafil and vardenafil are best taken on an empty stomach and start to act about 30 minutes after ingestion; their action lasts for 4–6 hours. Tadalafil has a longer duration of action (around 36 hours) and may be preferred by men who feel that the use of the other agents is 'cold-blooded' because it involves a degree of forward planning.

As all of these agents are vasodilators, they are absolutely contraindicated in men who take nitrates or nicorandil for angina, as the combination of such drugs with nitrates can produce catastrophic falls in blood pressure (Fisken, 2010). Generally speaking, men with ED and diabetes tend to need the highest available doses of these agents if they are to achieve a successful result — this means 100mg of sildenafil or 20mg of either tadalafil or vardenafil (Malavige and Levy, 2009). Side effects of PDE-5 inhibitors include headache, facial flushing, nasal stiffness and backache (in the case of tadalafil).

Local and injectable treatments

If an oral agent is not effective or is not tolerated, the next option is an injection of a locally-acting direct vasodilator — alprostadil (Caverject, Viridal). This drug is injected directly into the middle portion of the penile shaft by the person and will result in an erection within a few minutes, irrespective of sexual arousal or the integrity of the local nerve pathways. It is customary to give a test dose of alprostadil 2.5µg or 5µg to confirm that the person will respond, and then to escalate the dose as necessary. As one of the principal side effects of alprostadil is priapism (a prolonged erection), the dose chosen for regular treatment should be one that will produce a full erection lasting for about an hour.

If a man strongly dislikes the idea of giving himself an injection, alprostadil can alternatively be given as a pellet, which is inserted into the urethra using a nylon applicator; this system is known as MUSE (Medicated Urethral System for

Erections). MUSE is effective in some men, although it is generally less successful than injected alprostadil (Shabsigh *et al.*, 2000) and can produce uncomfortable side effects, chiefly burning pain within the penis or pain and stiffness in the thighs.

Vacuum devices

Men who do not respond well to PDE-5 inhibitors and who do not wish to use alprostadil can use a vacuum device, a physical method for achieving erection. These devices work reasonably well and are available on prescription for men with diabetes. However, some couples dislike using them because of the pre-planned nature of the treatment. Some users are also unhappy about the fact that the penis is cold and dusky-coloured when such a device is used.

Penile implants

Penile implants are a last-resort treatment. If an implant fails there is no possibility of any other treatment being offered (the person's own erectile tissue has to be cored out when the implant is inserted). They are also very expensive, costing several thousand pounds. Many primary care trusts will not pay for penile implants, and their cost is beyond the means of many people.

Testosterone replacement

The European Association of Urology guidelines (Kapoor *et al.*, 2007) recommend that if a man has a serum testosterone level of <8nmol/l, he should be offered supplementation; values >12nmol/l generally mean that treatment is not necessary.

Where serum testosterone is between 8–12nmol/l it is reasonable to give a 3-month trial of testosterone. However, the person must be advised that this will not necessarily make a difference to sexual function or general wellbeing.

Before testosterone is given, the man should be advised about its effects on the prostate. He should have a digital rectal examination and a blood test to measure prostate-specific antigen (PSA). If these are normal, PSA should be repeated annually.

Oral testosterone replacement is not advisable, as the available preparations are either poorly absorbed or may give rise to safety concerns. Most clinics offer treatment with transdermal testosterone (Testogel, Tostran, Testim) or injectable testosterone (Sustanon, Nebido), which can be self-administered following education. A testosterone implant is also another option, but such implants carry a risk of extrusion and of implant site infection (Fisken, 2010).

Assessment and treatments: female

When reviewing women with diabetes and sexual dysfunction, a physical examination should be carried out to assess the factors presented in *Table 4*.

Clitoral vacuum engorgement device

Some female sexual arousal and orgasmic disorders result from diminished blood flow to the clitoris, labia, and vagina, and stimulation with a mechanical vibrator may not achieve adequate engorgement because of poor blood flow from these diseased genital vessels. The woman may be offered a clitoral vacuum engorgement device, which uses a gentle vacuum to engorge the clitoris — even where blood vessels are affected by vascular disease. The ability to engorge the clitoris despite diminished genital blood flow may have important implications for treatment efficacy (Billups, 2002). This is recommended as a treatment option for women with diabetes (Diabetes UK, 2009).

Vaginal lubricants and moisturisers

Both psychological and physical factors can contribute to problems with arousal, resulting in vaginal dryness. This can be relieved with moisturisers and lubricants (Barnabei *et al.*, 2002). Long-lasting vaginal moisturisers are available, which are designed to relieve general vaginal dryness for several days, and a lubricant such as KY Jelly can be used in addition for sexual intercourse. Water-based and oil-based lubricants can easily be bought over the counter. Oil-based lubricants can last longer, but they cannot be used with latex condoms.

Table 4. Physical examination for sexual dysfunction in women with diabetes	
Physical examination	**Rationale**
Weight	To review for obesity and to enable lifestyle advice
Blood pressure	To review for hypertension; if already diagnosed, to review efficacy of prescribed antihypertensive medication
Hormone levels	To assess oestrogen levels and screen for the menopause
Urinalysis	To review for glucose as an indicator of diabetes control and for protein to explore the need for further investigation of infection and renal function

Sexual and relationship therapy

Sexual and relationship therapists have specialist training and work with couples to overcome sexual problems. Therapy enables couples to talk openly and discuss options, and educates them in techniques such as 'sensate focusing' (in which couples learn to touch each other in a sensual, rather than a sexual way), which can reduce tension and improve performance (Stephenson *et al.*, 2011). Such psychological support can be very helpful, but the practitioner needs to take a culturally and religiously-sensitive approach when suggesting this type of therapy.

Conclusions

Health practitioners have unique and important roles in the lives of people with diabetes. By using person-centred care planning techniques and working in partnership with individuals (Holdich, 2009) sensitive areas such as sexual dysfunction, which can be difficult to broach, can be made easier to discuss.

Embarrassment, fear and guilt can inhibit both men and women from talking about their sexual difficulties; if they are worried that their diabetes is implicated, they may find these problems harder to manage. Women with diabetes are at particular risk of depression, and screening for this is especially useful as it can reveal sexual dysfunction, enabling more open discussion of sexual health and wellbeing within diabetes care. For men, ED is a common, distressing and undertreated complication of diabetes. To detect ED often requires sensitive discussion with the individual.

Health professionals have a duty to offer holistic care to people with diabetes and it is recommended that sexual health and wellbeing are included during a consultation. Appropriate treatment options are available to both men and women with diabetes who are experiencing sexual dysfunction.

Key points

- Diabetes doubles the risk of sexual problems in women and men
- Erectile dysfunction (ED) is associated with diabetes; its prevalence rises with age and longer duration of diabetes
- Women with diabetes may experience sexual problems in four main areas: desire, arousal, dyspareunia (pain with intercourse) and orgasm
- Exploring sexuality and sexual wellbeing is part of a holistic approach to care and cannot be separated from other care issues
- It is important to be aware of cultural and religious sensitivities when discussing sexual health and wellbeing
- Management approaches include sexual and relationship therapy.

References

Althop S et al (2005) Outcome measurement in female sexual dysfunction clinical trials: review and recommendations. *J Sex Marital Ther* 31: 153-66

Bacon C et al (2002) Association of type and duration of diabetes with erectile dysfunction in a large cohort of men. *Diabetes Care* 25: 1458-63

Barnabei M et al (2002) Menopausal symptoms in older women and the effects of treatment with hormone therapy. *Obstet Gynecol* **100**(6): 1209-18

Basson R (2006) Sexual desire and arousal disorders in women. *New Eng J Med* **354**(14): 1497-1506

Billups K (2002) The role of mechanical devices in treating female sexual dysfunction and enhancing the female sexual response. *World J Urol* 20: 137-41

Clayton et al (2002) Prevalence of sexual dysfunction amongst newer anti depressants. *J Clin Psychiatry* **63**(4): 357-66

Diabetes Control and Complications Trial Research Group (1993) The effect of intensive treatment of diabetes on the development and progression of long-term complications in insulin-dependent diabetes mellitus. *N Engl J Med* **329**(14): 977-86

Diabetes UK (2009) Sex and diabetes. www.diabetes.org.uk/Guide-to-diabetes/Living_with_ diabetes/Sex-and-diabetes/

Diabetes UK (2010) Women and sexual dysfunction. www.diabetes.org.uk/Guide-to-diabetes/Living_with_diabetes/Sex-and-diabetes/Female-sexual-problems/

Dandona P et al (2006) Endothelial dysfunction in diabetes. In: Fonseca VA (ed.) Clinical Diabetes: Translating Research into Practice. Saunders Elsevier, Philadelphia:78

EDIC Research Group (1999) Epidemiology of Diabetes Interventions and Complications (EDIC). Design, implementation, and preliminary results of a long- term follow-up of the Diabetes Control and Complications Trial cohort. *Diabetes Care* **22**(1): 99-111

Enzlin P et al (2002) Sexual dysfunction in women with diabetes. *Diabetes Care* **25**(4): 672-77

Enzlin P et al (2009) Sexual dysfunction in women with type 1 diabetes. *Diabetes Care* **25**(4): 1-9

Fedele D et al (2000) Erectile dysfunction in type 1 diabetes and type 2 diabetes in Italy. *Int J Epidemiol* **29**(3): 524-31

Fisken R (2010) Assessment and treatments for erectile dysfunction in diabetes. *Practice Nursing* **21**(8): 416-20

Fonseca V, Jawa A (2005) Endothelial and erectile dysfunction, diabetes mellitus and the metabolic syndrome: common pathways and treatments. *Am J Cardiol* 96: 13-18

Gibson H (2009) Hypoglycaemia unawareness (Diabetes: evidence- based management 7). *Practice Nursing* **20**(5): 240-44

Giuliano F et al (2004) Prevalence of erectile dysfunction among 7689 patients with diabetes or hypertension or both. *Urology* 64: 1196-201

Kapoor D et al (2007) Clinical and biochemical assessment of hypogonadism in men with type 2 diabetes: correlations with bioavailable testosterone and visceral adiposity. *Diabetes Care* 30: 911-17

Katon W, Maj M, Sartorius N (2010) Depression & Diabetes, Wiley Blackwell, UK

Holdich P (2009) Patient-centred care planning (Diabetes: evidence-based management 3). *Practice Nursing* **20**(1): 18-23

Malavige L, Levy J (2009) Erectile dysfunction in diabetes mellitus. *J Sexual Med* 6: 1232-47

National Institutes of Health (1993) NIH Consensus Conference. Impotence. NIH Consensus Development Panel on Impotence. *JAMA* 270: 83-90

Nelson S (2009) Women and sex. In: Squire C, ed. The Social Context of Birth, 2nd edn. Radcliffe Publishing, Oxford

Phillips A, Wright J (2009) Achieving treatment concordance. (Diabetes: evidence-based management 9). *Practice Nursing* **20**(7): 353-57

Phillips A, Khan K (2010) Assessment and support of women with sexual dysfunction. *Practice Nursing* **21**(8): 416-19

Rosen L, Rosen R (2006) Fifty years of female sexual dysfunction research and concepts: from Kinsey to the present. In: Goldstein I et al eds. Womens Sexual Function and Dysfunction: Study, Diagnosis and Treatment. Taylor and Francis, New York: 3–10

Rubin R et al (2004) Recognising and treating depression in patients with diabetes. *Curr Diabetes Rep* **4**(2): 119-25

Sexual Dysfunction Association (2007) Sexual dysfunction and diabetes in women. www.sda.uk.net/advice.php

Shabsigh R et al (2000) Intracavernous alprostadil alfadex is more efficacious, better tolerated and preferred over intraurethral alprostadil plus optional ACTIS: a comparative, randomized, crossover, multicenter study. *Urology* 55: 109-13

Stephenson K et al (2011) The association between sexual motives and sexual satisfaction: gender differences and categorical comparisons, *Arch Sex Behav* 40: 604-18

Tuomilehto J, Rastenyte D (1997) Epidemiology of macrovascular disease and hypertension in diabetes mellitus. In: Alberti K, Zimmet P, DeFronzo R, Keen H, eds. International Textbook of Diabetes Mellitus. 2nd edn. Wiley, Chichester: 1559-83

Chapter 19

Neuropathic presentations of diabetes

Dr Ewan Masson

Introduction

Along with retinopathy and nephropathy, peripheral neuropathy is one of the big 3 'microvascular' complications of diabetes. Diabetes is the leading cause of peripheral neuropathy worldwide (Said, 2007). This chapter explains how neuropathic complications are caused, how they present, and what practitioners should be curious about when assessing people with diabetes. Presentations can be vague and neuropathy can be missed if the practitioner does not have a keen awareness to make the connections between presenting symptoms and possible neuropathy. This chapter is illustrated by Peter's case study, in which focused and prompt action was taken following an avoidable incident.

Aetiology

Although a number of biochemical theories have been put forward, these are all based on animal models of the acute, functional effects of hyperglycaemia (Morrow, 2004) rather than the long-term structural defects seen in most (but not all) people with diabetes, so these theories are fundamentally flawed. Therapeutic agents based on these theories have been universally disappointing.

Nerves are most unusual cells — effectively, a single cell passes from brain to spinal cord, and a single cell passes from spinal nerve root to skin receptor (which can be over a metre away!) as seen in *Figure 1a*. We are all familiar with the effects that pressure can have on peripheral nerves. For example, after leaning on the elbow, pins and needles may be felt in the hand, or numbness might develop down one side of the body after sleeping on that side. Longer-term pressure can result in more serious nerve damage, although the relief of noxious stimuli allows recovery. Regenerative phenomena are always seen in peripheral nerve biopsies; the integrity of nervous tissue, as any tissue, relies on the balance of everyday minor insult, versus capacity for repair (Pellettieri and Alvarado, 2007).

It has long been recognised that in diabetes, nervous tissue undergoes similar basement membrane and capillary changes to those seen in the retina and

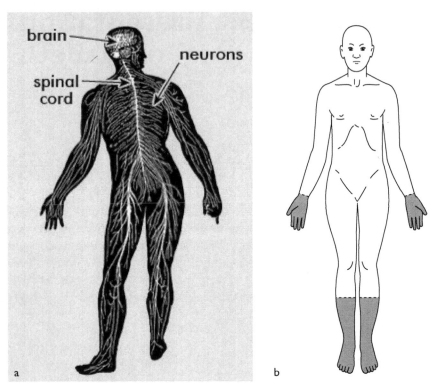

Figure 1. Individual neurons go from brain to spinal segment and then from spinal cord to skin receptor (a). The 'glove and stocking' distribution of sensory loss in diabetic peripheral neuropathy (b).

kidney (Britland *et al.*, 1990). This could reasonably be expected to diminish repair capacity more than normal ageing (which in itself diminishes peripheral sensation, though not usually causing a clinical problem) (Thomson *et al.*, 1993).

The longest nerves will be the most difficult to repair, which explains the typical 'glove and stocking' distribution of sensory loss in diabetic peripheral neuropathy (*Figure 1b*).

Practice points:
- Glycaemic control has some relationship to the progression of diabetic complications, and should be optimised where possible
- Smoking and alcohol are independent risk factors and should be addressed in a person-centred way to encourage understanding and empowerment of individuals, who may rely on smoking and alcohol to cope with other aspects in their lives (Hawthorne, 2009; Holdich, 2009).

Case Study

Peter is a 64-year-old retired publican, who lives alone. He was referred to the foot clinic 4 years ago when he was found to have loss of sensation to 10g monofilament by the practice nurse on annual foot screening. He also complained of some pins and needles and burning pains in both feet. The multi-disciplinary foot team included a podiatrist, a consultant diabetologist and a diabetes specialist nurse (DSN). Foot pulses were present and his feet were warm and well perfused. He had bilateral calluses over the 1st metatarsal heads, indicating high pressure. He also had deformities of diabetic neuropathy with subluxation of the metatarsal heads and clawing of the toes. Peter was classified as being at high risk for foot ulceration (NICE, 2004).

The diabetologist explained that damage to the nerves caused the burning sensations, the numbness and the change of foot shape. The podiatrist noted dry skin with cracking at the heels (a feature of diabetic neuropathy due to loss of sweating). After discussing the medication options for painful neuropathy, Peter felt that his symptoms were not severe enough to take drugs with potentially unpleasant side-effects. The DSN reviewed Peter's insulin and blood glucose monitoring and explained that diabetic neuropathy cannot be reversed, but that poor blood glucose control can make it worse.

To try and prevent ulceration, Peter was given advice regarding his foot care. In view of the foot deformity with obvious high pressure areas on the balls of the feet, Peter was advised on footwear to accommodate the altered shape of his feet and referred for insoles to reduce high pressure areas. His calluses were debrided. Peter was followed up every 3–4 months in the high risk podiatry clinic, and given an emergency number.

On his return from a holiday, Peter phoned to say that he had been walking more than usual and had developed a sore area under his right big toe. He put a dressing over it while away, but it had become worse and his foot was now red, swollen and throbbing. Peter was offered an appointment that afternoon and was found to have a neuropathic ulcer over his right first metatarsophalangeal joint with surrounding cellulitis, which was tracking up his leg. He had been feeling 'like he had flu', with shivers, and he was feeling 'generally off food'. His blood glucose readings had shot up, despite eating less. In view of his systemic symptoms and the obvious foot infection, Peter was admitted directly to hospital for bed rest, intravenous antibiotics and surgical review.

Types of neuropathy

Any nerve can be affected by diabetes. For example, a person complaining of double vision may have an ocular mononeuropathy due to diabetes, and would require onward referral to ophthalmology for investigation. However, for the purposes of this chapter, the mononeuropathies (single nerve palsies) are only of passing interest.

By far the biggest problem encountered in the community is distal sensorimotor neuropathy, which can present in a variety of ways. The principal problems are sensory loss sufficient to allow foot ulceration and the sometimes disabling phenomenon of peripheral neuropathic pain. There is also the issue of autonomic neuropathy, which usually presents with postural hypotension or gastrointestinal disturbances.

Practice points:
- People with diabetes should have an annual check for sensory loss by whatever means are available. Sensation is said to be protective against ulceration (Tan, 2010). If a 10g flexible monofilament can be felt, then the person can be categorised as at low risk of ulceration (Bowness, 2008)
- Vascular disease is a major cofactor in most cases of foot ulceration and should also be assessed at the annual foot check
- Sensory loss and/or signs of vascular disease are triggers for referral to podiatry for assessment (Bowness, 2008).

Neuropathic pain

This is a strange phenomenon, independent of the objective degree of sensory loss (Boulton, 1992). Fortunately it is only encountered by a relatively small proportion of individuals. Neuropathic pain can be intensely painful and its various characteristics are listed in *Table 1*.

The phenomenon of neuropathic pain is analogous to the experience of optical illusions. Consider the classic inkblot, which can be seen as a young lady looking one way or an old woman looking the other, or the various artworks of M. C. Escher (available at www.mcescher.com). The brain's main sensory function is to interpret the environment for navigation, safety and interaction. When faced with the former illusion, a double interpretation is possible as there is insufficient information for the observer to be certain of the form; a few stokes of the pen would resolve the dilemma, but in the absence of confirmatory information, we simply guess. In the latter, an excess of information deliberately leads us to confusion.

Table 1. Characteristics of neuropathic pain
■ Nocturnal exacerbation
■ Hyperaesthesia
■ Burning/freezing
■ Gnawing/aching
■ Lancinating jolts of pain
■ Dysaesthesia

So how does the sensory cortex react when its orderly set of inputs from peripheral sensory receptors is altered or removed by neuropathy? It simply guesses — if a person with neuropathy is 'lucky', the brain will guess correctly and the person's experience will be an awareness of numbness; others will be unaware of there being any problem at all, until painless ulceration occurs; some experience dysaesthesia in the form of annoying 'pins and needles'; and the 'unlucky' experience neuropathic pain.

This pain is unusual and hard to describe. Given the opportunity to choose pain descriptors from lists such as the McGill pain questionnaire (Masson *et al.*, 1989), people with neuropathy choose more descriptors than a control group with mechanical pain, and often choose contradictory words such as 'burning' and 'freezing' simultaneously. People with neuropathy may also describe their pain as 'shooting', 'stabbing', 'an electric shock', 'burning', 'tingling', 'tight', 'numb', 'prickling', 'itching' or a sensation of 'pins and needles'. The pain can come and go, or be there all the time. This illustrates the central nature of the sensory illusion.

Neuropathic pain is famously resistant to conventional analgesia. Interestingly, some centrally-acting drugs can offer relief, including antidepressants (amitriptyline, duloxetine) and anticonvulsants (gabapentin, pregabalin). These medications may alter the processing and interpretation of inputs. They should be titrated up slowly, and their effects need to be assessed. If the pain is difficult to manage and does not resolve, then assessment in a specialist diabetic foot or pain clinic is recommended.

In people with objectively intact nerves, acute sensory disturbance can also occur, particularly after a metabolic disturbance such as ketoacidosis. This pain is similar to that of chronic sensorimotor neuropathy. Fortunately, it is usually self-limiting.

Practice points:
- Medical treatments for neuropathic pain can be very disappointing. An explanation and reassurance is often the best first step
- Neuropathic pain correlates very poorly with objective sensory loss. Pain does not infer adequate sensation exists to prevent ulceration and thus an annual foot check is independent. People with neuropathy should be advised to undertake wherever possible a daily foot check to observe for change and to trigger seeking for help (Bowness, 2008).

Diabetic foot ulceration

Damage to the skin is usually intensely painful, easily localised and leads to an immediate change in behaviour. Consider the 'new shoe' phenomenon: people often buy shoes for their appearance rather than comfort. When the inevitable blisters appear, sometimes after only a few steps, behaviour changes in predictable ways — a change of shoes, applying a plaster, limping (a few stick it out and risk further damage). It takes quite a lot of sensory loss to present with a painless ulcer. Of course, sensory loss alone does not cause the skin defect — there has to be a

Figure 2. The relationship between social deprivation score and risk of amputation from diabetic foot disease in the East Riding of Yorkshire. Spearman's Rho 0.047, p = 0.002

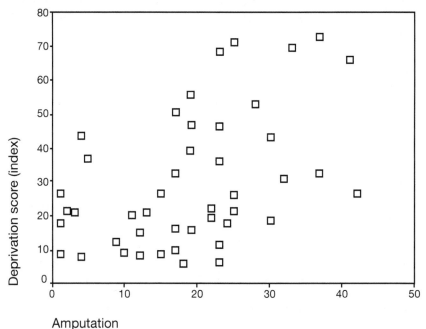

mechanical influence, either intrinsic to the foot or extrinsic, in the environment. Neuropathy may be seen as permissive of the process of ulceration, rather than its primary cause. The primary cause can often be removed or altered, which will lead to healing if the circulation is adequate.

However, most people attending diabetes foot clinics are older and have comorbid peripheral vascular disease, as well as other chronic health problems (Shaw and Zimmet, 1999). Many also come from socioeconomically deprived backgrounds (Holman, 2011). These patients should make us pay particular attention to the vulnerability of this population and consider factors such as home environment and nutrition. *Figure 2* illustrates the relationship between deprivation score (derived from statistics for various benefits, by area) and amputations related to diabetic foot disease in East Riding of Yorkshire.

Practice points:
- All new ulcers should be referred urgently to local podiatry services
- Foot sepsis should be suspected when a person with diabetes presents with signs of infection (fever, rigors) (Frykberg *et al.*, 2006)
- The neuropathic patient may not volunteer information about a foot problem (they may not be aware of it); removal of **both** shoes and socks is mandatory
- This patient group is often reticent to present to specialist services, so to identify new cases, the practice nurse, community nurse and GP must all remain vigilant.

Autonomic neuropathy

The autonomic nervous system controls many bodily functions that we are usually unaware of, including heart rate and the redirection of blood flow within the body (for example, shutting down the peripheral circulation when we are cold and increasing it when we are hot). The commonest presentations of autonomic dysfunction are:

- Erectile dysfunction (ED)
- Dizziness (and sometimes fainting) associated with changes in posture (postural hypotension) — particularly when getting out of bed
- Disturbances of gut function (gastroparesis).

Gastroparesis occurs with vagus nerve damage, which stops the muscles of the stomach and intestines working normally and alters normal digestion (http://digestive.niddk.nih.gov/ddiseases/pubs/gastroparesis/index.aspx). The effects on gut motility include failure of stomach emptying (which can cause discomfort, vomiting and problems with glycaemic control) and the bowel can also be affected, leading to constipation or diarrhoea and occasionally incontinence. Less often the bladder is affected, causing urinary retention and overflow incontinence. This can present as repeated urinary tract infections and sometimes long term catheterisation may be necessary.

Erectile dysfunction in diabetes can be contributed to by comorbidities such as vascular disease and low testosterone levels (Fisken, 2010) (please see *Chapter 18* for more information).

Practice points:
- Common drugs such as metformin can cause gut dysfunction, and may exacerbate symptoms of autonomic dysfunction
- ED in diabetes is associated with poor glycaemic control, which should be optimised. Many men with diabetes take medications which can contribute to ED (such as antihypertensives). In the absence of contraindications, men with ED should be offered a trial of a drug such as sildenafil (Viagra)
- Postural hypotension can be difficult to treat. Non-pharmacological measures should be tried first. Medication should be reviewed and compression stockings and ensuring adequate water intake may help

Conclusion

Practitioners should have a knowledge and awareness of neuropathic presentations of diabetes, which can be unusual — symptoms such as vomiting, indigestion or incontinence may require further investigation. The key to avoiding neuropathic complications of diabetes is good glycaemic control, and good advice on controlling blood glucose levels can help to prevent or delay glycosylation occurring and nerve damage presenting. Peter's case illustrates what is often an inexorable process, from presentation with a minor foot injury, through chronic ulceration to major sepsis and amputation. Alcohol is often a cofactor in the neuropathic process. The 'holiday foot', due to unusual activity, new shoes and sometimes thermal injury haunts every diabetic foot clinic. People need ongoing support and encouragement to comply with foot care and live with diabetes.

Key points

- Glycaemic control is related to the progression of diabetic complications and where possible, it should be optimised
- Medical treatments for neuropathic pain can be very disappointing; the best first step is often explanation and reassurance
- Practitioners should have an awareness of and curiosity regarding unusual presentations that are suggestive of neuropathic complications in people with diabetes.

References

Boulton A (1992) What causes neuropathic pain? *Journal of Diabetes and its Complications* 6: 58-63

Bowness D (2009) Diabetes: Evidence Based Management 8 Managing foot complications. *Practice Nursing* **20**(6): 296-301

Britland S et al (1990) Relationship of endoneurial capillary abnormalities to type and severity of diabetic neuropathy. *Diabetes* 39: 909-13

Fisken R (2010) Diabetes: Evidence Based Management 22 Assessment and treatment for Erectile Dysfunction in Diabetes. *Practice Nursing* **21**(8): 416-20

Frykberg R et al (2006) Diabetic foot disorders: a clinical practice guideline. *J Foot Ankle Surg* **45**(5): S2-66

Hawthorne G (2009) Diabetes: Evidence Based Management 4 A risk-management partnership *Practice Nursing* **20**(2): 86-90

Holman N (2011) Diabetes: Evidence Based Management 31 Using data to inform care needs planning for people with diabetes. *Practice Nursing* **22**(5): 258-63

Holdich P (2009) Diabetes: Evidence Based Management 3 Patient-centred care planning. *Practice Nursing* **20**(1): 18-23

Masson E et al (2004) A novel approach to the diagnosis and assessment of symptomatic diabetic neuropathy. *Pain* 38: 426-28

Morrow T (2004) Animal models of painful diabetic neuropathy: the STZ rat model. *Curr Protoc Neurosci*, Nov; Chapter 9:Unit 9.18.

NICE (2011) Neuropathic pain - pharmacological management: http://www.nice.org.uk/guidance/CG96

Pellettieri J, Alvarado A (2007) Cell Turnover and Adult Tissue Homeostasis: From Humans to Planarians. *Annual Review of Genetics* 41: 83-105

Said G (2007) Diabetic neuropathy: a review. *Nat Clin Prac Neuro* **3**(6): 331-40

Shaw J, Zimmet P (1999) The epidemiology of diabetic neuropathy. *Diabetes Rev* 7: 245-52

Tan L (2010) The clinical use of the 10g monofilament and its limitations: a review. *Diabetes Res Clin Pract.* **90**(1):1-7

Thomson F et al (1993) The clinical diagnosis of sensory neuropathy in elderly people *Diabetic Med* 10: 843-46

Chapter 20

Skin complications in diabetes

Anne Phillips

Introduction

Diabetes can affect every part of the body (Bilous and Donnelly, 2010) and it increasingly presents with skin complications. Poor glycaemic control affects the glycosylation of proteins, lipids and other organic molecules, which can have a profound effect on the structure of proteins in the skin and cause skin manifestations (Huntley and Drugge, 2010). As a result, the skin's integrity and its ability to repair damage and resist infection can be compromised. The skin is part of the integumentary system, which also includes hair and fingernails, and it is the largest organ of the human body. This chapter examines many diabetes-related skin manifestations, explaining their potential meaning and how they can be recognised. This gives practitioners an indication of what to look out for when working in partnership with people with diabetes.

It is estimated that 33% of people with diabetes will have a skin disorder either caused by or affected by their diabetes at some point in their lives (American Diabetes Association [ADA], 2011). Fortunately, if recognised and diagnosed early, most skin conditions can be prevented or treated. While some skin problems can affect anyone (such as impetigo or psoriasis), people with diabetes tend to get skin complications such as bacterial infections, fungal infections and pruritis more easily (Diabetes UK, 2011). There are other skin problems which can affect people with diabetes or pre diabetes, which include:

- Diabetic dermopathy
- Necrobiosis lipoidica diabeticorum
- Bullosis diabeticorum (diabetic blisters)
- Diabetic thick skin
- Digital sclerosis
- Diabetic yellow skin
- Eruptive xanthomatosis
- Acanthosis nigricans (associated with insulin resistance).

Comorbid conditions

Skin problems in diabetes can be associated with comorbid conditions. For example, atherosclerosis can cause the skin to become hairless, cool and shiny, the toes to become cold, the toenails to become thickened and discoloured and it can inhibit white blood cell activity, delaying healing (Bilous and Donnelly, 2010).

Bacterial infections

Several types of bacterial skin infection can affect people with diabetes, including styes (infections of the glands of the eyelid), boils, folliculitis (infections of the hair follicles), nail infections and carbuncles. These infections are all more common in people with diabetes and are usually caused by staphylococci (Diabetes UK, 2011). They can largely be prevented with good skin hygiene and good blood glucose control (Bilous and Donnelly, 2010). When reviewing people with diabetes, it is always worth reiterating the importance and impact of good glucose control (ADVANCE Collaborative Group, 2008).

Fungal infections

Fungal infections commonly occur in warm, moist skin folds. Problem areas include under the breasts, around the nails, between the fingers and toes, under the foreskin (in uncircumcised men) and in the armpits and groin.

In people with diabetes, many fungal infections are most commonly caused by *Candida albicans* (*C. albicans*), a yeast-like fungus which can cause itchy, moist, red rashes of tiny blisters and scales.

Common fungal infections include 'jock itch', 'athlete's foot' and ringworm and vaginal infections that cause itching. 'Jock itch' (tinea cruris) is a fungal infection of the groin, which causes the skin of the groin and scrotum to become reddened and discoloured; it is usually treated with the application of a topical antifungal cream and advice to keep the area clean and dry, to promote healing (Bjekic *et al.*, 2011, Ragunatha *et al.*, 2011).

Vulvo-vaginal candidiasis is usually accompanied by a white discharge and can be complicated by *C. albicans* in the colon. This is typically managed by stabilising blood glucose levels and giving treatments such as topical anti-fungal medications and/or 150mg oral fluconazole (Huntley and Drugge, 2010).

To raise awareness of the link between raised blood glucose levels and thrush-type infections can help develop the person's understanding of the need for tight glycaemic control (Bilous and Donnelly, 2010).

Angular stomatitis

Angular stomatitis is an infection at the corner of the mouth, which is commonly caused by *C. albicans* in children and also in some adults with diabetes, due to increased concentrations of salivary glucose. Its recommended treatment is stabilisation of blood glucose levels and the use of anti-candidal lozenges and/ or a topical imidazole cream (Diabetes UK, 2011; Bilous and Donnelly, 2010).

Candidal paronychia

Candidal infection of the hands and feet can present in different ways. Candidal paronychia (infection of the nail fold) begins at the lateral folds with erythema, swelling and separation of the fold from the lateral margin of the nail (Huntley and Drugge, 2010).

Athlete's foot

Trapped moisture promotes the growth of fungi and yeasts and is associated with repeated infections. Athlete's foot (tinea pedis) is one such infection, which causes flaking, itching and scaling of the skin; it can become a chronic problem.

To prevent infections, topical treatments can be used (such as antifungal creams) and it can also help to keep the web-spaces clean and dry (Singer *et al.*, 2010). In addition, working in partnership with people with diabetes and discussing good blood glucose control can help to alleviate and/or avoid recurrent infection (Phillips and Wright, 2009).

Nail plate infections

Dermatophyte (a group of fungi) or candidal infections of the nail plate or nail bed present as a distal yellowing, whitening and thickening of the nail. Apart from the obvious changes in nail appearance, this infection poses no risk to the individual with diabetes.

Mucormycosis

Individuals with poorly-controlled diabetes, possible ketosis and weakened immune systems are at greater risk of mucormycosis, a rare but potentially fatal fungal infection. This usually starts in the nasal cavity, from where it can spread to the eyes, skin and brain. Symptoms of cutaneous (skin) mucormycosis include having a single, painful, hardened area of skin that may have a blackened centre; if present, this needs to be excised urgently, to remove all the necrotic tissue (Dugdale and Vyas, 2010). Treatment of mucormycosis is with hospital admission and intravenous amphotericin (Pinto *et al.*, 2011).

Diabetic dermopathy

Diabetes causes microvascular changes, which can result in the development of light reddish brown-coloured oval or circular scaly patches on the skin (Holt *et al.*, 2010). Sometimes these are mistaken for 'age spots' or pretibial patches, as they often occur on the shins. Less commonly, they can be found on the front of the thighs, forearms, scalp and trunk. These spots are commonly seen in clinical practice and practitioners should be aware of their links to pre-diabetes and diabetes. The presence of four or more lesions is strongly suggestive of diabetes, so if a person who does not already have a diagnosis of diabetes presents with shin spots, they will be at increased risk of type 2 diabetes and should be investigated for impaired glucose tolerance (Reed, 2010).

Diabetic dermopathy tends to occur more commonly in older people, who have lived with diabetes for at least 10–20 years. However, it is relatively common and occurs in about 30% of people with diabetes (Diabetes UK, 2011). It is worth looking for at annual review appointments and asking people if they have noticed any skin changes since their last review. Diabetic dermopathy appears to be closely associated with raised levels of glycosylated haemoglobin, and indicates poor glycaemic control (Bilous and Donnelly, 2010). It is also associated with the microvascular changes that are seen in neuropathy, retinopathy and nephropathy, all of which are caused by hyperglycaemia and raised levels of glycosylation end products (Bowness, 2009; Holdich and Gillibrand, 2010; Robbins, 2010).

Necrobiosis lipoidica diabeticorum

Necrobiosis lipoidica diabeticorum (NLD) is thought to be caused by changes in collagen and fat underneath the skin, which cause the overlying skin to become thin and reddened. It occurs almost exclusively in white people (Huntley and Drugge, 2010). The onset of NLD is often gradual and it can go unnoticed until very visible, raised, red patches fully appear. NLD is thought to affect about 0.3% of people with diabetes and although it can occur at any age, it is more common in those aged 20–40 years (Hayat *et al.*, 2010; Diabetes UK, 2011). It is three times more common in women than in men and it can occur regardless of how well-controlled the individual's diabetes is (Diabetes UK, 2011). Most lesions are found on the lower legs and ulcerate if subjected to trauma.

NLD needs to be recognised as an emotionally distressing condition, as it causes the individual's diabetes to become 'visible' (Sampogna, 2004). Furthermore, healing rates are very poor. Over 3–4 years it resolves in just 20% of individuals (Hayat *et al.*, 2011; Diabetes UK, 2011). As illustrated by Julia's case, it is liable to be permanent (see *case study*). To reduce the emotional trauma of dealing with this very noticeable condition, skin camouflage is recommended; this is available on prescription and it can be very effective (Hayat *et al.*, 2010).

Bullosis diabeticorum

Occasionally, people with diabetes can erupt with blisters. These blisters can occur on the backs of fingers, hands, toes, feet, legs and forearms. They look similar to burn blisters and are often experienced by people with neuropathy, but who have generally good circulation. The blisters are large but painless and can present in two ways (DermNetNZ, 2009):

- **Intraepidermal bullae** — these are filled with clear, sterile viscous fluid and normally heal spontaneously within 2–5 weeks, without scarring or atrophy
- **Subepidermal bullae** — these are less common and can be filled with blood. Healed blisters may show scarring and atrophy.

It is important to ensure that blisters remain unbroken and that blood glucose levels are controlled. In addition, it is vital that the person is given reassurance, as this condition suggests that other glycation is occurring within the body.

Any individual with diabetes who presents with bullosis diabeticorum should be considered high risk, owing to diabetes and the vascular impact of prolonged hyperglycaemia presenting as these skin manifestations (Bilous and Donnelly, 2010).

Diabetic thick skin

It has been suggested that cross-linking of collagen is responsible for about 30% of people with diabetes having generally thicker skin; in some people, the dorsae of the feet are involved (Bilous and Donnelly, 2010; Huntley and Drugge, 2010). Clues that suggest such thickening include (Clark *et al.*, 1984; Huntley, 1986):

- Difficulty in tenting the skin
- Pebbled or rough skin on the knuckles or in the periungual region
- Decreased skin wrinkling following immersion in water.

About one third of people with type 1 diabetes will develop diabetic cheiroarthropathy (Bilous and Donnelly, 2010; Lebiedz-Odrobina and Kay, 2010), which results in reduced mobility of the hands and stiff, waxy, yellowed skin. This condition is also thought to be due to glycosylation and the effects of glycation end products (DermNet NZ, 2009). A simple test to assess for this at annual review is to ask the individual to put their hands together as if praying. The 'prayer sign' (an inability to hold the palms and fingers flat to one another) indicates the presence of diabetic cheiroarthropathy.

Dupuytren's contracture

Individuals with diabetic thick skin may also experience Dupuytren's contracture, which tightens the tendons in the hands and bends the fingers. Diabetic hand syndrome consists of thickened skin over the interphalangeal joints, complicated by painful, stiff hands. Rarely knees, ankles and elbows also get stiff. The only diabetes-related treatment for this is to attempt to normalise blood glucose levels (Diabetes UK, 2011).

Case study

Julia is a 23-year-old woman with type I diabetes. She presents to her practice nurse with a red, hairless patch on her right lower shin. She is very concerned about the appearance of this area as it is very noticeable when she wears skirts or cropped trousers, and it can also be seen through thin tights. Julia's HbA_{1c} is 8.2% (66mmol/mol) and she has a history of suboptimal diabetes control.

Julia's practice nurse suspects necrobiosis lipoidica diabeticorum (NLD) — a rare skin condition but one that she has seen previously in another young woman with type I diabetes. The practice nurse takes a digital photograph of the patch (with Julia's permission) and sends this to the local diabetes and dermatology department for their opinion. They confirm her suspicions and a diagnosis of NLD is confirmed.

The practice nurse reassures Julia and together they discuss Julia's blood glucose control and determine how they might try to gradually reduce her HbA_{1c} to a level below 7.5% (58mmol/mol). They also discuss the psychological impact of this red area on her shin, as she finds it very visually unappealing and distressing. The practice nurse asks Julia if she might consider trying some camouflage creams and they agree to give this a go. They work together to design ways in which Julia can mask the reddened area and begin to accept its presence.

Diabetic scleroderma

Diabetic scleroderma is rare and involves a markedly thickened dermis on the neck and the upper back, which sometimes extends to cover a wider area. This is more common in type 2 than in type 1 diabetes (Konohana *et al.*, 1985). The significance of this thickened skin condition is its link with microvascular complications in the retina (Bilous and Donnelly, 2010). Health professionals need to be aware of such presentations in people with diabetes, as they suggest that microvascular and likely macrovascular damage is already present.

These individuals are at high risk, so a careful approach to care is required, aiming for risk reduction, improved quality of life and careful and responsive symptom control (Bilous and Donnelly, 2010).

Yellow skin and nails

People with diabetes often develop a yellow skin hue, which is probably best observed on the palms of the hands and the soles of feet, as pigment is sparse in these areas (Norman, 2001). The yellow nail effect is best observed on the toenails.

A suggested cause of this yellowing is glycosylation end products. Huntley and Drugge (2010) proposed that the yellowness of skin and nails might be used as a quantifiable indicator of the degree of non-enzymatic glycosylation in other tissues within the body. Skin and nail colour can be used as a visual clue to suggest which diabetes-related micro- and macrovascular complications are likely to be present and need to be screened for. There is no treatment for skin yellowing; it is simply a clinical observation that should be made during opportunistic screening or annual review, and one which may be considered significant.

Eruptive xanthomatosis

While eruptive xanthomatosis can present in both men and women, it most commonly affects young men with type 1 diabetes. It appears as firm, yellow, waxy, itchy, pea-like bumps on the skin, which are surrounded by red halos. These are usually found on the face, buttocks, backs of arms and legs, and in the creases of the groin and the armpits.

Eruptive xanthomatosis may present when blood glucose levels are elevated and triglycerides also rise to high levels (ADA, 2010). It is also a complication of severe insulin resistance, which makes it difficult for the body to clear fat from the blood. People with extremely high triglycerides and blood glucose levels are also at high risk of pancreatitis (Digby *et al.*, 2011).

The individual with eruptive xanthomatosis needs to be supported, as they will feel frightened and unwell. The aims of treatment are to control cholesterol levels and reduce triglycerides, to protect against pancreatitis (Digby *et al.*, 2011). Good blood glucose control can help to resolve these troublesome bumps in a matter of weeks.

Acanthosis nigricans

Acanthosis nigricans is a condition to be mindful of during consultations with children and other people who do not have known diabetes. This is intrinsically linked with insulin resistance; it generally occurs in children and others who are overweight or obese, and it is a strong indicator of impaired glucose tolerance, impaired fasting glucose (Reed, 2010) and probable type 2 diabetes.

Brown or tan patches can appear on the sides or nape of the neck, armpits and groin. Sometimes they also occur on the hands, elbows and knees. The relationship between insulin and acanthosis nigricans is especially clear in the context of disordered insulin metabolism. Huntley and Drugge (2010) speculated that high plasma insulin levels contribute to the development of acanthosis nigricans. Classic insulin receptors and insulin-like growth factors have been found in cultured samples taken from the lesions, which supports this theory (Blackett *et al.*, 2011).

When a person presents with acanthosis nigricans, or it is noticed on general health assessment, it is worth discussing diabetes and offering an oral glucose tolerance test, for confirmation (MacArthur, 2008).

Conclusions

Diabetes has a number of skin manifestations and the effects of glucose control and glycosylation cannot be underestimated. This chapter has provided a summary of some of the unusual skin presentations that health professionals (and primary care diabetes teams in particular) may come across when caring for and working in partnership with the increasing numbers of people with diabetes.

People find skin presentations distressing, as they are obvious and visible. Therefore, it is essential that practitioners offer reassurance and share their knowledge of treatment strategies and coping mechanisms, and discuss the various options that are available with individuals like Julia.

It is important that practitioners realise that the effects of diabetes on the skin also offer suggestive prompts to the potential glycosolation that may be taking place elsewhere in the body. Skin complications can trigger screening for further diabetes-related micro- and macrovascular complications.

Key points

- Impaired regulation of glucose and glycoslation end products can make people with diabetes vulnerable to skin complications
- Skin complications are a trigger for practitioners to consider screening for micro- and macrovascular complications
- Healthcare practitioners may encounter increasing numbers of people with diabetes-related skin presentations.

References

Advance Collaborative Group (2008) Intensive blood glucose control and vascular outcomes in patients with type 2 diabetes. *N Eng J Med* 358: 2560-72

American Diabetes Association (2011) Skin Complications, http://www.diabetes.org/ living -with-diabetes/complications/skin-complications.html

Bjekic M et al (2011) Risk Factors for gential lichen sclerosus in men. *British Journal of Dermatology* **164**(2): 325-29

Bilous R, Donnelly R (2010) Handbook of Diabetes, 4th Ed, Chichester: Wiley-Blackwell.

Bowness D (2009) Diabetes Evidence Based Management – 8, Managing Foot Complications. *Practice Nursing* **20**(6): 296-301

Blackett et al, P (2011) Management of Pediatric Obesity and Diabetes. *Nutrition and Health* 2: 101-40

Clark C, Pentland B, Ewing D, Clark B (1984) Decreased skin wrinkling in diabetes mellitus. *Diabetes Care* 7: 224-27

Diabetes UK (2011) Guide to Other associated conditions – Skin (Necrobiosis) www.diabetes.org.uk

Digby M et al (2011) Eruptive xanthomas as a cutaneous manifestation of hyper-triglyceridema: a case report. *J Clin Aesthet Dermatol* **4**(1): 4-46

Dugdale D (2010) Mucormycosis http://www.nlm.nih.gov/medlineplus/ency/article/ 000649.htm (accessed: 02-03-11)

Hayat A et al, (2010) Updates in the management of cutaneous manifestations of diabetes mellitus. *World Applied Sciences Journal* **8**(4): 394-99

Holt R, Cockram C, Flyvbjerg A, Goldstein B (2010) Textbook of Diabetes: A Clinical Approach (Pickup, Textbook of Diabetes) Oxford: Wiley Blackwell

Huntley A (1986) Finger pebbles: A common finding in diabetes mellitus. *J Amer Acad Dermatol* 14: 612-17

Huntley A, Drugge R (2010) Diabetes in Skin Disease, http://www.telemedicine.org (accessed: 03-03-11)

Gillibrand W, Holdich P (2010) Evidence based diabetes management – 20, Assessment of retinopathy. *Practice Nursing* **21**(6): 305-09

Konohana A et al (1985) Glycosaminoglcans and collagen in the skin of a patient with diabetic scleroderma. *Keio J Med* 34: 221-26

Lebiedz-Odrobina D, Kay J (2010) Rheumatic presentations of diabetes mellitus *Rheumatic Disease Clinics of North America* **36**(4): 681-99

MacArthur C (2008) Diabetes Evidence Based Management – 1, Diagnosis and Risk Assessment. *Practice Nursing* **19**(11): 546-51

Norman A (2001) Dermal manifestations of diabetes. Norman R (ed). Geriatric Dermatology. New York, NY: Parthenon Publishing.

Phillips A, Wright J (2009) Achieving Treatment Concordance, Diabetes Evidence Based Management. *Practice Nursing* **20**(7): 353-57

Pinto M et al (2011) Hyperglycemic hyperosmolar state and rhino-orbital murcormyosis. *Diabetes Research and Clinical Practice* **91**(2): 37

Skin problems associated with diabetes mellitus. http://www.dermnetnz.org/systemic/diabetes.html (accessed: 02-03-11)

Sampogna F et al (2004) Association Between Poorer Quality of Life and Psychiatric Morbidity in Patients With Different Dermatological Conditions. *Psychosomatic Medicine* 66: 620-24

Singer A et al, (2010) Skin and Soft Tissue Injuries and Infections – A Practical Evidence Based Guide, PMPH: USA.

Ragunatha S et al (2011) Cutaneous disorders in 500 diabetic patients attending diabetic clinic. *Indian Journal of Dermatology* **56**(2): 160-64

Reed E (2010) Diabetes Evidence Based Management 15, Recognising pre-diabetes. *Practice Nursing* **21**(1): 28-32

Robbins V (2010) Diabetes, Evidenced Based Mangement – 16, Managing Diabetic Nephropathy. *Practice Nursing* **21**(2): 84-88

Chapter 21

Preconception care in diabetes

Dr Gillian Hawthorne

Introduction

While pregnancy outcomes for women with diabetes have improved from a perinatal mortality rate of 400 per 1000 people during the 20th century (Molsted-Pedersen, 2003), reports in European countries have shown that diabetic pregnancy continues to be high risk (Evers *et al.*, 2004; Jensen *et al.*, 2004). The Confidential Enquiry into Maternal and Child Health (CEMACH, 2005) reported diabetic pregnancy outcomes from England, Wales and Northern Ireland, showing a fivefold increase in stillbirth and a twofold increase in the risk of congenital anomaly (CEMACH, 2005). All congenital malformations can occur in maternal diabetes (Ramos-Arroyo *et al.*, 1992; Goto and Goldman, 1994; Martinez-Frias, 1994). In particular, cardiac defects are more prevalent in diabetic pregnancy (Wren *et al.*, 2003) and neural tube defects are also more common, including some rare defects such as sacral agenesis.

A key goal of preconception care in diabetes is to reduce the risk of congenital anomaly to the same as that in the background population. In type 2 diabetes, the risk of poor pregnancy outcome — including the increased risk of congenital anomaly — is the same or higher than in type 1 diabetes (CEMACH, 2005; Clausen *et al.*, 2005) and most women with type 2 diabetes are managed within primary care. This chapter recognises the importance of the practice diabetes team in preconception care.

Case study

Amy is 23 years old and works as a shop assistant in a newsagent's. After presenting with thirst and tiredness 2 years ago, she was diagnosed with type 2 diabetes. She has a strong family history of diabetes. She has always been overweight and her body mass index (BMI) is currently $31kg/m^2$. At her last annual review, her HbA_{1c} was 6.8% (51mmol/mol) and her GP noted that her total cholesterol was raised, at 6.7mmol/l, so she was started on simvastatin which was titrated up to 40mg once daily. Her diabetes is managed with metformin 500mg twice daily.

Amy got married last year, and she has not been using any contraception since the wedding. She has gained weight and says that both her and her husband are 'piling on the pounds'. She continues to smoke ten cigarettes a day. Her most recent HbA$_{1c}$ is 8.8% (73mmol/mol). Today, she has attended the surgery for a routine diabetes check; during the consultation it becomes clear, by chance, that she is actively trying to become pregnant.

Assessment

Amy is obese and a smoker. She has poorly-controlled diabetes. She is not currently using any contraception and she is actively trying for a family. She is on simvastatin and metformin.

Amy's knowledge and understanding of her diabetes need to be assessed. She needs to be aware of the impact of diabetes on pregnancy and she should be given preconception counselling. Her HbA$_{1c}$ is currently elevated at 8.8% (73mmol/mol) and until her glycaemic control has improved, she should be strongly counselled against pregnancy.

Preconception counselling

The CEMACH (2007) enquiry found an association between poor pregnancy outcomes and suboptimal preconception care, which included lack of discussion of diabetes-specific issues that relate to fetal risk during pregnancy. Preconception care aims to improve pregnancy outcomes and involves:

• Imparting relevant information to improve knowledge
• Modifying individuals' behaviour, based on this knowledge.

The National Institute for Health and Clinical Excellence (NICE, 2008) has published recommendations on the information and advice required for preconception care. Women with diabetes who are planning to become pregnant should be informed that maintaining good glycaemic control before conception and throughout pregnancy reduces the risks of congenital malformation, early and late miscarriage, stillbirth and neonatal death. Information and advice should be given on the risks of diabetes in pregnancy, weight loss (if BMI>27kg/m^2), hypoglycaemia and hypoglycaemia unawareness, retinal and renal assessment, and when to stop contraception and start folic acid 5mg once daily.

Amy needs to understand that her poorly-controlled diabetes is a high risk to pregnancy and that she can reduce her risks of miscarriage and congenital malformation by establishing good glycaemic control before conceiving. She needs to have information to make appropriate decisions about her management.

Her preconception counselling should include the following:

- She needs to be supported to stop smoking
- As her HbA_{1c} is elevated, she should be counselled against pregnancy at this time. In line with NICE (2008) recommendations, she should be advised to delay conception until her HbA_{1c} is less than 6.1% (43mmol/mol)
- Contraception should be started, to ensure that when pregnancy occurs it is actively planned and happens when her diabetes is well-controlled
- She should be given advice on lifestyle factors. Amy needs to understand the impact that diet and exercise can have on her glycaemic control and weight. To help her achieve her weight loss aims, referral to a diabetes specialist dietitian is recommended
- She should start taking folic acid 5mg once daily, to reduce the risk of congenital neural tube defects
- Amy should discontinue her simvastatin when she stops her contraception, as it is contraindicated in pregnancy. Until then, she should continue with this treatment to manage her cholesterol.

Medications contraindicated in pregnancy

Of particular note, simvastatin should be stopped when contemplating pregnancy (Joint Formulary Committee, 2009: 2.12). Other medications contraindicated in pregnancy that are commonly used by people with type 2 diabetes include angiotensin-converting enzyme (ACE) inhibitors (Lip *et al.*, 1997; Cooper *et al.*, 2006) and angiotensin-II receptor antagonists (Jacqz-Aigrain and Koren, 2005). These need to be stopped before conception and alternative medications, which are safe in pregnancy, should be introduced.

Evidence base for preconception care

Weight management
Obesity before pregnancy is associated with an increased risk of fetal macrosomia and perinatal mortality (CEMACH, 2002). The risk of late fetal death increases with pre-pregnancy BMI and early neonatal death is almost doubled in nulliparous women (Cnattingius *et al.*, 1998).

Table 1. Gestational age for anomalies	
Anomaly	**Weeks post-ovulation**
Caudal regression (sacral agenesis)	3
Neural tube defects	4
Cardiac anomalies	5–6
Anal and rectal atresia	6
Renal/ureteral anomalies	5
Situs inversus	4
From: Kucera, 1971.	

Folic acid

Folic acid is safe and should be taken by all women who are planning pregnancy. Folic acid 5mg has been shown to reduce the risk of neural tube defects (Expert Advisory Group, 1992). It should be started before conception and continued until the end of the first trimester.

Glycaemic control

The association between poor glycaemic control and increased risk of congenital anomaly is clearly established (Kitzmiller *et al.*, 1996). A study by Fuhrmann *et al.* (1983) demonstrated a major congenital malformation rate of 7.5% when women with diabetes did not receive preconception care and 0.8% when good glycaemic control was maintained preconceptually and throughout pregnancy. Furthermore, Steel *et al.* (1988) showed that a preconception service for women with diabetes was effective — those who attended the service had lower HbA$_{1c}$ values in the first trimester and a lower rate of congenital abnormality.

Further observational studies have reported the success of preconception care in reducing the congenital anomaly rate (Goldman *et al.*, 1986; Mills *et al.*, 1988; Damm *et al.*, 1989, Kitzmiller *et al.*, 1996). Results from the Diabetes Control and Complications Trial (DCCT, 1996) support the timely use of intensive therapy to reduce rates of congenital malformation. In this randomised controlled trial, one congenital abnormality occurred in the intensive group (HbA$_{1c}$ 7.4±1.3%) compared to eight congenital abnormalities in the group with conventional therapy (HbA$_{1c}$ 8.1±1.7%).

A meta-analysis of 14 cohort studies of preconception care by Ray *et al.* (2001) focused on the effects of glycaemic control. In total, major congenital malformations were assessed among 1192 offspring of mothers who had received preconception care and 1459 offspring of mothers who had not. The pooled rate of major anomalies was found to be lower in those who had received preconception care (2.1%) compared with those who had not (6.5%).

As fetal organogenesis is completed by 10 weeks of gestation, it makes sense that any abnormal organ development will have occurred by this point (Kucera, 1971) (*Table 1*). The aim of good glycaemic control during preconception is to prevent or reduce the occurrence of fetal abnormality in this initial phase of cellular proliferation and organisation.

Initial management

Amy's diabetes is poorly-controlled and before conceiving she needs to improve her glycaemic control to a target HbA_{1c} of <6.1% (43mmol/mol), in the absence of hypoglycaemia (see *Chapter 13*).

The practice nurse identifies that Amy's dietary understanding is poor, so she is referred to a specialist diabetes dietitian for advice and help. Amy has never attended a structured education course such as Diabetes Education and Self Management for Ongoing and Newly Diagnosed (DESMOND) and her understanding and knowledge of diabetes is patchy. It is clear that she did not know that diabetes could affect pregnancy and its outcome. The practice nurse arranges for Amy to attend an education course and to see the dietitian.

She also arranges an appointment with the GP, so that Amy can start contraception. In the meantime, she emphasises that Amy should not become pregnant until her diabetes control has improved. She suggests using barrier methods of contraception until Amy has started a more reliable form of contraception. She also stresses that if Amy should inadvertently become pregnant, she must let the practice know as soon as possible so that her referral to the obstetric antenatal service can be fast-tracked. An appointment is made for preconception care and counselling at the local preconception clinic.

Preconception care

The essential components of preconception care include review and consideration of the medical, obstetric and gynaecological history, advice on glycaemic control to optimize HbA_{1c} and screening for complications (NICE, 2008). Individualised blood targets are set for self-monitoring and the target for HbA_{1c} is set at <6.1% (43mmol/mol), with the HbA_{1c} monitored monthly. Women are counselled about the risks of congenital malformations. To reduce the risk of congenital malformation, the goal is to achieve the lowest HbA_{1c} possible without disabling hypoglycaemia.

Medications which are contraindicated in pregnancy are stopped or changed. Simvastatin is contraindicated in pregnancy, so Amy will have to stop this when she stops her contraception and plans for pregnancy. Metformin may be used before and during pregnancy, so this can be continued (Hawthorne, 2006). All sulphonylureas except for glibenclamide are contraindicated (Langer *et al.*, 2000; Gutzin *et al.*, 2003). If any intensification of therapy is required, insulin treatment is indicated.

Folic acid supplements (5mg/day) are started even before contraception is stopped. This is a safe medication that is effective in reducing neural tube defects in the baby.

Contraindications to pregnancy

Sometimes women with diabetes are strongly advised against pregnancy because of the risk to their own (maternal) health. Women with diabetes and known ischaemic heart disease need to be advised that pregnancy is very high risk for their health, so it should be avoided (Bagg *et al.*, 1999). Other complications of diabetes which can impact on pregnancy outcomes and maternal health include diabetic nephropathy (Biesenbach *et al.*, 1999; Dunne *et al.*, 1999; Rossing *et al.*, 2002), diabetic autonomic neuropathy and diabetic eye disease. Women need to be counselled about their individual risk in these situations.

Follow-up

Eight weeks later, Amy is now using contraception. She has attended a structured education course and found the information very helpful. The dietetic session arranged by the practice nurse was particularly useful. She has lost some weight and her HbA_{1c} has improved to 7.2% (55mmol/mol). She has set a date to stop smoking. The practice nurse encourages Amy and checks that she has an appointment booked for the preconception clinic. She learns that she does, in the next 2 weeks, and arranges for Amy to collect a prescription for folic acid 5mg once daily.

Three months later Amy attends the practice. She and her husband have been seen at the preconception clinic. She has stopped her simvastatin as advised, is on 5mg folic acid daily and she has just stopped her contraception. Her diabetes is now being treated with metformin 1g twice daily and insulin therapy, and she is monitoring her blood glucose at home. Her most recent HbA_{1c} was 6.8% (51mmol/mol). She continues to attend the preconception clinic every 2 months, and is actively trying for pregnancy. Eighteen months later, the practice nurse meets Amy and her 6-week-old healthy baby girl as they are leaving the surgery.

Conclusions

All women with diabetes who are of child-bearing age need to be aware that diabetic pregnancy is high risk and that there is an increased risk of congenital malformation in their offspring. Good glycaemic control in the preconception period has been shown to reduce this risk. Women with diabetes should plan their pregnancies and if they are not actively trying for pregnancy, they should be using a reliable form of contraception. Practice nurses should ask all pre-menopausal women with diabetes about the possibility of pregnancy.

Planning pregnancy entails optimisation of blood glucose control, starting on folic acid and reviewing medication, to ensure that any contraindicated treatments such as simvastatin or ACE inhibitors have been stopped. Women should be given advice and information about how diabetes affects pregnancy and how pregnancy affects diabetes. This is best provided by a local preconception service, so the woman should be referred to one.

Key points

- Diabetic pregnancy is high risk
- Women with diabetes should be supported to actively plan pregnancy
- Preconception counselling highlights the importance of good blood glucose control at conception and during pregnancy
- Preconception care improves pregnancy outcomes in women with diabetes.

References

Bagg W et al (1999) Pregnancy in women with diabetes and ischaemic heart disease. *Aust N Z Obstet Gynaecol* **39**(1): 99-102

Biesenbach G et al (1999) How pregnancy influences renal function in nephropathic type 1 diabetic women depends on their pre-conceptional creatinine clearance. *J Nephrol* **12**(1): 41-46

Confidential Enquiry into Maternal and Child Health (2002) Why mothers die. Royal College of Obstetricians and Gynaecologists, London

Confidential Enquiry into Maternal and Child Health (2005) Pregnancy in women with type 1 and type 2 diabetes in 2002-2003 England, Wales and Northern Ireland. Royal College of Obstetricians and Gynaecologists, London

Confidential Enquiry into Maternal and Child Health (2007) Diabetes in pregnancy: are we providing the best care? Royal College of Obstetricians and Gynaecologists, London

Clausen T et al (2005) Poor pregnancy outcome in women with type 2 diabetes. *Diabetes Care* **28**(2): 323-28

Cnattingius S et al (1998) Pre-pregnancy weight and the risk of adverse pregnancy outcomes. *N Engl J Med* **338**(3): 147-52

Cooper W et al (2006) Major congenital malformations after first-trimester exposure to ACE inhibitors. *N Engl J Med* **354**(23): 2443-51

Damm P, Molsted-Pederson L (1989) Significant decrease in congenital malformations in newborn infants of an unselected population of diabetic women. *Am J Obstet Gynecol* **161**(5): 1163-67

Diabetes Control and Complication Trial (1996) Pregnancy outcomes in the Diabetes Control and Complications Trial. *Am J Obstet Gynecol* **174**(4): 1343-53

Dunne F et al (1999) Pregnancy outcome in women with insulin-dependent diabetes mellitus complicated by nephropathy. QJM **92**(8): 451-54

Evers I et al (2004) Risk of complications of pregnancy in women with type 1 diabetes: nationwide prospective study in the Netherlands. *BMJ* **328**(7445): 915-18

Expert Advisory Group (1992) Folic acid and the prevention of neural tube defect. Department of Health, Scottish Office Home and Health Department, Welsh Office, Department of Health and Social Services, Northern Ireland, London

Fuhrmann K et al (1983) Prevention of congenital malformations in infants of insulin-dependent diabetic mothers. *Diabetes Care* **6**(3): 219-23

Goldman J et al (1986) Pregnancy outcome in patients with insulin-dependent diabetes mellitus with preconceptional diabetic control: a comparative study. *Am J Obstet Gynecol* **155**(2): 293-97

Goto M, Goldman AS (1994) Diabetic embryopathy. *Curr Opin Pediatr* **6**(4): 486-91

Gutzin S et al (2003) The safety of oral hypoglycemic agents in the first trimester of pregnancy: a meta-analysis. *Can J Clin Pharmacol* **10**(4): 179-83

Hawthorne G (2006) Metformin use and diabetic pregnancy-has its time come? *Diabet Med* **23**(3): 223-27

Jacqz-Aigrain E, Koren G (2005) Effects of drugs on the fetus. *Semin Fetal Neonatal Med* **10**(2): 139-47

Jensen D et al (2004) Outcomes in type 1 diabetic pregnancies. *Diabetes Care* **27**(12): 2819-33

Joint Formulary Committee (2009) British National Formulary 57. March. BMA and RPS Publishing, London

Kitzmiller J et al (1996) Pre-conception care of diabetes, congenital malformations and spontaneous abortions. *Diabetes Care* **19**(5): 514-41

Kucera J (1971) Rate and type of congenital anomalies among offspring of diabetic mothers. *J Reprod Med* **7**(2): 61-70

Langer O et al (2000) A comparison of glyburide and insulin in women with gestational diabetes mellitus. *New Engl J Med* **343**(16): 1134-38

Lip G et al (1997) Angiotensin-converting enzyme inhibitors in early pregnancy. *Lancet* **350**(9089): 146-47

Martinez-Frias M (1994) Epidemiological analysis of outcomes of pregnancy in diabetic mothers: identification of the most characteristic and most frequent congenital anomalies. *Am J Med Genet* **51**(2): 108-13

Mills J et al (1988) Lack of relation of increased malformation rates in infants of diabetic mothers to glycemic control during organogenesis. *N Engl. J Med* **318**(11): 671-76

Molsted-Pedersen L (2003) The Pedersen legacy. In: Hod M et al (eds) (2003) Textbook of Diabetes and Pregnancy, Martin Dunitz, London

National Institute for Health and Clinical Excellence (2008) Diabetes in pregnancy: Management of diabetes and its complications from pre-conception to the postnatal period. Clinical guideline 63. NICE, London

Ramos-Arroyo M et al (1992) Maternal diabetes: the risk for specific birth defects. *Eur J Epidemiol* **8**(4): 503-8

Ray J et al (2001) Preconception care and the risk of congenital anomalies in the offspring of women with diabetes mellitus: a meta-analysis. *QJM* **94**(8): 435-44

Rossing K et al (2002) Pregnancy and progression of diabetic nephropathy. *Diabetologia* **45**(1): 36-41

Steel J et al (1990) Can prepregnancy care of diabetic women reduce the risk of abnormal babies? *BMJ* **301**(6760): 1070-74

Wren C et al (2003) Cardiovascular malformations in infants of diabetic mothers. *Heart* **89**(10): 1217-20

Chapter 22

Caring for children and young people with diabetes

Carole Gelder

Introduction

International consensus guidelines recommend that children and young people with diabetes are cared for by a specialist team with 'training, expertise and understanding of both diabetes and paediatrics including child and adolescent development' (Pihoker *et al.*, 2008: 609). In practice, it often becomes more difficult to achieve this aim as teenagers with diabetes become adults.

Care pathways for teenagers may be unclear, and communication between specialist diabetes services and general practice may break down. In addition, as teenagers take on personal responsibility for their health and become independent from parents and more subject to the culture of their peers, there is a risk that critical aspects of their diabetes management may be neglected.

General practice is the first port of call when health concerns or illnesses arise. Therefore it is essential for the practice team to work collaboratively with specialist diabetes professionals who care for the individual. The National Service Framework (NSF) for Diabetes: Standards (Department of Health [DoH], 2001) stressed the importance of key stakeholders implementing agreed protocols, and recognised that early recognition of diabetic ketoacidosis in people with new onset and existing type 1 diabetes is an important responsibility of primary care. The DoH (2007a: 26) identified 'shared access to records and 24-hour access to specialist diabetes advice' as mechanisms to support such collaborative relationships.

In the case of Sarah (see *case study*), following such recommendations for collaborative working, diabetes management during adolescence and the transition from paediatric to adult teams will help practitioners in providing the support and psychoeducational interventions that Sarah needs to maintain good health in her adult life.

Incidence and prevalence

In the absence of a national diabetes register, accurate figures of prevalence are difficult to ascertain. However, a survey by the Royal College of Paediatrics and Child Health (RCPCH, 2009) found at least 22,783 children with type 1 diabetes under 17 years of age in England. The same study identified 328 children with type 2 diabetes. Although this number is much higher than in previous reports, it still accounts for less than 1% of the population of children and young people with diabetes; this chapter focuses on caring for children and young people with type 1 diabetes.

The prevalence of type 1 diabetes in children and young people is predicted to rise by 70% by 2020 (Patterson *et al.*, 2009). Furthermore, the National Diabetes Audit (2007/2008) showed that only 17.7% of children and young people with diabetes were achieving HbA$_{1c}$ values below 7.5% (58mmol/mol) — therefore, better ways of working must be explored.

The Best Practice Tariff for Paediatric Diabetes sets out mandatory care standards for paediatric diabetes service teams, to ensure quality care across the UK (NHS, 2012). These are available on the NHS Diabetes website:

http://www.diabetes.nhs.uk/

Working collaboratively

Despite recommendations for a specialist team approach (Pihoker *et al.*, 2008) complemented by shared access to records by key stakeholders (DoH, 2007a) paediatric diabetes teams remain chronically under-resourced (Edge *et al.*, 2005) and struggle to meet NSF standards (DoH, 2001). At the same time, 'primary care teams are unlikely to care for sufficient numbers of children and young people with diabetes to develop the necessary specialist competencies ... and are similarly ... unlikely to have adequate capacity to meet their needs' (DoH, 2007a: 26). As a result, children and young people can experience distinct rather than integrated pathways.

Table 1. Indications for same-day referral to hospital specialist team
■ Vomiting
■ Kussmaul breathing
■ Abdominal pain
■ Urinary ketones >1mmol/l
■ Blood ketones >0.6mmol/l
■ Dehydration
■ Drowsy, exhausted or confused
■ Blood glucose continues to rise despite extra insulin
Remember: Children on insulin pumps only use rapid-acting insulin; therefore diabetic ketoacidosis can develop rapidly. Children can and do die from diabetic ketoacidosis
From: Brink et al, 2007.

Nevertheless, specialist children's diabetes teams are working towards more intensive diabetes management including basal bolus regimens, insulin pump therapy, carbohydrate counting and psychoeducational interventions, as recommended by NICE (2004; 2008) and Brink *et al.* (2007). Such intensive forms of diabetes management impact on the school day. Staff act *in loco parentis* during the school day and therefore need the requisite knowledge and skills to support diabetes management — specifically, the supervision or administration of insulin at school.

Investment in structured education for school nurses, school staff and general practice staff is needed to ensure a long-term and sustainable support solution within the child's community.

Diabetic ketoacidosis

The incidence of diabetic ketoacidosis for all ages varies widely, from 15–70% in Europe (Wolfsdorf *et al.*, 2007). In children with established diabetes, the risk is 1–10% per patient per year (Hanas *et al.*, 2005).

Children and young people can become seriously unwell very quickly; therefore, same-day referral to a specialist team is strongly recommended (NICE, 2004) (*Table 1*). Young people with diabetic ketoacidosis should be treated according to the British Society for Paediatric Endocrinology and Diabetes (BSPED, 2009) best practice guideline. Children and young people with diabetic ketoacidosis should be managed in centres experienced in its treatment where vital signs, neurological status and laboratory results can be monitored (Wolfsdorf *et al.*, 2007).

Following diagnosis and recovery, children and young people are generally discharged from hospital with a named contact, planned home visits and regular outpatient appointments to see the specialist team. However, the prescription items dispensed from secondary care at discharge are limited. More frequent blood glucose testing equates with better control (Pihoker *et al.*, 2007) and to obtain items for home testing, families must book an early appointment in general practice. This can also provide a timely opportunity for the practice team to establish a good rapport with the family. While a consistent approach should be reinforced from the outset, some flexibility and understanding will be necessary as the individual's needs and prescription supplies requirements change with age.

Home testing of blood ketones can facilitate earlier detection and fewer hospital admissions when compared with urine ketone testing (Laffel *et al.*, 2006) and is recommended in all children and young people with diabetes (BSPED, 2009). Anecdotal evidence also suggests that adolescents find this method more socially acceptable. For babies and toddlers who are not toilet trained, there are

Table 2. High risk of diabetic ketoacidosis
The following raise the risk in children and young people
■ Poor glycaemic control
■ Previous diabetic ketoacidosis
■ Adolescent girls
■ Eating disorders
■ Parental abuse
■ Omission of insulin
■ Insulin pump therapy that is interrupted for any reason
From: Hanas et al, 2005.

practical benefits to obtaining a urine sample. The risk of diabetic ketoacidosis is higher in certain groups (*Table 2*).

Sarah (*case study*) admits to regularly omitting her insulin. Wolfsdorf *et al.* (2007:38) argued that 'insulin omission either deliberate or inadvertent is the cause in most cases [of diabetic ketoacidosis] and there is usually an important psychosocial reason for this'. Therefore, Sarah should be referred to the diabetes team psychologist or the local child and adolescent mental health service. As she may not have associated her vaginal thrush with poor glycaemic control, this should be explained to her and an antifungal should be prescribed.

A good quality diabetes service should have local agreements in place to facilitate communication and all key stakeholders should have online access to information about diabetes, shared protocols and decision support trees (DoH, 2007).

Adolescence

During adolescence, young people strive to accept responsibility for themselves and for making independent decisions (Arnett, 2001). Their behaviour fluctuates — at times they act responsibly and at others they are childlike and unsure. It is important that young people feel listened to, but there must be clear boundaries. On serious matters, such as the high risk of diabetic ketoacidosis that accompanies insulin omission, they need non-negotiable parenting, which sets clear long-term goals (Court *et al.*, 2008).

When transferring responsibility from parent to young person, it has been found that gradual negotiation through a process of interdependence (Giordano *et al.*, 1992; Schilling *et al.*, 2002) improves resilience and metabolic outcomes (Grey *et al.*, 2001) and supports self-efficacy (La Greca *et al.*, 1990; RCPCH,

---

Case study

Sarah attends an appointment with her practice nurse. She is almost 16 years old and was diagnosed with type 1 diabetes when she was 5 years old. She requests a repeat prescription of insulin and mentions to the practice nurse that she keeps having vaginal thrush. When the nurse checks on the computer system, she notices that Sarah has not had a prescription of insulin for 6 months, nor has she attended the diabetes transition clinic with the specialist team in this period.

During the consultation, the practice nurse notices a 'pear drops' smell on Sarah's breath (acetone). Sarah reports having felt tired for several weeks and that she regularly falls asleep after school. She comments that she does not see the point of testing her blood glucose and admits to missing some of her mealtime insulin injections.

The practice nurse provides equipment for Sarah to test her blood glucose and blood ketone levels. Sarah's blood glucose level is found to be 23mmol/l and her blood ketone level is 2.5mmol/l. The practice nurse explains the implications of these results to Sarah. She explains that a blood ketone level above 0.6mmol/l indicates insulin insufficiency and that a level above 3mmol/l requires prompt assessment by the specialist diabetes team at the local hospital's diabetes centre, with possible admission to hospital.

Tears start to form in Sarah's eyes and she shows a discoloured mark on her shin. She has searched the internet and is frightened this is a skin complication of her diabetes. She has recently enrolled on a dance course at her local college and confides that her worst fear is that she will not be able to realise her dream of a career on the stage.

2003; DoH, 2007; Court *et al.*, 2008). The importance and value of fitting in with peers should not be underestimated. With peer support, many young people feel confident carrying equipment and injecting insulin in front of their friends; they may sometimes even invite them along to clinic appointments.

Transition

Standard 6 of the NSF for diabetes (DoH, 2001) recommends that 'all young people will receive a smooth transition of care organised with them and at an age appropriate to them'. It has since been recommended that this transition takes place not at a specific age, but between the ages of 16–25 years (RCPCH, 2003; Royal College of Nursing, 2004; DoH, 2007a).

To prevent Sarah from being one of the 40% who are lost to follow-up at this vulnerable age (Fleming *et al.*, 2002), the practice nurse and GP need to communicate with her key worker in secondary care. This person may have a role within a dedicated transition service, or they may be part of a paediatric or adult team. Ideally, this communication should be two-way, facilitated by access to each other's records. A minimum requirement to ensure recall is a database that alerts practitioners when someone fails to attend clinic (Court *et al.*, 2008; DoH, 2007a).

The 'You're welcome' quality criteria (DoH, 2007b) are intended to help services become more accessible to young people. They recommend additional training in communicating with young people and in health promotion for people with general, acute and long-term conditions. This training covers areas such as confidentiality, consent, staff training, health promotion and child and adolescent mental health services. Young people are more likely to ask their GP or practice nurse about sexual health issues than the specialist diabetes team (Matyka and Richards, 2009) and as Viner and Barker (2005) found, behaviours set down in adolescence are carried through to adulthood — getting communication right at this stage is pivotal to future long-term health.

Psychoeducational interventions

Relationships between young people and health professionals must be renegotiated in adolescence if they are to survive (Viner and Barker, 2005). Trusting, non-judgmental relationships which help the individual to set small achievable targets have been identified as the most effective (Delamater, 2007). Adolescents have also reported better self care when health professionals are motivating (Skinner *et al.*, 2000; Kyngas *et al.*, 1998).

As Sarah was diagnosed when she was 5 years old, it is highly likely that education at that time was focused on her parents and this must now be reviewed. At present there are no evidence-based structured paediatric education programmes which meet the national criteria (DoH and Diabetes UK, 2005). However, there is evidence to support certain psychoeducational interventions (*Table 3*), which have been found to have small to moderate benefits in adolescents (Hampson *et al.*, 2001) equivalent to a 0.5% reduction in HbA_{1c} (Winkley *et al.*, 2006).

Encouragingly, there is also growing evidence that health professionals from the multidisciplinary team can learn and effectively use many of these psychoeducational interventions (Hampson *et al.*, 2001; Delamater, 2007).

Table 3. Psychoeducational interventions for adolescents with diabetes
■ Health-related behaviour change
■ Problem solving
■ Coping skills
■ Person-centredness
■ Communication skills
■ Cognitive restructuring
■ Conflict resolution
■ Family involvement
■ Skills-based training
■ Motivational and solution-focused strategies
■ Stress management
From: Hampson et al, 2001; Delamater, 2007.

Continuing care

Advice and support offered by the diabetes specialist team about type 1 diabetes can be backed up and extended by GPs and practice nurses in areas of health promotion, including alcohol and drug use, smoking and sexual health — an area in which practice nurses have particular experience.

In line with NICE recommendations, children and young people should be offered routine monitoring and review of their management, as well as regular screening (*Table 4*). GPs and general practice nurses can complement this monitoring by identifying when repeat prescriptions are not collected and alerting the specialist team to this.

Clinical targets for children and young people have moved closer to those recommended for adults (*Table 5*). This is encouraging as children and young people diagnosed with diabetes face a reduced life expectancy of about 23 years (DoH, 2001). Therefore, it is essential that management is optimised as early as possible.

Access to HbA_{1c} results at the clinical consultation is routine within many paediatric teams and has been advocated by NICE (2004). Interestingly, early analysis of results from the Hvidøre Study Group on Childhood Diabetes showed that the most significant impact on HbA_{1c} was achieved when the team, child or young person and parents all shared the same goals (Skinner, 2007). This can be supported in practice by routinely sending clinic letters with the jointly-agreed goals of all three parties to the child and family, and copying the letter to general practice.

Table 4. Routine checks for adolescents with type 1 diabetes
■ **Every 3 months**
• Haemoglobin A_{1c}
• Height
• Weight
• Injection sites
■ **Every 12 months**
• Retinopathy (>12 years or if diagnosed >5 years ago)
• Microalbuminuria,
• Blood pressure
• Thyroid disease
• Foot care
■ **Every 3 years**
• Coeliac disease
From: National Institute for Health and Clinical Excellence, 2004.

Conclusions

To provide optimal support to young people like Sarah and prevent them being lost to follow up during the transition of care at this vulnerable age, collaborations between primary and secondary care must continue to develop. Information technology facilitating the two-way exchange of information, which enables access to shared records, protocols and decision support trees is pivotal in supporting integrated care pathways.

Children and young people with diabetes should not be treated as small adults, as they are different and have more complex needs. Both at diagnosis and in existing diabetes, diabetic ketoacidosis can lead to a sudden deterioration in health, so same-day referral to a specialist team is paramount.

Probably the most important first step in developing a good therapeutic relationship and optimising care is to listen to the child or young person and their family and to agree shared clinical targets with the entire team.

Table 5. Blood glucose targets for children and young people	
■ HbA$_{1c}$	<7.5% (<58mmol/mol)
■ Preprandial blood glucose	4–8mmol/l
■ Postprandial blood glucose	<10mmol/l
From: National Institute for Health and Clinical Excellence, 2004.	

Key points

■ Collaboration with the specialist children's diabetes team is essential for effective team-working

■ Children and young people with diabetes can become unwell very quickly and same-day referral to the specialist team is paramount

■ The most significant improvements in HbA$_{1c}$ can be achieved when all members of the health professional team share the same goals.

References

Arnett J (2001) Emerging Adulthood: The Winding Road from Late Teens through to the Twenties. Open University Press

Brink S et al S (2007) Sick day management in children and adolescents with diabetes. ISPAD Consensus Guidelines. *Pediatr Diabetes* 8: 401-7

British Society of Paediatric Endocrinology and Diabetes (2009) Guidelines for the management of diabetic ketoacidosis. www.bsped. org.uk/professional/guidelines/docs/DKAGuideline.pdf

Court J et al (2008) Diabetes in Adolescence. ISPAD Consensus Guidelines. *Pediatr Diabetes* 9: 255-62

Delamater A (2007) Psychological care of children and adolescents with diabetes. ISPAD Consensus Guidelines. *Pediatr Diabetes* 8: 340-48

Department of Health (2001) Diabetes: National Service Framework for Diabetes: Standards. The Stationery Office, London

Department of Health (2007a) Making Every Young Person with Diabetes Matter. Report of the Children and Young People with Diabetes Working Group. April. DH, London

Department of Health (2007b) You're Welcome Quality Criteria: Making Health Services Young People Friendly. DH, London

Department of Health, Diabetes UK (2005) Structured Patient Education in Diabetes: Report from the Patient Education Working Group. DH, London

Edge J et al; Youth and Family Advisory Committee of Diabetes UK (2005) Diabetes services in the UK: Fourth national Survey: Are we meeting NSF Standards and NICE guidelines? *Arch Dis Child* 11: 1005-9

Fleming E et al (2002) The transition of adolescents with diabetes from the children's health care service: a review of the literature. *J Clin Nurs* 11(5): 560-67

Giordano B et al (1992) The challenge of transferring responsibility for diabetes management from parent to child. *J Pediatr Health Care* 6(5): 235-39

Hampson S et al (2001) Effects of educational and psychosocial interventions for adolescents with diabetes mellitus: a systematic review. *Health Technology Assessment* 5(10): 1-79

Hanas R et al (2005) Predisposing conditions and insulin pump use in a 2-year population study of pediatric ketoacidosis in Sweden. *Diabetes* 54(suppl 1): A455

Kyngas H et al (1998) Adolescents perceptions of physicians, nurses, parents and friends: help or hindrance in compliance with diabetes self- care. *J Adv Nurs* 27: 760-69

La Greca A et al (1990) Developmental and behavioural aspects of diabetes management in youngsters. *Child Health Care* 19: 132-39

Laffel L et al (2006) Sick day management using blood 3-hydroxybutyrate (3-OHB) compared with urine ketone monitoring reduces hospital visits in young people with T1DM: a randomised clinical trial. *Diabet Med* 23: 278-84

Matyka K, Richards J (2009) Managing children with type 1 diabetes in collaboration with primary care. *Diabetes and Primary Care* 11(2 Suppl): 117-22

NHS Diabetes (2012) Best Practice Tariff for Paediatric Diabetes (diabetes in children and young people aged 18 and under) - information for parents, children and young people. http://www.diabetes.nhs.uk/networks/paediatric_network/best_practice_tariff_for_paediatric_diabetes/ [accessed 30-3-12]

National Institute for Health and Clinical Excellence (2004) Type 1 Diabetes: Diagnosis and Management of Type 1 Diabetes in Children and Young People. Clinical guideline 15. NICE, London

Patterson C et al; EURODIAB Study Group (2009) Incidence trends for childhood type 1 diabetes in Europe during 1989–2003 and predicted new cases 2005–20: a multicentre prospective registration study. *Lancet* 373(9680): 2027-33

Pihoker C et al (2008) The delivery of ambulatory diabetes care: structure processes and outcomes of ambulatory diabetes care. ISPAD Consensus Guidelines. *Pediatric Diabetes* 9: 609-20

Royal College of Nursing (2004) Services for children and young people: Preparing nurses for future roles. RCN, London

Royal College of Paediatrics and Child Health (2003) Bridging the Gaps: Healthcare for Adolescents. RCPCH, London

Royal College of Paediatrics and Child Health (2009) Growing up with Diabetes: Children and Young People with Diabetes in England. March. RCPCH, London

Schilling L et al (2002) The concept of self-manangement of type 1 diabetes in children and adolescents: an evolutionary concept analysis. *J Adv Nurs* **37**(1): 87-99

Skinner C et al (2000) Diabetes during adolescence. In: Snoek FJ, Skinner C, eds. Psychology in Diabetes Care. John Wiley and Sons, Chichester

Skinner (2007) Psychosocial research revealed by the Hvidøre Study Group: Changing diabetes through DAWN Youth. Novo Nordisk, Denmark

Winkley K et al (2006) Psychological interventions to improve glycaemic control in patients with T1DM: systematic review and meta-analysis of randomised controlled trials. *BMJ* 333: 65-68

Wolsdorf J et al (2007) Diabetic ketoacidosis. ISPAD Consensus Guidelines. *Pediatr Diabetes* 8: 28-43

Viner R, Barker M (2005) Young people's health: the need for action. *BMJ* 330: 901-3

Chapter 23

Caring for vulnerable adults with diabetes

Julie Oldroyd

Introduction

Caring for adults with complex diabetes who are dependent and housebound presents a number of challenges and obstacles for the diabetes team. It also presents particular challenges for providing equitable and accessible diabetes care. There can be a tendency to exception report people who are housebound and who cannot access primary care (*Table 1*). The aim of this chapter is to demonstrate the benefits of taking a collaborative multidisciplinary approach and using personalised care planning to improve outcomes.

Housebound patients

The needs of the older person are now being more widely recognised. The National Service Framework (NSF) for Older People (DoH, 2001) advocates a flexible and integrated care package for dependent people with diabetes — one that takes the individual's holistic needs into consideration and that allows autonomy and empowerment.

Much attention is centred on caring for individuals in the community, with an emphasis on self care. Supporting people with long-term conditions is costly, which is perhaps the main driver for efforts to build a self-caring society. Although the DoH (2006: 24) encourages health professionals to 'support and empower people to self-manage their condition', self care is a particular challenge in older people, especially in those with language barriers and co-morbidities.

Care for people with diabetes who are dependent or housebound varies according to the structure of the local primary care team. Some practices may not be able to readily identify the individuals on their patient list who are housebound. While practice nurses and district nurses can visit people in their homes, such visits are often time-limited and primary care staff may lack the experience and skills required to support the individual with complex problems alone; they may need to draw on the experience of the specialist team. However, the ability and availability of members of the specialist team to attend joint home visits varies. Indeed, due to the complexity of their needs it might be easier to exception report people such as Bhahimbi (see *case study*).

Developing a 'diabetes housebound team' can enable the practice to offer people who are dependent and housebound regular reviews. Initially, the practice nurse may be required to arrange joint home visits with the diabetes specialist nurse and then liaise as required, following personalised care planning. To involve the GP via a virtual review (a comprehensive discussion in the patient's absence) can support the practice nurse and provide a holistic review.

Farooqi and Sorrie (2005) studied the monitoring of people with diabetes who were housebound, mobile and over 75 years of age, and found that monitoring standards were significantly lower (p<0.001) in this group. Forbes *et al.* (1996) acknowledged that district nurses require the support of the specialist team in caring for older people with diabetes who are housebound and that this group may 'miss out on advances being made in the diabetes medical treatment field'. NHS Diabetes (2011) further acknowledges the 'disparity of care for older people residing in care homes and the housebound' along with 'lower standards of monitoring'.

Personalised care planning

Personalised and integrated care planning is about addressing an individual's full range of needs, taking into account physical and mental health, personal, family, social, economic and educational circumstances, and ethnic and cultural background (DoH, 2009).

NICE (2009) advocates 'patient-centred care' with professionals and patients working in partnership. The National Diabetes Support Team (2008) identifies the benefits to people of personalised care planning as:

* Being more likely to stick with the decisions made, because they have been involved in making them
* Having a better understanding of their condition and the clinician's agenda.

The benefits to health professionals include more satisfying consultations and allowing the individual to take more responsibility.

Table 1. Exception reporting
Exception reporting was introduced into the Quality and Outcomes Framework (QOF) in order to allow practices to pursue the quality improvement agenda and not be penalised, where, for example, patients do not attend for review, or where a medication cannot be prescribed due to a contraindication or side-effect.
From: British Medical Association and NHS Employers, 2006.

The National Diabetes Support Team (2008) highlights that, for personalised care planning to be effective, people must have access to information about services and time to consider their preferences and make decisions that are appropriate to them. Barriers to achieving this include language, literacy, learning difficulties and being housebound or unregistered. To undertake effective personalised care planning requires training and advanced consultation skills. NICE (2011) includes care planning in its quality standards for adults with diabetes, and has published the quality statement 'people with diabetes participate in annual care planning which leads to documented agreed goals and an action plan'. The Year of Care Pilot (2011) reported that the implementation of a care-planning approach results in 'a better experience for people with diabetes and health care professionals alike', and that individuals reported being 'able to address some of the lifestyle issues they may have been struggling with for years'.

Case management

Taylor (2003) found that older people with diabetes living at home or in care homes received inadequate or no diabetes care. To provide a holistic framework of care for such individuals, health and social services professionals need to work together (Smith *et al.*, 1996). Ishani *et al.* (2011) suggested that practitioner case management working using evidence-based treatment algorithms improved multiple cardiovascular risk factors.

Integrated working requires highly-developed communication and collaboration skills. It can be time-consuming and difficult to organise and as more individuals become involved in a person's care, it becomes increasingly complex. One individual, the case manager, is required to take the lead. For integrated working to be successful, all stakeholders must be fully committed and working towards shared goals. Determination and patience are necessary, but rewards are substantial when goals are achieved. The sharing of patient records greatly assists integrated working, so IT solutions should be deployed. In Bhahimbi's case, communication was greatly enhanced as all of the main stakeholders had access to his medical records via SystmOne, a shared patient records system.

The King's Fund (2004) reviewed the costs of case management and found that comparisons were difficult to make, as some studies reported an increase in costs and others a decrease. While practitioners' time commitments escalated, the subsequent reduction in accident and emergency attendances, hospital admissions, risk of hypoglycaemic complications and need for district nursing and community matron visits made case management cost-effective, and potentially cost-saving.

The DoH (2006: 13) reports that, 'intensive, ongoing and personalised case management can improve the quality of life and outcomes for these patients.'

Treating to target and older people

A number of trials investigating the effects of tight blood glucose and blood pressure control suggest that polypharmacy is the route to prevention of diabetic complications (Diabetes Control and Complications Trial [DCCT], 1993; United Kingdom Prospective Diabetes Study [UKPDS] Group, 1998a, 1998b; Kjeldson *et al.*, 1998; Gerstein and Yusuf, 2000). However, trials mostly exclude older adults, who generally have many comorbidities and the effects of ageing. There is scant evidence to support aggressive treatment in this age group. Corsonello *et al.* (1999) found that antihypertensives were not associated with an increased risk of hypoglycaemia in older adults treated with insulin. Svensson *et al.* (2004) focused on acute coronary syndrome, and concluded that avoidance of hyper- and hypoglycaemia in this group was of equal importance. However, Sinclair, (2009) acknowledged that hypoglycaemia in older people can be catastrophic, and symptoms of hypoglycaemia may be wrongly attributed to communication difficulties after a stroke or dementia.

The Diabetes Outcomes in Veterans (DOVE) study (Murata *et al.*, 2003) reported high levels of vascular disease and poor HbA_{1c} levels (>8.0%/63.9mmol/mol) in its older adult population. Poor outcomes were found to be associated with severity of disease, comorbidities, psychosocial and economic factors, as well as lifestyle and psychological indicators, highlighting the need to individualise treatment for older people.

Meneilly (2006) suggested that diabetes in older people is metabolically different to that in younger people and argued that it should, therefore, be treated differently. He called for more research, claiming that there are gaps in our understanding of the progression of diabetes and its appropriate treatment in older people. Diabetes and its vascular, neuropathic and psychological complications cause significant morbidity and mortality across all age groups (Sinclair, 2009). Specifically, Chelliah and Burge (2004) suggested that renal function is often compromised in older people, which interferes with drug elimination and places them at risk of severe hypoglycaemia; the risk of hypoglycaemia is raised in patients taking more than five medications, and those taking ACE inhibitors.

Klepping (2000) discussed the physiological changes which affect drug distribution in older people, namely an increase in fat tissue, reduced body water, decreased lean body mass, and reduced plasma albumin — all of these

---

Case study

Bhahimbi is a 75-year-old Indian man who was diagnosed with type 2 diabetes 24 years ago. He lives alone and has multiple complications — a history of acute myocardial infarction followed by heart failure, acute coronary syndrome, chronic renal failure and polymyalgia rheumatica. His condition is complicated further by social isolation, deprivation and difficulty with English.

Following several hospital admissions for erratic blood glucose control, with both hypo- and hyperglycaemia, his practice nurse referred him to the community diabetes specialist nurse team. His most recent HbA_{1c} was 10% (86mmol/mol). Bhahimbi has hypoglycaemia unawareness and a disparity was found between his insulin regimen and dietary pattern (see *Tables C1* and *C2*).

The diabetes specialist nurse, district nurse and community matron all attended an initial home visit to see Bhahimbi and his daughter, and they liaised with the hospital social worker by telephone. This joint consultation elicited a number of issues to consider for the plan of care.

A personalised care-planning consultation then took place. Bhahimbi's experiences were given equal weight with the health professionals' perspectives. Goals were identified, an agenda was negotiated and actions were agreed upon (*Figure C1*). The care intervention aims were to improve diabetes control while reducing the risk of hypoglycaemia, and to regain a self-caring, independent lifestyle. His insulin was changed to a daily regimen supported with glimepiride.

A 'virtual review' with the GP revealed that Bhahimbi's prednisolone should have been reduced to a maintenance dose of 10mg several months previously. After liaising with the community pharmacist, this was gradually reduced, which brought his blood glucose under control, and target levels were reached. Bhahimbi was able to adopt a more independent lifestyle with minimal professional support.

---

changes predispose older people to adverse drug reactions. Decreased hepatic and renal elimination can also compromise drug metabolism. In recognition of such changes, Louis *et al.* (2005) advised that the glomerular filtration rate (GFR) should be assessed before administering any drug in older people.

Hudson and Boyter (1997) associated poor drug absorption with delayed gastric emptying, disrupting the process by which an oral drug enters the digestive system and is metabolised by the liver (first-pass metabolism) before reaching its target via the circulation. Such factors complicate issues regarding blood glucose control and should evoke caution when prescribing.

Denneboom *et al.* (2007) considered the need to regularly monitor prescribing and medications in older people, suggesting that regular 'treatment reviews with case conferences lead to greater uptake of clinically-relevant recommendations'.

Bhahimbi's story

The care-planning process helped to elicit key points relating to Bhahimbi's diabetes care. He was able to articulate his fear of hypoglycaemia and its possible impact, and avoidance of hypoglycaemia became Bhahimbi's main 'care planning goal'. Further exploration and discussion of his regular eating pattern revealed that he was eating a large number of biscuits and had a stock of 13 bottles of Lucozade, which reflects his skill in adapting to being over-insulinised. Lowe and Raynor (2000) found that non-adherence can be unintentional — for example, it can relate to sensory or manipulation difficulties or to cognitive dysfunction; individuals may sometimes appear confused and causes of non-adherence can remain hidden. However, older people are generally as capable as the young at making rational decisions regarding adherence (Lowe and Raynor, 2000).

Horne *et al.* (2005) suggest that intentional non-adherence develops from past experiences, with beliefs, expectations and fears of side effects impacting on compliance. They reason that intentional non-adherence can be regarded as a form of empowerment. Shilitoe (1994: 63) recommended that health professionals should respect an individual's choices, even if they contradict their professional view. Shilitoe defined empowerment as 'to value and promote [the person's] active participation in management'.

The professionals' story

Health professionals face a dilemma — to reduce the risks of developing complications, they must achieve tight control of blood pressure and blood glucose, but they must avoid hypoglycaemia. While safety is paramount, evidence of the benefits of good control highlights the importance of supporting people to achieve it.

Involving Bhahimbi's daughter made it possible to highlight the importance of the care plan, and facilitated joint decision-making. Working together, the practice nurse and Bhahimbi prioritised the need to avoid hypoglycaemia over the target of 'good diabetes control'.

When Bhahimbi had settled into a daily regimen of insulin detemir 30 units/ml

Table C1. Bhahimbi's diet and routine	
3am	Rises and prepares for mosque
4am	Tea and toast
5–6am	Attends mosque
6–8am	Back to bed
8am	Insulin and cereal
12pm	Curry + chapattis
4pm	Insulin + sandwich
7–8pm	Curry + chapattis
9–10pm	Tea + biscuits
10–3am	Sleep

Table C2. Assessment	
Insulin	
Morning	Novomix 30–60iu
Evening	Novomix 16iu
Supervised by district nurses	
Home blood glucose monitoring ranges	
Before breakfast	5–9mmol/l
Mid-afternoon	1.9mmol/l (hypoglycaemia)
Before evening meal	7–18mmol/l
Injection sites	Abdomen, no evidence of lipohypertrophy

and glimepiride 4mg, his glycaemic control began to deteriorate. There were no obvious reasons for this. A virtual review was conducted by his diabetes specialist nurse (the case manager), the GP and the practice nurse, which included a full medication review.

Bhahimbi had been diagnosed with polymyalgia rheumatica 2 years previously and prednisolone 10mg was being used to treat this. While steroids are considered to be the cornerstone of treatment, lower doses are required for maintenance (Gonzalez-Gay *et al.*, 2006). It was decided that instead of altering his anti-diabetic regimen, his steroid dose should be reduced. This reduction caused no deterioration in health. Polymyalgia rheumatica is self-limiting, and further steroid reductions were possible, which enabled insulin dose reductions.

That the GP and practice nurse were included in Bhahimbi's case management brought his story full circle. He has had many hospital admissions and is under the care of a number of hospital departments. In this complex situation, the person is rarely reviewed holistically, taking all parameters into consideration; each area is usually reviewed independently.

A 'virtual review' with the team requires time and organisation but brings many benefits, including improved understanding of the complexities faced by the team, support for the case manager, true partnership working and improved outcomes.

Following implementation of the actions identified at the care planning consultation and virtual review, Bhahimbi gained independence. He was able to self-inject daily insulin and he started attending reviews with his practice nurse and GP again, negating the need for regular home visits.

Table 2. Suggested components of an effective service for people with diabetes who are dependent and housebound
■ Identification of a dedicated 'diabetes housebound team' including: • Administrator   • Healthcare assistant   • Practice nurse   • GP   • District nurse and/or community matron
■ Register of housebound people with diabetes
■ Administrative recall system to arrange for bloods when due
■ Administrative system to pass on blood results to case manager
■ Identification of 'case manager'
■ Identification by case manager of all key stakeholders
■ Good communication channels with stakeholders
■ Sharing of patient records
■ Joint reviews as appropriate
■ Personalised care-planning reviews
■ Support of GP
■ Adoption of virtual review

Figure C1. Diabetes care plan for Bhahimbi

Individual's story	*Professional's story*
• Fear of severe hypoglycaemia • Fear of hospital admission • Desire to self care and for independent living	• Need to ensure safety • Need to improve diabetes control • Need to reduce complication risk • Aim for self-caring

Learning about diabetes	*Managing diabetes*	*Living with diabetes*	*Other health and social issues*
Change to a non-coding meter with time and date setting. To test before insulin and if feeling 'low'	Home care to prompt regular use of dosette box for oral medications	Update knowledge of recognition and treatment of hypoglycaemia	Review treatment of other conditions

Information shared and discussed

Negotiated agenda
Consideration of safety and avoiding hypoglycaemia outweighs need for tight blood glucose control. Regaining independence and self-caring remain priorities. Need to tailor insulin regimen to pattern of diet, and arrange district nurse support at appropriate times. To keep to same type of insulin pen device to avoid new learning experience. Support and supervision to continue.

Action: Diabetes specialist nurse	*Action: District nurse team*	*Action: Home care team*	*Action: Bhahimbi*
Change insulin to detemir 30 units/ml twice daily (pen device remains as current disposable FlexPen)	Supervise evening insulin dose initially	4pm visit to make drink and ensure evening meal is prepared and planned for 7pm	Try to follow healthy diet, and have fruit for snacks rather than biscuits

Reviewed negotiated agenda
- Gradually reduce steroids to a safe maintenance dose, reassessing impact of reduction regularly
- Liaise with community pharmacist re: changes to dosette box
- Diabetes specialist nurse to make insulin dose reductions, and consider withdrawal of insulin if target blood glucose levels achieved (5–7mmol/l) when taking minimal insulin dose
- Follow-up care: when both polymyalgia rheumatica and diabetes are considered controlled and stable, community matron to make monthly review home visits, with liaison between diabetes specialist nurse as required. Full diabetes review due in 6 months

Conclusions

Personalised care planning balances the health professional's perspective and the individual's concerns and when used as part of an effective multidisciplinary service for people with diabetes who are housebound and who have complex needs, it can have a number of important health benefits (*Table 2*). To plan care in this way permits clarity in complex cases and clear objectives and goals are set, which can be communicated between all of the care providers involved. In Bhahimbi's case this resulted in improved outcomes.

Bhahimbi's case is complex — he has multiple co-morbidities, is housebound, was having frequent hospital admissions with resulting changes in medication, and he also had a language barrier. To address these elements necessitates regular, consistent, holistic care and an understanding of each disease process and its treatment. For multidisciplinary working to be effective, systematic organisation, dedication, persistence and flexibility are necessary from all team members, including the patient and his or her family.

The general practice involved in Bhahimbi's case had a housebound register, a designated housebound team and a recall system, and was supported by record sharing and time allocated for virtual reviews. This is an effective model of care but one that requires understanding and adoption by the whole primary care team. Where specialist teams are based in secondary care, this model may be augmented by sharing records between primary and secondary care.

Key points

- Personalised and integrated care planning enables the full range of an individual's needs to be addressed
- A 'virtual review' (i.e. a comprehensive discussion of a person's case by members of the multidisciplinary team) supports the practice nurse's role and provides evidence of holistic care
- Non-adherence may be intentional as a result of experiences, beliefs, expectations and fear of side effects. It may also be regarded as a form of patient empowerment
- Non-adherence may also be unintentional — it can be a result of sensory and manipulatory difficulties or cognitive dysfunction.

References

British Medical Association, NHS Employers (2006) Guidance on exception reporting. October. http://tinyurl.com/dzeu3d

Chelliah A, Burge M (2004) Hypoglycaemia in elderly patients with diabetes mellitus: causes and strategies for prevention. *Drugs Aging* **21**(8): 511-30

Corsonello et al (1999) Antihypertensive drug therapy and hypoglycaemia in elderly diabetic patients treated with insulin and/or sulfonylurea's. *Eur J Epidemiol* **15**(10): 893-901

Cribb A, Barber N (1997) Prescribers, patients and policy. The limits of technique. *Health Care Analysis* **5**(4): 292-98

Denneboom W et al (2007) Treatment reviews of older people on polypharmacy in primary care: cluster controlled trial comparing two approaches. *Br J Gen Pract* **57**(542): 723-31

Department of Health (2001) National Service Framework for Older People. The Stationery Office, London

Department of Health (2006) Supporting people with long term conditions to self care. DH, London

Department of Health (2009) Supporting People with Long Term Conditions: Commissioning Personalised Care Planning. DH, London

Diabetes Control and Complications Trial Research Group (1993) The effect of intensive treatment of diabetes on the development and progression of long-term complications in insulin-dependent diabetes mellitus. *N Engl J Med* **329**(14): 977-86

Farooqi A, Sorrie R (2005) Monitoring of elderly housebound and mobile diabetic patients in 31 Leicestershire practices: A comparative study. *Practical Diabetes International* **16**(4): 114-16

Forbes et al (1999) Housebound older people are missing out on diabetes care. Nursing Times ISSN: 0954-7762

Gerstein H, Yusuf S (2000) The HOPE study and diabetes. *Lancet* **355**(9210): 1183-84

Gonzalez-Gay M et al (2006) Giant cell arteritis and polymyalgia rheumatica: pathophysiology and management. *Drugs and Ageing* **23**(8): 627-49

Higashi T et al (2005) Quality of care is associated with survival in vulnerable older patients. *Ann Intern Med* **143**: 274-81

Horne R et al (2005) Concordance, Adherence and Compliance in Medicine Taking. Report for the National Co-ordinating Centre for NHS Service Delivery and Organisation R&D (NCCSDO)

Hudson S, Boyter A (1997) Pharmaceutical care of the elderly. *The Pharmaceutical Journal* 259: 686-88

Ishani A et al (2011) Effect of nurse case management compared with usual care on controlling cardiovascular risk factors in patients with diabetes. *Diabetes Care.* **34**(8): 1689-94

The King's Fund (2004) Case-Managing Long-Term Conditions. What Impact Does It Have in the Treatment of Older People? The King's Fund, London

Kjeldsen S et al (1998) Hypertension optimal treatment (HOT) study: home blood pressure in treated hypertensive subjects. *Hypertension* 31: 1014-20

Klepping G (2000) Medication review in elderly care homes. *Primary Care Pharmacy* **1**(4): 105-8

Kyle V, Hazelman B (1993) The clinical and laboratory course of polymyalgia rheumatica/giant cell arteritis after the first two months of treatment. *Ann Rheum Dis* 52: 847-50

Louis et al (2005) Predicting and preventing adverse drug reactions in the very old. *Drugs Aging* **22**(5): 375-92

Lowe C, Raynor D (2000) Intentional non-adherence in elderly patients: fact or fiction? *The Pharmaceutical Journal* 265: R19

Meneilly G (2006) Diabetes in the elderly. *Med Clin North Am* **90**(5): 909-23

Murata G et al (2003) Risk factor management in stable, insulin- treated patients with Type 2 diabetes: The Diabetes Outcomes in Veterans Study. *J Diabetes Complications* **17**(4): 186-91

National Diabetes Support Team (2008) Partners in Care: a guide to implementing a care planning approach to diabetes care. NDST

NHS Diabetes Knowledge and Information Repository (2011) Care Homes, Hospices and Housebound.

National Institute for Health and Clinical Excellence (2009) Type 2 diabetes: newer agents for blood glucose control in type 2 diabetes. Short clinical guideline 87, May. NICE, London

National Institute for Health and Clinical Excellence, 2011. Quality statement for diabetes in adults. NICE, London

Pederson T (1994) Randomised Trial of Cholesterol Lowering in 4444 Patients with Coronary Heart Disease: the Scandinavian Simvastatin Survival Study (4S). *Lancet* 344: 1383-89

Shilitoe R (1994) Counselling People with Diabetes. BPS Books, Leicester

Sinclair, A. (2009). Diabetes in Old Age. 3rd Edition. Chichester: Wiley-Blackwell.

Smith P, Forbes A (1996) Coordinators of care. *Nursing Times* **92**(16): 55-57

Svensson et al (2005) Association between hyper- and hypoglycaemia and 2 year all-cause mortality risk in diabetic patients with acute coronary events. *Eur Heart J* **26**(13): 1255-61

Taylor A (2003) Diabetes care in care homes and for the housebound. *Journal of Diabetes Nursing* November 1

Year of Care, (2011) Report of findings from the pilot programme. London http://www.diabetes.nhs.uk/year_of_care/

United Kingdom Prospective Diabetes Study Group (1998a) Intensive blood-glucose control with sulphonylureas or insulin compared with conventional treatment and risk of complications in patients with type 2 diabetes (UKPDS 33). *Lancet* **352**(9131): 837-53

United Kingdom Prospective Diabetes Study Group (1998b) Effect of intensive blood-glucose control with metformin on complications in overweight patients with type 2 diabetes (UKPDS 34). *Lancet* **352**(9131): 854-65

Chapter 24

Suspecting diabetes in people living with a learning disability

Anne Phillips

Introduction

There has been widespread agreement that people with learning disabilities have poorer health than the rest of the population (Department of Health [DoH], 2008). In the UK, there are 9 million people with some form of learning disability, and it is estimated that 270,000 of these people have type 2 diabetes (Diabetes UK, 2009b).

Compared with the general population, the prevalence of diabetes is much higher in people with learning disabilities such as Down's syndrome (Smith, 2001). It is important for health practitioners to be aware of this association and to know how to ensure that these people receive person-centred care appropriate to their needs.

Health action planning

NHS initiatives such as the learning disabilities White Paper (DoH, 2001) and Valuing People: A New Three Year Strategy for People with Learning Disabilities (DoH, 2008) have paved the way for people living with a learning disability to receive care that is more appropriate to their individual needs. The Valuing People strategy recommends health action planning to deliver individualised care (DoH, 2009). According to the DoH (2002) a health action plan details the actions needed to maintain and improve the health of an individual and any help needed to accomplish these. It is a mechanism to link the individual and the range of services and supports they need, if they are to have better health. This approach to planning care around the needs of the individual is enshrined in the NHS Year of Care for People Living with Diabetes (Centre for Clinical Management Development, 2009).

Where the focus of a consultation is a change in health behaviour, it is essential that the therapeutic alliance between the practitioner and the person is based on respect, empathy and trust. People's health needs must be clearly communicated and addressed. To enable this, the Valuing People White Paper (DoH, 2001) recommended appointing a health facilitator to help practices identify people with learning disabilities, and liaise with primary care services on their behalf. NHS Diabetes (2011) further advocated that people with learning disabilities should be invited for an annual health review within their GP practice, and that screening for diabetes should be a part of this health review.

Learning disability

The term 'learning disability' is used in children and adults to describe difficulty in picking up new skills, both intellectual and social. A learning disability is not a disease or an illness, and is not acquired in adulthood or as a result of injury or disease — a learning disability is evident from childhood. There may be a variety of causes (*Table 1*) but in many cases the cause is unclear.

It can be misleading and inappropriate to label individuals, as each learning disability condition or syndrome has different associated symptoms and behaviours, and the way in which these manifest depends on the individual. To formulate an appropriate health action plan, it is very important to go beyond a mere diagnostic label when defining and categorising a learning disability. Assessment of its impact and the level of support and care required must be based on the individual's needs and social context, not the diagnosis (Rowlinson, 2009).

Table 1. Causes of learning disability
■ **Genetics**
• Fragile X syndrome
• Klinefelter's syndrome
• Tourette's syndrome
■ **Chromosomal abnormalities**
• Down's syndrome
• Prader-Willi syndrome

Down's syndrome

About 1 in every 1000 newborn babies has Down's syndrome. Although antenatal screening has been available in the UK since 1989, the number of babies being born with Down's syndrome has increased since 2000. Figures from the National Down Syndrome Cytogenetic Register show that the proportion of newborns with Down's rose by approximately 15% between 2000 and 2006 (Down's Syndrome Association, 2008); 749 babies with this chromosomal abnormality were born in 2006. Life expectancy for these people is increasing, owing to improved knowledge of the syndrome and its complications and better access to healthcare, for example, through health facilitation (DoH, 2002).

Down's syndrome and diabetes

Insulin resistance can develop many years before there are any symptoms of diabetes. Evidence suggests that, in particular, women with Down's syndrome who are obese show high levels of insulin resistance from adolescence onwards, before diabetes is diagnosed (Van Goor *et al.*, 1997; Roizen and Patterson, 2003).

Health action planning

Sally's experience (*case study*) illustrates how health action planning can be used to facilitate care of the person with Down's syndrome who is at risk of diabetes. Sally has significant risk factors for type 2 diabetes, with impaired fasting glucose (IFG) and elevated total cholesterol and LDL cholesterol. Diabetes UK (2009a) recommends that all those with IFG should be offered lifestyle advice and have an oral glucose tolerance test, to exclude diabetes.

Taken together, Sally's obesity, hypertension, Down's syndrome and evidence of insulin resistance and PCOS put her at high risk of developing type 2 diabetes. A thorough health screen will be necessary to enable the development of a health action plan together with Sally, which will help her to manage her symptoms and reduce her weight and blood pressure and hence, her risk of diabetes.

Communication

It is important to use plain language and pictures when communicating with people with learning disabilities, such as Sally, to facilitate their understanding and participation in health decision-making (DoH, 2007). Health professionals

Case study

Sally is 24 years old and works at a local horticultural nursery. Sally has Down's syndrome, and since her mid-teens she has been gaining weight. She lives at home with her older adult parents; she is their only child. Sally has a boyfriend, who also works at the nursery. Sally attends the surgery with Amy, her health facilitator, to discuss contraception.

Sally cannot read or write, and she needs help with interpreting instructions and planning her work at the nursery. The practice nurse knows Sally well, so she keeps all the information clear and uses plain language and pictures to help Sally understand and take part in making decisions about her health. Sally has insight into her situation, and is able to discuss her options with the practice nurse.

Sally's health facilitator, Amy, works with Sally's health professionals to help her gain access to health services and have her individual health needs met.

Over the last 10 years, Sally has developed central obesity and her body mass index is now $31 kg/m^2$. Her blood pressure is elevated, at 138/78mmHg. Amy and the practice nurse are concerned because Sally's Down's syndrome, obesity and hypertension all increase her risk of developing type 2 diabetes. The practice nurse decides to conduct a full preventive health screen, as insulin resistance can develop without clinical signs long before diabetes is diagnosed.

The practice nurse begins by talking to Sally about contraception. She learns that Sally likes her boyfriend Phil very much, and would like to have a sexual relationship with him. However, Sally expresses concern about her parents, who are unwell, and she knows that she needs to stay with them as when she is not working at the nursery she helps them at home. The practice nurse asks Sally about her periods. Sally reports having very occasional bleeds and that these happen about three times a year.

With Sally's permission, the practice nurse takes some blood to review her cholesterol, triglycerides, blood glucose, HbA_{1c}, full blood count, urea and electrolytes and thyroid function (*Table C1*). Sally's results include markers suggestive of insulin resistance. Sally also requires an oral glucose tolerance test.

The practice nurse notices that Sally has developed some facial hirsutism and acne, signs of polycystic ovary syndrome in the presence of obesity. The practice nurse tests for luteinising hormone (LH), follicle stimulating hormone (FSH), testosterone and sex hormone-binding globulin. Ideally, this test should be conducted in the first week of the menstrual cycle but as Sally has infrequent must ensure that care plans include goals that the person chooses, as well as relevant and appropriate advice (Morton, 2009). A health facilitator can help with creating a health action plan (Coding and Solomon, 2007).

Thyroid function

About 10% of women develop a thyroid problem at some time in their lives; thyroid problems are less common in men (Rubello *et al.*, 1995). In half of people with Down's syndrome, thyroid disease develops before the age of 8 years. Of the remaining population with Down's syndrome, over 8 years, a further 30% will develop thyroid disorders before the age of 25 years. As Sally is 24 years old, it is worth testing her thyroid function.

periods, opportunistic testing is valid. Her LH:FSH ratio is 5:1, which is suggestive of PCOS.

The practice nurse completes the consultation by offering advice on nutrition, weight loss and physical activity and scheduling a follow-up appointment.

Table C1. Sally's significant blood test results

Blood test	Normal value	Sally's result	Clinical indication
Total cholesterol	<4mmol/l	6.5mmol/l	Sally has depressed HDL cholesterol, and elevated total and LDL cholesterol, which suggests hyperlipidaemia, a CVD risk factor and insulin resistance
	HDL	*HDL*	
	>1.2mmol/l	*<0.8mmol/l*	
	LDL	*LDL*	
	<3mmol/l	*3mmol/l*	
Uric acid	110–360µmol/l	358µmol/l	Elevated uric acid levels increase the risk of CVD and diabetes
Fasting plasma glucose (FPG)	3.5–5.5mmol/l	6.8mmol/l	Sally has impaired fasting glucose (defined as FPG of 6.1–7mmol/l)

HDL = high density lipoprotein; LDL = low density lipoprotein.

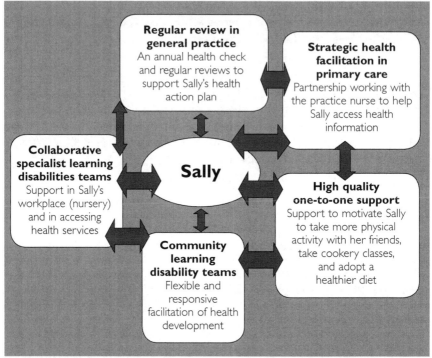

Figure 1. The health action planning model (DoH, 2009) adapted for Sally

Polycystic ovary syndrome

Polycystic ovary syndrome (PCOS) is a common disorder and its associated symptoms include glucose intolerance and insulin resistance, which are strong possible precursors of diabetes (Bacha *et al.*, 2009). Acne, obesity and hirsutism are all signs of PCOS.

An elevated ratio of luteinising hormone (LH) to follicle stimulating hormone (FSH), usually greater than 3:1, supports the diagnosis of PCOS. In PCOS, serum LH is raised and serum FSH is lower than in a normal menstrual cycle. However, Cho *et al.* (2005) found that the ratio of LH to FSH varied as much in women with normal ovaries as it did in those with PCOS. Metformin can reduce the LH:FSH ratio to 1:1.

Testing for PCOS should include testosterone, although serum testosterone seldom exceeds 4.8nmol/l in women with PCOS. A testosterone level above 4.8nmol/litre indicates further endocrinological investigations to exclude other causes of androgen hypersecretion (e.g. Cushing's syndrome, adrenal and ovarian tumours) (Bacha *et al.*, 2009; Balen *et al.*, 1995).

Hyperinsulinaemia is recognised as a fundamental disturbance of PCOS in many women — a subgroup have 'metabolic PCOS' which can be considered a pre-diabetes state. Clinically, this subgroup is most easily identified by their central obesity, strong family history of diabetes and menstrual disturbance (Kelly, 2000). On checking Sally's family history, it is revealed that her maternal grandmother had type 2 diabetes.

To lower the risk of women with PCOS developing diabetes and coronary artery disease in later life, it may be necessary to consider measures to reduce insulin resistance at an earlier stage. The incidence of insulin resistance is higher in women with PCOS, whether they are obese or not. In Sally's case, where the risk of developing diabetes is raised further by having Down's syndrome, the importance of effective partnership working and health action planning cannot be overemphasised (DoH, 2002).

An important complicating factor in PCOS is that some cell types may develop insulin resistance (most commonly muscle and fat) whereas others may not. Hence, the ovaries, pituitary and adrenal glands of women with insulin resistance are stimulated by far higher levels of insulin than desired, which causes elevated LH and androgens — a phenomenon which is referred to as 'selective resistance' (Book and Dunaif, 1999).

To treat insulin resistance and PCOS, the drug of choice is metformin (see *Table 2*).

Table 2. Actions of metformin in insulin resistance and polycystic ovary syndrome
■ Decreases the absorption of dietary carbohydrates through the intestines
■ Reduces the production of glucose by the liver
■ Increases the sensitivity of muscle cells to insulin, and helps the body to transport glucose with relatively less insulin, thus lowering circulating insulin levels
■ Appears to reduce insulin, testosterone and glucose levels, which in PCOS can reduce acne, hirsuitism, abdominal obesity, amenorrhoea and other symptoms, and promote regular ovulation
From: Tsilchorozidou et al, 2002.

Contraception

Metformin facilitates regular ovulation in women with PCOS, which increases the likelihood of conception (Tsilchorozidou *et al.*, 2002). The common contraception options for these women are the progestogen-only pill and progestogen injection. For a woman with a learning disability such as Sally, a dosette box can be used to ensure that she takes the progestogen-only pill as indicated, along with any other medications (metformin in Sally's case).

Conclusions

Sally's review and screening enable significant risk factors to be identified and Sally, Amy and the practice nurse work together with the community learning disability team to formulate an achievable health action plan, which is reviewed at regular intervals (*Figure 1*). The practice nurse liaises with Amy and the community learning disability team, which works with Sally and supports her and her parents at home, and shares the information that Sally needs treatment for her insulin resistance and help losing weight and keeping physically active. The community learning disability team organises a successful walking club for people with learning disabilities and Sally expresses a wish to take part when she is told about this. She also mentions that she would like to learn how to cook, so the team facilitates her attendance at a cookery club which promotes healthy eating.

The community learning disability team liaises with Sally, Amy and the practice nurse about an afternoon session to inform people with learning disabilities about diabetes and their risk factors. At this session, pictures and multimedia tools are used to help communicate health information in a timely and appropriate manner.

It is important that health services are made accessible to people with learning disabilities. The identification of significant risk factors for pre-diabetes, as in Sally's case, provides an ideal opportunity for health promotion advice and health action planning, which involves the person in decision making and enables their understanding of how to manage their health more effectively.

DVD for people with learning disabilities and diabetes
Diabetes UK in partnership with Speakup (2009) have produced a DVD for people with learning disabilities which covers a range of topics including an explanation of what type 2 diabetes is, how to prevent it, how to manage and understand it, and the benefits of healthy eating and physical activity. This DVD is available free online at: https://www.diabetes.org.uk/OnlineShop/

Key points

- Working in partnership with people with learning disabilities can facilitate successful health action planning
- Diagnosis of pre-diabetes provides an opportunity for health action planning to help people improve their long-term health
- Screening for insulin resistance can highlight opportunities for health promotion.

References

Balen A et al (1995) Polycystic Ovary Syndrome: the Spectrum of the Disorder in 1741 Patients. *Hum Reproduction* **10**(8): 2107-11

Bacha F et al (2009) What are the differences between normal glucose tolerance, impaired glucose tolerance, and type 2 diabetes? *Diabetes Care* **32**(1): 100-5

Book C, Dunaif A (1999) Selective insulin resistance in the polycystic ovary syndrome. *J Clin Endocrinol Metab* **84**(9): 3110-16

Centre for Clinical Management Development (2009) Definition of Year of Care. www. dur.ac.uk/ ccmd/yoc/definition

Cho L et al (2005) The Biological Variation of those with LH/FSH Ratio in Normal Women and Those with Polycystic Ovarian Syndrome. *Endocrine Abstracts* 9: 80

Coding M, Solomon J (2007) Evaluating Health Checks. *Learning Disability Practice* **10**(4): 32-38

Department of Health (2001) Valuing People: A New Strategy for Learning Disability for the 21st Century. White Paper, 20 March. The Stationery Office, London

Department of Health (2002) Action for Health: Health Action Plans and Health Facilitation. The Stationery Office, London

Department of Health (2007) Good Practice Guidance on Working with Parents with a Learning Disability. The Stationery Office, London

Department of Health (2008) Valuing People Now: A New Three Year Strategy of People with Learning Disabilities. The Stationery Office, London

Department of Health (2009) Health Action Planning and Health Facilitation for People with Learning Disabilities: Good Practice Guidance. March. The Stationery Office, London

Down's Syndrome Association (2008) Births with Down's syndrome increase. 24 November www.downs-syndrome.org.uk/news-and-media/press- releases/2008/487-births-increase.html

Diabetes UK (2009a) Care recommendations: New diagnostic criteria for diabetes. http://tinyurl.com/yf3adg2

Diabetes UK (2009b) Diabetes UK launches DVD to help people with learning disabilities. Press release, 23 April. http://tinyurl.com/cus6qd

Kelly G (2000) Insulin resistance: lifestyle and nutritional interventions. *Altern Med Rev* **5**(2): 109-32

Morton A (2009) Celebrating the year of care. [Suppl: Diabetes Year of Care: Roadmap for Partnership: Putting Patients in Charge.] *Health Service Journal* 12 March (Suppl): 1-13

NHS Diabetes (2011) Commissioning for people with learning disabilities who have diabetes, June, NHS Diabetes.

Roizen N, Patterson D (2003) Down's syndrome. *Lancet* **361**(9365): 1281-89

Rowlinson J (2009) About learning disabilities. www.aboutlearningdisabilities.co.uk

Rubello D et al (1995) Natural course of subclinical hypothyroidism in Down's syndrome: prospective study results and therapeutic considerations. *J Endocrinol Invest* **18**(1): 35-40

Smith D (2001) Health Care Management of Adults with Downs Syndrome. *Am Fam Physician* **64**(6): 1031-38

Tsilchorozidou T et al (2002) Efficacy of metformin for ovulation induction in polycystic ovary syndrome. *Endocrine Abstracts* 3: P228. www.endocrine-abstracts.org/ea/0003/ea0003p228.htm

Van Goor G et al (1997) Increased incidence and prevalence of diabetes mellitus in Down's syndrome. *Arch Dis Child* **77**(2): 183

Chapter 25

Supporting people with diabetes-related stress, anxiety and depression

Phil Holdich and Dr Warren Gillibrand

Introduction

Psychological distress and depression can affect a person's motivation and ability to cope with diabetes self-management (Snoek and Skinner, 2006; Katon *et al.*, 2010), impacting on adherence to prescribed medications, appropriate diet, physical activity and blood glucose monitoring (Fisher *et al.*, 2007; Gonzalez *et al.*, 2007). People with diabetes and comorbid mental health problems such as depression can have poorer glycaemic control and a higher risk of morbidity and mortality (Williams *et al.*, 2004; Fisher *et al.*, 2007; Katon *et al.*, 2010).

Studies such as the DAWN (Diabetes Attitudes Wishes and Needs) study (Alberti, 2002) have shown that many nurses and physicians do not recognise depression, anxiety and emotional problems in people with diabetes (Alberti, 2002; Pouwer *et al.*, 2005). Health professionals are often preoccupied with metabolic outcomes (Alberti, 2002), while people with diabetes have to achieve a balance between keeping well and living a normal life (Dunning, 2009). The practitioner should be supportive and help the person with diabetes to maintain this balance (Dunning, 2009). All health professionals should be aware of potential mental health issues in people with diabetes.

Assessing care needs

Recognising and managing anxiety, stress and depression may be associated with improved function and better outcomes in people with long-term conditions such as diabetes (National Institute for Health and Clinical Excellence [NICE], 2009); careful, sensitive questioning and good listening skills can help. The importance of good management is illustrated by the case of Mrs Jones (see *case study*). Although she is not necessarily clinically depressed, the loss of her husband, early signs of complications (retinal changes) and a comorbid illness (hypothyroidism) may have psychological and physical effects on her diabetes management.

Gonzalez *et al.* (2007) reported that non-adherence to diabetes treatment is associated with depression. Furthermore, a comorbid, long-term condition may exacerbate mood changes and anxiety in people with diabetes, and compromise self-management (Piette and Kerr, 2006).

Although it may come as no surprise that trying to manage more than one condition can impact on diabetes, this factor can be overlooked by health professionals (Piette and Kerr, 2006; Katon *et al.*, 2010). It is of particular consideration in older adults, as the risk of having more than one long-term condition increases exponentially with age (Department of Health, 2008).

Bruce *et al.* (2005), who reported the incidence of depression and mortality for the Fremantle Diabetes Study (a prospective study of patients with type 2 diabetes) suggested a correlation between the development of diabetic complications and the onset of depression. However, the aetiology of diabetes-related depression remains unclear; it is not known if it develops physiologically (for example, by increasing counter-regulatory hormones) or as a result of the

---

Case study

Mrs Susan Jones is a 63-year-old woman who has had type 2 diabetes for 15 years. Until her husband died last year, she had been a regular attender at the practice diabetes clinic, but she has missed her last two appointments before attending this time. She is usually a talkative and active lady, with well-controlled diabetes. However, today she appears tired and uncommunicative and her weight has increased significantly. Her eyes were screened over a year ago, finding background retinopathy. She has hypothyroidism for which she takes levothyroxine 50mg.

Table C1. Susan's biometric data and current medication	
Biometric data	**Current medication**
HbA$_{1c}$ 10.2% (88mmol/mol)	metformin 500mg, twice daily gliclazide 80mg, twice daily
Cholesterol 5.4mmol/litre	
Blood pressure 146/82mmHg	

psychological burden of disease.

Williams *et al.* (2004) suggested that effective care for depression may impact positively on self-care ability and, ultimately, on health outcomes. However, in order to help Mrs Jones it is important to assess her mental state using a simple screening tool for depression.

Anxiety and depression

Cohen *et al.* (1994) identified that while health practitioners can focus more on the physical impact of diabetes, people living with the disease can experience its psychological effects more than its physical effects. The UK National Psychiatric Morbidity Survey (Das-Munshi *et al.*, 2007) found that common mental disorders, including anxiety and depression, were more common in people with diabetes; they also found associations with female gender, recent life events (in the past 6 months), comorbid physical illness and disability. This reinforces the need to identify vulnerable individuals, such as Mrs Jones, who may be at risk of developing mental health problems.

The issue of people with diabetes experiencing anxiety as a psychological outcome has received some debate in the literature (Ridder *et al.,* 2009). Indeed, anxiety in diabetes was first delineated as a major theme by one of this chapter's authors, in a qualitative study of people with type 1 and type 2 diabetes (Gillibrand and Flynn 2001). Low levels of anxiety have been reported in a number of different contexts, which suggests the involvement of both environmental (service intervention) and personal (patient-oriented) factors (Adriaasne *et al.*, 2002). Because anxiety is often linked with other diabetes-related psychosocial issues, including stress, coping and depression, its own impact on quality of life is sometimes overlooked. Health professionals should regularly explore the personal perspectives of people with diabetes. In a study of people with type 1 and type 2 diabetes, it was found that younger participants with type 2 diabetes were most likely to report anxiety (Karlsen *et al.*, 2002). Early intervention may prevent anxiety escalating.

Macrodimitris and Endler (2001) examined condition-specific coping strategies and how they relate to glycaemic control and psychological outcomes in type 2 diabetes. They found that emotional preoccupation and palliative coping were associated with anxiety and depression, whereas perceived control was associated with a reduction in anxiety and depression and better glycaemic control. Perceived control was considered key to psychological and physical adjustment, which highlights the importance of psychological issues in diabetes care.

Depressive illness and diabetes-related stress

A major depressive episode can be persistent and debilitating (NICE, 2009). When compared with the general population, depression is twice as common in people with diabetes and two to three times more common in women (Anderson *et al.*, 2001; Rubin *et al.*, 2004; Bruce *et al.*, 2005; Katon *et al.*, 2010). It often goes unrecognised by the person affected and practitioners alike and is under-diagnosed and under-treated in as many as 50% of cases (Anderson *et al.*, 2001; Rubin *et al.*, 2004). However, not all people with diabetes who present with depressive-type symptoms are clinically depressed; some may be experiencing emotional and diabetes-related distress (Fisher *et al.*, 2007). Furthermore, screening tools for depression may not detect emotional stress that is specific to living with a long-term condition such as diabetes (Fisher *et al.*, 2007). Indeed, Gilbody *et al.* (2006) found that cross-sectional surveys of depression identified people who were experiencing 'transient distress', which would often resolve within a few weeks. This supports the recommendation to 'watch and wait' before intervention in those identified as having 'mild' depression (NICE, 2009). Furthermore, NICE (2009) describes depression as a 'broad and heterogeneous diagnosis'; for people with diabetes, this may be within a range of different types of emotional distress and poor psychological wellbeing (Alberti, 2002). Symptoms may range from persistent sadness to suicidal ideation (*Table 1*). The main characteristics are a marked lowering of mood and a loss of interest or pleasure in usual activities (anhedonia). These characteristics may be indicated by the person's responses to two simple screening questions (see below).

Table 1. Symptoms of depression
■ Persistent, sad, irritable or 'empty' mood
■ Loss of interest in activities once enjoyed, including sexual intercourse
■ Significant change in appetite or body weight
■ Difficulty in sleeping, waking early or oversleeping
■ Feelings of worthlessness, helplessness or guilt
■ Decreased energy, fatigue or feeling 'lacklustre'
■ Restlessness and irritability
■ Difficulty concentrating and remembering
■ Recurring thoughts of death or suicide
From: National Institute of Health and Clinical Excellence, 2009

Screening

There are a number of screening tools for psychological and emotional health. While many of these have research value, they can be unwieldy for use in practice. Furthermore, when people are expecting a practitioner to help them manage the physical symptoms of their diabetes, it may appear threatening and inappropriate to introduce a psychological inventory (Hermanns *et al.*, 2006). Practitioners should be aware of this when asking about mood. To lead into psychological questioning, they may begin with questions about how the person with diabetes feels about his or her diabetes, such as:

- How are you finding living with diabetes?
- Do you think that the way you are feeling affects your self-care (such as diet, monitoring and exercise)?
- Are there other aspects of your life that are taking priority at the moment?

Once this type of dialogue is established, it may then be appropriate to introduce some specific questions that may help to identify any depressive illness (NICE, 2009):

- During the past month, have you often been bothered by feeling down, depressed or hopeless?
- During the past month, have you often been bothered by having little interest or pleasure in doing things?

NICE (2009) and Katon *et al.* (2010) advise caution, to avoid a 'symptom count'. However, if the person answers 'yes' to either of these questions, the person should be referred to an experienced mental health assessor, who can review the individual's mental state and physical and social functioning, to identify if he or she is likely to have a depressive illness. A more comprehensive assessment may be implemented using the Diagnostic and Statistical Manual of Mental Disorders (DSM-IV) inventory of depressive symptoms (American Psychiatric Association, 1994) (*Table 2*).

Initial management

Mrs Jones has a number of risk factors for depression, which may alert health practitioners to explore whether or not she is depressed (Pouwer, 2009). As an older woman with diabetes she fits a high-risk profile, and she has recently had a major life event (her husband's death) (Phillips and Wright, 2010). Mrs Jones is likely to be grieving and she may benefit from counselling if she is finding this

Table 2. Definitions of depression (from DSM-IV*)	
Sub-threshold depressive symptoms	Fewer than five symptoms of depression
Mild depression	Few, if any, symptoms in excess of the five required to make the diagnosis, and symptoms result in only minor functional impairment
Moderate depression	Symptoms or functional impairment are between 'mild' and 'severe'
*DSM-IV is published by the American Psychiatric Association (1994) From: National Institute of Health and Clinical Excellence, 2009	

difficult to cope with. She also has a comorbid condition (hypothyroidism) and early diabetic eye disease. She may need to be given an opportunity to discuss how she perceives her future and what she feels she can do to reduce the onset of diabetic retinopathy.

Physiological problems can influence and be influenced by mental state, and any such problems need to be addressed. For example, hypothyroidism can contribute to weight gain and general lethargy, which can affect motivation; a thyroid function test might reveal that Mrs Jones' levothyroxine needs to be increased. Hyperglycaemia can also affect energy levels and motivation, and can either cause or be caused by low mood. Another possibility is that Mrs Jones may not be adhering to her medications; exploring if and how she takes her oral hypoglycaemic medications, together with her current food intake and activity level, should reveal whether or not they are working effectively.

A change in treatment is recognised as a risk factor for depression in diabetes (Katon *et al.*, 2010) and should be avoided unless indicated (for example, where metformin is not tolerated). However, in Mrs Jones' case, there is scope to increase the dose of metformin to 1g twice daily and gliclazide to 160mg twice daily.

Despite her increase in weight, it is probably unhelpful to estimate Mrs Jones' body mass index at this stage, as this is likely to reinforce her low mood. The focus should be on exploring her current eating habits and where she feels she might be able to make some small and achievable changes.

While it may appear that Mrs Jones is unable to cope with her diabetes, it might be possible to identify and reinforce some of her personal strengths, which may impact positively on self-care.

Coping

Fisher *et al.* (2007) and Katon *et al.* (2010) suggested that when addressing personal and diabetes-related stress, practical problem solving and the reinforcement of coping strategies are likely to be more meaningful and effective than treatments specific to depression.

Miller (2000) described how people with long-term conditions respond to stressors across various domains, which she refers to as 'power resources' (*Figure 1*). She describes that these power resources may be weakened by the experience of having a long-term condition and that through recognising and understanding what they are, health practitioners are able to provide more useful and specific support, enabling people like Mrs Jones to better manage their diabetes during periods of emotional distress.

Figure 1. Coping strategies and power resources. From Miller (2000).

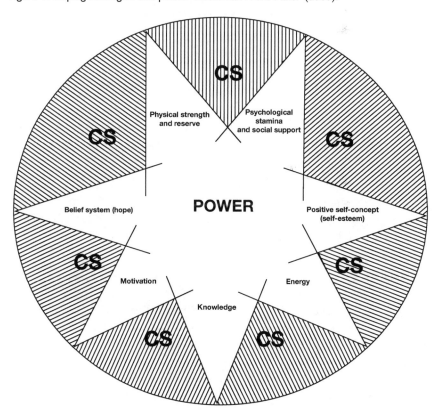

Some relatively simple interventions may be helpful, such as helping Mrs Jones to recognise and understand her low mood, while reassuring her that what she is feeling is quite common and will usually subside. Her diabetes is not well-controlled, so she will feel lethargic and generally unwell. Helping her to reduce her blood glucose levels may improve her 'energy levels' and motivation. She has clearly been successful at managing her diabetes previously, and discussing this with her may help to improve her self-esteem.

Figure 2. The 'step' approach to managing depression

Focus of the intervention	Nature of the intervention
STEP 4: Severe and complex* depression; risk to life; severe self-neglect	Medication, high-intensity psychological interventions, electroconvulsive therapy, crisis service, combined treatments, multiprofessional and inpatient care
STEP 3: Persistent subthreshold depressive symptoms or mild to moderate depression with inadequate response to initial interventions; moderate and severe depression	Medication, high-intensity psychological interventions, combined treatments, collaborative care† and referral for further assessment and interventions
Step 2: Persistent subthreshold depressive symptoms; mild to moderate depression	Low-intensity psychosocial interventions, medication and referral for further assessment and interventions
Step 1: All known and suspected presentations of depression	Assessment, support, psychoeducation, active monitoring and referral for further assessment and interventions

*Complex depression includes depression that shows an inadequate response to multiple treatments, is complicated by psychotic symptoms, and/or is associated with significant psychiatric comorbidity or psychosocial factors.

†Only for depression where the person also has a chronic physical health problem and associated functional impairment.

From: National Institute for Health and Clinical Excellence, 2009

These are positive interventions that do not require specialist input, although support or supervision from a specialist practitioner is helpful (Pouwer, 2009).

Through understanding self-efficacy and coping skills and by helping individuals to recognise and manage stressors, practitioners can support people with diabetes during periods of distress and low mood. Some techniques are borrowed from cognitive behavioural therapy approaches and require some skill and practice, but should be within the remit of motivated care providers for people with diabetes (Peyrot and Rubin, 2007). However, for those individuals who screen positive for depression, there is specific guidance for the management of the condition (NICE, 2009).

Management options

NICE (2009) recommends a 'step' approach to the management of depression. Based on best evidence, this guides management in relation to the severity of depressive symptoms (*Figure 2*). The best management depends on a person-centred approach to care, which enables openness and trust between the health professional and the person with diabetes.

Initially, non-drug therapies are favoured for all but persistent or severe depression. Indeed, 'watchful waiting' may be adequate for subclinical or mild depression — so long as the health professional remains in contact with the person. Ideally, there should be a follow-up clinic appointment or a phone call within the first 2 weeks.

More formal management may require referral for 'talking therapies', such as cognitive behavioural therapy (which focuses on the thinking patterns that cause symptoms) or counselling and psychotherapy (which explore concerns and relationships and encourage personal reflection).

A range of antidepressants may be used in people with diabetes, including selective serotonin reuptake inhibitors (SSRIs), which are associated with less weight gain and some improvement in insulin sensitivity (Rubin *et al.*, 2008). However, to avoid side effects and problems relating to early withdrawal, careful monitoring and management are required.

Adjunctive treatments which can also be helpful include exercise and strategies to improve sleep patterns, such as avoiding alcohol and excessive eating at bedtime (NICE, 2009).

Conclusions

There is good evidence for psychological, social and physical interventions that health practitioners can implement to support the person with diabetes-related stress or depression. Primary care is well-positioned to offer these people comprehensive care. However, care is often suboptimal as a result of poor recognition of depression, inadequate management (for example, a lack of integration with specialist mental health services) and inconsistent monitoring (Williams *et al.*, 2004; Gilbody *et al.*, 2006).

This may be improved by more systematic educational interventions involving combined case management and integration with secondary care (National Prescribing Centre, 2005; Gilbody *et al.*, 2006). In the shared care of people with diabetes who have complex needs, this is a logical extension of good practice.

Key points

- Psychological distress can impact profoundly on diabetes self-management
- Screening for anxiety, depression and diabetes-related distress requires sensitive questioning
- The support of health professionals is vital for good management and recovery
- NICE (2009) recommends a 'step' approach for the management of depression.

References

Adriaanse, M et al (2002), Screening for Type 2 diabetes: an exploration of subjects' perceptions regarding diagnosis and procedure. *Diabetic Medicine* 5: 406-11

Alberti G (2002) The DAWN (Diabetes Attitudes, Wishes and Needs) Study. *Pract Diabetes Int* 19: 22-24

American Psychiatric Association (1994) Diagnostic and Statistical Manual of Mental Disorders. 4th edn (DSM-IV). APA, Washington

Anderson R et al (2001) The prevalence of comorbid depression in adults with diabetes. A meta-analysis. *Diabetes Care* 24(6): 1069-78

Bruce D et al (2005) A prospective study of depression and mortality in patients with type 2 diabetes: the Fremantle Diabetes Study. *Diabetologia* 48: 2532-39

Cohen M et al (1994), Explanatory Models of Diabetes - Patient Practitioner Variation. *Social Science & Medicine* 38(1): 59-66

Das-Munshi J et al (2007) Diabetes, Common Mental Disorders, and Disability: Findings From the UK National Psychiatric Morbidity Survey. *Psychosomatic Medicine* 69: 543-50

Department of Health (2008) Raising the Profile of Long-Term Conditions Care. A Compendium of Information. DH, London

Dunning T (2009) Care of People with Diabetes. A Manual of Nursing Practice. 3rd edn. Wiley Blackwell, Chichester

Fisher L et al (2007) Clinical depression vs distress among patients with type 2 diabetes. Not just a question of semantics. *Diabetes Care* 30: 542-48

Gilbody S, Sheldon T, Wesley S (2006) Health policy: should we screen for depression? *BMJ* 332: 1027-30

Gillibrand W, Flynn M (2001) Forced externalisation of control in people with diabetes: a qualitative exploratory study, *J Adv Nurs* **34**(4): 501-10

Gonzalez J et al (2007) Depression, self-care and medication adherence in type 2 diabetes: relationships across the full range of symptom severity. *Diabetes Care* **30**(9): 2222-27

Hermanns N et al (2006) How to screen for depression and emotional problems in patients with diabetes: comparison of screening characteristics of depression questionnaires, measurement of diabetes-specific emotional problems and standard clinical assessment. *Diabetologia* 49: 469-77

Karlsen B, Bru E, Hanestad B (2002) Self-reported psychological well-being and disease-related strains among adults with diabetes. *Psychology and Health* **17**(4): 459-73

Katon W, Maj M, Sartorius N (2010) Depression and Diabetes, Wiley Blackwell, UK

Macrodimitris S, Endler N (2001) Coping, control, and adjustment in Type 2 diabetes. *Health Psychology* **20**(3): 208-16

Miller J (2000) Coping with Chronic Illness: Overcoming Powerlessness. 3rd edn. FA Davis Company, Philadelphia

National Prescribing Centre (2005) The management of depression in primary care. MeReC Briefing. Issue No. 31. NPC/NHS, London

National Institute for Health and Clinical Excellence (2009) Depression in Adults with a Chronic, Physical Health Problem. Treatment and Management. Clincal Guideline 91. NICE, London

Peyrot M, Rubin R (2007) Behavioral and psychosocial interventions in diabetes. *Diabetes Care* **30**(10): 2433-40

Phillips A, Wright J (2010) Recognising the impact of mental well being on self-management of physical conditions. *British Journal of Wellbeing* 1(6): 30-35

Piette J, Kerr E (2006) The impact of co-morbid, chronic conditions on diabetes care. *Diabetes Care* 29(3): 725-31

Pouwer F (2009) Should we screen for emotional distress in type 2 diabetes mellitus? *Nature Rev Endocrinol* 5: 665-71

Pouwer F et al (2005) Nurses' recognition and registration of depression, anxiety and diabetes-specific emotional problems in outpatients with diabetes mellitus. *Patient Educ Counsel* 60(2): 235-40

Ridder D et al (2008) Psychological adjustment to chronic disease. *Lancet* 372(9634): 246-55

Rubin R et al (2008) Elevated depression symptoms, antidepressant medicine use and risk of developing diabetes during the Diabetes Prevention Programme. *Diabetes Care* 31(3): 420-26

Rubin R et al (2004) Recognizing and treating depression in patients with diabetes. *Curr Diabetes Rep* 4(2): 119-25

Snoek F, Skinner T (2006) Psychological aspects of diabetes management. *Medicine* 34(2): 61-62

Williams J et al (2004) The effectiveness of depression care management on diabetes-related outcomes in older patients. *Ann Intern Med* 140: 1015-24

Chapter 26

Diabetes and older people: ensuring individualised practice

Stephen Phillips

Introduction

Diabetes mellitus is increasingly common in older people — partly because diabetes outcomes and risk management strategies have improved (Hawthorne, 2009) and partly because people are living longer and healthier lives (Office for National Statistics [ONS], 2011).

This chapter investigates the impact of diabetes in older people and the ethical considerations when making decisions regarding the care of older people (Reed *et al.*, 2004). It is important, but sometimes difficult, to balance a person's individual needs with the need to achieve national targets for diabetes, such as those in the Quality and Outcomes Framework (QOF) (British Medical Association, 2011).

To do no harm and achieve good outcomes, care must be person-centred and not target-driven. Practice nurses, GPs and community nurses are at the forefront of providing older people with individualised diabetes care, and this chapter explores the determinants of this care.

Prevalence

Diabetes is being diagnosed at an increasing rate across the whole population, but especially in the older population (Sinclair, 2009). It is estimated that there are over 3 million people aged 16 years and over with diabetes in England (a prevalence of 7.4%) and almost one third of these people may remain undiagnosed (Yorkshire and Humber Public Health Observatory [YHPHO], 2010). In Scotland, its prevalence is 6.7% and in Wales it is 9% (YHPHO, 2010). Owing to rising rates of obesity and an ageing population, the prevalence of diabetes in the UK is expected to continue to increase (YHPHO, 2010).

Demographics

It has been estimated that by 2034, roughly 87,900 people in the UK will be aged over 100 years (ONS, 2011). The Nursing and Midwifery Council expects this figure to reach 250,000 by 2050 (NMC, 2009). The ONS (2011) has revealed that at least one quarter of the UK's population is currently aged 50 years or more, and that by 2031 more than 1 in 5 members of the UK population (about 15.8 million older people) will be aged 65 years or more. There are associations between age and increased incidence of type 2 diabetes and comorbidities of diabetes (Williams, 2009); 14.3% of people with diabetes are aged between 55–74 years, and 16.5% are over 75 years (YHPHO, 2010). Diabetes UK (2010) estimates that someone with diabetes is admitted to hospital from residential care every 25 minutes. These demographic and disease prevalence changes have substantial implications for the health of the older population and the work of diabetes primary care teams.

Impact of diabetes on older people

Although the prevalence of hypertension and hypercholesterolaemia and the incidence of mortality from cardiovascular and cerebrovascular disease are markedly declining, the prevalence of diabetes remains high and is expected to rise further, especially in the older population (King *et al.*, 1998; Allender *et al.*, 2008).

Diabetes, together with its vascular, neurological and psychological complications, causes significant morbidity and mortality across all age groups. As diabetes becomes increasingly common in older people, some of its under-appreciated complications need to be addressed (Sinclair *et al.*, 2009; Sinclair, 2011). These include cognitive disorders (such as dementia), physical disabilities that can cause or be caused by falls, fractures, and other conditions that are common in older people, such as arthritis (Schwartz *et al.*, 2001; Gregg *et al.*, 2002; Jolley, 2009).

These less well-recognised complications impair quality of life, lead to a loss of independence, increase the demands on ageing caregivers, and may be of greater concern to older people with diabetes than more commonly-recognised vascular and neurological complications (Gregg *et al.*, 2002).

Communicating risks

The risks of diabetic complications increase with the duration of diabetes. Therefore, self-care strategies are important in older adults, where risks are likely to be high (Hewitt *et al.*, 2011). For realistic and safe care planning, older people need to have a good understanding of their condition and should be sufficiently cognitively aware and motivated to make informed decisions about their health (Holdich, 2009). This is often difficult to achieve, which is where rigid adherence to QOF targets or tight HbA$_{1c}$ control can be detrimental (Hall and Haslam, 2010). Evidence of cognitive impairment has been found in around one quarter of people taking insulin aged over 75 years, which significantly reduced their ability to understand the actions required in the event of low blood glucose or acute infection (Hewitt *et al.*, 2011).

Disability

Diabetes is associated with greater risk of disability relating to mobility and being able to perform daily tasks (Gregg *et al.*, 2000; Gregg *et al.*, 2002). Findings from the National Health and Nutrition Examination Survey (NHANES) indicated that older people with diabetes had about 2–3 times the prevalence of an inability to walk 400 metres, to do housework, to prepare meals independently and to manage money (Gregg *et al.*, 2000). One in four women with diabetes aged 60 years or over reported being unable to walk 400 metres, compared to less than one in six women without diabetes of the same age.

Women with diabetes appear to become disabled at about twice the rate of women without diabetes, and they also have an increased risk of hip fractures and falls (Gregg *et al.*, 2002; Schwartz *et al.*, 2001). The association between diabetes and physical disability is explained in part by the typical complications of diabetes, including coronary heart disease, peripheral arterial disease and visual impairment. However, even after controlling for these factors, a 60% greater prevalence of disability remains (Gregg *et al.*, 2000; Gregg *et al.*, 2002).

Diabetes and dementia

Type 2 diabetes is associated with an increase in cognitive impairment and earlier development of both Alzheimer's disease and vascular dementia (Biessels *et al.*, 2006; Luchsinger *et al.*, 2007). The most common form of dementia affecting people with diabetes is vascular dementia (Jolley, 2009), which is thought to be intrinsically linked to the vascular complications of diabetes. As diabetes is a risk factor for cerebrovascular disease and stroke, it can also cause cognitive impairment through ischaemic brain damage (Bruce *et al.*, 2008).

There are a number of possible mechanisms by which diabetes may accelerate cognitive decline and the development of dementia, including insulin resistance, disturbances of insulin homoeostasis in the brain, hyperinsulinaemia and the generation of advanced glycation end products (Zimmett *et al.*, 2001). Diabetes is also associated with damage to the central nervous system (CNS) and cognitive deficits, which can range from moderate to severe depending on the quality of glycaemic control (Moireria *et al.*, 2007).

Insulin affects a number of brain functions including cognition and memory. Insulin resistance, the accumulation of advanced glycation end products and/ or changes in cerebral signaling have all been linked with development of earlier-onset Alzheimer's disease (Moireria *et al.*, 2007, Bruce *et al.*, 2008). The development of dementia is also increased by hypertension in middle age (Qiu *et al.*, 2005), obesity (Gorospe and Dave, 2007) and dyslipidemia (Reitz *et al.*, 2004), which are independent, modifiable risk factors for diabetes, vascular disease and dementia.

Strachan (2010) suggested that very high blood glucose concentrations are associated with poor memory, ill health and mood changes. This may be due to alterations in cerebral blood flow (such as cerebral microvascular disease) causing osmotic changes in neurons. Indeed, diabetic retinopathy is a surrogate marker of cerebral microvascular disease, and people with retinopathy are likely to have a longer duration of diabetes and hypertension (Gillibrand and Holdich, 2010).

Case study 1

Rachel is an 81-year-old widow with type 2 diabetes and a history of angina and neuropathy. She was found wandering around her local town in a disorientated state. Following emergency ambulance intervention for the acute assessment and management of hypoglycaemia, she was referred for reassessment at her local general practice with her practice nurse. Rachel is unable to remember what happened prior to this episode, and she is afraid that it might happen again.

Rachel does not test her own blood glucose levels and she no longer drives. Her most recent HbA$_{1c}$ (recorded at the practice) is 6.5% (48mmol/mol). She is prescribed metformin 500mg BD and gliclazide 80mg BD.

A mini mental health assessment was undertaken during her consultation and the results of this indicate early signs of cognitive dysfunction. The practice nurse is concerned that Rachel may be having difficulty remembering to take her medications and possibly her meals. She suggests a dosette box to Rachel and asks her to bring a friend or neighbour along for another appointment.

After discussion with Rachel, the practice nurse also discontinues her sulphonylurea medication (gliclazide) to reduce her risk of hypoglycaemia, as Rachel's recent experience of hypoglycaemia has left her feeling unsafe, frightened and at risk. Rachel is happy with these suggestions and agrees to return in a week's time so that her practice nurse can assess how she is coping.

The evidence that diabetes is a risk factor for dementia is of considerable importance (Sinclair *et al*, 2000) — given the increasing prevalence of diabetes (YHPHO, 2010) and the increasing longevity of the population (ONS, 2011) this is a major public health concern. Many individuals who are at risk of or living with dementia often reside in care homes (Sinclair *et al.*, 2000), and may experience the difficulties of diabetes control within care establishments (Diabetes UK, 2010; Phillips and Phillips, 2011). To identify those at particular risk may help target early treatment strategies (Department of Health, 2010). This can be seen in the case of Rachel, where the intervention of her practice nurse was pivotal (*case study 1*).

Hypoglycaemia

Hypoglycaemia is one of the most common side effects of taking diabetes medications such as insulin and sulphonylureas (MacArthur, 2010; NHS Diabetes, 2010). It occurs in 7.7% of all inpatient admissions and leads to increased mortality and length of stay (NHS Diabetes, 2010). While all people who take insulin or sulphonylureas are at risk of hypoglycaemia, older patients taking sulphonylureas are more significantly at risk of developing severe hypoglycaemia (MacArthur, 2010).

Hypoglycaemia is a serious condition at all ages. It may be underestimated in the older person as symptoms can be attributed to other conditions, such as confusion due to dementia or communication difficulties after a stroke. This can have catastrophic consequences and can result in death (Sinclair, 2009).

In advanced age, hypos can occur for a variety of reasons, such as acute illness or as a complication of long-term comorbidities. Therefore, strategies to reduce the older person's risk of hypoglycaemia need to consider a range of factors. Being prescribed five or more medications increases the risk of falls and hypoglycaemia (Hawthorne, 2009) and a very large number of older people with diabetes are prescribed polypharmacy (NHS Diabetes, 2010; Phillips and Phillips, 2011). Additionally, hypoglycaemic risk is raised considerably if the older person has chronic kidney disease (where the excretion of drugs is impaired) and poor nutrition. Prescribers need to be mindful that when medications are prescribed, they may not work as expected and may increase the risk of hypogycaemia.

Practice nurses, GPs and community nurses need to be aware of the risks of hypoglycaemia in older people, especially in those who live alone. Its implications should be discussed with all older people with diabetes.

A partnership approach can facilitate safe decision-making for individuals with diabetes (Holdich, 2009). Stakeholders should be aware that rigid adherence to QOF guidance (2011) for HbA$_{1c}$ targets can be risky in older people, as aggressively medicating to reduce HbA_{1c} levels considerably increases the risk of hypoglycaemia.

Health practitioners must also be aware of any underlying macrovascular diseases, as strokes and myocardial infarctions can directly result from hypoglycaemia (Sinclair, 2009). Repeated hypoglycaemic episodes are associated with a high risk of falls and hospital admissions due to fractured neck of femur, and can result in a lack of independence and self-confidence in the older person with diabetes (Schwartz *et al.*, 2001; Sinclair, 2009; Phillips and Phillips, 2011).

Other potential complications of hypoglycaemia in older adults include compromised nutritional status, neglected periodontal health (Dunning, 2009) and a deficient cognitive ability affecting self-treatment (Velayudhan *et al.*, 2010).

Other risk factors for hypoglycaemia include:

- Recovery and increased activity after illness
- Major amputation
- Abrupt discontinuation of steroid therapy.

The timing of meals can increase the risk of hypoglycaemia considerably, which may be an issue if the person relies on support care workers or meals on wheels. Older people may be experiencing comorbidities secondary to their diabetes, which can cause eyesight problems, falls, depression, and poor oral intake, all of which can necessitate closer monitoring is required (Sinclair, 2009).

Symptoms of hypoglycaemia

Individuals are usually alerted to low blood glucose levels by symptoms such as sweating, shaking and hunger (NHS Diabetes, 2010). In older people these symptoms can be suppressed, so blood glucose levels can be very low by the time individuals become aware that they are low. The intensity of symptoms is often low and cognitive function may be impaired, so the older person with diabetes may not be aware of symptoms, as in the case of Ray (*case study 2*), or they may not be able to self-treat (Sinclair, 2009). Hypoglycaemia unawareness is due to the loss of autonomic warning signs, which include sweating, shaking, hunger and anxiety (Gibson, 2009); when these are not detected, hypoglycaemic episodes can be mismanaged by the older person and/or their carers (Gibson, 2009; MacArthur, 2010).

When caring for people who are at risk, close monitoring and awareness are essential. The practice nurse and primary care diabetes team need to assess and address common issues in older people with diabetes, which include poor eyesight, polypharmacy, poor nutrition, weight loss, poorly-fitting dentures, mobility difficulties, low mood and activities of daily living (Phillips and Wright, 2009). Management should be based on safety and individually-tailored care, rather than QOF targets (Hall and Haslam, 2010).

Care homes

NHS Diabetes (2010) previously highlighted the key features of good care for older people with diabetes, which include appropriate screening mechanisms, individualised care plan development, appropriate blood glucose control and the coordination of available specialist services. While these principles of excellence in care are admirable, the provision of care is at the mercy of local commissioners and is at risk if not on their current priority agenda (Da Costa, 2010). To bring health and social care professionals together to ensure that older people with diabetes get the best possible care, NHS Diabetes and the Institute of Diabetes for Older People (IDOP) have launched the 'Older people network' (2012). This network can target deficits in care, to improve standards.

Case study 2

Ray is a 72-year-old retired teacher. He has had type 1 diabetes for 36 years and has always managed this very well. He uses a basal bolus regime.

Since the death of his wife 6 months previously, Ray has found it increasingly difficult to be motivated, his appetite has reduced and he has lost interest in eating. He was recently admitted to hospital following an acute hypoglycaemic episode, which he was unable to treat. He reported that he did not recognise any hypo symptoms.

Following discharge, Ray comes to see his practice nurse and together they plan a system of care to enable him to regain control. Ray agrees to test his blood glucose levels pre-meal and to reduce his total daily insulin dose by 10% due to his recent hypo and the suggestion that there may have been other hypo episodes, which he may not have recognised.

Ray is having difficulty preparing meals at home, so they discuss social care arrangements which may help him continue to manage independently at home. Ray is happy with this suggestion, and the practice nurse arranges a referral to social services, as well as contacting his local Age UK voluntary befriending scheme. They arrange a follow-up appointment for a fortnight's time, to review his situation.

The Diabetes UK (2010) report 'Diabetes in care homes — Awareness, screening, training', found that 6 out of 10 care homes in England with residents with diabetes failed to provide their staff with training about the condition. Diabetes UK (2010) has further reported that a person with diabetes is admitted to hospital every 25 minutes from residential care, due to failings in screening and training. Without appropriate training, staff are unable to manage the complex problems of diabetes, cognitive impairment and other conditions and unable to provide the care that residents need.

Conclusions

The prevalence of diabetes in the older adult population is increasing, and considering growing evidence that diabetes is a risk factor for dementia (Sinclair *et al.*, 2009), the importance of good diabetes management is of particular concern in this group.

To promote safety and reduce the risk of hypoglycaemia, which can be especially dangerous in older people, it is essential that care is individualised (Sinclair, 2009). Care planning must be done in partnership with the person. The cases of Rachel and Ray illustrate how fundamental the role of the health practitioner working with people with diabetes really is.

Key points

■ To ensure safety and avoid hypoglycaemia, care must be individualised, not target driven
■ NHS Diabetes and the Institute of Diabetes for Older People (IDOP) are championing older people's diabetes care to enable best practice
■ Individual assessment and personalised care planning are paramount for maintaining safety of older people with diabetes.

References

Allender S et al (2008) Patterns of coronary heart disease mortality over the 20th century in England and Wales: possible plateaus in the rate of decline. *BMC Public Health* 8: 148

Biessels G et al (2006) Risk of dementia in diabetes mellitus, a systematic review. *Lancet Neurol* 5(1): 64-74

British Medical Association (2011) Summary of 2011/12 QOF indicator changes, points and thresholds. http://tinyurl.com/672y3eb (accessed 21 March 2011)

Bruce D et al (2008) Predictors of cognitive decline in older individuals with diabetes. *Diabetes Care* **31**(11): 2103-07

Da Costa S (2010) Does the NHS White Paper signal a raw deal for older people. *Journal of Diabetes Nursing* **14**(8): 310

Department of Health (2010) Living well with dementia. A National Dementia Strategy. http://tiny.cc/vv68p (accessed 1 March 2011)

Diabetes UK (2010) Diabetes in Care Homes. Awareness, Screening, Training. http://tiny.cc/7bif0 (accessed 1 March 2011)

Dunning T (2009) Peridontal disease – the overlooked diabetes complication. *Nephrology Nursing Journal* **36**(5): 489-96

Gorospe E, Dave J (2007) The risk of dementia with increased body mass index. *Age Aging* 36: 23-29

Gibson H (2009) Hypoglycaemia unawareness. *Practice Nursing* **20**(5): 240-44

Gillibrand W, Holdich P (2010) Assessment of retinopathy. *Practice Nursing* **21**(6): 305-9

Gregg E, Natayan V (2000) Type 2 diabetes and cognitive function: are cognitive impairment and dementia complications of type 2 diabetes? *Clin Geriatr* 8: 57-72

Gregg E et al (2002) Complications of diabetes in elderly people. *BMJ* **325**(7370): 916-17

Hall G, Haslam D (2010) Tailoring care in type 2 diabetes. *Journal of Diabetes Nursing* **14**(Suppl): 8

Hawthorne G (2009) A risk management partnership. *Practice Nursing* **20**(2): 86-90

Hewitt J et al (2011) Self management and patient understanding of diabetes in the older person. *Diabetic Medicine* **28**(1): 117-22

Holdich P (2009) Patient-centred care planning. *Practice Nursing* **20**(1): 18-23

Jolley D (2009) The epidemiology of dementia. *Practice Nursing* **20**(6 suppl): S4-S6

King H et al (1998) Global burden of diabetes, 1995–2025: prevalence, numerical estimates and projections. *Diabetes Care* **21**(9): 1414-31

Luchsinger J et al (2007) Relation of diabetes to mild cognitive impairment. *Arch Neurol* **64**(4): 570-75

MacArthur C (2010) Hypoglycaemia in type 2 diabetes. *Practice Nursing* **21**(2): 84-88

Moreira P et al (2007) Brain mitochondrial dysfunction as a link between Alzheimer's disease and diabetes. *Journal of the Neurological Sciences* 257: 206-14

NHS Diabetes and The Institute of Diabetes for Older People (2012) Older People Network. http://www.diabetes.nhs.uk/networks/older_people_network/

NHS Diabetes (2010) Safe and effective use of insulin in hospitalised patients. http://www.diabetes.nhs.uk (accessed 21 March 2012)

Nursing and Midwifery Council (2009) Guidance for the Care of Older People. http://tiny.cc/fbqmg (accessed 1 March 2011)

Office for National Statistics (2011) Population estimates. UK population grows to 61.8 million. http://tiny.cc/2f1iw (accessed 1 March 2011)

Phillips S, Phillips A (2011) Diabetes, blood glucose levels and comorbidities. *Nursing and Residential Care* **13**(87): 368-72

Phillips A, Wright J (2010) Assessing the impact of mental wellbeing on self-management. *British Journal of Wellbeing* **1**(6): 30–5

Qiu C et al (2005) The age dependent relation of blood pressure to cognitive function and dementia, *Lancet Neuro* **4**: 487-99

Reed J et al (2004) Health, Well-Being and Older People. The Policy Press, Bristol

Schwartz A et al (2001) Older women with diabetes have an increased risk of fracture: a prospective study. *J Clin Endocrinol Metab* **86**(1): 32-38

Sinclair A et al (2000) Cognitive dysfunction in older subjects with diabetes mellitus: impact on diabetes self management & use of care services. All Wales Research into Elderly (AWARE) Study. *Diabetes Res Clin Practice* **50**(3): 203-12

Sinclair A (2009) Diabetes in Old Age (3rd edn). Wiley-Blackwell, Oxford

Sinclair A (2011) Diabetes care for older people: A practical view on management. *Diabetes and Primary Care* **13**(1): 29-38

Strachan M (2011) The brain as a target organ in type 2 diabetes: exploring the links with cognitive impairment and dementia. *Diabetic Medicine* **28**: 141-47

Velayudhan L et al (2010) Risk of developing dementia in people with diabetes and mild cognitive impairment. *Br J Psych* **196**(1): 36-40

Williams J (2009) Diabetes and the older adult: what care do they need and what do they receive? *Journal of Diabetes Nursing* **13**(8): 308-10

Yorkshire and Humber Public Health Observatory (2010) APHO Diabetes Prevalence Model: Key findings for England. http://tinyurl.com/2wjkckp (accessed 1 March 2011)

Zimmett P, Alberti K, Shaw J (2001) Global and societal implications of the diabetes epidemic. *Nature* **414**(6865): 782-87

Chapter 27

Reassessing people who have been diagnosed with diabetes below age 25

Julie Cropper and Maggie Shepherd

Introduction

This chapter outlines how possible cases of maturity-onset diabetes of the young (MODY) can be identified in general practice, using four cases to illustrate its main features. MODY is caused by a change in a single gene, and as such it is known as 'monogenic diabetes'. It is characterised by three key features (Stride and Hattersley, 2002):

- Non-insulin dependent diabetes
- Early onset (below the age of 25 years)
- Autosomal dominant inheritance.

MODY accounts for 1–2% of cases of diabetes in the UK but it is frequently misdiagnosed (Shepherd, 2001), which leads to inappropriate treatment and inadequate follow-up of family members, who may also be affected or at risk of developing diabetes.

All health professionals who are involved in diabetes care have a responsibility to ensure that diagnosis is accurate. An awareness of the features of MODY can help health professionals to recognise people who may have been misdiagnosed with either type 1 or type 2 diabetes.

Genetic testing

A diagnosis of MODY can be confirmed by molecular genetic testing. If it is confirmed then treatment can be changed — in many cases individuals successfully transfer from insulin to low-dose sulphonylureas (Pearson *et al.*, 2003).

Non-genetic tests

Non-genetic tests, such as the urine C-peptide creatinine ratio (UCPCR) and pancreatic autoantibody tests can aid differential diagnosis. These are widely accessible at minimal cost (see www.diabetesgenes.org for details).

C-peptide is a measure of endogenous insulin production. The UCPCR (calculated from a postprandial urine sample) gives an idea of whether or not an individual is producing their own insulin, and if so how much (Bowman, 2010). In people with type 1 diabetes of more than 5 years' duration, a UCPCR of <0.2nmol/mmol (indicating no insulin production) would be expected. A result above this level indicates some endogenous insulin production. Therefore,

---

Case study 1

Mrs S was diagnosed with type 1 diabetes aged 15 years, when she presented with glycosuria, polydipsia and polyuria. She was of normal weight, a random blood glucose was 22mmol/l and she had a trace of ketonuria. Due to her age, symptoms and BMI, she was assumed to have type 1 diabetes and was started on insulin treatment.

Twelve years later, she moved home and was reassessed by her new diabetes nurse specialist. When asked about her family history, she said that her father had been diagnosed with diabetes aged 28 and was treated with insulin. His brother was diagnosed at 35 and treated with tablets. Their mother was diagnosed aged 45 but her treatment was unknown. The family recalled she had some visual loss as a result of her diabetes (*Figure C1*).

In view of this family history of autosomal dominance, a urinary C-peptide creatinine ratio (UCPCR) test was requested. A result of 1.2nmol/mmol indicated that Mrs S was still producing insulin, despite 12 years of diabetes. As a consequence of this test result, a blood sample was sent for genetic testing, and a hepatocyte nuclear factor 1-alpha (HNF1A) mutation was identified. Mrs S was diagnosed with HNF1A MODY.

The new diagnosis meant Mrs S was able to transfer from insulin injections to low-dose sulphonylureas (gliclazide 40mg twice daily), which improved both quality of life and HbA$_{1c}$ (8.4%/68mmol/mol to 6.9%/52mmol/mol). Other family members with diabetes were offered genetic testing, which indicated that her father and uncle had the same HNF1A mutation. Genetic counselling was offered to the 'unaffected' family members with a 50% risk of having HNF1A.

UCPCR can be useful when differentiating between type 1 diabetes of over five years' duration and MODY (Besser, 2011).

Type 1 diabetes is characterised by the presence of pancreatic autoantibodies; around 70% of people with type 1 diabetes have multiple islet cell antibodies at diagnosis, indicating an autoimmune cause (McDonald, 2011). However, the prevalence of glutamic acid decarboxylase 65 (GAD65) and islet antigen pancreatic autoantibodies is <1% in MODY (McDonald, 2011). Antibody tests are therefore an excellent means of distinguishing type 1 diabetes from MODY. These tests should preferably be performed at diagnosis, as antibodies are known to decrease over time.

MODY subtypes

The descriptions below and the case studies presented throughout this chapter illustrate the main features of hepatocyte nuclear factor 1-alpha (HNF1A), hepatocyte nuclear factor 4-alpha (HNF4A), hepatocyte nuclear factor 1-beta (HNF1B) and glucokinase (GCK) MODY. In all cases, the correct molecular genetic diagnosis was made many years after the initial diagnosis of diabetes.

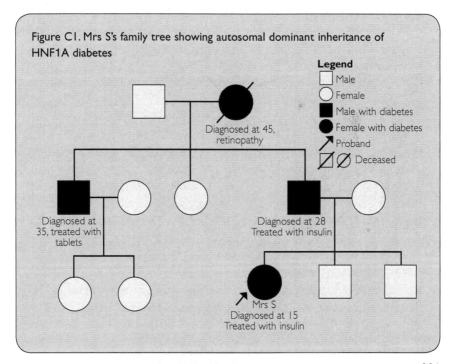

Figure C1. Mrs S's family tree showing autosomal dominant inheritance of HNF1A diabetes

Hepatocyte nuclear factor 1-alpha (HNF1A) MODY

HNF1A MODY is the commonest cause of MODY in the UK, accounting for 65% of cases (Frayling, 2001). People with HNF1A typically present with symptoms as teenagers or young adults and, consequently, are often misdiagnosed as having type 1 diabetes (Lehto, 1997; Møller, 1998; Hathout, 1999; Shepherd, 2001; Lambert, 2003). They have a low renal threshold for glucose (Menzel, 1998; Stride *et al.*, 2002) and progressive beta cell failure, which leads to increasing hyperglycaemia throughout life.

People with HNF1A are extremely sensitive to sulphonylureas (Pearson, 2000; 2003). They may be successfully treated with very low doses for many years, achieving good glycaemic control and lower risks of hypoglycaemia than with insulin treatment (Shepherd 2003; 2009). However, individuals with HNF1A

Case study 2

Mr L was diagnosed with diabetes at the age of 28, with lethargy, polyuria and polydipsia. His BMI was 29kg/m², random blood glucose was 16mmol/l and there was no ketonuria. He was started on insulin.

The consultant requested glutamic acid decarboxylase and islet antigen-2 antibodies tests to confirm the type of diabetes, which were both negative, suggesting that the cause was not autoimmune.

Mr L's sister had been diagnosed with diabetes at 32 and his mother had developed diabetes aged 44 (*Figure C2*).

At the time of Mr L's diagnosis, his wife was pregnant. James was born at 40 weeks, weighing 4.12kg. He was hypoglycaemic and his random blood glucose was 1.0mmol/l, which remained low despite feeding. He was started on diazoxide, which was continued until he was 9 months old.

The consultant suspected that Mr L might have MODY and asked the local genetic diabetes nurse for advice, who suggested testing for hepatocyte nuclear factor 4-alpha (HNF4A) MODY in view of the macrosomia and neonatal hypoglycaemia. Molecular genetic testing confirmed HNF4A MODY in Mr L, his sister, his mother and James.

Mr L and his sister were successfully transferred to sulphonylurea treatment, but their mother opted to remain on insulin. Mr and Mrs L were advised that James was likely to develop diabetes when he became older and were counselled about future pregnancies.

---

can expect to progress to insulin treatment over time.

Complications are common in HNF1A, including early myocardial infarction, and good glycaemic control is required to reduce the risk of these (Steele, 2010).

HNF1A should be considered in those diagnosed with diabetes below age 25, with a parent also diagnosed with diabetes — particularly when there is evidence of endogenous insulin production or other features, such as sensitivity to low dose sulphonylureas (*case study 1*).

Hepatocyte nuclear factor 4-alpha (HNF4A) MODY

HNF4A MODY accounts for approximately 5% of MODY. It presents in a similar way to HNF1A MODY, although there may be a slightly later age of onset (Pearson, 2005). As with HNF1A MODY, people are often sensitive to sulphonylureas (Fajans and Brown, 1993).

Macrosomia (birth weight >4kg) and transient neonatal hypoglycaemia are common, and caused by hyperinsulinism *in utero* (Fajans and Bell, 2007; Pearson *et al.*, 2007). Birth weight can be increased if the HNF4A mutation is inherited

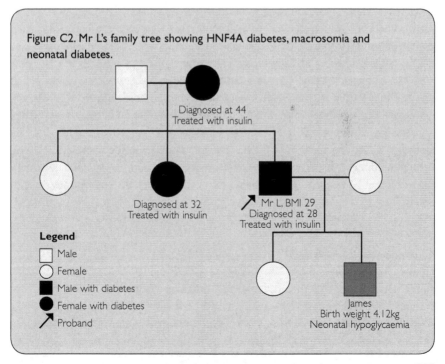

Figure C2. Mr L's family tree showing HNF4A diabetes, macrosomia and neonatal diabetes.

by the fetus, irrespective of parental diabetes. It is important that HNF4A is recognised in parents (even fathers) as it has implications for the management of pregnancy and delivery.

HNF4A should be considered when a baby is born with macrosomia and neonatal hypoglycaemia to a parent with diabetes. Individuals who are identified with HNF4A are at very high risk of developing diabetes in later life, so annual monitoring from childhood is recommended (*case study 2*).

Hepatocyte nuclear factor 1-beta (HNF1B) MODY

HNF1B MODY is characterised by renal cysts, or other developmental renal disease, and diabetes — it is also known as 'renal cysts and diabetes' (RCAD) (Bingham *et al.*, 2001; Edghill *et al.*, 2006).

Renal cysts often present before the diabetes and may be detected on fetal ultrasound scans — individuals with HNF1B MODY have also been identified with single, absent or horseshoe kidneys (Bingham and Hattersley, 2004). While renal function may be normal, some individuals progress to dialysis or renal transplant (Bingham *et al.*, 2001; Stride and Hattersley, 2002). Other features of HNF1B MODY include uterine malformations, such as bicornuate uterus or uterus didelphys (which can lead to recurrent miscarriages), and other genital tract malformations (Horikawa 1997; Bellanné-Chantelot *et al.*, 2005; Edghill *et al.*, 2006). Hyperuricaemia and gout may also occur (Bingham *et al.*, 2001).

Half of those with HNF1B mutations develop early onset diabetes, which presents in a similar way to HNF1A MODY. However, those with HNF1B MODY are more insulin resistant and usually require insulin treatment (Shepherd, 2010).

The possibility of HNF1B should be considered in anyone with diabetes and renal cysts and in those with the other features described above. Although insulin treatment is usually required, confirming the genetic diagnosis can explain the variation in features within these families and enable appropriate genetic counselling (*case study 3*).

Glucokinase (GCK) MODY

GCK MODY is characterised by mild hyperglycaemia from birth, which remains stable and does not require treatment (Stride and Hattersley, 2002). If insulin or oral hypoglycaemic agents are used and then stopped, HbA_{1c} levels usually remain stable (Gill-Carey *et al.*, 2007). It is often detected on routine screening, such as antenatal screening (Spyer *et al.*, 2001) or employment medicals.

Case study 3

Emma was diagnosed with diabetes when she was 16 years old. She had typical symptoms and was started on insulin. She was already under the care of the renal team, as she had been born without a right kidney.

Her paediatrician had recently attended a presentation by the local genetic diabetes nurse and asked her to assess Emma, as Emma's mother also had diabetes, having been diagnosed when she was 25 years old (*Figure C3*).

When the genetic diabetes nurse investigated the family history, she was told that Emma's mother had renal cysts, as did Emma's maternal aunt who was investigated for recurrent miscarriages and found to have a bicornate uterus. Emma's maternal grandfather was known to have diabetes, although no details were available.

The genetic diabetes nurse requested HNF1B testing, which confirmed HNF1B mutations in Emma, her mother and her aunt. Although Emma and her mother still require insulin, the diagnosis provided an explanation for the renal problems, uterine malformation and diabetes within the family and enabled genetic counselling about the condition and its implications.

Figure C3. Emma's family tree showing HNF1B diabetes and renal cysts

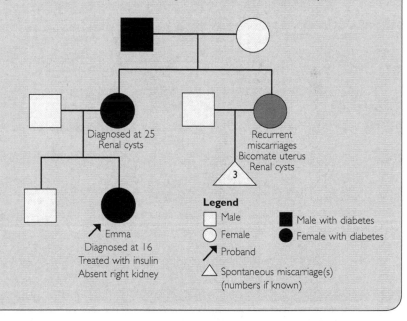

Legend

☐ Male   ■ Male with diabetes
○ Female   ● Female with diabetes
↗ Proband
△ Spontaneous miscarriage(s) (numbers if known)

Case study 4

Mrs T was diagnosed with gestational diabetes during her pregnancy, aged 23 years, and was treated with insulin.

During a visit to her GP for a postnatal glucose tolerance test, she mentioned to the practice nurse that her brother had been diagnosed with diabetes when he was admitted to hospital after a motorcycle accident, and that her father had been told that he had 'borderline diabetes' during an army medical many years ago (*Figure 4*).

On the basis of her family history and an oral glucose tolerance test result of 6.3mmol/l fasting and 7.8mmol/l at two hours, her GP contacted the local genetic diabetes nurse.

Molecular genetic testing confirmed a glucokinase (GCK) mutation in Mrs T, her father and her brother, which enabled her brother to be taken off treatment. Following discussion with the genetic diabetes specialist nurse, Mrs T's sister (now 20 years old) is considering whether or not to have a fasting blood glucose test, before contemplating a genetic test to see if she has inherited the GCK mutation from her father.

Figure C4. Mrs T's family tree showing GCK MODY and incidental diagnosis of diabetes.

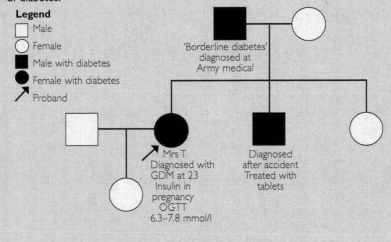

Legend
- ☐ Male
- ◯ Female
- ■ Male with diabetes
- ● Female with diabetes
- ➚ Proband

'Borderline diabetes' diagnosed at Army medical

Mrs T
Diagnosed with GDM at 23
Insulin in pregnancy
OGTT
6.3–7.8 mmol/l

Diagnosed after accident
Treated with tablets

Fasting blood glucose is typically 5.5–8.0mmol/l and HbA_{1c} levels are usually around the 'top end' of normal, rarely exceeding 7.5% (Ellard *et al.*, 2008). Microvascular complications are rare (Velho 1997; Ellard 2008). GCK MODY can affect birth weight, although this depends on who has the mutation (the mother or father) and whether or not the fetus has inherited it (Hattersley *et al.*, 1998).

GCK MODY should be considered in individuals with mild, stable hyperglycaemia, which may have been detected incidentally, who have HbA_{1c} and fasting glucose in the ranges identified above and no complications. Treatment of hyperglycaemia with oral agents or insulin is not required; HbA_{1c} levels remain stable in people with GCK MODY if insulin or oral hypoglycaemic agents are stopped (Gill-Carey *et al.*, 2007). Confirming this diagnosis can enable treatment cessation and appropriate counselling for other family members (*case study 4*).

Conclusions

Increased awareness of the features of MODY can lead to the identification of people who have previously been misdiagnosed with type 1 or type 2 diabetes. Each MODY subtype has its own particular characteristics which, in combination with the key features of MODY, can potentially be identified by an alert health professional.

A young age of diagnosis combined with a family history of any type of diabetes can raise questions about the diagnosis, and non-genetic tests such as UCPCR or pancreatic antibodies can help when deciding whether or not genetic testing is appropriate.

All of the people in the case studies presented in this chapter benefited from having the correct molecular genetic diagnosis. In some cases, insulin treatment could be stopped, and glycaemic control and quality of life improved; in others, the correct diagnosis provided an explanation for the diabetes within the family and other features which had not previously been considered to be related. To ensure an accurate diagnosis is the responsibility of all health professionals involved in diabetes care.

Further information about monogenic diabetes, genetic testing (including how to access UCPCR and pancreatic antibody tests) and local genetic diabetes nurses is available online at www.diabetesgenes.org

Acknowledgments: this chapter was funded by a National Institute of Health Research fellowship and is supported by the Peninsula Clinical Research Facility, University of Exeter

Key points

■ People diagnosed below the age of 25 years who have a parent with diabetes should be assessed to ensure that the cause and type of diabetes has been correctly identified

■ Urinary C-peptide/creatinine ratio (UCPCR) and pancreatic antibody tests aid the accurate diagnosis of such patients, because they help to differentiate between type 1 diabetes and MODY

■ Practice nurses and GPs can identify possible cases of monogenic diabetes many years after an initial diabetes diagnosis, and should discuss such cases with a local genetic diabetes nurse before referral for genetic testing

■ A confirmed molecular genetic diagnosis of monogenic diabetes can lead to treatment changes and improvements in glycaemic control and quality of life.

References

Bellanné-Chantelot C et al (2005) Large genomic rearrangements in the hepatocyte nuclear factor-1beta (TCF2) gene are the most frequent cause of maturity onset diabetes of the young type 5. *Diabetes* **54**(11): 3126-32

Besser R et al (2011) Urinary C-peptide creatinine ratio is a practical outpatient tool in discriminating long duration type 1 diabetes from HNF1A MODY. *Diabetes Care* **34**(2): 286-91

Bingham C, Hattersley A (2004) Renal cysts and diabetes syndrome resulting from mutations in hepatocyte nuclear factor-1beta. *Nephrol Dial Transplant* **19**(11): 2703-8

Bingham C et al (2001) Mutations in the hepatocyte nuclear factor-1beta gene are associated with familial hypoplastic glomerulocystic kidney disease. *Am J Hum Genet* **68**(1): 219-24

Bowman P et al (2010) Single sample urinary C-peptide creatinine ratio (UCPCR) is a reproducible alternative to serum C-peptide in patients with type 2 diabetes. *Diabet Med* **27**(Suppl 1): A63

Edghill E et al (2006) Mutations in hepatocyte nuclear factor-1beta and their related phenotypes. *J Med Genet* **43**(1): 84-90

Ellard S et al (2008) Best practice guidelines for the molecular genetic diagnosis of maturity-onset diabetes of the young. *Diabetologia* **51**(4): 546-53

Fajans S, Bell G (2007) Macrosomia and neonatal hypoglycaemia in RW pedigree subjects with a mutation (Q268X) in the gene encoding hepatocyte nuclear factor 4alpha (HNF4A). *Diabetologia* **50**(12): 2600-1

Fajans S, Brown M (1993) Administration of sulphonylureas can increase glucose-induced insulin secretion for decades in patients with maturity-onset diabetes of the young. *Diabetes Care* **16**(9): 1254-61

Frayling T et al (2001) Beta cell genes and diabetes: molecular and clinical characterization of mutations in transcription factors. *Diabetes* **50** (Suppl 1): S94-S100

Gill-Carey O et al (2007) Finding a glucokinase mutation alters patients' treatment. [Abstract.] *Diabet Med* **24**(Suppl 1): 6

Hathout E et al (1999) A case of hepatocyte nuclear factor-1 alpha diabetes/MODY3 masquerading as type 1 diabetes in a Mexican-American adolescent and responsive to a low dose sulphonylurea. *Diabetes Care* **22**(5): 867-68

Hattersley A et al (1998) Mutations in the glucokinase gene of the fetus results in reduced birth weight. *Nat Genet* **19**(3): 268-70

Horikawa Y et al (1997) Mutation in hepatocyte nucelar factor 1 beta gene (TCF2) associated with MODY. *Nat Genet* **17**(4): 384-85

Lambert A et al (2003) Identifying hepatic nuclear factor 1alpha mutations in children and young adults with a clinical diagnosis of type 1 diabetes. *Diabetes Care* **26**(2): 333-37

Lehto M et al (1997) Characterization of the MODY3 phenotype. Early-onset diabetes caused by an insulin secretion defect. *J Clin Invest* **99**(4): 582-91

McDonald T et al (submitted 2010) Pancreatic autoantibodies can discriminate MODY from type 1 diabetes. *Diabet Med* (in press)

Menzel R et al (1998) A low renal threshold for glucose in diabetic patients with a mutation in the hepatocyte nuclear factor-1alpha (HNF-1alpha) gene. *Diabet Med* **15**(10): 816-20

Møller A et al (1998) Mutations in the hepatocyte nuclear factor-1alpha gene in Caucasian families originally classified as having Type 1 diabetes. *Diabetologia* **41**(12): 1528-31

Pearson E et al (2007) Macrosomia and hyperinsulinaemic hypoglycaemia in patients with heterozygous mutations in the HNF4A gene. *PLoS Medicine* **4**(4): e118

Pearson E et al (2005) Molecular genetics and phenotypic characteristics of MODY caused by hepatocyte nuclear factor 4alpha mutations in a large European collection. *Diabetologia* **48**(5): 878-85

Pearson E et al (2003) Genetic cause of hyperglycaemia and response to treatment in diabetes. *Lancet* **362**(9392): 1275-81

Pearson E et al (2000) Sensitivity to sulphonylureas in patients with hepatocyte nuclear factor-1 alpha gene mutations: evidence for pharmacogenetics in diabetes. *Diabet Med* **17**(7): 543-45

Shepherd M et al (2010) Differential diagnosis: Identifying people with monogenic diabetes. *J Diabetes Nurs* **15**(1) (in press)

Shepherd M et al (2009) A genetic diagnosis of HNF1A diabetes alters treatment and improves glycaemic control in the majority of insulin-treated patients. *Diabet Med* **26**(4): 437-41

Shepherd M et al (2003) No deterioration in glycaemic control in HN-1alpha maturity onset diabetes of the young following transfer from long-term insulin to sulphonylureas. *Diabetes Care* **26**(11): 3191-92

Shepherd M (2001) Recognising maturity onset diabetes of the young. *J Diabetes Nurs* **5**(6): 168-72

Spyer G et al (2001) Influence of maternal and fetal glucokinase mutations in gestational diabetes. *Am J Obstet Gynecol* **185**(1): 240-41

Steele A et al (2010) Increased all-cause and cardiovascular mortality in monogenic diabetes as a result of mutations in the HNF1A gene. *Diabet Med* **27**(2): 157-61

Stride A et al (2002) The genetic abnormality in the beta cell determines the response to an oral glucose load. *Diabetologia* **45**(3): 427-35

Stride A, Hattersley A (2002) Different genes, different diabetes: lessons from maturity-onset diabetes of the young. *Ann Med* **34**(3): 207-16

Velho G et al (1997) Identification of 14 new glucokinase mutations and description of the clinical profile of 42 MODY-2 families. *Diabetologia* **40**(2): 217-24

Chapter 28

Managing diabetes in palliative and end of life care

Theresa Smyth and Dion Smyth

Introduction

During the last decades of the 20th century, the demographics of disease and dying changed fundamentally. Advances in medicine, therapeutic technologies and supportive care successfully transformed many previously acute causes of death into chronic and incurable illness, such that we now often only come to death after a long period of progressive decline (Lynn, 2005).

There are over 15 million people in the UK living with a long-term condition, such as diabetes mellitus (DoH, 2010); according to Diabetes UK (2012) the known diagnosed population is now in excess of 3 million people. In the UK, more than half a million people die each year, most of whom are over the age of 75 years (DoH, 2008). In 2010, 493,242 deaths were registered in England and Wales (ONS, 2011); 53,967 in Scotland (Registrar General, 2011) and 14,500 in Northern Ireland (NISRA, 2010). Most of these deaths occurred in people with a long-term condition, and it has been suggested that 6–9% of those dying have diabetes mellitus (Rowles *et al.*, 2011).

About half of all people do not die in their preferred place of care (Gomes and Higginson, 2006). At present, the majority of deaths (58%) occur in institutional settings (such as NHS hospitals), approximately 18% occur at home, 17% in care homes, 4% in hospices and 3% elsewhere (DoH, 2008). More than half (54%) of the complaints to the Healthcare Commission about hospital care were associated with aspects of end of life care (Healthcare Commission, 2007). Similarly, dissatisfaction with and wide disparities in access to specialist palliative care services have been reported, with only 5% of all referred people having a diagnosis of non-malignant disease (Payne *et al.*, 2004).

Effective, equitable end of life care that facilitates choice and control should be available to all, regardless of medical diagnosis and place of care (DoH, 2008). Some authors suggest that palliative care is an international human right (Brennan, 2007; Gwyther *et al.*, 2009) as are elements of palliative care, such as adequate access to appropriate pain relief (Lohman *et al.*, 2010).

What is palliative care?

The World Health Organization (WHO, 2002) defines palliative care as 'an approach that improves the quality of life of patients and their families facing the problem associated with life-threatening illness, through the prevention and relief of suffering by means of early identification and impeccable assessment and treatment of pain and other problems, physical, psychosocial and spiritual'. Some of the fundamental principles of palliative care are outlined in *Table 1*.

While palliative care may once have been considered synonymous with, or relegated to terminal care, Sepúlveda *et al.* (2002) suggest that the principles and practices of palliative care do not belong solely to discrete stages at the end of life but should be applied as soon as feasible in the course of any chronic, ultimately fatal illness. Accordingly, 'end of life care' refers primarily to care of the dying and incorporates all elements of the daily life of a person in the last part of their life — the final weeks, days and hours.

The challenge of palliative care

The management of diabetes at the end of life has been variously reported as a continuing 'challenge' (Budge, 2010); 'complex' (McCoubrie *et al.*, 2005) and 'inconsistent' (Quinn *et al.*, 2006a; Ford-Dunn *et al.*, 2006). It is acknowledged that palliative care in people with diabetes is perceptibly different from the treatment of people who do not have advanced illness (McPherson, 2008). Vandenhaute (2010) suggests that caregivers have an inclination to overmedicate at a time where interventions are likely to be invasive, irksome, inopportune, and ineffective. All the same, the prevailing philosophy, individual person-centred opinion, political priorities and professional impetus emphasise that compassionate end of life care is the concern of all practitioners, not just palliative care specialists (NCHSPCS, 2002; DoH, 2008; RCN, 2011). As the emphasis of healthcare provision shifts from hospitals to primary care, across the health continuum (Pellett, 2009), it is imperative that practitioners such as practice nurses, GPs and community nurses are able to discuss, plan, and deliver high-quality end of life care to people.

Communicating about palliative care

The vast majority of people with diabetes have longstanding type 2 diabetes (Diabetes UK, 2010) and many of these individuals will already be known to diabetes practice teams. Diabetes is also a common comorbidity of other

Table I. Principles of palliative care practice
■ Provides relief from pain and other distressing symptoms
■ Affirms life and regard dying as a normal process
■ Practices with the intention to neither hasten nor postpone death
■ Integrates the psychological and spiritual aspects of a person's care
■ Offers a support system to help people live as actively as possible until death
■ Offers a support system to help the family cope during the person's illness and in their own bereavement
■ Uses a team approach to address the needs of people and their families, including bereavement counselling if indicated
■ Good palliative care improves quality of life and may also positively influence the course of illness
■ Palliative care is applicable early in the course of illness, in conjunction with other therapies that are intended to prolong life, such as chemotherapy or radiation therapy, and includes those investigations needed to better understand and manage distressing clinical complications

complex diseases such as cancer (Smyth and Smyth, 2005a; Psarakis, 2006) and it can arise as a result of diabetogenic treatments, such as the use of glucocorticosteroids (Smyth and Smyth, 2004; Dunning *et al.*, 2010). Whatever the aetiology, it is reasonable to expect that many people with diabetes and their families will have been managing their diabetes independently and well for some time. The change in emphasis associated with end of life care — from disease modification and management to the improvement and maintenance of quality of life, and death — can be confusing and distressing for individuals (Ronaldson and Devery, 2001; Randall and Wearn, 2005). This is especially relevant if people are not sufficiently aware of their situation, not involved in the decision-making process, or if they lack accurate information about what palliative care involves. People and their families may perceive the cessation of disease-modifying treatments and relaxation from dietary restrictions and rigorous blood glucose monitoring and control to be a lack of professional concern, or abandonment (McCoubrie *et al.*, 2005; Back *et al.*, 2009).

Impact of caring for the dying

Nurses have a vital role in care of the dying. By enabling communication about the conceptual shift towards palliative or end of life care, they provide comfort and increase the person's awareness and progress of the illness journey and care trajectory (Wittenberg-Lyles *et al.*, 2011). Even so, it is recognised that caring for the dying, listening to or talking to a person about their impending death and acknowledging and understanding a person's preferences for end of life care is a source of significant stress and anxiety for many practitioners (Marks, 2005; Costello, 2006; Burnard *et al.*, 2008; Thompson-Hill *et al.*, 2009). In one study, which explored the experiences of GPs and community nurses discussing individuals' preferred places of death, the majority of professionals revealed they found it a difficult area of practice (Munday *et al.*, 2009).

The delivery of effective, high-quality palliative care depends on confident and competent communication skills (Malloy *et al.*, 2010). Equally, being suitably prepared may mitigate the potentially distressing effects of dealing with death and dying. Therefore, before any pragmatic clinical considerations of managing diabetes at the end of life can be addressed, practitioners should reflect on their communication skills and continuing professional development needs. There are various resources to assist the practitioner, including the Royal College of Nursing (2011) publication 'Route to success: the key contribution of nursing to end of life care', which provides a useful compendium of links to assessment tools, policy documents and clinical guidance from organisations such as the Liverpool Care Pathway and Preferred Priorities for Care.

Clinical management of diabetes at the end of life

Blood glucose values

Angelo *et al.* (2011) remarked that there is a dearth of evidence-based medical literature regarding best practice in the management of people with diabetes who are at the end of life, and the optimal approach remains uncertain. This notwithstanding, there are some general observations and consensus guidelines which suggest that stringent glycaemic control via regular invasive blood glucose monitoring is of dubious benefit (if not downright burdensome) and that it may potentially be harmful if it causes symptomatic hypoglycaemia (Rowles *et al.*, 2010; Angelo *et al.*, 2011). A blood glucose target range of 5–15mmol/l is reasonable (Smyth and Smyth, 2005b; Rowles *et al.*, 2011), as illustrated by the advice given to Tom and his wife, Alice (*case study*).

Case study

Tom is a 68-year-old retired mechanic, who lives with his wife, Alice. Six months ago he was diagnosed with lung cancer with extensive metastases, which is associated with a poor prognosis; he is aware of his prognosis and wants to 'live as much as possible' while he can. Tom has lived with type 2 diabetes mellitus since the age of 42 years.

Tom's weight has decreased over the past few months; his body mass index (BMI) was previously 31kg/m² but this is now 26kg/m². He complains of having 'no appetite' and when he feels like eating he wants 'just small amounts'.

Tom's diabetes is treated with biphasic human insulin twice daily and he also takes metformin 1000mg twice daily. He has had several hypoglycaemic episodes recently, during which his wife had to administer Glucagel to help him recover. Although Tom does not want to eat, Alice is now anxious about ensuring that he has regular meals, which is a source of some tension between the couple.

Tom has always striven to maintain good glycaemic control to prevent complications of diabetes, but the practice nurse and the community nurse now discuss how preventing the extremes of glycaemic control (hypoglycaemia and hyperglycaemia) may be more appropriate. She advises Tom to stop taking his metformin as this can cause gastrointestinal discomfort and reduced appetite and she changes his twice-daily biphasic insulin to a once-daily long-acting insulin analogue. She reassures both Tom and Alice that eating a 'pleasurable' diet when Tom feels like it is fine. They agree that Tom should continue checking his blood glucose but 'just once a day', aiming to keep his blood glucose between 5 and 15mmol/l. The practice nurse provides him with some simple titration guidelines so that he can adjust the insulin himself, should it be above or below this range.

Type 1 diabetes

Rowles *et al.* (2011: 27) emphasise that insulin withdrawal is 'likely to lead to death' in people with type 1 diabetes, who have absolute insulin deficiency due to autoimmune destruction of pancreatic beta cells. Therefore, insulin should be continued — preferably with a simplified regimen, such as using a once-daily long-acting insulin analogue, a twice-daily isophane insulin, or a twice-daily fixed mixture. They also recommend seeking the advice and guidance of a specialist diabetes team for help with individualised care planning, rather than adhering to generic treatment procedures; this is especially valid for people with type 1 diabetes.

Type 2 diabetes

In people with type 2 diabetes, like Tom, medication should be used to prevent symptoms of hyperglycaemia; this usually means maintaining blood glucose levels below 15mmol/l.

Infections and steroid use can cause marked hyperglycaemia, which can lead to dehydration and the development of hyperosmolar hyperglycaemic state (HHS); this is associated with some unpleasant symptoms, including polyuria, polydipsia and confusion (but not ketosis) and can lead to death. As palliative care is defined by the 'impeccable assessment and management of symptoms' and 'intends neither to hasten nor postpone death' (WHO, 2011), treatment to correct hyperglycaemia is appropriate and justified.

Towards the end of life, individuals suffering from advanced cancer or other chronic illness often become anorexic. Should this occur, oral medication is to be discontinued, as in Tom's case, due to the risk of hypoglycaemia with insulin-secreting agents (such as sulphonyureas) and the gastrointestinal side effects of metformin (Angelo, 2010).

Individuals with type 2 diabetes who are treated with insulin may be able to discontinue this aspect of treatment, as their endogenous insulin may well accommodate the reduced dietary intake, weight and energy demands; should they become symptomatic, insulin can be reinstated, such as a once-daily long acting insulin analogue (Rowles *et al.*, 2011).

HbA$_{1c}$ and blood glucose recording

While HbA$_{1c}$ is ordinarily used as a measure of diabetes control, this is largely irrelevant in end of life care as the question or concern of long-term complications is essentially of no real therapeutic value or consequence (Smyth and Smyth, 2005; McPherson, 2008); the frequency of blood glucose monitoring can also be reduced, to daily or twice-daily, even in type 1 diabetes. However, the avoidance of acute complications of diabetes such as hyperglycaemia, diabetic ketoacidosis and HHS is important to the overall goal of maintaining quality of life (Smyth and Smyth, 2005).

Diabetic ketoacidosis

Diabetic ketoacidosis is a life-threatening complication, which occurs in type 1 and type 2 diabetes when there is an absolute or relatively severe insulin insufficiency; this results in body fat being used as a fuel source, which causes a build-up of acid and ketones (by-products of fat metabolism). Older patients with type 2 diabetes can present with HHS, which is distinguished by hyperglycaemia, hyperosmolarity and dehydration without significant ketoacidosis; this is also associated with significant mortality (Hemphill *et al.*, 2011). Clearly, close collaboration between primary care staff and diabetes and palliative care specialists is vital (Quinn *et al.*, 2006b). It is reiterated that professionals must sensitively communicate changes in management to the person concerned and their family in a way that does not imply that the situation is hopeless or that 'nothing more than can be done', but rather in a way that helps the person and their family to shift their focus to one of everyday coping and quality of life matters (Olsson *et al.*, 2010).

Prognostication and palliative care

Estimations of prognosis can aid people and their families in self-directed decision-making and provide them with opportunities to make provisions for their future care needs. However, various papers have reported on the inconsistencies and intricacies of end of life prognostication, highlighting a consistent overestimation of duration of survival by doctors (Glare *et al.*, 2003; Head *et al.*, 2005).

With due regard to this caveat, a prognosis-based system for prioritising treatments, which considers the severity of people's conditions and their circumstances, has been advocated in the literature (Angelo *et al.*, 2011). Assorted tools to aid prognostication, such as the Palliative Performance Scale (Anderson *et al.*, 1996) have also been produced to provide objective data regarding the individual's predicted prospects. A brief discourse on the various tools is available on the Gold Standards Framework website (search for 'prognostic indicators'): www.goldstandardsframework.org.uk

Angelo *et al.* (2011) propose three groups:

- Advanced disease but relatively stable
- Impending death or organ or system failure
- Actively dying.

For those whose condition is stable, and who are mainly ambulant and independent, the following might be considered:

- Continuation of the current regimen (but the practitioner should open an honest conversation about reducing the intensity of glycaemic control)
- Instructions on hypoglycaemia prevention
- Stop HbA_{1c} monitoring

- Reduce the frequency of blood glucose monitoring
- Maintain reasonable hyperglycaemia prevention (blood glucose <10mmol/l)
- Prescription of a relaxed 'pleasure-based' diet, where the individual eats for satisfaction and gratification, only limiting highly-concentrated carbohydrate.

To this we might add that where appropriate, the practitioner should initiate candid conversations about the individual's preferred priorities for care, possibly using the pro forma available on the National End of Life Care Plan website:

www.endoflifecareforadults.nhs.uk/tools/core-tools/preferredprioritiesforcare

During transitional stages, when disease advances and performance status is reduced, people become dependent and intake can be reduced; the importance of glycaemic control is less obvious at these times and the prevention of hypoglycaemia is considered more important. People with type 1 diabetes may need to reduce insulin doses, especially if renal or hepatic failure is manifest, as insulin will not be metabolised and gluconeogenesis will be hindered. People with type 2 diabetes may also have to decrease their anti-diabetic treatment, due to reduced oral intake and/or organ involvement that compromises the activity and safety of drugs. Blood glucose monitoring can generally be stopped in type 2 diabetes and its routine practice can be stopped in type 1 diabetes, using it only as a decision-making tool.

When the individual is actively dying — a stage characterised by the need for total care with activities of daily living, multiple organ failure and no capacity for enteral intake (eating and drinking) — Angelo *et al.* (2011) suggest that consensus is lacking but 'most practitioners' would withdraw all hypoglycaemic agents, including insulin in a person with type 1 diabetes. This raises significant moral, ethical and legal considerations, which are beyond the scope of this chapter. However, it is vital that good communication is maintained between all health professionals, the person (where able) and their family and/ or carers. This also highlights one of the key principles of contemporary end of life care: that realistic, anticipatory planning and preparation for the dying process, which includes the elicitation of preferred priorities for care and the person's decisions regarding the direction of care, can obviate any potential dilemma or distress.

Conclusion

Looking after people with diabetes who are at the end of life can be an immensely rewarding experience for all practitioners who are involved in the provision of care. NHS Diabetes (2011) has published guidance for healthcare providers, entitled 'Commissioning Diabetes End of Life Services', bringing together guidance, policy, commissioning guides, links to care pathways and examples of how end of life care can be improved for people with diabetes. A number of different teams in both community and acute settings provide end of life care services and it is essential that care is coordinated through a care-planning process.

As with other areas of diabetes care, the management of individuals who are at the end of life should include an assessment of their physical, emotional and psychological wellbeing, and there should be timely access to appropriate medical, nursing and psychological interventions. Other essential components of care for people nearing the end of life include support for their carers and families, the provision of timely information and access to spiritual care services.

Considered planning, honest conversations and clear explanations can make the experience of dying much more meaningful. Traditionally, there has been a fear of stopping insulin and other medications but as this chapter illustrates, careful decision making, good explanations and a focus on quality of life can be enabling to practitioners and people receiving end of life care.

Key points

- Realistic anticipatory planning and preparation for the dying process, which includes elicitation of the person's preferred priorities for care and decisions regarding the direction of care, can obviate any potential dilemma or distress
- The provision of effective, equitable end of life care that facilitates choice and control should be available to all, regardless of medical diagnosis and place of care
- Practitioners should reflect upon their communication skills and continuing professional development needs.

References

Back A et al (2009) Abandonment at the End of Life From Patient, Caregiver, Nurse, and Physician Perspectives: Loss of Continuity and Lack of Closure. *Archives of Internal Medicine* **169**(5): 474-79

Brennan F (2007) Palliative care as an international human right. *Journal of Pain and Symptom Management* **33**(5): 494-99

Budge P (2010) Management of diabetes in patients at the end of life. *Nursing Standard* **25**(6): 42-46

Burnard P et al (2008) A comparative, longitudinal study of stress in student nurses in five countries. *Nurse Education Today* **28**(2): 134-45

Costello J (2006) Dying well: nurses' experiences of 'good' and 'bad' deaths in hospital. *Journal of Advanced Nursing* **54**(5): 594-601

Department of Health (2008) End of Life Care Strategy: Promoting high quality care for all adults at the end of life. Executive Summary Department of Health. London.

Department of Health (2010) Improving the health and well-being of people with long term conditions. Department of Health. London.

Diabetes UK (2010) Diabetes in the UK 2010: Key statistics on diabetes. Diabetes UK. London

Diabetes UK (2011) Key diabetes statistics and reports: Diabetes prevalence 2010. http://diabetes.org.uk/About_us/Media-centre/Key-diabetes-statistics-and-reports/Diabetes-prevalence-2010/ [accessed 31/12/10]

Dunning T et al (2010) Guidelines for managing diabetes at the end of life. Nurses Board of Victoria. Melbourne.

Ford-Dunn S et al (2006) Management of diabetes during the last days of life: attitudes of consultant diabetologists and consultant palliative care physicians in the UK. *Palliative Medicine* 20: 197-203

Glare P et al (2003) A systematic review of physicians' survival predictions in terminally ill cancer patients. *BMJ* 327: 1-6

Gomes B, Higginson I (2006) Factors influencing death at home in terminally ill patients with cancer: systematic review. *BMJ* 332: 515-21

Gwyther L et al (2009) Advancing palliative care as a human right. *Journal of Pain and Symptom Management* **38**(5): 767-74

Healthcare Commission (2007) Spotlight on complaints: a report on second stage complaints about the NHS in England. Healthcare Commission. London.

Head B et al (2005) Prognostication In Hospice Care: Can The Palliative Performance Scale Help? *Journal Of Palliative Medicine* **8**(3): 492-502

Hemphill R et al (2011) Hyperosmolar hyperglycaemic state. available at www.emedicine.medscape.com/article/1914705-overview

Hubert H (1977) Last Speech of Hubert H. Humphrey, November 1, 1977, Washington, D.C.

Lohan D et al (2010) Access to treatment as a human right. *BMC Medicine* **8**(8): 1-9

Lynn J (2005) Living Long in Fragile Health: The New Demographics Shape End of Life Care. *Hastings Center Report* **35**(6 suppl): s14-s18

NCHSPCS (2002) Definitions of supportive and palliative care: Briefing 11. National Council for Hopsice and Specialist Palliative Care Services. London

NHS Diabetes (2011) Commissioning Diabetes End of Life Care Services: NHS Diabetes. Leicester

Malloy P et al (2010) Beyond Bad News: Communication Skills of Nurses in Palliative Care. *Journal Of Hospice And Palliative Nursing* **12**(3):166-74

Marks J (2005) Addressing end of life issues. *Clinical Diabetes.* **23**(3): 98-99

McCoubrie R et al (2005) Managing diabetes mellitus in patients with advanced cancer: a case note audit and guidelines. *European Journal of Cancer Care* 14: 244-48

McPherson M (2008) Management of diabetes at end of life. *Home Healthcare Nurse* **26**(5): 276-78

Munday D et al (2009) Exploring preferences for place of death with terminally ill patients: qualitative study of experiences of general practitioners and community nurses in England. *BMJ* 338: 214-18

NISRA (2011) Statistical Bulletin: Deaths In Northern Ireland (2010) available at www.nisra.gov.uk/archive/demography/.../births_deaths/deaths_2010.pdf [accessed 31/3/11]

Office for National Statistics (2011) Death Registrations available at http://www.statistics.gov.uk/cci/nugget.asp?id=95213 [accessed 31/7/11]

Olsson L et al (2010) Maintaining hope when close to death: insight from cancer patients in palliative home care. *International Journal of Palliative Nursing* **16**(12): 607-12

Payne S et al (2004) Overview. In Payne, S, Seymour, J & Ingleton, C (eds) Palliative care nursing: principles and evidence for practice OUP. Maidenhead.

Pellett C (2009) Provision of end of life care in the community. *Nursing Standard* **24**(12): 35-40

Psarakis H (2006) Clinical challenges in caring for patients with diabetes and cancer. *Diabetes Spectrum* **19**(3): 157-62

Quinn K et al (2006a) Diabetes management in palliative care. *Australian Nursing Journal* **13**(8): 29

Quinn K et al (2006b) Diabetes management in patients receiving palliative care. *Journal of Pain and Symptom Management* **32**(3): 275-86

RCN (2011) Route to success: the key contribution of nursing to end of life care. RCN. London

Registrar General (2011) Chapter 3 – Deaths in Scotland's Population 2010 The Registrar General's Annual Review of Demographic Trends, 156th Edition. available at www.gro-scotland.gov.uk/files2/stats/annual-review-2010/j176746-05.htm

Ronldson S, Devery K (2001) The experience of transition to palliative care services: perspectives of patients and nurses. *International Journal of Palliative Nursing* **7**(4): 171-77

Rowles S et al (2011) ABCD position statement on diabetes and end of life care. *Practical Diabetes International* **28**(1): 26-27

Sepúlveda C et al (2002) Palliative Care: The World Health Organization's Global Perspective. *Journal of Pain and Symptom Management* **24**(2): 91-96

Smyth D, Smyth T (2004) Steroid induced diabetes. *Cancer Nursing Practice* **3**(10): 15-19

Smyth D, Smyth T (2005a) The relationship between diabetes and cancer. *Journal of Diabetes Nursing* **9**(7): 269-73

Smyth T, Smyth D (2005b) How to manage diabetes in advanced terminal illnesses. *Nursing Times* **101**(17): 30-32

Wittenberg-Lyles E et al (2011) The shift to early palliative care: a typology of illness journeys and the role of nursing. *Clinical Journal of Oncology Nursing* **15**(3): 303-310

World Health Organization (2011) WHO definition of palliative care. http://bit.ly/9wlPS6

Chapter 29

Leadership and successful team working in diabetes care

Lorna Storr and Anne Phillips

Introduction

As you will have read throughout this book, the essence of good diabetes care is effective team working in its various forms. The partnership between practitioners and people with diabetes respects people's rights and promotes safe, evidence-based decision making (Phillips and Wright, 2009). Teamwork within the multidisciplinary diabetes care team is essential for good care. Each team member plays an important role. This final chapter explores how effective leadership, 'leaderfulness' (Raelin, 2003) and teamwork are critical for the delivery of high-quality, safe diabetes care, whereby:

> '...high quality leadership, management (and teamwork) at all levels are essential elements for a National Health Service which is capable of delivering the highest possible quality of care to patients and the best possible deal for taxpayers...'
>
> (The Kings Fund, 2011:3)

Many studies across several industries, including healthcare, suggest that effective leadership and teamwork are key determinants of performance (Baker, 2011). Competent and committed leaders are essential for enabling an organisation to shift from 'good' to 'great' (Collins, 2001 [as cited by Baker, 2011]). Additionally, team-orientated organisations are able to respond efficiently and effectively in the fast-changing environments that most organisations now encounter (Aston Organisation Development Ltd, 2004). Considering the rising prevalence of diabetes and pre-diabetes, coupled with ever-changing NHS organisation and funding structures, this is particularly relevant to diabetes care.

At the time of writing, Britain's public services are facing unprecedented challenges amid profound structural, political, economic and social changes, a loss of confidence in politics and a competitive market economy. Organisations are becoming increasingly complex and inequalities in wealth, poverty and wellbeing continue to rise. Changing demographics and an ageing population present further demands and challenges, especially as the prevalence of diabetes is increasing in socially and economically deprived communities (YHPHO, 2011) and within ageing populations (Sinclair, 2011; Phillips and Phillips, 2011). As if this weren't enough, we are striving for a sustainable future in terms of climate and energy production and our society is experiencing a recession, with a loss of market confidence. There has never been a greater need for resourcefulness and creativity in the provision of diabetes care, and never a greater need for competent and committed leaders to make the 'good' become 'great' (Collins, 2001 [as cited by Baker, 2011]).

As information and communication technologies rapidly evolve (Storr, 2004; Darzi, 2008; Hartley and Benington, 2011), as do our opportunities for information giving and improving communication. Examples of information technology initiatives include SystmOne and Telehealth, which aim to improve communication within and between NHS organisations (Moore *et al.*, 2011), create greater patient participation initiatives (Hannan, 2010), and provide more self-management choices.

In 2010, colleagues of ours at King's College London conducted a UK-wide diabetes care scoping exercise (Forbes *et al.*, 2010). This project recognised the need to involve people with diabetes in their care decisions and for diabetes services to be organised and delivered in an effective manner to allow this to happen. Researchers concluded that care organisation is essential to the delivery of diabetes care nationally. They also made key recommendations, which comprised:

- The development of integrated models of individual and population level access to identify individual care needs and to develop care provision
- The development of more effective and efficient models of ongoing self-care support, including education, that respond to patient preferences
- The development of better systems that provide information on clinical performance and care efficiency, to enhance care delivery
- The development of commissioning models that reinforce greater integration and efficiency in care organisation and delivery (including inequalities in care).

(Forbes *et al.*, 2010:107)

All of these elements require leadership and team working, with the philosophy of turning diabetes care services from 'good' to 'great'.

Defining leadership

Leadership is not a person or a position, but a complex, paradoxical and moral relationship between individuals and groups. It is based on trust, obligation, commitment, emotion and a shared vision of the good — no one can be a leader without willing followers (Storr, 2004).

Despite a plethora of research and literature on the subject, it seems there is no definitive, robust and conclusive definition of 'leadership'. However, there are three commonly-recurring themes:

- It is a process of getting things done through others, based on an interactive relationship (what it is)
- Mutual goals are achieved by influence and emotions (how it is exercised)
- It is a process for creating change and improving quality (why it is needed; its purpose).

Hardacre *et al.* (2011) suggest that to achieve an elevated goal or vision, change must occur. It can be argued that:

- For change to occur, a risk must be taken
- To encourage risk taking, a supportive climate must exist
- A supportive climate is demonstrated by day-to-day leadership behaviour.

Therefore, the relationship between leaders and followers can be powerful and value-laden. Leaders can enable teams to achieve their mutual goals, which results in change. However, given the inevitable uncertainty and turbulence within this process, there are risks (Storr, 2004).

Examples of leadership in diabetes care include leading change within care delivery, supporting colleagues and teams so they are able to embrace change without fear, and inspiring, processing and progressing new evidence as 'early adopters' (Cherry *et al.*, 2011; Reynolds and Lawless, 2011). Examples of 'leaderfulness' (Raelin, 2003) in diabetes care include the partnership approach between practitioner and individual, including information giving and shared care planning (Holdich, 2009), and the facilitation of effective and safe decision making and realistic achievable goal setting (Furze *et al.*, 2008).

How are leaders effective?

Leaders help people to connect and find meaning at work by:

- Increasing self-awareness
- Restoring and building optimism, confidence and hope
- Promoting transparent decision making and relationships that build trust and commitment among team members
- Fostering inclusive structures and positive ethical climates.

(Avolio and Gardner, 2005)

In essence, in diabetes care this can be achieved though honest communication, valuing the opinions of others and respecting differences, creating an environment of synergy and fostering the value of teamwork, with the individual with diabetes at the centre of the team.

Team working — so what?

'Team working in healthcare promotes resilience, innovation, quality and safety.'
(West, 2011).

Teams do not work in isolation, individuals do, and solitary working does not provide effective care for people with diabetes. There needs to be clarity of roles within teams and an environment of trust, safety and support, which can be achieved through communication. Teams that are governed through fear cannot be effective. So what is team working and how do teams add value to diabetes care?

- Team-based organisations are *responsive* and can adapt to rapidly-changing environments which many now face
- Teams promote *improved quality* by offering diverse perspectives and ideas, comprehensive and high-quality decision making, creativity and innovation
- Teams can *challenge assumptions* which enable a climate of *radical change* to develop. Risks can be explored and analysed in order to *improve services* and ways of working
- Teams help to create a *learning organisation* which stimulate growth and improvement amongst team members
- Teams provide a vehicle for the delivery of *organisational strategy*, through synergy and valuing each others opinions and differences

- Teams can *achieve goals* and desired outcomes by organising and coordinating the work of individuals and groups
- Teams provide *complex networks* for sharing knowledge. This *optimises organisational intelligence, cross-fertilisation* and ensures that information is processed effectively to develop diabetes care, to reflect key elements as highlighted through the work of Forbes *et al.* (2010)
- *Staff satisfaction* (and performance) improves in teams. There are *higher levels of involvement and commitment* and lower stress levels — this is of particular importance given the rapid nature of change and uncertainty in the current economic climate.

(Aston Organisation Development Ltd, 2004; West, 2004).

Teamwork can also be extremely rewarding.

Practice development

Leadership and teamwork, in their various forms, make positive contributions to the outcomes and care experiences of people with diabetes; they also promote staff satisfaction, professional confidence and practice development.

Diabetes care environments are often complex and challenging and practitioners are constantly seeking to demonstrate best practice and to improve the quality of care delivery services. This can be exhausting at times — adopting one set of working strategies, only to have it quickly replaced with another. This has been a common theme within NHS for a number of years now, as we constantly seek to develop, refine and improve care. As practices evolve in this way, the NHS can be described as undergoing a metamorphosis.

Conclusion

Good leadership enables teams to work effectively and offer a higher standard of care. There are many different types of teamwork — between members of the practice diabetes team, between hospital-based staff and between practitioners and the person with diabetes. All are important. There needs to be a clarity of roles within teams and an environment of trust, safety and support, which can be achieved through good communication.

Self-management is an integral part of effective diabetes care and education and a team-based approach that promotes and develops this will enable people with diabetes to have better care experiences and achieve better outcomes.

With increasing numbers of people being diagnosed with diabetes, we are facing a monumental opportunity. It is through excellence in team working, organisation, communication and enablement that we see the best results for people with diabetes who work in partnership with us as practitioners. This is the essence of great diabetes care.

Key points

- Diabetes care relies on effective team working (in its various forms)
- Leadership can enable teams to achieve mutual goals, resulting in change; for diabetes care services to shift from 'good' to 'great', competent and committed leaders are essential
- A team-based approach which promotes and develops self-management will enable better care experiences and lead to better outcomes.

References

Aston Organisation Development Ltd (2004) The Aston Team Performance Inventory, Aston Organisation Development Ltd: Birmingham

Avolio, B and Gardner W (2005) Authentic Leadership Development: Getting To the Root of Positive Forms of Leadership. *Leadership Quarterly* 16: 315-38

Baker, G (2011) The Roles of Leaders in High-Performing Health Care Systems, Commission on Leadership and Management in the NHS, The Kings Fund: London

Cherry B et al (2011) Experiences with electronic health records: early adopters in long-term care facilities. *Health Care Management Review* 36(3): 265-74

Darzi. (2008) High quality care for all: NHS Next Stage Review final report. The Stationary Office. London.

Forbes A et al (2010) The Organisation and delivery of diabetes services in the UK: a scoping exercise. Report for the National Institute for Health Research Service Delivery and Organisation Programme, SDO Project (08/1809/249)

Furze G et al (2008) The Clinician's Guide to Chronic Disease Management for Long Term Conditions: A Cognitive Behavioural Approach, M&K Publishing:UK.

Hannan A (2010) Providing patients online access to their primary care computerised medical records: a case study of sharing and caring. *Informatics in Primary Care* 18: 41-49

Hardacre J et al (2011) What's leadership got to do with it?, Health Foundation: London

Hartley J, Benington J (2011) Recent Trends in Leadership – Thinking and Action in the Public and Voluntary Service Sector, Commission on Leadership and Management in the NHS, The Kings Fund: London

Holdich P (2009) Diabetes evidence based management: Patient-centred care planning. *Practice Nursing* 20(1): 18-23

Moore P et al (2011) Medicines reconciliation using a shared electronic health record. *Journal of Patient Safety* 7(3): 148-54

Phillips A, Wright J (2009) Diabetes evidence based management: Achieving treatment concordance. *Practice Nursing* **20**(7): 353-57

Phillips S, Phillips A (2011) Diabetes evidence-based management: Diabetes and older people – ensuring individualised practice. *Practice Nursing* **22**(4): 70-74

Raelin J (2003) Creating Leaderful Organizations: How to Bring Out Leadership in Everyone. San Francisco: Berrett-Koehler

Reynolds S, Lawless B (2011) Creating process and policy change in health care. In: Textbook of Rapid Response Systems. De Vita M et al (Eds). Springer Sciences and Business Media: Canada.

Sinclair A (2011) Diabetes care for older people: A practical view on management. *Diabetes and Primary Care* **13**(1): 29-38

Storr L (2004) Leading with Integrity: a Qualitative Research Study. *Journal of Health Organisation and Management* **18**(6): 415-34

The Kings Fund (2011) The Future of Leadership and Management in the NHS – No More Heroes, The Kings Fund: London

West M (2004) The Secrets of Successful Team Management, Duncan Baird Publishers: London

West M (2011) Changing Cultures: Quality and safety in healthcare. Paper delivered to: Department of Health Sciences, University of York, Lancaster University Management School and The Work Foundation

Yorkshire & Humber Public Health Observatory (2011) AHPO Diabetes Prevalence Model. Available at: http://www.yhpho.org.uk/default.aspx?RID=81090 [last accessed: 27-3-12]

Index

acanthosis nigricans   228
ACE *see* angiotensin-converting
   enzyme
ACEi *see* angiotensin converting
   enzyme inhibitor
ACR *see* albumin-creatinine ratio
adherence *see* medication, adherence
adolescence   244–5
albumin-creatinine ratio   187
albuminuria   187
alcohol   137
aliskiren   185, 189
alpha-blocker   113
Alzheimer's disease   291–3
angiotensin converting enzyme
   inhibitor   185, 188–90
angiotensin II receptor blockage   185,
   189–90
angular stomatitis   223
annual assessment   60
anti-diabetic agents   88, 95–6
anti-diabetic treatment   85–97
antidepressants   285
anxiety   277–86
ARB *see* angiotensin II receptor
   blockage
athlete's foot   223

bacterial infections   222
beta-blocker   113
Bhahimbi case study   257–61
biguanides   88–90

blood glucose   143–4, 149, 314, 316
   children and young people   249
   tests   2
blood pressure   109–14, 117–18
   control   17–18, 42–3, 46, 190
   drug management   112–13
body mass index   24
bullosis diabeticorum   225

calcium channel blocker   112–13
candidal paronychia   223
cardiovascular risk   64
care homes   295–6
care plan   261
care planning sheet   62–3
children and young people   241–9
   collaborative working   242–3
   continuing care   247–8
   psychoeducational
      interventions   246–7
   routine checks   248
   transition of care   245–6
cholesterol   43
chronic kidney disease   184, 186
CKD *see* chronic kidney disease
combination therapies   96
consultation   122–5, 127–8
   map   123
   skills   124
contraception   236, 274
coping strategies   81, 283
costs of diabetes   6

dementia 291–3
demographics 289–90
depression 125–6, 277–86
  definitions 282
  initial management 281–2
  screening 281
  step approach 284–5
  symptoms 280
DESMOND 30, 53–4
diabesity 73–82
  investigations 79
  multidisciplinary approach 79–80
  referrals 76–7
  specialist service 76
  treatment aims 75
diabetes prevention 6
diabetes-related stress 280
diabetes review 59–63
diabetic dermopathy 224
diabetic nephropathy 183–93
  diagnosis 187–8
  referral 192
  risk factors 183
  treatment 188–91
diabetic peripheral neuropathy 212
diabetic retinopathy *see* retinopathy
diabetic scleroderma 227
diabetic thick skin 225–6
diagnosis 1–11, 85
  benefits of 5–6
  late 1
  newly-diagnosed 51–2
  support following 51–6
dietary change 25–6
dietetic support 52–3
dietitian 25–6, 28, 30, 79, 129
disability 291
diuretics 112–13
dizziness 217
Down's syndrome 269–72
DPP-4 inhibitors 94

driving 147–8
drug history 79
Dupuytren's contracture 226
DVLA 148

ED *see* erectile dysfunction
empowerment 47
end of life care 311–19
  clinical management of
    diabetes 314–18
  prognostication 317–18
energy balance 36–7
erectile dysfunction 78, 196, 198–9,
  203–4, 217–18
eruptive xanthomatosis 227–8
ethnic minorities 54–5
European Health Insurance Card 133
evidence base 41–2
exception reporting 254
exenatide 92–3
exercise 25–6
  aerobic and anaerobic 33
  benefits of 27
  intensity 34
  recommendations 34–6
  resistance 34
  type 1 diabetes 37–8
feet 161–70
  advice for those at risk 168
  behaviour modification 169
  care pathway 166–7
  deformity 165–6
  ischaemia 165
  peripheral neuropathy 165
  peripheral vascular disease 165
  preventive care 162–4
  risk classification 167–8
  risk factor management 169
  ulceration 161–2, 216–17
fibrates 116
fluid 38–9

folic acid   234
food   38–9
food diaries   28–9, 81
fungal infections   222

gastroparesis   217–18
genetic diabetes *see* monogenic
diabetes
genetic testing   299
gestational diabetes   8–10
gliclazide   89
glimepiride   89
glipizide   89
GLP-1 receptor agonists   93–4
   see also glucagon-like peptide-1
glucagon-like peptide-1   91–2
glucose dependent insulinotropic
   peptide   91–2
glucose intolerance   2
glycaemic control   77–8, 87, 101,
   190, 234–5
glycaemic excursion
glycaemic memory   18
glycaemic target   87–8, 102
guardian drugs   67–8

haemodialysis   192
HbA$_{1c}$ 16–19, 104–5 316
health action planning, learning
   disabilities   267–8
healthy eating   23–30
high serum triglycerides   116
housebound patients   253–4
hyperglycaemia, exercise and   38
hyperinsulinaemia   273
hypertension   43, 64, 67, 109
hypo *see* hypoglycaemia
hypoglycaemia   139–56
   addressing   154–5
   causes   140
   consequences   144–5

defined   139–40
driving   147–8
drugs and   140
exercise and   38
financial costs of   146
identifying   154
impaired awareness of   142–3, 152
mortality   146–7
older people   293–5
practice development   155–6
prevalence   140–2
questionnaire   153
risk factors   147, 294
secondary care   155
symptoms   141, 145–6, 294–5
type   1 diabetes 141–2, 149–50
type   2 diabetes 142
hypoglycaemia unawareness   294

IFG *see* impaired fasting glucose
IGT *see* impaired glucose tolerance
impaired fasting glucose   6, 7
impaired glucose tolerance   6, 7, 15
incretin agents   92–3, 95
incretin effect   90–2
incretin enhancers   94
incretin mimetics   92–4
information technology   324
insulin
   adjustment   38
   effect on brain function   292
   management   80
   regimen   81
   storage   136
insulin therapy
   assessment   103
   considerations   105–6
   . evidence base   103–5
   management options   102
   optimising   101–7
   withdrawal of   315, 318

intermediate hyperglycaemia   2–3

ischaemia   165

ketoacidosis   1, 243–4, 316–17
kidney
  diabetes and   187
  failure   186–7
  functions   184
  hormonal functions   184–5
kidney disease, chronic   184, 186

leadership   323–8
  definition   325
  effectiveness   326
learning disabilities   267–75
  causes   268
  communication   269, 271
legacy effect   18
lifestyle changes   111, 117, 190–1
lipid management   115–18
liraglutide   92–3

maculopathy   177
maturity-onset diabetes of the
      young   299–308
  glucokinase   304, 306–7
  hepatocyte nuclear factor   1-alpha
      302–3
  hepatocyte nuclear factor   4-alpha
      303–4
  hepatocyte nuclear factor   1-beta
      304–5
  subtypes   301–7
medication   80
  adherence   67, 104, 121, 257, 278
  guardian drugs   67–8
  review   66–7
meglitinides   89–90
MET *see* metabolic equivalent of task
metabolic equivalent of task   34, 36

metformin   88–9, 95, 273
microvascular and macrovascular
      complications   16–17
microvascular risk   64
misconceptions   152
mobility assessment   79
MODY *see* maturity-onset diabetes of
      the young
monogenic diabetes   8, 299–308
mortality   17–19
motivational interviewing   82
mucormycosis   223
myocardial infarction   16–18

nail plate infections
nateglinide   89
necrobiosis lipoidica
      diabeticorum   224–5
nephrologists   191–2
nephropathy   183–93
neuroglycopaenia   141
neuropathy   211–18
  aetiology   211–12
  autonomic   217–18
  pain   214–16
  types of   214
NLD *see* necrobiosis lipoidica
      diabeticorum
non-genetic tests   300

obesity   24, 73–4, 111, 233–4
  medication for   26
older people   256–8, 289–96
  communicating risks   290–1
  disability   291
  hypoglycaemia   293–5
  impact on   290

palliative care   311–19
  communicating about   312–13
  defined   312

impact of 314
principles of 313
patient satisfaction 56
PCOS *see* polycystic ovary syndrome
PCR *see* albumin-creatinine ratio
penile implants 206
peripheral neuropathy 165
peripheral vascular disease 17–18,
   165
peritoneal dialysis 192
person-centred planning 59–68
personalised care planning 254–5
PHQ-9 Depression Scale 125, 127
physical activity 25–6, 33–9
  see also exercise
polycystic ovary syndrome 272–3
potassium-sparing diuretic 113
preconception care 231–7
  assessment 232
  counselling 232–3
  evidence base 233–5
  folic acid 234
  follow-up 236–7
  glycaemic control 234–5
  initial management 235
  pregnancy 231–7
  contraindications 236
  medications contraindicated 233
prevalence 6–7, 73–4
  children and young people 241–2
  older people 289
protein-creatinine ratio 187
proteinuria 187–8
psychoeducational
   interventions 246–7
psychological issues 23, 78, 81, 127
psychosocial support 121–30

questionnaires 127

RAAS *see* renin-angiotensin-

aldosterone-system
renal function 186
renal replacement therapy 192
renal threshold 4–5
renin-aldosterone system blocker 112
renin-angiotensin-aldosterone-
   system 185
repaglinide 89
retinopathy 173–9, 292
  advanced 177
  background 174
  education 177–8
  pre-proliferative 176
  progression 173–4
  proliferative 176–7
  screening 178–9
risk 41–7, 104
  arterial 116–17
  assessment 41
  calculators 45
  communication 44, 65–6
  factors 7
  framing 44–5
  perception of 44
  setting goals 45
  sharing goals 43–4

secondary diabetes 8–9
self-management 81
self-monitoring 66
sexual dysfunction 195–208
  clitoral vacuum engorgement
   device 207
  female 196–7, 199–202
  health practitioners and 202–3
  hypoglycaemia 200–1
  lubricants 207
  male 196, 198–9, 203–6
  medication 205–6
  penile implants 206
  psychological factors 200–2

sexual and relationship therapy   208
testosterone replacement   206
treatment   204–8
vacuum devices   206
significant event report   55
sitagliptin   94
skin complications   221–9
  bacterial infections   222
  comorbidities   222
  fungal infections   222
sleep apnoea   82
sleep deprivation   78
smoking, stopping   6, 42, 46
statins   115–16, 190
stress   277–86
  coping   283
stroke   17–18
structured education   52–3
sulphonylureas   89–90, 96
symptoms   2

team working   326–7
testosterone replacement   82, 206
therapeutic alliance   46
thiazolidinediones   90, 96
thyroid function   271–2
transplantation, kidney   192
travel   133–8
  air   134–5
  checklist   133
  insulin and   135–6
type 1   diabetes 1–3
  end of life care   315
  hypoglycaemia   141–2, 149–50

type 2   diabetes 1–3
  anti-diabetic treatment   85–97
  end of life care   316
  hypoglycaemia   142
  intensive glycaemic
    management   15–20
types of diabetes   8–10

UCPCR *see* urine C-peptide creatinine
  ratio
UK Prospective Diabetes Study   15–
  17
urine C-peptide creatinine ratio   300

vacuum devices   206
vildagliptin   94
vulnerable adults   253–62
  Bhahimbi case study   257–61
  case management   255–6
  housebound patients   253–4
  older people   256–8
  personalised care planning   254–5

waist circumference   24
weight gain   16, 75
  see also obesity
weight loss   23–30
  benefits   27, 77

yellow skin and nails   227